Also by Richard Ellis

THE BOOK OF WHALES

DOLPHINS AND PORPOISES

THE BOOK OF SHARKS

GREAT WHITE SHARK
(WITH JOHN MCCOSKER)

MEN AND WHALES

MONSTERS OF THE SEA

MONSTERS
of the SEA

RICHARD ELLIS

ROBERT HALE • LONDON

ISBN 0 7090 5634 6

Robert Hale Limited
Clerkenwell House
Clerkenwell Green
London ECIR OHT

Manufactured in the United States of America

A Note on the Illustrations

MANY OF THE illustrations used throughout this book were taken from the original sources, such as Aldrovandi (1555), Gesner (1551–58), or Rondelet (1560), but reproduced in more recent publications. For those that were drawn and published over four centuries ago, the problem of copyright would seem to be inapplicable, and I have—where possible— identified the original source and not where the reproduction was found. For the other illustrations, such as movie stills, recent animals, mermaids, sea-cows, blobs and globsters, etc., the credits appear on pages 427–9.

CONTENTS

PREFACE

ALTHOUGH I DIDN'T realize it when I began this study, there has been a long progression of writers who have chosen to tackle the subject of sea monsters. I refer particularly to the more recent studies, where the authors attempted to differentiate between real and imaginary creatures, as opposed to the earlier writers, like Aldrovandi, Belon, and Olaus Magnus, who may very well have believed in all the creatures they wrote about, including the dragon, unicorn, griffin, mermaid, siren, and kraken.

Among my predecessors along this convoluted road are A. C. Oudemans, Henry Lee, Frank Lane, Willy Ley, Richard Carrington, Herbert Wendt, and the indefatigable Bernard Heuvelmans. I have referred to their works often, but I hope that my stew has its own flavor. This book is about sharks, whales, octopuses, squid, and various sea serpents, and I discovered that another contemporary writer includes all of these creatures (and many more that I have not touched on) in his voluminous works. Arthur C. Clarke, best known as an author of science fiction—*2001: A Space Odyssey*, for example—shares my fascination for all sorts of large sea creatures, real and imaginary, and has probably written more (and better) about the giant squid than any other writer of fiction.

One of the more influential writers on the subject of monsters was (and still is, I hope) a friend: Peter Benchley seems to have anticipated my interest in various monsters and has helpfully written novels that include three of the creatures I chose to investigate (the shark in *Jaws;* the giant squid in *Beast;* the manta ray in *The Girl of the Sea of Cortez*). The sperm whale makes a brief appearance in *Beast,* but the octopus and the manatee have managed to avoid Benchley's attention, and I suspect that the octopus—especially if there really *is* one that is 200 feet long—will not maintain its isolated anonymity for long. (Actually, Benchley may have already mentioned it; in *Beast*, the tale of something attacking and dragging fish traps deep in Bermuda waters is based on octopus, not squid, lore.

I owe Jules Verne, who died in 1905, an apology. I once suggested to my agent the possibility of an annotated version of *Twenty Thousand Leagues Under the Sea*. I was so agitated over Verne's apparant ignorance of matters ichthyological, teuthological, and cetological that I felt the need to publish the truth as I knew it. As it turned out, there already *was* an annotated version, written by Walter J. Miller (which I didn't know about when I made my suggestion), published in 1976, so I have taken this opportunity to identify the errors having to do with the biology of whales, sharks, squid, and manatees. I have probably been too harsh in my disparagement of Verne's material, since I admire his work and have enjoyed reading his books for what they are: fiction largely unencumbered by fact.

Peter Benchley saw much of this book in its early stages and made many useful comments. I believed I knew enough about whales and sharks for this enterprise, but for cephalopods I shamelessly insinuated myself on many people who probably had a lot better things to do than teach me the rudiments of invertebrate biology. For their advice and counsel (and reprints), I would like to thank Clyde Roper of the Smithsonian Institution; Ron O'Dor of Dalhousie University in Halifax; Claude Morris of the Memorial University of Newfoundland; Eric Hochberg of the Santa Barbara Museum of Natural History; Bruce Carlson of the Waikiki Aquarium; John Arnold of the University of Hawaii; Martina A. C. Roeleveld of the South African Museum; and Bernd-Ulrich Budelmann and Roger Hanlon of the University of Texas. Malcolm Clarke published extensively while at the Marine Biological Association at Plymouth, England, but he has now retired, which, I am happy to say, has given him time to answer my numerous queries, mostly about the lives and intermingled destinies of squid and whales.

In the matter of sharks and medicine, Bob Hueter of the Mote Marine Laboratory was very helpful, and Genie Clark of the University of Maryland was, as always, a good critic and a good friend. Others who gave me guidance on various aspects of monsterology were Howard Hall, Alex Kerstitch, John McCosker, Gary Mangiacopra, and Ricardo Mandojana. Janey Winchell and the staff of the Peabody Museum of Salem were generous with their time and materials, and Stuart Frank of the Kendall Whaling Museum opened his photo files to me, enabling me to find pictures of monsters that no one believed existed. The "news" articles about Nessie's baby, the attack of the monster squid, the woman who married a shark, and the folks who were rescued by a giant octopus are all from the *Weekly World*

News, and I am grateful for their permission—and for their sense of humor.

Once again, I spent a lot of time in the library of the American Museum of Natural History (AMNH), where Nina Root, the librarian, made the vast facilities of that institution available to me. It is no easy task to locate obscure references in difficult languages, but Sarah Granato and Annette Springer of the AMNH library were unfailingly helpful and cheerfully supportive. At the same museum, Jim Atz gave me advice, counsel, references, and rare bibliographic materials that contributed greatly to my monster studies. The Minolta Company kindly permitted me to reproduce the painting by J. Lofaro, and Rhoda Kalt allowed me to use the shark and dinosaur illustrations by her grandfather, Charles R. Knight. As soon as I saw the "Nissin cup noodles" ad with the giant squid, I realized that I had to reproduce it in this book; Nissin Foods (USA) made it possible. I am especially grateful to Greg Aaron, the editor of my children's book *Physty,* who located the N. C. Wyeth painting of the battle with the giant squid, and to the Free Library of Philadelphia for making it available. A very special note of gratitude is offered to Glen Loates, whose generosity resulted in the inclusion in this book of his marvelous drawings of giant squid and sperm whales. Because of his consuming interest in *Architeuthis,* Glen worked closely with the late Frederick Aldrich of Memorial University, Newfoundland, and his experiences and enthusiasm have helped me substantially with my still-limited understanding of the giant squid.

There are not very many places one can go with the expectation of seeing monsters; nevertheless, I did visit Loch Ness to see what I could observe. On this trip, as well as my meandering expedition through life, I was accompanied by Stephanie Guest, who has the remarkable ability to turn fantasy into reality.

This book is dedicated to Forrest G. Wood, who died in 1991 and was a monster hunter par excellence. Some sixty years after the event, Woody "broke" the story of the monster octopus on the St. Augustine beach and set the stage for this book. He was a good friend and adviser (dare I use the word mentor?), and I am truly sorry he was not around to see it published.

—RICHARD ELLIS
New York, 1994

AN INTRODUCTION TO SEA MONSTERS

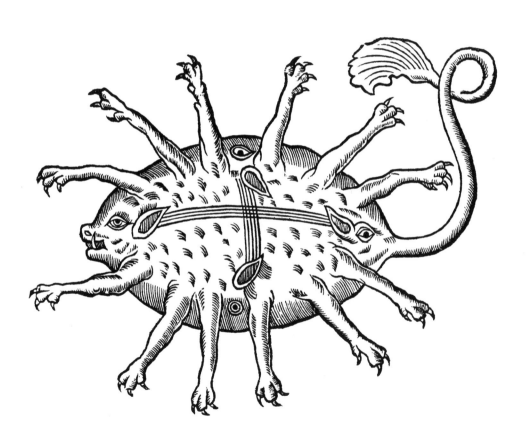

$\mathcal{A}$ COUPLE OF YEARS AGO, I was industriously working on a book about the Atlantic Ocean. I had researched the history of discovery (Leif Ericsson, Christopher Columbus, Amerigo Vespucci, et al.), commercial fishing (the Basques, French, Portuguese, etc.), Atlantic oceanography (William Beebe, the submersible *Alvin*, etc.), and the flora and fauna of the Atlantic (mostly fauna). Nothing about the fauna was more intriguing than the unexpected appearance on Newfoundland beaches of numerous giant squid in the late nineteenth century. From 1870 to 1880, some fifty of these monsters washed ashore, and some of them even attacked fishermen in small boats. I thought this story would make a wonderful addition to my study of the Atlantic, especially since it had occurred in Newfoundland waters, but then I learned that the next giant squid invasion took place in New Zealand. I could either ignore the New Zealand squid or extend the boundaries of my study of sea monsters.

I chose the latter path and temporarily abandoned Ericsson and William Beebe for man-eating octopuses, seductive mermaids, gigantic leviathans, sea serpents, and other legendary mysteries of the deep. Instead of the hyperbole and hysteria that I thought I would find as I pursued the tangled trails of sea monsters, I found a surprisingly coherent history wherein perceptions of monsters conformed to a broad but recognizable pattern through time. (I did, of course, encounter a certain amount of hyperbole and hysteria, which made the study that much more interesting.) Early sea monsters were first deemed hazards to ships and men, sinking the former and consuming the latter. Many monsters disappeared into the mists of legend, but others persevered, taking their place among the scientifically authenticated inhabitants of the world's oceans. Once they were identified as corporeal entities and no longer considered "monsters," they were integrated into the natural history of the period. They were often reviled, but they were almost always hunted, sometimes for food, sometimes for revenge, sometimes out of malice.

For the most part, historians of early man have been concerned with the discovery, occupation, and exploitation of the land, since that commodity is particularly useful to those who would settle it, farm it, or simply cross it to get from one place to another. Terrestrial travelers, to be sure, can be subjected to every conceivable kind of intemperate condition, from snowstorms and biting cold to blistering heat and drenching rain; from sleet storms, high winds, volcanoes, tornadoes, and earthquakes to hostile wildlife, but for the most part, the land under the feet of the traveler remains solid and unmoving—a secure connection and a reassuring purchase with mother earth.

The sea, with no semblance of stability, was often considered only as a way to get from place to place. Composed of an alien, cold substance, the sea is given to dangerous storms and treacherous currents, and in some places, its abyssal depths plumb the very limits of our terrestrial consciousness. And even if the poor seaman had some idea of where he was going or how to get there, the fathomless oceans were populated by gigantic monsters just waiting to gobble him up. So it is not surprising that early man turned his eyes inward toward the land—the trees, the plains, and the mountains—and not toward the intimidatingly limitless horizon of the sea. No good could come of venturing onto a watery plain that could lead only to misfortune. To the first man who gazed out over an expanse of endless water, the sheer size of the vista and the distance to the horizon must have been awe-inspiring and completely terrifying.

Certainly the primal fear of early mariners was that they would become lost or disappear forever. Because of this not unreasonable anxiety, early seafarers never sailed far enough from the nearest landfall to lose sight of it. Even though accounts of the fears of Columbus's seamen are probably apocryphal—they did not, after all, anticipate that their captain would sail them off the end of the world—they were certainly made nervous by the steady westering that put the only land they knew farther and farther astern. When the pioneering Portuguese navigators sailed south along the coast of West Africa in the early fifteenth century, they firmly believed that the nearer they came to the equator, the hotter the temperature would get, until the hellfires of the Torrid Zone would cause them to turn black and their ships to burst into flames. And even if they survived such meteorologic calamities, there would always be sea monsters waiting for them.

We meet the sea monster early in history, when the "great fish" swal-

lows Jonah. We will never know the type of animal that ingested him after he was cast into the sea, but the roster of candidates is impressive. Elasmohistorians vote for the shark (Guillaume Rondelet, a French naturalist who lived from 1507 to 1566, has even named the species; he maintains that it was a great white), while cetologists tend to favor the sperm whale. The eighteenth-century Swedish naturalist Carolus Linnaeus suggested that the "enormous fish" was a grouper.

A portion of a 1570 map of Iceland showing many of the monsters that seafarers might expect to encounter

If the name and nature of the swallower of Jonah is unresolved, the "leviathan" in the Book of Job is a major biblical conundrum. In his inquisition about the relative powers of man and God, the Lord asks Job if he can

> draw out leviathan with an hook? or his tongue with a cord which thou lettest down? Canst thou put an hook into his nose? or bore his jaw through with a thorn? . . . Shall the companions make a banquet of him? . . . Canst thou fill his skin with barbed irons? or his head with fish

spears? . . . Who can open the doors of his face? his teeth are terrible round about. His scales are his pride, shut up together as with a close seal. One is so near to another, that no air can come between them. They are joined one to another, they stick together, that they cannot be sundered. By his neesings a light doth shine, and his eyes are like the eyelids of the morning. Out of his mouth go burning lamps, and sparks of fire leap out. Out of his nostrils goeth smoke, as out of a seething pot or caldron. . . . He maketh the deep to boil like a pot: he maketh the sea like a pot of ointment. He maketh a path to shine after him; one would think the deep to be hoary. Upon earth there is not his like, who is made without fear. . . .

Some of this description bespeaks a whale ("Out of his nostrils goeth smoke. . . . He maketh the deep to boil like a pot: he maketh the sea like a pot of ointment. He maketh a path to shine after him . . ."), but it is difficult to reconcile such things as "His scales are his pride, shut up together as with a close seal" or "Out of his mouth go burning lamps, and sparks of fire leap out" with anything but a dragon. Since the description is not intended

*I*t is difficult to classify this seventeenth-century German artifact, which purports to show Jonah in the whale but is comprised of a wooden effigy in the mouth of a 30-inch dried shark. Note the remarkable resemblance of this shark to the one on p. 323, from Aldrovandi's 1613 *De Piscibus*.

*T*he illustration by Rockwell Kent that introduces Melville's chapter on "The Monstrous Pictures of Whales" in the 1930 edition of *Moby-Dick*

to refer to a specific creature, rather to demonstrate the Lord's power over the most powerful and frightening of creatures, the admixture of terrestrial and aquatic characteristics is understandable. A self-appointed authority on sea monsters, Herman Melville equates the dragon of St. George with a whale: ". . . in many old chronicles whales and dragons are strangely jumbled together and often stand for each other," but in his *In the Wake of the Sea-Serpents,* the Belgian zoologist Bernard Heuvelmans tries in vain to identify the leviathan, suggesting a "snake, crocodile, jackal, whale, dragon, and great fish." Whatever leviathan actually was—it seems unlikely that it was a jackal—some very large and ominous creatures lived in the ocean.

The blue whale, which has been known to reach a length of 100 feet and a weight of 200 tons, is the largest animal ever to have inhabited this planet, and for seafarers, the sight of a heretofore unsuspected creature that was considerably longer than their ships (the *Santa Maria* was seventy-seven feet long) must have been startling indeed. It would not be until the eighteenth century that the harmless nature of this leviathan would be recognized.

The first explorers to venture across the open ocean must have seen monsters that defied the imagination. Let us assume that a Portuguese navigator of the year 1450 had departed from Lisbon on an exploratory voyage to Africa. His little ship passes Madeira, and then, in the vicinity of the Canaries, his crew sights a humpback whale. (Before they were eliminated by the whalers, humpbacks were quite common off the coast of West Africa.) What are they to make of this bizarre animal? It is about 50 feet long—almost as long as the *caravela*—with a face covered with lumps and bumps, long, white-blotched flippers, and a powerful spout that issues from the top of its head. It continually leaps out of the water and crashes back, an activity that would be hard for these seamen to interpret as anything but threatening.

Thoroughly frightened by this exuberant sea monster, the captain brings his ship about and heads for home. The stories that the sailors tell upon their return emphasize the terror inspired by this long-winged demon, and before long, artists have begun to interpret their descriptions. By the sixteenth century, then, illustrations of sea monsters have become common, and sailors have no reason not to believe that gigantic ship-sinking creatures inhabit the distant oceans. In 1539, Olaus Magnus drew the *Carta marina*, the first detailed map of Scandinavia, and populated the oceans with an assembly of monsters, several of which are seen performing aggressive acts.

The mere presence of large creatures in the sea, however, was not enough to deter mariners; the beasts had to be equipped with some device for attacking ships. Olaus Magnus suggested that it was the spout of "the biggest and most monstrous creature in the Indish Ocean" that was responsible:

> The *Physeter* or *Pristis* is a kind of whale, two hundred cubits long, and is very cruel. For, to the danger of seamen, he will sometimes raise himself above the sail-yards, and casts such floods of waters above his head, which he had sucked in, that with a cloud of them he will often sink the strongest ships, or expose the mariners to extreme danger. The beast hath also a large round mouth, like a lamprey, whereby he sucks his meat or water, and by his own weight cast upon the fore or hinder deck, he sinks and drowns a ship.

In *Historia de Gentibus Septentrionalibus*, he illustrated these phenomena, and the drawings were repeated by his followers for years.*

Since monsters are expected to be larger than life—a foot-long monster is almost oxymoronic—at one time or another, almost every large sea creature was considered dangerous. The largest sharks—in fact, the largest of all fishes, bony or cartilaginous—are the whale shark (*Rhincodon typus*) and the basking shark (*Cetorhinus maximus*), measuring 50 and 40 feet long, respec-

---

*Despite appearances, whales do not take in or expel water from their blowholes. In *Sea Fables Explained*, Henry Lee referred to this erroneous depiction as "spouting from their blowholes one or more columns of water, which, after ascending skyward to a considerable distance, fall over gracefully as if issuing from the nozzle of an ornamental fountain." The spout is actually a mist of warm condensed air, made visible as it expands after coming into contact with the cooler air into which the whale exhales.

tively. (The largest dangerous shark is the great white, reaching a maximum known length of 23 feet.) It is possible to imagine early seafarers being terrified of such gigantic animals, especially the whale shark, which is covered with a striking geometric pattern of pale spots and has a broad mouth that can be six feet wide. Whale sharks have tiny teeth and eat only plankton, which they strain from the water using a series of gill rakers, not unlike the baleen sieve of some whales, but the first man to see a fifty-foot-long fish with a six-foot-wide mouth can probably be excused for not immediately recognizing its benign nature. The basking shark, found in cooler climates than the tropical whale shark, is also a plankton feeder but more likely to be seen in large numbers, which itself might be cause for trepidation among the uninformed.

There are several marine creatures that are large enough to have frightened uneducated observers, but as we learned more about them, they turned out not to be monsters after all. One animal, with a wingspread of 22 feet or more, was initially perceived as a true terror of the deep but turned out to be a harmless, graceful, gentle giant, eagerly sought by scuba divers for a free ride on its broad back. It is the manta ray, the largest of all rays, and with its pointed wings, whiplike tail, strange-looking cephalic "horns," and a remarkable propensity to throw itself out of the water, it was known for years as "devilfish." The manta is not the only member of the family *Mobulidae,* commonly known as devil rays; there are several poorly defined species, but the largest is thought to be *Manta birostris,* found in the tropical western Atlantic.

Because of their imposing size and strength, devil rays were not always recognized as being harmless to anything but plankton, and they were feared and reviled by the people who first saw them. In 1919, the *National Geographic* ran "Devil-fishing in the Gulf Stream," by John Oliver La Gorce, in which the author described the feeding habits of the manta as follows:

> When the giant ray dashes into a school of fish, the head fins are of great assistance in obtaining food, for like the arms of a boxer, they are in constant motion, whirling about and sweeping living prey into a yard-wide mouth with amazing facility as the giant hurls its body around in its natural element.

Later in the same article, La Gorce identifies some

authentic reports of the devil-fish's running afoul of the anchor chain. True to instinct, it clasps the chain tight by wrapping its tentacula [*sic*] horns or feelers about it, applies its tremendous strength, lifts the heavy chain as if it were a feather, and starts to sea with the anchor, chain and ship, to the amazement and terror of the crew. . . .

All that is nonsense, of course, since the manta actually feeds by swimming slowly through schools of plankton and inhaling the microorganisms with the help of the guiding cephalic fins. But in the early decades of this century, there was little understanding of the biology of the manta and even less sensitivity to the plight of the hunted animal.* When La Gorce and his cronies harpooned a dolphin for sport off Bimini, the game was interrupted when the captain spotted a disturbance in the distance. It turned out to be a huge manta, which they harpooned with three irons, and when the giant ray did not succumb, they shot it with a high-powered rifle. "It was a grand battle," wrote La Gorce, "full of thrills for each of us, although a little tough on the devil-fish."

During his pioneering underwater exploration of the Red Sea, Hans Hass encountered large schools of mantas. (The 1952 book about his adventures is called *Manta: Under the Red Sea with Gun and Camera.*) At that time it was still not obvious that these giant rays were harmless, so Hass entered the realm of the "monsters" (his term) armed with a harpoon as well as a camera. At one point, a large manta made straight for him:

> He didn't seem to see me at all. He came fluttering along, as though in a blissful trance. I took several photographs, focusing nearer and nearer, but the giant continued to swim calmly on. . . . He actually touched me, and at the same instant spun around, his flukes whipping, and gave me a terrific thump on the back. I thought my spine had broken in two. Though the jaws of these creatures might not be dangerous—I had just carefully observed them and there was only one sparse row of teeth along the lower mandible—their movements in fright were certainly so.

Starting in the Sea of Cortez around 1976, scuba divers found that the giant rays were so docile that they could be ridden like a living flying carpet as they swam gently through the clear waters. Many divers did it—and had themselves photographed doing it—but perhaps the best known of these manta riders was Peter Benchley, whose picture (taken by Stan Waterman) serves as the author photo on the back cover of *The Girl of the Sea of Cortez,*

---

*By the time Marine Studios (later Marineland of Florida) opened in St. Augustine in June 1938, the curators had managed to capture two mantas for exhibition. They had so little information on the feeding habits of the giant rays that they crammed the mantas' mouths with mullet until they died.

*U*sing two remoras as handlebars, a diver rides a 20-foot manta like an underwater motorcycle.

his 1982 novel. In this novel, Benchley changes tactics to the point where the large sea creature—in this case, a manta that had become entangled in a fisherman's net—is rescued by a girl named Paloma, but unlike the shark in *Jaws,* the ray is the good guy. Like Androcles' lion, the manta saves the girl's life and even thanks her for cutting him free of the net by taking her to a previously undiscovered oyster bed, where, we assume, giant pearls abound.

As we shall see, some sea monsters have been revealed to exist relatively recently, and some of the so-called sea serpents have not been verified in a way that would satisfy skeptics, let alone scientists. But the marine crypto-zoologist is nothing if not an optimist and is encouraged by two creatures, one of which was believed to have been extinct for 70 million years; the other was not known to exist at all until one turned up under most unusual circumstances in 1976.

The story of the coelacanth is well known, and some elements of it pertain to our study of monsters. In December 1938, about five miles offshore from the South African city of East London, near the mouth of the Chalumna River, fishermen of the trawler *Nerine* had hauled in a five-foot-

*T*he coelacanth, a lobe-finned
fish that was believed to have
been extinct for 70 million years
until one was found off South
Africa in 1938

long fish. It was steely blue in color, with large, bony
scales and fins that appeared to be on leglike stalks.
It was first examined by Marjorie Courtenay-
Latimer, curator at the East London Museum, and
because she could not place it in any known category, she realized that it
was something special indeed. She contacted J. L. B. Smith, a professor of
chemistry at Rhodes University at Grahamstown and an enthusiastic amateur ichthyologist, and told him of her discovery. He guessed—correctly, as
it turned out—that the fish was of a type that was believed to have thrived
300 million years ago and became extinct approximately 70 million years
ago, at the same time as the disappearance of the dinosaurs.

Despite subsequent popular publications, the fish was not the one that
had been extinct for so long; it was a relative. In Devonian deposits, paleontologists had uncovered and identified fossils of lobe-finned fishes of the
order Crossopterygii: a fish known as *Macropoma* from the Cretaceous
period and another, somewhat later version, *Undina,* from the Jurassic.
Both closely resembled the fish that Courtenay-Latimer had examined in
that they had two dorsal fins, paired pectoral and pelvic fins, and a curious
protrusion from the symmetrical caudal fin. Smith named the fish *Latimeria chalumnae:* the genus after Miss Courtenay-Latimer, the species after
the river.

World War II interfered with Smith's plans to obtain another specimen
(all he had of the first was the skull and a taxidermist's mount of the skin),
and a second did not turn up until 1952. In the thirty-four years from 1938
to 1972, sixty-six coelacanths were caught and examined by scientists. (This

figure does not include those caught and not reported by fishermen of the Comoro Islands, where most specimens have been collected.) They have even been observed (from a submersible) swimming along the ocean's bottom at a depth of three hundred feet, and in 1972 a live coelacanth was caught by fishermen off Grand Comore and its behavior carefully observed by scientists before it died. Because of the remote nature of the coelacanth's known habitat (there may be more somewhere else, but no one has much of an idea where to look), there is no information on the number of these fishes that exists. Some ichthyologists have therefore suggested that there be a moratorium on catching them, at least until such time as we can obtain some responsible population figures. It would be a shame to find out that we have lost the coelacanth simply because scientists are so interested in finding out how it managed to last so long.

All this is interesting to paleoichthyologists and evolutionists (because of the structure of their limbs, the earlier coelacanths are believed to have given rise to the first amphibians and are therefore listed in the ancient ancestry of reptiles and mammals), but what does any of this have to do with monsters? A five-foot-long fish isn't really much of a monster. That the coelacanth was believed to have been extinct for 70 million years and then turned up completely unexpectedly gives eternal hope to monster buffs. If there is a "living fossil" like the coelacanth, why not a plesiosaur or a *Basilosaurus?* On rare occasions, monster watchers know (or think they know) what they are looking for, but in most cases, a sighting, or as in the case of the coelacanth, the first specimen, is a complete surprise.

Indeed, another very large, completely unexpected, unknown animal appeared off the Hawaiian island of Oahu in November 1976. The U.S. naval research vessel *AFB-14* was conducting oceanographic experiments in water that was some fifteen thousand feet deep, twenty-five miles off the Kaneohe coast. When the time came to haul in the parachute sea anchors (deployed to keep the ship in position in water where it is too deep to anchor), the crew of the vessel saw that instead of an orange-and-white cargo chute, they were hauling in a very large shark. On deck, it was weighed at 1,653 pounds and measured at a total length of 14.6 feet. A young ensign immediately realized that she had never seen anything like this creature—and, as it turned out, neither had anyone else.

The carcass was brought to the Waikiki Aquarium, where it was examined by the director, Dr. Leighton R. Taylor. It was nicknamed "Megamouth" because it had a large mouth with microsopic teeth and floppy, rubbery lips. When it was examined at the aquarium and the Bishop

*T*he first specimen ever seen of the 13-foot megamouth shark (*Megachasma pelagios*), hoisted high above the dock in Hawaii on November 17, 1976

Museum in Honolulu, the shark was found to be a plankton feeder. It was named *Megachasma pelagios* ("deep water bigmouth"), and the carcass was stored in a special sarcophagus at the Bishop Museum.

Because it had swallowed the parachute (mistaking it for a swarm of plankton?) at approximately five hundred feet, it was assumed that this species had probably never appeared at the surface, nor did it have any reason to do so. Moreover, a plankton feeder would not take a baited hook, which explains why none had ever been caught before. However, since the remarkable discovery of the first Megamouth, four more have appeared: The second one (a male like the first) was caught in a gill net off Santa Catalina Island, Southern California, in 1984; the third male washed ashore at Mandurah, Western Australia, in 1988, and number four was discovered on a beach at Hamamatsu, Japan, in 1989. In October 1990, a healthy male was snagged by a gill-net fisherman off Dana Point, California, and before it was released, it was filmed and tagged.

Perhaps even more than the coelacanth, Megamouth buoys the spirits of monster watchers. After all, here is a very large fish whose existence was completely unsuspected. Throughout Hawaiian history—from the early days of the Polynesian sailing canoes, through the Pacific explorers of the eighteenth and nineteenth centuries, and past World War II in the Pacific (when there was considerable naval action off Hawaii)—no hint of the existence of this fish had ever appeared. If such a creature can be brought to the surface—and if its appearance can then be confirmed by four others in a fifteen-year period—the possibility of a proper sea serpent cannot be dismissed.

The history of monsters has been surprisingly consistent. Most of them began as myths, and in the cases of those discussed at length in this book, they acquired a corporeal reality as their true existence became known. The mermaid metamorphosed into the manatee; Leviathan became the whale; the polyp is the octopus; and the kraken is now known to us as the giant squid. Of all the monsters in this study, only the shark retained the name and form with which it insinuated itself into human awareness. Some of the monsters then regained their mythological status, but in an unprecedented manner. Most of us no longer believe that there are unknown monsters or relict dinosaurs waiting to be discovered. The Loch Ness monster still lurks beneath the cold waters of its highland lake, awaiting the photograph or the carcass that will confirm its existence.

THE LOCH NESS MONSTER

I N THE SUMMER of 1992, I stood on the shore of Loch Ness in the highlands of Scotland. It is a deep, tranquil lake surrounded by yew, birch, and fir trees on gentle hills that roll down to the water. Known to its promoters as "the most famous lake in the world," Loch Ness gives no sense of the complicated controversy that revolves around its most notorious inhabitant. Although you cannot see anything beneath the surface (indeed, there may not be anything below it), there are enough indicators to suggest that something quite unusual is going on there. In Inverness, the loch's northern terminus, there are signs recommending a boat ride to look for "Nessie"; or you can remain in your car and follow the "Monster Trail," which consists of a circumnavigation of the twenty-four-mile-long loch, with lay-bys every mile or so that provide plenty of opportunities to pull off the road and stare at the loch's wind-rippled surface. The loch is actually part of the Great Glen, a deep fault that cuts across the width of Scotland at about a forty-five-degree angle, comprised of the connected lochs of Ness, Lochy, and Linnhe. Tourists may visit the Official Loch Ness Monster Exhibition Centre, opened in 1980. As described in the official brochure,

it has grown to encompass the National Archive and has become the centre for research at the Loch. The exhibition is a multi-media presentation lasting forty minutes. Dramatic use of stage lighting, photography, historical tableaux, video, audio and specially composed music, help set the scene. Ten themed areas tell the story of the monster from 565 AD to the present day. Prepare yourself for forty minutes of sheer fascination and mystery.

*A*t the Official Loch Ness Monster Exhibition Centre at Drumnadrochit, there is a "monster" in the pond that can be activated for movie cameras and camcorders for ten pence.

Appended to the museum is a series of gift shops selling kilts, sporrans, tams, ties, and other Scottish souvenirs, but specializing in *objets* with some representation of the monster in any one or all of its permutations. There are scary monsters on T-shirts, funny monsters on ashtrays, cute monsters on bibs, and postcards with all of the above. You can also purchase books, videos, audiotapes of the museum's "specially composed music," key chains, cigarette lighters, hats, and tea towels. Outside the gift shop is a pond containing a thirty-foot-long model of the monster, which can be activated for the benefit of cinematographers and children for ten pence.

Although it cannot be legitimately classified as a sea monster, the Loch Ness monster is perhaps the most famous of all cryptozoological creatures. Its controversial history requires—indeed, has begotten—a small library,*

---

*In addition to the thousands of newspaper and magazine articles, some of the books about the Loch Ness monster are *The Loch Ness Monster and Others*, Rupert T. Gould, 1934; *More Than a Legend*, Constance Whyte, 1957; *The Elusive Monster*, Maurice Burton, 1961; *Loch Ness Monster*, Tim Dinsdale, 1961; *The Great Orm of Loch Ness*, F. W. Holiday, 1969; *In Search of Lake Monsters*, Peter Costello, 1974; *The Monsters of Loch Ness*, Roy Mackal, 1976; *The Loch Ness Story*, Nicholas Witchell, 1976; *The Loch Ness Mystery Solved*, Ronald Binns, 1984; *The Enigma of Loch Ness*, Henry H. Bauer, 1986; *The Loch Ness Monster: The Evidence*, Steuart Campbell, 1991.

and learned societies debate its existence, affiliations, shape, size, respiration, and eating habits. As will be seen, most other water monsters appear once, usually in a remote corner of a remote ocean. Of all monsters, only Nessie has spawned such a history of sightings, and since Loch Ness is far more accessible than, say, Cape Horn, a steady stream of researchers has headed for the shores of the lake to establish base camps for every imaginable sort of surface and underwater investigation.

The first appearance of a monster in that cold lake—its temperature at the lower levels averages forty-two degrees Fahrenheit—occurred back in the sixth century. It seems that St. Columba, a Scottish holy man, witnessed the burial of a swimmer who had been killed by some sort of water beast, but because he needed to cross the loch, he sent one of his companions to fetch a boat that was on the other side. Upon seeing the swimmer threatened by the beast in the loch, Columba made the sign of the cross and exhorted the animal to "think not to go further, touch not that man!" Thereupon the beast retreated, swimming backward more rapidly than it had been swimming forward.

As with almost every other aspect of Nessie research, someone has decided to study this one in detail. In the journal *Cryptozoology,** Charles Thomas, the director of the Institute of Cornish Studies at the University of Exeter, wrote an article entitled "The 'Monster' Episode in Adomnan's Life of St. Columba." After a detailed analysis of the Latin text (and harsh criticism for those who have "simply repeated assertions already published by others"), Thomas concludes that the "disturbance" was probably caused by a stray marine mammal, probably a walrus or a bearded seal.

Even though most monster stories—and certainly their repetition over time—suffer from exaggeration, this interpretation seems to err on the side of caution, since the text, as translated by Thomas himself, seems as good an account of a monster as we are likely to find anywhere. Here is the relevant passage from what Thomas calls his "fresh and completely literal translation":

> But the beast, not so much satiated by what had gone before [the attack on the first man] as whetted for prey, was lurking at the bottom of the

Cryptozoology is published by the International Society of Cryptozoology (ICS), which was founded in 1982 by a group of scientists from various disciplines. The first president of the ISC was Bernard Heuvelmans, who wrote this credo in the first issue of the journal: "Cryptozoology is the science of 'hidden' animals. While paleontology discovers and describes organisms of the past, cryptozoology attempts to do the same with unknown animals of the present. . . . The task of cryptozoology consists of demythifying the content of information in an attempt to make the inventory of the planet's fauna as complete as possible."

river. Feeling the water above it disturbed by the swimming, and suddenly coming up to the surface, it rushed with great roaring and with a wide open mouth at the man swimming in the middle of the stream-bed.

While it is true that pinnipeds have been known to roar, they do not spend much time "lurking at the bottom of the river," and none of the species that Thomas suggests for the actual monster (gray seal; harbor seal) are known to attack, let alone kill, people. From Columba's time to the present, however, some sort of monster has been appearing irregularly, and in various forms, in Loch Ness.

Morphologically related to some offshore "sea monsters" sighted in the latter half of the nineteenth century, a "monster" appeared in Loch Ness at the beginning of the twentieth century, which culminated—if that is the right word for an event that may or may not have occurred—with the celebrated "photograph" taken by a surgeon named R. Kenneth Wilson in 1934. (That it is a photograph seems beyond doubt, but exactly what it is a photograph *of* has been perplexing people for years. In addition to the monster,

*T*he most famous "Nessie" photograph of all: the "surgeon's photograph" supposedly taken by Dr. Kenneth Wilson in 1934. It has been revealed that this picture was a fake, staged and photographed by a frustrated filmmaker and big-game hunter named Marmaduke Arundel Wetherell.

other candidates include a seal, an otter, a killer whale, a pilot whale, a bird, a tree trunk, gas bubbles, and even an elephant.) Before Wilson took his photograph, however, something had been sighted swimming in the loch. In 1933, many Scotsmen claimed (and subsequently swore under oath to the veracity of their claims) to have seen an animal that dived and reappeared, leaving a wake as it moved.

Mr. and Mrs. George Spicer, motoring alongside the loch at Inverfarigaig on July 22, 1933, reported that a huge creature had crossed the road in front of them. They described it as having a thick body and no legs, rather like a huge snail with a long neck. It appeared to be carrying a small lamb or a young deer. Six months later, Arthur Grant of Drumnadrochit declared that he had spotted a large lizardlike creature crossing the road, illuminated in the headlights of his motorcycle. He drew a picture of what he had seen and sent it to Prof. Antoon Cornelis Oudemans, a Dutch scientist who had published the definitive work on the subject in 1892, *The Great Sea-Serpent.* Oudemans believed that it was a large seal and urged the British government to capture it for science, but nothing was done.* Then Comdr. Rupert T. Gould, a popular radio personality, headed for Loch Ness on a motorcycle, interviewed everyone who claimed to have seen the monster, and in *The Loch Ness Monster and Others,* published in 1934, declared that it was a saltwater sea serpent that had wandered into the loch from the sea.

To place the most common descriptions of the monster in a historical (or more accurately, a prehistorical) perspective, let us conduct a paleontological search for the creature that fits the descriptions most often applied to the Loch Ness monster. During the Mesozoic era, a period that lasted approximately 100 million years, the dinosaurs ruled the earth—and, it would appear, the oceans as well. A large group of long-necked plesiosaurs swam with broad, paddle-like flippers, and because they were air-breathing reptiles, they poked their heads out of the water to inhale. A plesiosaur looks much like the creature that most cryptozoologists conjure up when they try to place a long-extinct animal in Loch Ness: a dinosaur that looks, as the nineteenth-century amateur paleontologist William Conybeare wrote, "like a snake threaded through the body of a turtle." However, until the "sightings" of the nineteenth and twentieth centuries of the various ple-

---

* There have been verified records of seals in Loch Ness, but they were only common harbor seals, which can reach a length of five feet and have been seen in and around the lochs of Scotland. From November 1984 to June 1985, a seal was observed swimming in Loch Ness and photographed by Gordon Williamson, a respected naturalist. (The photographs appear in the *Scientific Reports of the Whales Research Institute of Tokyo,* no. 39, 1988.) After sporadic appearances over a seven-month period, the seal was shot by salmon fishermen.

*A*lthough the snakelike neck is now believed to be in error, Charles R. Knight painted this elasmosaur fishing in Cretaceous waters.

siosaurs (there is fossil evidence for some eight or nine species, divided into two groups, the plesiosaurs and the shorter-necked, larger-headed plio-saurs), there was no reason to believe that they had not died out, along with all the other dinosaurs, by the end of the Cretaceous period, some 65 mil-lion years ago.

On the jacket of *Animal Legends,* author Maurice Burton is described as "a well-known zoologist and authority on animal behavior." In this 1957 book, he devotes a chapter to "Marvelous Eels and the Loch Ness Mon-ster" in which he discusses the biology of eels and then suggests that Nessie may be a gigantic representative of that tribe:

> I suggested tentatively that the Monster, assuming it was a living organ-ism, might be a large eel. My reasons for taking this view were three-fold. First, we have to visualize something of large size that lived habitually below the surface of the water, yet was capable of staying on the surface with the head out of the water for extended periods of time, and might even be capable (as some eyewitnesses claim) of coming on land. Sec-

ondly, it must be long in the body and capable of traveling at fair speed. Thirdly, it must be powerful, to create the wash of which all eyewitnesses speak. The only animal I could think of was a giant eel, one of greater proportions than any known to science.

In 1960, Tim Dinsdale, a dedicated monster watcher and amateur photographer, filmed what he claimed was the monster swimming across the loch. His short film shows something moving, but even a frame-by-frame laboratory analysis of the film by the Royal Air Force (RAF) could only verify that it was "an animate object" and could not establish its size. Then scientists from the University of Birmingham picked up movement deep in the loch with a new type of sonar, but they were unable to decide if the shadows on their screens were schools of fishes or something else. Under the leadership of David James, the Loch Ness Phenomena Investigation Bureau, Ltd. (LNPIB) was formed in 1963 in an attempt to organize the hordes of curious tourists who visited Loch Ness during the summer. They were given binoculars, survey sheets, and instructions on what to do if and when they made a sighting. Clem Skelton was one of the field marshals of the LNPIB, and since he spent more time than almost anyone else on the site (he and his wife lived year-round in a tent on the shore), he had accumulated more Nessie sightings than anyone else. (He claims to have nearly bumped into it while rowing across the loch one night in June 1964.)

F. W. "Ted" Holiday was by his own description a dedicated monster seeker since the age of twelve. (He collected press clippings and wrote to the "authorities" of the time, like George Spicer, who had seen Nessie crossing the road in front of his motorcar.) After a wartime stint in the RAF, Holiday returned to his obsession and in 1962 mounted a one-man expedition to Loch Ness. (He writes, "Forming a one-man expedition is easy. You assemble your equipment, arrange your family affairs, and push off into the blue.") Shortly after setting up his camp, he saw the Loch Ness monster:

> It was thick in the middle and tapered at the extremities. It was sort of blackish-grey in colour. To demonstrate that it was no trick of light refraction, it moved steadily from one side of the leat [a leat is a brook or stream] to the other and then back again. . . . Its size, judging from the width of the leat, was between 40 and 45 feet long. No details were visible nor did any portion of it again break surface. It was simply an elongated shape moving purposefully to and fro at the edge of the deep water.

On the basis of this sighting (not to mention his previous predisposition to believe in the monster), Holiday became a staunch advocate of Nessie; only

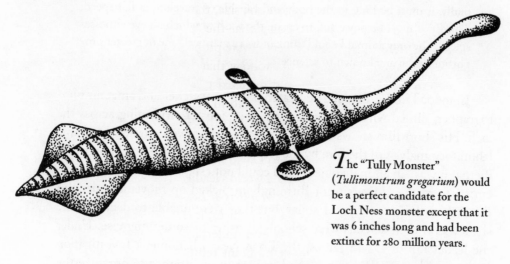

*T*he "Tully Monster" (*Tullimonstrum gregarium*) would be a perfect candidate for the Loch Ness monster except that it was 6 inches long and had been extinct for 280 million years.

he suggested that it was some sort of gigantic worm, which he referred to as an "orm." (He wrote that it looked "like a huge black slug.") Unhappy with the pejorative associations of the word "monster," Holiday decided to call it (and his book) "The Great Orm of Loch Ness."* There are marine worms (*Lineus* spp.) that can be stretched to a length of 100 feet, but they are about an inch in diameter, making them unlikely candidates for sea monsters.

Holiday organized a photographic expedition in 1965, but it was not as successful as his first, for there were no sightings and no photographs of the orm. But then Roy Mackal, an American molecular biologist, came to see Holiday at Loch Ness, bearing a photograph of a long-extinct, segmented invertebrate called *Tullimonstrum gregarium,* the "common Tully monster." *Tullimonstrum* is indeed a bizarre animal, with no known affiliations, but it was only six inches long, and the only record of its existence was a gathering in what would become the shales of Mazon Creek, Illinois, where it lived some 280 million years ago. (It was named for Francis J. Tully, a fossil collector from Chicago who brought the first specimens to that city's Field Museum, where they were described and named by Eugene S. Richardson.)

But if invertebrate paleontologists could not make sense out of *Tullimonstrum,* it was exactly what Ted Holiday was looking for. It looked as if it had a long neck, a small head, two paddle-like flippers, a long body, and a flattened, triangular tail; in other words, a miniature Loch Ness monster.

*In his introduction to Holiday's book, Ivan Sanderson has no problems whatever with the verified existence of Nessie. He writes: ". . . and I should here emphasize that we *now have absolute proof that they exist and that they are animals.* . . . This is the straightforward question: 'What can roar about the surface of any body of water at ten knots, without a sail, leaving a clear "V"-shaped bow-wave but no prop-wash?' Yet this is just what these things have not only been reputed to do, but have been filmed doing."

(Holiday conveniently chose to ignore the size, the backboneless nature of the beast, and most curiously, the fact that the "protrusions"—which he wanted so much to think of as flippers—were probably eyes.) The shape of this little invertebrate suggested to Holiday that "wormlike animals with the appearance of a plesiosaurus did once exist," and he wrote, "No-one knows whether the Orm of Loch Ness is a form of *Tullimonstrum;* but talking most unscientifically, I would bet my shirt that it is."*

Upon finding himself in the Scottish highlands in 1965, Roy Mackal went to Loch Ness, where he ran into David James (and Ted Holiday) and almost immediately became one of the world's leading monster scholars. By 1976 he had published the 392-page *Monsters of Loch Ness.* With its profusion of charts, diagrams, tables, and appendices, it is one of the most comprehensive studies of the controversy ever undertaken. After an exhaustive search of the literature and a point-by-point refutation of everyone else's theories, Mackal suggests that the best candidates are either a 20-foot-long, 2,500-pound eel or a gigantic descendant of an eellike amphibian, an embolomere or a urodele.† There is no doubt in Mackal's mind that the Loch Ness monster exists: "To those who are conservatively inclined," he writes, "the eel idea will no doubt be more appealing. The evidence has led me to believe that the best possible candidate is a gigantic aquatic amphibian, probably some evolutionary descendant of an embolomere. Be that as it may, we must recognize that whatever the identity of the animals in Loch Ness, they exist—independent of man's prejudices or beliefs."

Nessie research did not really flower until the development of new techniques for locating objects under water, particularly automated cameras and side-scanning sonar. The latter is a system involving a torpedo-shaped transmitter that can be towed at depth; it sends out lateral pulses and can therefore scan hundreds of yards on either side. Using this system, images can be obtained of large objects far beyond the depth capabilities of human divers. (It was side-scanning sonar that enabled oceanographers to locate the sunken ship *Titanic* in 1985.) Even if the monster did not surface—and evi-

---

*In *Wonderful Life: The Burgess Shale and the Nature of History,* a book about the unclassifiable fossils of the Burgess Shale of British Columbia, Steven J. Gould refers to *Tullimonstrum* as another of the "oddities"—also referred to as "Problematica"—in the fossil record, creatures whose morphology and associations defy understanding because they are so unlike anything else that is known. If, however, it is anything like the other segmented worms—and as far as we know, it is not—the flattened, triangular element, which Holiday wanted to represent the animal's tail, would be its head.

†According to Romer's *Vertebrate Paleontology,* an embolomere was an amphibian "water-dwelling fish predator" common in the Carboniferous period, and a urodele was an amphibian ancestor of current salamanders and newts. Both are known only from fossil evidence that is some 200 million years old.

*T*he tower of Urquhart Castle is sixty-four feet high, which gives a sense of scale to this photograph by P. A. McNab of something moving through the water in Loch Ness in 1955.

dently it didn't for several decades—the new technology would enable scientists to take its picture, anyway. (At its deepest point, Loch Ness is over eight hundred feet deep, and it contains a vast amount of peat particles in suspension, rendering its brownish waters almost opaque just below the surface.)

Dr. Robert Rines, director of the Academy of Applied Science (AAS) in Boston, assembled a cadre of diverse specialists in an all-out quest to obtain a photograph of Nessie. Included on some of the AAS expeditions to Scotland were Harold "Doc" Edgerton of MIT, the inventor of high-speed strobe photography, who would contribute his expertise to the project, and various sonar operators and technicians. One of the expeditions was joined by Sir Peter Scott, naturalist, artist, and ex-president of the World Wildlife Fund, who believed that the animals needed a scientific name to protect them "if and when their existence was established beyond doubt." In a letter published in the journal *Nature* (January 15, 1976), Scott named it *Nessiteras rhombopteryx*, or "Ness monster with rhomboidal fin."*

They took plenty of photographs, but only by using "computer enhancement" could they even suggest that the pictures showed a monster, or even part of one. Nevertheless, Mackal called the Rines photos "the most

*There are some who believe that Sir Peter Scott might not have been completely serious about his involvement with Nessie, since *Nessiteras rhombopteryx* turns out to be an anagram of "Monster hoax by Sir Peter S."

significant photographs to date of our Loch Ness animal." Indeed, there is a picture taken during the 1972 expedition that appears to show some sort of an appendage (whether tail or flipper cannot be determined) of an animal that is otherwise unidentifiable.* (This is the photo that Peter Scott used as the basis for his *Nessiteras*.) In 1975, Rines obtained another series of photographs, but although one of them was said to show most of a long-necked creature, the image was so indistinct that only by a great leap of faith could one make an animal out of it. (Mackal accepts this photograph, along with another four out of the seventeen that purport to show some aspect of Nessie, as "positive evidence" of its existence.) Despite the concerted efforts of the true believers—the scientists, the laymen, and the technicians—Nessie remains tantalizingly out of reach, and out of focus.

Even the *National Geographic,* employing technological and financial resources that far exceeded those of any previous expeditions, came up empty. In 1976, the magazine mounted a full-scale assault on Loch Ness. According to the 1977 article "Loch Ness: The Lake and the Legend" by William Ellis, "They positioned highly sophisticated camera gear below the surface. They played recorded beeper sounds meant to attract the most elusive of lake life. They set sonar to work, scanning the cold depths. They used mathematics and electronic wizardry. . . . *National Geographic* dispatched a team of underwater photographers and divers, together with Dr. Robert D. Ballard of the Woods Hole Oceanographic Institution."†

National Geographic photographers David Doubilet and Emory Kristof positioned elaborate camera rigs below the surface, some equipped with sonar sensitive enough to release the shutter at the slightest movement. When the waters of the loch were lit with underwater lights, they glowed with an eerie brown color, "like Scotch whiskey," because of the peat suspension. Doubilet and Kristof took pictures of many moving fish (a larger than expected population of arctic char lives in Loch Ness) and teapots and shoes on the bottom, but no monster.

An article in the winter 1982 issue of the *ISC Newsletter* (a quarterly publication of the International Society of Cryptozoology) begins with the words "It has not been a good year for Nessie." First, Maurice Burton, a

---

* In September 1984, the popular science magazine *Discover* published an article entitled "The (Retouched) Loch Ness Monster" in which two engineers, Rikki Razdan and Alan Kielar, examined the original photograph of the flipper that Rines had sent to the Jet Propulsion Lab; "to their astonishment, the images were grainy and indistinct, and bore little resemblance to flippers." The article set off a furious exchange of charges and countercharges, most of which appeared in the *ISC Newsletter* in 1984.

† If anyone could have located Nessie, it was Bob Ballard. After the *National Geographic*'s Loch Ness expedition, he went on to find the *Titanic* in 1985 and the *Bismarck* in 1989.

British mammalogist, published a three-part article in *New Scientist* in which he retracted his theory that the monster was an eel and wrote that a giant otter was probably responsible for most of the creature sightings. Then *New Scientist* published an article by Robert P. Craig entitled "Loch Ness: The Monster Unveiled" in which the author argued that sunken pine logs are brought to the surface by the trapped gases of decay, but since the gases escape when the log bobs to the surface, it sinks again. (The *Newsletter* article is entitled "Log Ness Monster?")

One of the most articulate and entertaining books on Scottish lake monsters is not about Nessie at all. Rather, the authors discuss Nessie, but only as a means of demonstrating that such phenomena exist and that we cannot discount all the eyewitness observations. The subject of the study by Elizabeth Montgomery Campbell and David Solomon is Morag, the monster of Loch Morar. In *The Search for Morag*, Campbell and Solomon, both members of the Loch Ness Investigation, present a lucid introduction to Scottish monsters, including one of the best historical summaries of the Loch Ness events. They then recount some thirty-two descriptions of Morag, the earliest being from 1897 and the latest from 1973, the year their book was going to press. It would appear that Morag is not unlike Nessie; it has a small head, a long neck, and occasionally a humped back and is anywhere from 12 to 40 feet in length. Also like Nessie, Morag could be an invertebrate, a fish, a seal, a shark, a plesiosaur, or an inanimate object, like a log or a mat of vegetation. Morag has not been the beneficiary of Nessie's photogenic celebrity. Despite an occasional concentration of cameras on the loch's shores, the Loch Morar Survey has failed to photograph the monster. Finally, although the existence of Morag has not been proved, Montgomery and Solomon show a deep concern for its preservation—and for the continuation of investigations:

> If support of the right kind is forthcoming, responsible investigation has a real hope of discovering the truth. If it is not, then yet another species may be condemned to join those such as the dodo and the trusting Steller's sea cow which man has succeeded in exterminating. But if these creatures are allowed to become extinct like so many before them, it will not be because they have died out through neglect. It will be because they have been ridiculed to death.

Adrian Shine, now a permanent resident of the Loch Ness area, has been the leader of the Loch Ness and Morar Project, which has been conducting annual searches in the loch for fourteen years. In October 1987, he organized Operation Deepscan, which consisted of a fleet of twenty power-

A "monster" ad for
Minolta copiers. The caption
reads "There are times when
faster is decidedly better."

boats, each equipped with a sonar fish finder, that would travel down the
loch "line abreast," pinging as they went. After a north-to-south sweep that
took nine hours, the fleet made the return journey the next day. They located
some "interesting mid-water targets," but Shine announced (to the three
hundred newsmen from twenty-two countries and to fifteen national television networks) that they would probably be disappointed in their hope for a
"media monster," because he believed that Nessie was a big fish. Tim Dinsdale, who shot the only film footage that purports to show Nessie, died later
that year. J. Richard Greenwell, editor of the *ICS Newsletter,* wrote a moving
obituary that ended with: "Like all those before him, Tim Dinsdale's essence
has joined the rich if mainly unwritten historical continuum of Loch Ness."

In 1991, Steuart Campbell collected all the stories, photographs, videos,
and sonar printouts and published a book he called *The Loch Ness Monster:
The Evidence.* To "save space and to avoid the problem of whether or not to
refer to a 'monster,' " he refers to Nessie as "N" and Loch Ness as "L Ness,"
so we get peculiar constructions like this: "Many believe that N entered L
Ness through an underwater tunnel," but otherwise Campbell's study is

complete, unbiased, and useful for a systematic analysis of N in L Ness. He is particularly good on geology, and he writes (immediately following the sentence used above as an example), "Since L Ness is 16m above sea level, any tunnel large enough to take N would drain the lake down to sea level. There is no tunnel. Nor are there underwater caves; L Ness lies in a glaciated valley ground smooth by aeons of glaciers."

After a thorough review of the eyewitness accounts, the photographs (enhanced and otherwise), and the sonar and video material, Campbell weighs in with his own personal view:

> Not only does the evidence show that N does not exist, N's existence is not probable. . . . The null hypothesis is supported in a curious way by Binn's observation that the more L Ness is watched, the less N shows itself. This is what would be expected if N does not exist. If the reports are merely due to misinterpretations of the commonplace at distances too great to allow proper identification and/or by inexperienced observers, then saturating the surroundings with skilled observers is bound to reduce or even elimi-nate reports of N. . . . The popular N is indeed an incongruous mix of reptile and mammal, of fish and amphibian, of vertebrate and inverte-brate, of long-necked and short-necked plesiosaur, of seal, whale, eel, etc. It is a chimaera, no more real than the centaur or the griffin.

Curiously, Campbell's book is being sold at the Official Loch Ness Monster Exhibition Centre, and we can only hope that those monster-seeking tourists don't read it too carefully. It would take all the fun out of the search for Nessie if too many people read Campbell's last sentence: "In my view there is absolutely no reason why anyone should believe in the exis-tence of lake-monsters."

Unfortunately, the very circumstances that make Nessie watching so popular (the availability of suitable vantage points; the limited size of the lake) are likely to be the undoing of the monster stories. If the creature is a plesiosaur, then it has to surface to breathe, like a whale. If, on the other hand, it is some sort of a fish, it could remain permanently submerged, but the idea of a 60-foot-long fish with a long neck and a small head has never been seriously proposed. (There is no fish that has a neck.) That leaves the invertebrates—the worms and slugs—and while there are indeed gigantic invertebrates (the giant squid is one), the idea of a 50-foot eel or a 60-foot slug does not fall comfortably into any scientific frame of reference cur-rently employed. (That they don't, of course, is grist for the cryptozoolo-gist's mill: They hasten to point out that until 1857 nobody really believed in the giant squid and until 1938 everyone thought that the coelacanth had

WEEKLY WORLD

NEWS

pril 14. 1992   75¢/80¢ CANADA   18259

70-foot mom and 2,000-lb. infant are doing fine!

LOCH NESS MONSTER

Photo taken just hours after birth!

HAS A BABY!

*F*ront-page news in the *Weekly World News*

been extinct for 70 million years.) Then there is the problem of the enclosed nature of the loch: At one time, it may have been open to the sea, but it is now completely landlocked, some fifty-five feet above sea level, and nothing can swim in or out. Assuming that there has been one monster (or even, as some have imagined, a small family) in the loch, it stands to reason that more than a single photograph or movie would have been taken over the past sixty years, especially considering the army of dedicated monster watchers who have steadily patrolled the gorse-covered shores with their cameras at the ready. Moreover, unless we are willing to believe that one animal has been living in the loch for several hundred years, we have to find a way to explain how a single monster might reproduce.

As this book was being set in type, a startling news story broke in Britain, rendering much of the previous chapter obsolete. Rather than modify it, however, I have elected to let it stand as written, grateful for the opportunity to include this addendum, which was written in March 1994.

The 1934 "Surgeon's Photograph" (reproduced on p.22 of this volume) was believed for sixty years to be *prima facie* evidence of the existence of some sort of a monster in Loch Ness, since it was clearly a photograph of *something*, and the photographer, R. Kenneth Wilson, was a respected Harley Street gynecologist, whose honesty was beyond question. Despite frequent questions about the subject, the spotless reputation of the photographer lent an air of almost unassailable credibility to the picture, which was first published in the *Daily Mail* on April 19, 1934.*

On March 13, 1994, the London *Sunday Telegraph* published this headline across the front page: REVEALED: THE LOCH NESS PICTURE HOAX. The story, written by James Langton, detailed a complicated plot involving a filmmaker and big-game hunter named Marmaduke Arundel Wetherell, his son and stepson, a London insurance broker named Maurice Chambers, and yes, Dr. R. Kenneth Wilson. "Wetherell," according to the article, "was already well known to the public after footprints of the 'monster' he found on a beach in Loch Ness in December 1933 were revealed by the Natural History Museum to have been made by a dried hippo foot—perhaps part of an umbrella stand." (In his 1989 study *The Loch Ness Story*, Nicholas Witchell, a BBC newsman, wrote, "It is not clear to this day whether Mr. Weatherall [*sic*] actually conspired with the young sons of the

---

* Wilson's photograph of the monster has been endlessly analyzed, but computer technology has now made the photograph a much less reliable confirmation of reality than it used to be. By digitizing photographs, technicians can now refashion them to show anything they want, such as the Eiffel Tower in London or a plesiosaur in Loch Ness. There is no way to identify such an enhanced photograph, so even if a picture of Nessie should appear in a magazine, it would prove nothing.

foot's owner to bring about the hoax, or whether he too had been taken in by it," but given the recent turn of events, his complicity seems virtually assured.) In any event, this unlikely expedition was sent to Loch Ness by the *Daily Mail* to check on reports of the monster, and to bring some evidence of it back to London. When no monster appeared, they decided to make one.

The hoax was revealed by Wetherell's stepson, Christian Spurling, who died at the age of ninety in November 1993. After "Duke" Wetherell's hippo footprints had been soundly ridiculed in the press, he evidently returned from Scotland determined to "give them their monster." The model made by Christian Spurling was about a foot high, made of plastic wood, and mounted on a toy submarine that had a lead keel to give it stability. They brought it to a quiet bay in Loch Ness, where it was photographed by Wetherell—the "surgeon's photograph" was therefore not taken by the surgeon. The plates were then given to Dr. Wilson, a friend of Maurice Chambers, whose participation was intended to lend credibility to the event. Wilson brought them for development to a chemist's shop in Inverness, claiming that he had taken the pictures.

Once the press reproduced the "Surgeon's Photograph," the thing got completely out of control, and obviously the only thing the conspirators could do was remain mute. And with the exception of Spurling, they took the secret to their graves. Wetherell and Chambers were gone by the mid-fifties, and the surgeon died in Australia in 1969. And what became of the foot-high "monster" that launched a thousand expeditions, caused sixty years of controversy, and spawned hundreds of books, articles, and arguments? When Wetherell and his son Ian had photographed it, they heard someone approaching, so "Duke" put his foot on it and sank it. Somewhere off the shore of Loch Ness, in water probably only a few feet deep, lies the most famous monster of all. Undoubtedly, a whole new series of expeditions will set out to find the "real" Nessie, a plastic-wood figurehead on a tin submarine.

SEA SERPENTS

WHEN THE PRIEST Laocoön tried to dissuade his countrymen from allowing the wooden horse of the Greeks to be brought into the walled city of Troy, two fearsome serpents came out of the sea, wrapped themselves around Laocoön and his two sons, and squeezed the life out of them. There are those who say that Poseidon sent the serpents because Laocoön sided with the Trojans, but whatever the reason, the Trojan horse was brought into the city, and Troy fell to the Greeks. The battle with the serpents was immortalized in marble in a heroic Hellenistic sculpture (now in the Vatican Museum) and was described in Book II of the *Aeneid* by the Roman epic poet Virgil around 30 B.C.:

> Laocoön, who was chosen by lot to be a priest of Neptune, happened at this moment to be sacrificing a fine bull at the altar of the cult, when, and I sicken to recall it, two giant arching sea-snakes swam over the calm waters from Tenedos, breasting the sea together and plunging towards the land. Their fore-parts and their blood-red crests towered above the waves; the rest drove through the ocean behind, wreathing monstrous coils, and leaving a wake that roared and foamed. And now, with blazing and blood-shot eyes and tongues which flickered and licked their hissing mouths, they were on the beach. We paled at the sight and scattered; they forged on, straight at Laocoön. First each snake took one of his two little sons, twined round him tightening, and bit, and devoured the tiny limbs. Next they seized Laocoön, who had armed himself and was hastening to the rescue; they bound him in the giant spirals of their scaly length, twice round his middle, twice round his throat; and still their heads and necks towered above him. His hands strove frantically to wrench the knots apart. Filth and black venom drenched his priestly bands.

ℒaocoön and his two sons attacked by two fearful sea serpents that came out of the sea.
The event was chronicled in Virgil's *Aeneid* and immortalized in marble by Greek
sculptors of the second century B.C.

Les Marins Monstres & Terrestres, from Olaus Magnus's 1648 *Historia de Gentibus Septentrionalibus* (History of the People of the Northern Regions)

In the ensuing years, sea serpents appeared throughout the world's oceans, and for reasons unknown, they were frequently beheld and described by clergymen. Olaus Magnus (1490–1557), the Catholic archbishop of Sweden, was influential as a historian and a cleric, but his name will be forever associated with sea monsters. He wrote *Historia de Gentibus Septentrionalibus* (History of the People of the Northern Regions), which appeared in English in 1658 as *A Compendious History of the Goths, Swedes & Vandals, and other Northern Nations*. The descriptions and drawings that appeared on his maps firmly established the existence of many fabulous creatures and were copied, reproduced, and modified for centuries, thus assuring his place as one of the most important figures in the history of zoology. He described the *Soe Orm* as follows:

A very large Sea-Serpent of a length upwards of 200 feet and 20 feet in diameter which lives in rocks and in holes near the shore of Bergen; it comes out of its cavern only on summer nights and in fine weather to destroy calves, lambs, or hogs, or goes into the sea to eat cuttles, lobster, and all kinds of sea crabs. It has a growth of hairs of two feet in length hanging from the neck, sharp scales of a dark brown color, and brilliant flaming eyes.

One of the best-known drawings in Olaus Magnus's work is the one known as *Les marins monstres & terrestres, lelquez on trouve en beaucoup de lieux es parties septentrionales* (The sea and land monsters that are found in many northern places). This woodcut, supposedly the work of Hans Rudolph Manuel Deutsch, who was active in Switzerland around the middle of the sixteenth century, reproduced many of Olaus Magnus's illustrations but added many new ones. *Les Marins Monstres* then became the basis for Conrad Gesner's *Historia Animalium* (1551–58), which is considered to be the basis of modern zoological classification. As Daniel Boorstin wrote in *The Discoverers:*

> . . . his *Historia Animalium,* following Aristotle's arrangement, supplied everything known, speculated, imagined, or reported about all known animals. Like Pliny, he provided an omnium-gatherum, but now added the miscellany that had accumulated in the intervening millennium and a half. A shade more critical than Pliny, he still did not deflate tall tales, as when he showed a sea serpent three hundred feet long.

Of course, Gesner included many of the creatures originally depicted by Olaus Magnus, which were then repeated, often without change, by the Renaissance encyclopedist Edward Topsell, whose *Historie of Foure-Footed Beastes* appeared in 1607. Although Topsell's marine "beastes" have no feet whatsoever, they are recognizably the drawings of Olaus Magnus. Ulysses Aldrovandi (*De Piscibus,* 1613) and John Jonstonus (*Historia Naturalis,* 1649) followed Olaus Magnus with their encyclopedias, and they faithfully repeated his drawings and fanciful stories.

Most often, the verification of these creatures came from seafarers' tales, embellished by equal parts of ignorance and fear. Less frequently, the evidence washed up on the beach, but even then, spectators were more than a little inclined to improvise and fantasize, particularly because many of these creatures had never been seen before and resembled nothing that landsmen had ever encountered, even in their most frightening nightmares. Think of the first person to come across a dead whale or a giant squid, animals with no terrestrial analogues.

Even though they have rarely been seen alive—and even more rarely by people who know what they are seeing—the ribbonfish, or oarfish (*Regale-*

cus glesne), may be responsible for some of the more dramatic sea-serpent stories. (Because of the "blood-red crests" of Laocoön's serpents, Heuvelmans has suggested that Virgil may have been referring to this fish.) Known to reach a length of 22 feet, the oarfish is a laterally flattened creature with a coral-red

This creature was found washed up on a Bermuda beach in 1860. Because it was 16 feet long and had a bright red crest, it is not surprising that it was described as a sea serpent. It is actually a harmless and toothless fish known as the oar-fish or ribbon-fish.

"cockscomb" of spines on its head and a red dorsal fin that runs the length of its body. It is so poorly known that few ichthyologists would venture to guess at its habits, but an oarfish swimming at the surface with its crest erect could easily bring the classical image of a sea serpent to mind.

No one but a trained ichthyologist would recognize an oarfish at the surface, so if we assume that this creature sometimes pokes its head out of the water while swimming at the surface, we might be able to account for some serpent sightings. We don't even know how big it gets: Gerald Wood's *Guinness Book of Animal Facts and Feats* lists oarfish measuring 45 and 50 feet, but there is no evidence to back up such claims. Regardless of its length, it would not make a very formidable sea serpent, since it is a fragile, almost transparent creature that is totally harmless. But because of its spectacular appearance on the beach (and occasional appearance in the water), several authorities—such as ichthyologist J. R. Norman of the British Museum—have firmly identified it with sea-serpent stories. In *A History of Fishes,* Norman wrote that "the Sea Serpents of Aristotle, Pliny, and other classical authors seem to have been nothing more than gigantic eels. The monster described as having the head of a horse with a flaming red mane is the Oar-fish or Ribbon-fish, a species which probably grows to more than fifty feet in length, and may sometimes be seen swimming with undulating movements at the surface of the sea."

Some sea-serpent sightings stand out, usually because they have been confirmed by reputable observers, while others gain verisimilitude because they have been corroborated by a significant number of "reliable" witnesses. (In his 1968 book *In the Wake of the Sea-Serpents*, Heuvelmans lists 587 "real, apparent, or pretended sightings of great unknown sea-animals, serpentine in some respect," but we will touch only on the best known or best documented of these.)

The Danish missionary Hans Egede, who eventually became the bishop of Greenland, visited that icy island early in the eighteenth century in hopes of converting the natives to Christianity. Two settlements were established, the first in 1721 and the second in 1723. While the Greenland Eskimos proved to be unsusceptible to the faith that was being foisted on them, they were disastrously susceptible to the smallpox virus carried by one of the Danish missionaries, and most of them died. Egede's story is told in his *Det gamle Grønlands nye Perlustration* (published in 1741), which contains the following episode:

As for other Sea Monsters . . . none of them have been seen by us, or any of our Time that ever I could hear, save that most dreadful Monster, that showed itself upon the Surface of the Water in the year 1734, off our colony in 64 degrees. The Monster was of so huge a Size, that coming out of the Water its Head reached as high as the Mast-Head; its Body was as bulky as the Ship, and three or four times as long. It had a long pointed Snout, and spouted like a Whale-Fish; great broad Paws, and the Body seemed covered with shell-work, its skin very rugged and uneven. The under Part of its Body was shaped like an enormous huge Serpent, and when it dived again under Water, it plunged backwards into the Sea and so raised its Tail aloft, which seemed a whole Ship's Length distant from the bulkiest part of its Body.

By this time the Dutch and the British were energetically slaughtering the bowheads off Greenland and Baffin Island for their baleen plates and oil, so Egede must have been familiar with whales. He had Pastor Bing draw a picture of the monster that was reproduced in his *Perlustration* (published in English as *A Description of Greenland* in 1745), and since Egede was known to be a sober, reliable observer, the picture thus became one of the earliest illustrations of a sea monster based on a reliable eyewitness account.

Clergymen seemed to have a particular affinity for sea monsters (or perhaps it was vice versa), for our next witness is Bishop Erik Ludvigsen Pontoppidan of Bergen, author of *The Natural History of Norway*, published

in 1755. The good bishop firmly believed in the kraken, which he called "Kraken, Kraxen, or, as some name it, Krabben," and maintained that the fishermen he spoke to told him it was a mile and a half in circumference. He took the deposition of a certain Captain von Ferry, who claimed to have seen a "sea-snake" passing his ship in August 1746. Upon being informed of the presence of the serpent, von Ferry came about in order to get nearer to it. At the bishop's request, he described it in a letter written to the court of justice at Bergen:

> The head of this sea-serpent, which it held more than two feet above the water, resembled that of a horse. It was of a greyish color, and the mouth was quite black and very large. It had large black eyes, and a long white mane, which hung down to the surface of the water. Besides the head and neck, we saw seven or eight folds, or coils, of this snake, which were very thick, and as far as we could tell, there was a fathom's distance between each fold.

Another worthy included in the bishop's *Natural History* was Governor Benstrup, who saw a monster quite different from Captain von Ferry. Benstrup's version, which he illustrated, shows a long, snakelike creature, with several bends in its body showing above the surface, which he likened to "a string of buoys." The two sea serpents included in Bishop Pontoppidan's discussion seem to have nothing in common except the folds, but Heuvelmans is ready to believe in both of them: "Thus we see that in the middle of the eighteenth century at least two large sea-monsters, both partly ser-

A curiously Muppet-like sea serpent

pentiform, but certainly different in anatomy, were found in northern waters and were rivals for the title of great sea-serpent."

Even sightings that occur in the same area seem to happen in sequence, often within a couple of years of each other. Soon after the furor of the Norwegian monsters had subsided, an Englishman named Charles (later Captain) Douglas, sailing off Lapland in the HMS *Emerald,* on one of the first European oceanographic voyages, interrogated the Norwegians about the kraken and the sea serpent, and while no one could tell him anything about the kraken, they knew a lot about what they called "Stoor Worms." Douglas recounted one sighting, described by the master of a Norwegian vessel, of three of the worms, "floating upon the surface of the sea, twelve parts of the back of the largest appearing above water; each part being in length about six feet . . . so that upon the whole he judged the animal could not be less than twenty-five fathoms long, and about one in thickness." From Douglas's description (which was read to the Royal Society in 1770), the "worms" might very well be the arms of a giant squid, either dead or dying.

We are at a loss to explain these ecclesiastical sightings. The bishops probably saw something—and may even have believed that they had seen sea serpents—but over time, their descriptions have been the inspiration for much ridicule of the association of church and monster. But there were some sightings that could not be so easily dismissed, because the carcass appeared on the beach. The most famous of these carcasses washed ashore in 1808 on the Shetland island then known as Stronsa, now called Stronsay.

A farmer named John Peace saw some sort of dead animal cast up on the rocks. Believing at first that it was a dead whale, he rowed out to examine it and discovered that it was a beast with a small head, a long neck, a thin tail, and paired fins. Although it was badly decomposed, it was measured at 55 feet in length. Further examination revealed that the bones were of a gristly nature, except the backbone, which was the only solid bone in the body. It had five or six toes on each paw and seemed to be covered with hair. Because the carcass was getting smashed beyond recognition on the rocks, a man was asked to make a drawing of the creature, and he drew a six-legged sort of a dinosaur, with a long neck and tail and with a ridge or fin running the length of its back. He either could not imagine what its head looked like or chose to draw only what he saw, for he made the head a skull. At a meeting of the Wernerian Natural History Society in Edinburgh, Patrick Neill read a communication to the members at their meeting of November 19, 1808, which concluded, "No doubt could be entertained that this was the kind of animal described by Ramus,* Egede, and Pontoppidan, but which scientific and systematic naturalists had hitherto rejected as spurious and ideal."

Neill, eager for a place in zoological history, bestowed a name on the Stronsa beast, *Halsydrus* ("sea water snake"), but when the story and some samples of the skin and cartilage reached a London surgeon and amateur naturalist named Everard Home, he was quick to point out that the samples were obviously from a basking shark. In fact, all the elements that had so enticed those who would have made this into a sea serpent are referable to a basking shark carcass.

The basking shark, now known as *Cetorhinus maximus,* is one of the largest fishes in the world, reaching a maximum known length of 40 feet. It is a filter feeder, straining plankton through an elaborate screen of gill rakers in its large gill arches. Basking sharks are so common in the waters of northern Scotland that there have been many shark fisheries there, including an effort in the late 1940s by Gavin Maxwell (the author of *Ring of Bright Water*), who wrote up his adventures as *Harpoon Venture*. The "small

---

*Johann Ramus was a Norwegian historian whose *Norvegica antiqua* (1689) contained the following description: "Anno 1687, a large Sea-snake was seen by many people in Dramsfiorden; and at one time by eleven persons together. It was very calm weather; and so as soon as the sun appeared and the wind blew a little, it shot away just like a coiled cable that is suddenly thrown out by sailors; and they observed that it was some time in stretching out its many folds."

*D*escribed and illustrated in *Harper's Weekly*, October 24, 1868, this "wonderful fish" is obviously a basking shark— except for the hind legs.

head" might have been the cartilaginous skull of the great shark, and the "long neck" would be the spinal column with the gill rakers missing. (They are usually the first elements to decompose in a shark.) Although it is somewhat more problematic to explain six legs, two of them are easily referred to the pectoral fins and two more to the pelvic fins. (And if the shark were a male, it would have had the paired intromittent organs known as "claspers," tubes of rolled cartilage that occur in no animals other than sharks, and could easily be mistaken for a pair of hind legs in a decomposed specimen.) Since the spinal column of a shark supports only the upper lobe of the tail fin, it is possible for the lower lobe to disintegrate before the upper, thus giving the skeleton the appearance of having a long, serpentlike tail. The skin of a shark often decomposes into stringy filaments, which would explain the appearance of "hair."*

Sea serpents were also beginning to appear across the Atlantic. The first American reference can be found in John Josselyn's 1674 *An Account of Two Voyages to New England*, in which he mentions ". . . a sea-serpent or snake

---

*In 1868, a 30-foot-long creature, described as "part beast and part fish," was captured near Eastport, Maine. From the illustration in *Harper's Weekly* (see above), it is obvious that the "wonderful fish" is indeed a basking shark, but the description says that "one third of its length from its tail, in connection with small fins, it has two huge legs, terminating in web feet." These are obviously the claspers, but the illustrator, Charles R. Barry, has followed the description and turned them into feet that look not unlike those of a lion.

*T*he first American sea serpent, sighted off Cape Ann, Massachusetts, in 1639. Although it was done much earlier, this drawing bears a remarkable similarity to those of the Gloucester monster that appeared in the same vicinity in 1817.

that lay coiled on a rock" at Cape Ann, Massachusetts, in 1639, a creature also mentioned by one Obidiah Turner, who described "a monster like unto this which did there come out of the sea and coil himself upon the land." In 1802, in the Gulf of Maine, the Reverend Abraham Cummings followed one around that he described thus:

> His head was rather larger than that of a horse, but formed like that of a serpent. His body we judged was more than sixty feet in length. His head and as much of his body as we could discover was all of a blue colour except a black circle round his eye. His motion was at first but moderate, but when he left us and proceeded towards the ocean, he moved with the greatest rapidity. . . .

In the summer of 1817, in the vicinity of Gloucester, Massachusetts, almost everybody seems to have spotted some sort of monster in the harbor. A broadside published in Boston on August 22 was entitled "A Monstrous Sea Serpent: The largest ever seen in America" and included many of the descriptions of the monster up to that time:

> There was seen on Monday and Tuesday morning playing around the harbor between Eastern Point and Ten Pound Island, a SNAKE with his head and body about eight feet out of water, his head is in perfect shape as

large as the head of a horse, his body is judged to be about FORTY-FIVE or FIFTY FEET IN LENGTH. It is thought that he will girt about 3 feet round the body, and his sting is about 4 feet in length.

It was first seen by some fishermen, 10 or 12 days ago, but it was then generally believed to be a creature of the imagination. But he has since come within the harbor of Gloucester, and has been seen by hundreds of people. He is described by some persons who approached within 10 or 15 yards of him, to be 60 or 70 feet in length, round, and of the diameter of a barrel. Others state his length variously, from 50 to 100 feet.

On the tenth, two women and a number of fishermen saw a sea serpent entering the harbor. Six days later, Timothy Hodgkins, returning from Newburyport with three companions, saw what they first took to be a school of pilot whales, but upon closer examination, the whales looked more like the humps of a sea monster:

> His head was elevated from three to five feet; the distance was about six feet from his neck to the first bunch; we counted twenty bunches, and we supposed them on average about five feet apart, and his whole length could not be less than one hundred and twenty feet. . . . His body was the size of a sixty- or eighty-gallon cask, his head large as a barrel. . . . There was nothing that appeared like fins or gills. We did not discern his tail.

Also on the sixteenth, a large number of people saw the monster near the Squam lighthouse. A fleet of whaleboats took after it, but it sounded, and they never saw it again. On the nineteenth, Capt. Richard Rich, commanding a whaleboat in the harbor, darted his iron into the monster as it swam under his boat, but after a run of about fifty yards, the harpoon pulled out. Summarizing the sightings to August 23, the Boston *Centinel* published this composite description:

> Gentlemen who have been in Gloucester, and attended to the accounts of those who have seen him at different times, and in different situations, think there can be no doubt that the animal is a serpent, in kind; that he is at least eighty, and more probably a hundred feet long, and nearly the size of a flour barrel at the widest place. . . . He does not wind laterally along, as serpents commonly do, but his motion is undulatory, or consisting of alternating rising and depression, somewhat like the motion of a caterpillar. Capt. Beach, who appears to have examined him very often, and sometimes in favorable situations, says his head is the size of a common bucket. He has seen him with his mouth open, his under jaw and teeth like a shark's, his head round, with apparently very thick scales and its whole appearance very terrific.

$\mathcal{A}$ contemporaneous illustration of the 1817 Gloucester sea serpent. Were all the people who claimed to see this creature victims of mass hallucinations, or were they part of some "monstrous" practical joke?

Because so many people claimed to have seen the serpent, the Linnaean Society of New England formed a special investigating committee consisting of John Davis, a judge; Jacob Bigelow, a doctor; and Francis Gray, a naturalist. They ordained Lonson Nash, a justice of the peace, to take sworn statements from as many people as he could who claimed to have seen the Gloucester monster. Nash collected eight affidavits in Gloucester and three more in Boston. In one of these sworn statements, a ship's carpenter named Matthew Gaffney described how he fired at the monster, which headed straight for him and passed beneath his boat. "His motion was vertical," said Gaffney, "like a caterpillar." (The Linnaean Society's Questionnaire appears as Appendix A of this volume.)

Throughout August, various people spotted the sea serpent in and around Gloucester. R. W. Dexter covers the August sightings in his 1986 summary of the Cape Ann visits: On the tenth, Lydia Wonson watched it cavort in front of her house on Eastern Point, and William Row observed it as it came into a cove at Rocky Neck accompanied by two sharks. On August 14, twelve people were standing near the windmill at Fort Point, and all of them viewed the sea serpent. Three days later, from the same vantage point, William Saville saw forty or fifty feet of it in distinct bunches. Then

Captain Corlis caught sight of it from his sailboat, from a distance of thirty feet. In a letter published some thirty-one years after the fact (in the Boston *Daily Advertiser* on November 25, 1848), Col. S. G. Perkins wrote to his friend John P. Cushing that he had seen the serpent stretched out in shallow water on August 22, 1817, and that it was about 100 feet long.

The serpent was not observed again in Gloucester that year, but a month later, two boys were playing on the beach near Cape Ann when they found a three-foot-long blacksnake with humps on its back. The Linnaean Society Board of Inquiry decided that the reason the giant snake had been so close to shore was that it was laying its eggs. The "serpent" was purchased by a Captain Beach, who presented it to the Linnaean Society for dissection. The committee examined the specimen and, in what Chandos Michael Brown describes as "a near sacramental act of taxonomic classification," spontaneously invented a whole new genus.

The Boston *Centinel* for October 4, 1817, ran a letter from Lonson Nash to the Honorable D. H. Humphreys as "additional and irrefragable evidence of the existence of the aquatic or amphibious animal which has recently been the subject of much conversation." In this letter, Nash described the "Young Serpent that was yesterday killed" as "about three feet and a half in length, and in the largest part perhaps three inches in circumference; and has thirty-two distinct bunches on his back." Although the "baby sea serpent" was remarkably similar to the common blacksnake (*Coluber constrictor*), it was named *Scoliophis atlanticus* ("Atlantic humped snake"), and the true believers had their evidence at last. They had a monster (albeit a baby), and they were now prepared to taunt the skeptics who had made such fun of them. Unfortunately, Alexandre Lesueur, a naturalist who specialized in reptiles and fishes, read the committee's report, examined the specimen, and told them that it was, after all, only a deformed specimen of the common blacksnake.

In August 1818, the same Captain Rich who had attempted to harpoon the monster the year before organized several of the witnesses who had seen the serpent before into a hunting party. They set out on a calm day toward a spot where the monster had been previously spotted, and when they sighted a disturbance on the water, they gave chase. As reported by Nathan Hale in the Boston *Weekly Messenger* for September 10, Rich said that he had chased the serpent, "but by following it up closely we have ascertained that the supposed Serpent is no other than the wake of such a fish as we have taken." (Earlier, Rich and his crew had caught a "Thunny or Horse Mackeral," and he was convinced—as were many others—that the "serpent" was simply a disturbance in the water caused by a large fish.)

But if the Gloucester sea serpent decamped temporarily from Massachusetts waters, it never completely disappeared. It would surface, more or less irregularly, over the remaining years of the nineteenth century, and despite the foolishness that led to the identification of a snake as its "spawn," the sightings have never been satisfactorily explained. It often entered the literature as a reality, as exemplified by its appearance in 1834 in Henry Dewhurst's *Natural History of the Order Cetacea.* Dewhurst's book includes a couple of sea serpents, one of which is the monster from Gloucester. He introduces it by saying it is "one of those unknown animals which occasionally puzzle the zoologist when they make their appearance," and after the usual description (snakelike head, folds like wooden buoys, 100 feet long, etc.), he writes that it remained in Gloucester harbor for about three weeks and then disappeared.

One of the most unusual—and persistent—elements of many early sea-serpent sightings is the presence of humps or bunches. From Bishop Pontoppidan's kraxen to the Gloucester monsters, the descriptions include a vertical flexion of the back, often likened to the locomotion of a caterpillar. With the exception of caterpillars—of which the inchworm is one—no known animals move this way. Sea snakes and other snakes in the water move in the same fashion as they do on land; by pushing against either aquatic or terrestrial resistance along a horizontal plane. (A snake in a tree does more or less the same thing, often using the roughness of the bark for purchase.) Other possibilities, including quadrupedal reptiles and mammals, fishes, and eels, move according to recognized systems. It is therefore most unusual to attribute such an impractical (and perhaps mechanically impossible) mode of travel to the sea serpent. Of course, there is always the possibility that these still undiscovered animals have developed a way of moving that, like their very existence, defies biology as we know it.*

As Heuvelmans says, "1817 was a lucky year for the sea-serpent." This was the year that the French-American naturalist Constantin Samuel Rafinesque-Schmaltz bestowed a proper name on it, *Megophias,* meaning "big snake." (His description was published in the *Philosophical Magazine* in an article entitled "Dissertation on Water-Snakes, Sea-Snakes, and Sea-Serpents.") Rafinesque (as he is commonly known) lists nine sea snakes and

---

*In *The Wake of the Sea-Serpents,* Heuvelmans refers to a private correspondence with Ivan Sanderson, who suggested that "the humps may actually be hydrostatic organs, air-filled sacs attached to the larynx and inflatable at will. . . . The number of these sacs, the size of which would be limited for mechanical reasons, would increase with the size of the individual. This would explain the great difference of opinion of witnesses about their number and size." Heuvelmans says that "this ingenious theory would explain much and is most attractive," but does not make clear how an animal so equipped would move.

writes of the Massachusetts monster, "It is evidently a real sea snake, belonging to the genus *Pelamis,* and I propose to call it *Pelamis megophias,* which means Great Sea Snake Pelamis.* It might, however be a peculiar genus, which the long equal scales seem to indicate and which a closer examination might have decided: in that case the name of *Megophias monstrosus* might have been appropriated to it."

In August 1819, the Gloucester Sea Serpent (or "an animal of similar nature") reappeared in Nahant (Massachusetts), where "it was stationary for four hours near the shore, and two hundred persons assembled to view it." In a letter published in the *Columbian Centinel* dated August 21, James Prince ("Esq. Marshal of this District") described his observations of the serpent:

> His head appeared about three feet out of water; I counted thirteen bunches on his back—my family thought there were fifteen—he passed three times at a moderate rate across the bay, but so fleet as to occasion a foam in the water—and my family and self, who were in a carriage, judged that he was from fifty and not more than sixty feet in length. . . . Nor my dear Sir, do I undertake to say he was of the Snake or Eel kind; though this was the general impression of my family, the spectators and myself. Certain it is, he is a very strange animal. I have been accustomed to see *Whales, Sharks, Grampuses, Porpoises,* and other large fishes, but he partook of the appearances of neither of these.

According to Heuvelmans's exhaustive analysis, the period from 1817 to 1847 was the high point of American monster sighting. Sea serpents of one sort or another were observed more or less regularly off the coast of Massachusetts and many other locations on the Atlantic coast of North America, including Maine, Halifax (Nova Scotia), Charleston (South Carolina), and the Gulf of Mexico. Heuvelmans writes, "Mass reports from the east coast of the United States agree so well as to be almost monotonous." The monotony was resoundingly shattered in 1845 by Albert C. Koch, a German collector who put on exhibit at the Apollo Saloon on Broadway a full skeleton of what he called *Hydrarchos sillimani,* or "Silliman's Master-of-the-Seas." (Benjamin Silliman, a professor at Yale, was honored in this manner because he had recognized the existence of the sea serpent in 1827 and also

---

*There are, of course, fully aquatic snakes (family Hydrophiidae), and the most common is *Pelamis platurus,* the yellow-bellied sea snake. Sea snakes are true reptiles and breathe air, but they are able to remain submerged for considerable periods of time. They are venomous but not particularly aggressive and average about 4 to 5 feet in length. All known species are found in Indo-Pacific waters.

because "Dr." Koch probably felt that the distinguished professor's name would lend credibility to his project.)

In a pamphlet published in 1845 to accompany the exhibit, Koch wrote that he found the entire skeleton in Clarksville, Alabama, in "a stratum of yellowish lime rock . . . thrown to the surface by volcanic action." He further maintained that the vertebrae "were found and dug out in the natural order in which they lay, and in which they are again put together in the skeleton as exhibited." As exhibited, *Hydrarchos* was a serpentine skeleton 114 feet in length, with the open-mouthed skull raised high off the floor and with several pairs of arched ribs and paddle-like forelimbs. "This relic," wrote Dr. Koch, "is without exception the largest of all fossil skeletons . . . reminding us most strikingly, of the various statements made by persons, in regard to having seen large serpents in different parts of the ocean, which were known by the name of Sea Serpents." So much for those doubting Thomases who did not believe in sea serpents; here we have the actual skeleton of "a huge Sea Serpent, or reptile, answering not only in its colossal size, but also in other respects remarkably the description given of a monster, which many respectable citizens have stated under oath that they have seen swimming alive on the ocean." Koch even went so far as to describe the behavior of *Hydrarchos:*

*I*n 1845, Dr. Albert Koch published his description (accompanied by this illustration) of *Hydrarchos,* a 114-foot-long "gigantic fossil reptile" that he claimed to have found in Alabama. Unfortunately, it turned out to be a fake; he had assembled the bones of no fewer than five fossil whales.

The supposition that Hydrarchos frequently skimmed the surface of the water, with its neck and head elevated, is not only taken from the fact that it was compelled to rise for the purpose of breathing, but more so from the great strength and size of its cervical or neck vertebra; and the comparatively small size of its head, which could, with the greatest ease, be maintained in an elevated position, when in the act of carrying a Shark or a Saurier, while struggling for its life, to free itself from the dreadful grasp with which it had been elevated from its native element, to serve as a morsel to this blood thirsty monarch of the waters.

At the end of this paean to Koch's sea serpent, the author included quotes from various publications. As a result his claims were vindicated and his paleontological skills applauded. It took more than a little audacity, however, to include this encomium from the New York *Evangelist:*

But there is no hoax in this. If it *were* a humbug, Dr. Koch would make his fortune from the stupendous ingenuity, science and skill evinced in its construction. As it is, it takes some time to overcome the incredulity of the people. But it is only those who have *not* seen the monster that can indulge in the slightest questioning as to its genuineness and authenticity. And Dr. Koch deserves the thanks of the whole country, and of all men of science of the world, for that persevering sagacity and industry with which he has brought this prodigious skeleton to light and produced it in public. He is himself a man of true science, most unassuming and affable, far from all trickery and ostentation, a German with true German simplicity and thoroughness.

Of course, it *was* a humbug, and if Koch is to be remembered for any of the characteristics the writer bestowed upon the doctor, it would be for the "stupendous ingenuity" with which he perpetrated and publicized this gigantic hoax. (It seems more than a little likely that the author was the "unassuming and affable" Koch himself.) When Harvard anatomist Jeffries Wyman (who had just published the first scientific description of the gorilla) examined the "sea-monster," he identified it as an artfully assembled collection of bones from at least five fossil specimens of zeuglodon, a 45-foot-long ancestral whale. In his exposé of Koch's counterfeit monster, Wyman wrote, "These remains never belonged to one and the same individual, and . . . the anatomical characteristics of the teeth indicate that they are not those of a reptile but of a warm-blooded mammal."

When Silliman insisted that his name be removed from this fraudulent composite, Koch simply changed the name of his serpent to *Hydrarchos harlani,* naming it this time after Dr. Richard Harlan, another zoologist who had recently discovered a fossil whale known as *Basilosaurus*. Koch packed up his monster and headed for Europe, where, according to Willy Ley, "the fraud was exposed again." Sir Richard Owen wrote in 1848, "The fossil vertebrae and skull which were exhibited by Mr. Koch in New York and Boston as those of the great sea-serpent, and which are now in Berlin, belonged to different individuals of a species which I had previously proved to be an extinct whale."

The ship *Plumper's* "sea-serpent" was reported in the *Illustrated London News* on April 10, 1849, but the actual sighting occurred at the end of 1848. The article, which was signed "A Naval Officer," contained the following description:

> . . . being due west of Oporto [Portugal] I saw a long black creature with a sharp head, moving slowly, I should think about two knots, through the water in a north westerly direction, there being a fresh breeze at the time, and some sea on. I could not ascertain its exact length, but its back was about twenty feet if not more above the water; and its head, as near as I could judge, from six to eight . . . the creature moved across our wake towards a merchant ship barque on our lee quarter, and on the port tack. . . .

*A*board HMS *Plumper* off the Portuguese coast in 1848, the crew spotted this "long black creature." Was this another giant squid?

In 1848, the frigate *Daedalus* was sailing off the Cape of Good Hope when the crew spotted

> an enormous serpent, with head and shoulders kept about four feet constantly above the surface of the sea, and as nearly as we could approximate by comparing with the length of what our main topsail yard would show in the water, there was at the very least 60 feet of the animal a *fleur d'eau,* no portion of which was, to our perception, used in propelling it through the water, either by vertical or horizontal undulation.

This description came from Peter M'Quhae, the *Daedalus*'s captain, who was responding angrily to a request from the Admiralty that he confirm or deny the rumors about a sea serpent. M'Quhae went on to write that its diameter was "15 or 16 inches behind the head, which was, without any doubt, that of a snake," and that "it had no fins, but something like the mane of a horse, or rather a bunch of seaweed, washed about its back." The *Illustrated London News* ran the story, accompanied by drawings done from M'Quhae's description, and the *Daedalus* monster entered the lists as one of

*O*ne of the illustrations that accompanied the original report of a "sea serpent" sighted from the ship *Daedalus* in 1848 off the Cape of Good Hope. Part of the text reads "That there is such a creature, however, there can be but little doubt, as his appearance has so often been alluded to."

the best-described serpents of all time. Sir Richard Owen—who so disbelieved Charles Darwin that he tried to have him excommunicated—attempted to argue that the animal was really a gigantic seal.

To his dying day, Owen refused to admit even the slightest possibility that monsters might exist outside the zoological framework that he understood. In response to one "sighting," Owen wrote, "The observers have no expert knowledge of zoology; their observation is, therefore, without merit," and of M'Quhae's sighting he wrote, "It is very probable that no one on board the *Daedalus* ever before beheld a gigantic seal swimming freely in the open ocean." With his penchant for bombastic overstatement, Owen finished off his critique (which was published in the *Times* [London]) with the statement: "A larger body of evidence from eye-witnesses might be got together in proof of ghosts than of the sea-serpent." In his response (also printed in the *Times*), M'Quhae accused Owen of flagrantly misquoting him and wrote:

> Finally, I deny the existence of excitement, or the possibility of optical illusion. I adhere to the statement, as to form, colour, and dimensions, contained in my official report to the Admiralty; and I leave them as data whereupon the learned and scientific may exercise the "pleasures of imagination" until some more fortunate opportunity shall occur of making a closer acquaintance with the "great unknown"—in the present instance assuredly no ghost.

Richard Owen was born in 1804, and as a surgeon's apprentice, he was performing autopsies on the cadavers of prisoners as a teenager. After medical training at Edinburgh, he was named Hunterian Professor at the Royal College of Surgeons and acquired such a formidable reputation that his opinion was sought on all things anatomic. In addition to his talents for vertebrate morphology and his organizational skills, Owen was close to the royal family (he taught natural history to the children of Queen Victoria), and he was chosen for the monumental task of setting up a national museum of natural history in South Kensington. Although he wrote and published prodigiously and pioneered studies of the fossil animals of Britain and the comparative anatomy of vertebrates, he will probably be best remembered for his unwavering opposition to Darwin's *Origin of Species.* Owen reviewed Darwin's book, and Darwin responded by saying, "It is extremely malignant, clever, and I fear will be very damaging. . . . It requires much study to appreciate all the bitter spite of many of the remarks against me. . . ." (Of Owen's presentation, John Noble Wilford wrote, "He was pompous. He disliked being called the English Cuvier because he

believed himself superior to the Frenchman. He held himself to be infalli-
ble, and delivered opinions accordingly, as pronouncements freighted with
obscure polysyllables.") Owen went to his grave believing that God had
created the dinosaurs—a word he coined in 1841—and that people who
believed in sea serpents were as misguided as Darwin.

While the identity of the *Daedalus*'s "prehistoric saurian" remained
unresolved, more monsters began to appear, and because M'Quhae's had
been encountered off South Africa, they were no longer restricted to the
North Atlantic. Not surprisingly, then, in 1849 a "large marine mammal,
with the head and general figure of an alligator, except that the neck was
much longer, and instead of legs the creature had four large flappers,"
appeared to George Hope, an officer on HMS *Fly* in the Gulf of California. In his discussion of this event (in the British journal *Zoologist*), Edward
Newman wrote, ". . . the present existence of huge marine mammals closely
related to the Enaliosauri of by-gone ages . . . appears to me in all respects
the most interesting Natural History fact of the present century, completely
overturning as it does some of the most favourite and fashionable hypotheses of geological science."

In April 1852, in the British journal *Zoology*, there appeared an article
entitled "Reported Capture of the Sea-serpent," written by a Capt. Charles
Seabury of the New Bedford whaler *Monongahela*.* Sailing in the tropical
South Pacific, the lookouts spotted a sea serpent undulating through the
water, which Seabury described as "moving like the waving of a rope when
held and shaken in the hand." He exclaimed, "It is a sea-serpent!" and he
told his men that they had to capture it, for "our courage was at stake—our
manhood, and even the credit of the whole American whale-fishery." They
lowered the boats and took after it, but even with several harpoons in it, the
serpent towed the boat for sixteen hours before they were able to lance it.
To prove that theirs was not another unfounded monster story, they dried
out the 103-foot-long, blubber-covered snake, preserved the head ("long
and flat, with ridges"), the teeth ("94 in the jaws, very sharp, all pointing
backward and as large as one's thumb"), and various other components of
the beast and continued on their voyage. In the newspaper accounts, "Cap-

---

* The story, which runs to four densely packed pages, is followed by information on its origin
and the opinion of the journal's editor: "*New York Tribune*, copied in the *Times* of March 10, 1852.
(Very like a hoax, but well drawn up. E.N.)" According to Starbuck's authoritative *History of the
American Whale Fishery*, the New Bedford whaler *Monongahela*, Capt. *Jason* Seabury commanding,
really existed and was indeed lost in the Arctic in 1853. The account of the sea serpent appeared in
various newspapers (and the journal *Zoology*) before the disappearance of the ship, so the author of
the dispatches will probably never be known. It seems unlikely that Captain Seabury sent the stories and changed his own first name.

tain Seabury" explained that he gave the letters describing the events to the captain of the brig *Gipsy,* which explains how the news was disseminated, but alas, the *Monongahela* was not destined to deliver her precious cargo. She was lost the next year with all hands.

Perhaps the greatest sea serpentologist of all times was Antoon Cornelis Oudemans, a Dutchman who was by training an entomologist, specializing in acarology, the study of mites and ticks. His passion was sea serpents, however, and before long he was publishing popular articles on his favorite animals—in which he unequivocally believed. He wrote that the *Daedalus'*s serpent was a mammal, and even though there was absolutely no evidence except the sailors' stories to substantiate such zoological brashness, he invented a plesiosaur-shaped (therefore, long-necked) zeuglodon, which he named *Zeuglodon plesiosauroides.* (Later, he would recant the notion that a sea serpent could be a primitive whale, an idea that he attributed to the impetuousness and ignorance of his youth.) In 1885, on the basis of his work with mites, he was made director of the Royal Zoological and Botanical Gardens at The Hague, where he again steeped himself in his hobby, spending all his free time in accumulating information on sea serpents.

The result of this research was the publication in 1892 of *The Great Sea-Serpent,* the most comprehensive tome ever written (until Heuvelmans's) on the subject. Oudemans uses the arguments of the early clerics, Olaus Magnus and Pontoppidan, to support his belief in the existence of sea serpents, and he accepts their stories almost without reservation. He quotes Olaus Magnus at some length, endorses his tale of a 200-foot-long serpent that lives in caves along the shores of Norway, and rejects only the bishop's description of the serpent emerging in fine weather to devour livestock. ("We consider its devouring hogs, lambs and calves, and its appearance on summer nights on land to take its prey, to be a fable," he wrote.) In trying to answer Pontoppidan's question about why the larger serpents frequent only the northern seas, Professor Oudemans says, "To this question I answer that the Creator of all beings disposes of the dwellings of His creatures in different places by His wise intentions, which are not known to us."

In his magnum opus, Oudemans lists 162 specific cases of serpent sightings, even though some are only represented by short letters to newspapers. After reprinting the evidence, he then dismisses most of the cases because they do not agree with his theory. (In a surprisingly ungenerous discussion of Oudemans's book, Frank Bullen, no slouch himself when it came to fabrication, wrote, "It seems to be rather a feature with scientific men of a certain class to build a theory first, then mould the evidence or suppress it to fit the theory, and utterly ignore any explanation but their own.") The "various explanations hitherto given" (and therefore not applicable to Oudemans's definition of a sea serpent) include: a row of porpoises, giant eels, *Scoliophis* (the blacksnake), sea snakes, basking sharks, whales, dinosaurs such as ichthyosaurus and plesiosaurus, a row of sperm whales, ancestral whales, for example, *Basilosaurus*, land snakes seen at sea, seaweed, floating dead trees, flights of low-flying birds, large turtles, giant cuttlefish or calamaries, and a manatee. After a labored analysis of the material, he concludes that most of the verified sightings were of the same animal: *Megophias*, the giant snake of Rafinesque. But, says Oudemans, even though we have to use Rafinesque's nomenclature, the sea serpent is not a snake at all; it is a mammal: "It will be quite superfluous," he wrote, "to tell my readers to which order of animals I think this *Megophias megophias* belongs. It runs like a red thread through my whole volume, and I firmly believe that it belongs to the order of *Pinnepedia*."*

Oudemans's book contains a plaintive call for help from anyone who has seen (or might see) a sea serpent:

> Voyagers and sportsmen conversant with photography are requested to take the instantaneous photograph of the animal; this alone will convince zoologists, while all their reports and pencil-drawings will be received with a shrug of the shoulders.
>
> As these animals are very shy, it is not advisable to approach them with a steamboat.
>
> The *only* manner to kill one *instantly* will be by means of *explosive* balls, or by harpoons laden with nitro-glycerine; but as it most probably will sink, when dead, like most of the Pinnipeds, the harpooning of it will probably be more successful. . . .
>
> If but barely possible, preserve the whole skeleton, and the whole skin, but if this is utterly impracticable, keep the cleaned skull, the bones of one of the fore-flappers and those of one of the hind-flappers, four or five vertebrae of different parts of the backbone, neck, and tail; and preserve the skin of the head, and a ribbon of about a foot breadth along the whole back of the neck, the trunk, and the tail.

When the book was released, the critics were less than kind. The *Times* (London) wrote: "At first sight it looks like an elaborate scientific treatise

*Heuvelmans spends a not inconsiderable number of pages disputing Oudemans's conclusion, since he believes that there are a number of possibilities, including the marine saurian, the super-otter, the many-finned serpent, the many-humped serpent, the yellow-bellied serpent, the supereel, and the father of all turtles, all of which "occupy quite distinct ecological niches and cannot compete except where these habitats meet, which agrees perfectly with the laws of nature."

and so no doubt is it seriously regarded by its author; but, on closer examination, it rather presents itself as a cumbrous and elaborate, albeit quite unconscious, joke." Oudemans left the Royal Zoological and Botanical Gardens to take a teaching position at the Dutch city of Sneek, where he worked on his massive study of acarology, and when the commotion over the Loch Ness monster broke out in 1933, he tried to convince the British government to capture it, for he was convinced that Nessie, like all other monsters, was a giant seal. Oudemans died on January 14, 1943, without, alas, ever having seen a sea serpent or even an "instantaneous photograph" of one.

By the late 1880s, the serpent was back in New England waters. In his "Chronological Table of Sightings" for 1886 and 1887, Heuvelmans includes Rockport, Cape Cod, and Gloucester, Massachusetts; Fort Popham, Maine; and the "East Coast of U.S." as the locations of sightings, "real, apparent and claimed." The Rockport sighting was reported in a letter to the Boston *Journal*, dated August 13, 1886, in which G. B. Putnam, master of the Franklin School in Boston, wrote:

> Mr. Poole called my attention to his snakeship at once, and as he passed directly by my cottage I was able with an excellent marine glass to observe his movements. . . . The head was frequently raised out of the water, and the movement was a vertical one, showing some ten to fifteen ridges at once. I should say that he was at least eighty feet in length. . . . After he had disappeared, and while we were still looking, a school of porpoises passed, so that we had a chance to compare their appearance with that of the serpent. I speak of this, as it has often been said that the former was mistaken for the latter. I shall never doubt that the sea serpent is a fact.

In response to this sighting, P. T. Barnum sent the following letter to the Boston *Journal:* "The Pigeon County testimony proves what has before been previously established, the existence of monster sea-serpents, and I hope ere long to pay $20,000 for one, as named in my offer through your columns last week."

Seal or saurian, real or imaginary, nothing inhibited sailors from reporting strange things in the ocean. On December 4, 1893, the *Umfili* was sailing off the coast of West Africa when her crew spied a "Monster Fish of the Serpent shape, about 80 feet long with slimy skin and short fins about 20 feet apart on the back." Several passengers saw the long-necked beast, including Captain Cringle, First Mate Powell, and members of the crew. The *Umfili's* reports were dismissed by the press and the scientific establishment, prompting Captain Cringle to write, "I have been so ridiculed about the thing that I have many times wished that anybody else had seen the sea-monster rather than me."

In August 1905, Maj. Gen. H. C. Merriam of the U.S. Army sighted a sea serpent while sailing off Wood Island, Maine, and wrote a letter to Dr. F. A. Lucas, director of the American Museum of Natural History in New York. The letter (reproduced in its entirety in the appendix to V. C. Heilner's *Salt Water Fishing*) contains this description of a "monster serpent":

> Its head was several feet above the surface of the water, and its long body was plainly visible, slowly moving toward our boat by sinuous or snake-like motion. . . . It had no dorsal fin unless it was continuous. The color of its back appeared to be brown and mottled, shading down to a dull yellow on the belly. The head was like that of a snake, and the part shown above the surface—that is the neck—appeared to be about 15 to 18 inches in diameter. If it had any pectoral fins we did not observe them. I estimated its length at 60 feet or more.

In 1905, as if to dispel Owen's criticism that it was never scientists that saw these monsters, two naturalists, E. G. B. Meade-Waldo, and M. J. Nicoll, on a scientific cruise aboard the Earl of Crawford's steam auxiliary yacht *Valhalla*, sighted a dark brown animal with a great frill on its back off the coast of Brazil. In the *Proceedings of the Zoological Society of London*, Meade-Waldo published his observations:

> I looked and saw a large fin or frill sticking out of the water, dark sea-weed-brown in colour, somewhat crinkled on the edge. It was apparently about 6 feet in length and projected from 18 inches to 2 feet from the water. I could see, under the water to the rear of the frill, the shade of a considerable body. I got my field glasses on to it (a powerful pair of Goerz Trieder), and almost as soon as I had them on the frill, a great head and neck rose out of the water in front of the frill; the neck did not touch the frill in the water, but came out of the water in *front* of it, at a distance of not less than 18 inches, probably more. The neck appeared about the thickness of a slight man's body, and from 7 to 8 feet was out of the water. . . . The head had a turtle-like appearance, as had also the eye. I could see the line of the mouth, but we were sailing pretty fast, and quickly drew away from the object, which was going very slowly. It moved its head from side to side in a peculiar manner; the colour of the head and neck was dark brown above, and whitish below—almost white, I think.

Michael Nicoll's similar description was published alongside that of Meade-Waldo, and Nicoll also contributed a drawing, which is reproduced here.

In 1906, a year after Meade-Waldo and Nicoll had observed their snakelike creature, a

In 1904, when Michael Nicoll, a naturalist aboard the yacht Valhalla, sighted a sea serpent off Brazil, he drew this illustration, which was reproduced in the Proceedings of the Zoological Society of London.

certain Captain Koopman was aboard a merchant vessel steaming from the Mediterannean to Montevideo, and less than a hundred kilometers south of the Meade-Waldo sighting, he saw a sea serpent. (The story is told by Paul LeBlond in the 1983 issue of *Cryptozoology*.) Equipped with a telescope that he was using to observe a sailing ship in the distance, Koopman saw "an enormous beast, whose length I approximated at about 60 meters. . . . The monstrous head and a number of enormous dorsal fins sticking out above water level, as well as its wide wake, showed me the nearly horizontal posture of the giant sea-dragon or serpent." The proximity of the two locations is of interest, since Captain Koopman did not know anything about the earlier dragon and refrained from telling his shipmates about his monster "for fear of ridicule." (Koopman published his memoirs much later, and the relevant passage—in Dutch—was made available to LeBlond in 1982.)

May 22, 1917: The British merchant cruiser *Hilary* is participating in the North Sea blockade of German shipping. F. W. Dean, captain of the *Hilary,* is informed that there is some sort of an "object" on the starboard quarter. Dean orders the gun crews to make ready but first decides to have a closer look. Thirty yards away, Dean sees an animal with

the head . . . about the shape of, but somewhat larger than that of a cow, though with no observable protrusions such as horns or ears, and was black except for the front of the face, which could be clearly seen to have a strip of whitish flesh, very like a cow has, between its nostrils. . . . From the back of the head to the dorsal fin no part of the creature showed above water, but the top edge of the neck was just level with the surface, and its snake-like movements could be clearly seen. . . . The dorsal fin appeared like a black triangle, and when the creature was end on, the fin seemed to be very thin and apparently flabby. . . . The fin was estimated to be about four feet high when in the position highest out of the water.

The *Hilary* steamed past the monster, and when it was about a thousand yards astern, Captain Dean ordered his crews to fire their six-inch guns. Two shots landed, very near the animal, but "quite failed to disturb its equanimity." The third gun crew scored a direct hit; the wounded creature dove in a flurry of foam and was never seen again. In *The Case for Sea-Serpents*, Rupert T. Gould reports on his discussions with Captain Dean, but when the possibility is raised that it might have been a basking shark, Gould asserts: "It was most certainly not a shark." Summarizing the controversy, Heuvelmans says, "The *Hilary* monster, in fact, seems to be our old friend the New England sea-serpent, caught once again basking on the surface."

But Gavin Maxwell discusses the *Hilary* incident in *Harpoon Venture*, his book about his basking shark–fishing endeavors in the Hebrides, and makes quite a convincing case for the shark. First Dean made a sketch of what he had seen; then Gould sent Dean a little drawing of a basking shark to see if it looked anything like Dean's monster. It didn't. But then Maxwell

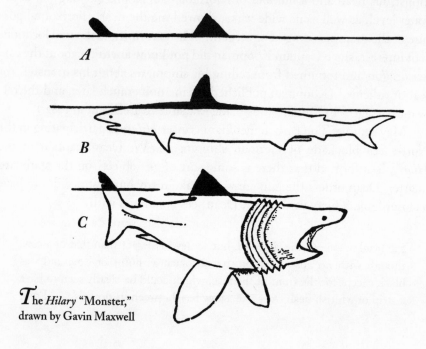

The *Hilary* "Monster," drawn by Gavin Maxwell

tried his hand at drawing, and he produced a perfectly serviceable "explana-tory sketch" of just how Dean's drawing could be made into a shark. Maxwell wrote, "The bottom sketch, C, represents my own explanation of Captain Dean's drawing, nor in his lengthy quoted description can I see anything but my old friend, the basking shark." Not only is this basking-shark territory, but in Maxwell's book there are several photographs that even explain the "strip of whitish flesh between the nostrils." Basking sharks appear to have a white strip on the underside of their snout, and while it is difficult to imagine a naval officer turning a shark's nose into a cow's head—even without ears—it is coincidental enough to explain almost all the elements in Dean's description.

Van Campen Heilner was a sport fisherman who wrote *Salt Water Fish-ing* in 1937 and saw it reprinted (with a preface by Ernest Hemingway) in 1953. In addition to tales of marlin, tuna, swordfish, sharks, and tarpon, he included an appendix entitled "Sea Serpents" in which he wrote, "Believing sincerely in the existence of a creature or creatures as yet undescribed by sci-ence, I have endeavored to track down every account which has come to my notice." He wrote hundreds of letters, but of all the replies, he considered only a couple worthy of inclusion in his book. One was the tale of General Merriam's 1905 sighting (see p. 64); the other was a letter to him from a Captain Sylvestre of the French Line steamer *Cuba*, which had been some eight hundred miles southwest of the Azores in July 1934. (Heilner also reproduces the letter in the original French and apologizes for any errors in his translation.) At 5:20 a.m., in calm seas, the watch officer and two helms-men saw "an enormous animal making a leap out of the water. His length could have been estimated at 20 to 25 meters, his width 4 to 5 meters, a small head and a long and thin neck. . . . At each appearance the animal raised its flexible neck out of the water and the head seemed to look at the ship; the leap out of the water was so rapid that it was impossible to discern the exact shape of the body and tail." Of Captain Sylvestre's beast, Heilner wrote, "I cannot prove the existence of a sea serpent nor can anyone disprove it. . . . My personal conclusion is that there is too much evidence on record in favor of some creature of unclassified form and species to be lightly dis-missed by the stroke of a pen."

In the 1930s, the attentions of serpentologists were directed toward a cold, deep lake in Scotland where all sorts of strange creatures were said to be appearing. Many of the pelagic "monsters" are probably related to Nessie, since she has been variously described as an otter, an eel, a snake, a plesiosaur, and some other creatures that no one thought to locate in the Atlantic or Pacific. Since neither Nessie nor any of the other versions of the sea serpent has been shown to exist, perhaps this is the moment to examine the data critically. Certainly the single animal theory of Oudemans makes the most sense—even if the gigantic seal doesn't—because otherwise we would have to follow Heuvelmans and postulate an entire menagerie of monsters, some mammalian, some reptilian, some dinosaurian, and some of completely unknown affiliations. Even allowing for the verification of the giant squid and the surprise discovery of the coelacanth, we cannot extrapolate an assortment of gigantic animals that only appear sporadically and in such odd places. Mammals and reptiles would have to surface regularly to breathe; reptiles (at least as we understand them now) could not live in the cold waters of the North Atlantic, and to the best of our knowledge, no large dinosaurs have survived.

Perhaps influenced by the publicity attendant upon the publication of the "surgeon's photograph" of the Loch Ness monster in 1934, the first officer of the Cunard liner *Mauretania* reported a monster "65 feet long, 2 feet across the head, and 6 feet broad amidships" while cruising the Caribbean. As quoted in the *New York Times* on February 11, Officer S. W. Moughton said, "Its color was a shiny jet black. . . . I could not distinguish the eyes, as the monster kept its head on a slant from the *Mauretania* as if it were braced sharply against the breeze. Before I could get Chaunce out of the chart room, the head and shoulders had disappeared. I have no doubt that this was the sea serpent of the type that has been written about for hundreds of years."

Even when most of the possibilities are exhausted, an occasional creature appears that seems to defy identification. Such was the "New Zealand Monster," which was hauled up in the trawl net of a Japanese fishing vessel in April 1977. Brought onto the deck of the *Zuiyo Maru*, a mackerel trawler fishing off New Zealand, was a badly decomposed carcass that was 32 feet long and weighed approximately 4,000 pounds. After it was measured and photographed, pieces were snipped off for tissue samples, and it was dumped overboard so as not to contaminate the ship's catch. "It's not a fish, whale, or any other mammal," said Prof. Yoshinori Imaizumi of the National Science Museum in Tokyo.

Other experts weighed in with the usual suspects: Dr. Bobb Schaeffer, a paleoichthyologist at the American Museum of Natural History in New York, said, "It's baloney. Every ten years or so, something is found, usually in the Pacific, and people think it's a dinosaur. And it always turns out to be a basking shark or an adolescent whale." Alwyne Wheeler of the British Museum of Natural History agreed with his fellow ichthyologist and said it was the remains of a basking shark: "Sharks are cartilaginous fish," he said.

*T*his carcass was hauled aboard a Japanese fishing boat off New Zealand in 1977. After many misidentifications as a dinosaur, sea serpent, and sea monster, it turned out to be the decomposed carcass of a basking shark.

"When they start to decompose after death, the head and gills are the first to drop from the body. . . . Greater experts than the Japanese fishermen have been foiled by the similarity of shark remains to a plesiosaur."

Despite what would appear to have been a great desire to identify the carcass as that of a sea monster, it turned out to be a basking shark, after all. Before the carcass was discarded, one of the crewmen lopped off a piece of a fin, which contained the horny fibers (*ceratorichia*) that characterize the elasmobranchs, and these were later identified as those of *Cetorhinus maximus*. Still, if you squint at the photographs taken by a fisheries inspector aboard the *Zuiyo Maru*, they look a lot more like a rotten dinosaur than an old shark.

In an unpublished study, zoologists Paul LeBlond and John Sibert have collected an impressive dossier on their "observations of large unidentified marine animals in British Columbia and adjacent waters." Rather than relying on press reports, as Heuvelmans had to do, LeBlond and Sibert "went directly to eye-witnesses for information" and therefore limited their study to creatures sighted after 1969, only in the waters adjacent to their base in Vancouver. They sent a questionnaire to "marinas, lighthouse-keepers, fishing clubs, and to all local newspapers on the British Columbia coast," and their quest was soon picked up by national and international newspapers, including the *New York Times*.

There is not space enough to paraphrase their evidence, which relates to twenty-three eyewitness accounts, but perhaps an excerpt from their conclusion will suffice:

> From 23 direct eye-witnesses and seven second-hand reports, we have isolated 23 sightings which could not definitely or even speculatively be accounted for by animals known to science. On the basis of differences in the size of the eyes and in body shape, these animals have been classified into three categories. The first type of animal has very large eyes, a horse-shaped head, a long (5–10 ft.) neck and a body showing three humps. It is covered with short fur looking somewhat like coconut fiber. This creature resembles Heuvelmans' Merhorse, except for the absence of a mane. The second type is very similar to the first in general body build except that the eyes are much smaller and often go unnoticed; some specimens have a long floppy mane running at the back of their neck and short giraffe-like horns are also observed. The third animal is definitely serpentine in form, swimming with loops of its body emerging above the surface of the water. A jagged fin runs along its back and its head is described as sheep-like.

Now along comes *Cadborosaurus*.

Named for the British Columbia region known as Cadboro Bay, this creature is virtually unique in the literature because it comes accompanied by a photograph. (The photograph is somewhat ambiguous, and it would be possible to see something other than what its sponsors claim to see, but the reader is advised to read the description and arrive at his own conclusions.) The first sighting is believed to have occurred in 1933, when a Victoria lawyer and his wife were cruising in Cadboro Bay. They noticed "an immense head shaped like a camel's . . . that was rearing out of the water on the north side of the bay." Later that same year, two members of the B.C. Provincial Government saw the same apparition, and in 1934, fishermen reported that there were *two* monsters in the bay, the smaller one about 60 feet long. In *The Wake of Sea Serpents*, Heuvelmans discusses "Caddy" at some length, including—but not documenting—all sorts of sightings. Here are a couple of examples: "On 13 February 1953 some ten people saw him, from different points of view, as he swam for more than an hour in Qualicum Bay." And: "In 1960 a Sidney couple said they saw Caddy on Boxing Day. He was half a mile off the town and heading southwards, raising his head 8 feet out of the water."

𝒫 hotograph taken in October 1937 showing "Cadborosaurus," collected from the stomach of a sperm whale that had been brought to the Naden Harbour whaling station in Vancouver. It was described as having a "head like that of a horse, a snake-like body, and a finned, spiny tail."

Marine scientists Paul LeBlond (University of British Columbia) and E. L. Bousfield (Royal B. C. Museum) now enter the story, collecting and publishing not only the information on the 1937 specimen of *Cadborosaurus* but also "field observations and sketches made during the last century by more than 50 witnesses. . . ." LeBlond and Bousfield list twenty-eight sightings of what they are assuming is the same creature and discuss at some length its possible affiliations:

> Evidence to date indicates that this cryptid species is a vertebrate animal. It embodies major characteristics of both Reptilia and Mammalia, but it is not clearly classifiable within existing sub-categories of either. In gross aspects of its large, elongate form, fore-flippers, and bifurcate tail "Cadborosaurus" is similar to, but more slender than, reconstructions of the fossil whale known as Zeuglodon (Eocene, 30 m.y.b.p. [million years before present]) which apparently evolved from early terrestrial creodonts.

In the April 1993 issue of *Pacific Northwest,* writer Jessica Maxwell interviewed LeBlond and Bousfield and described more of the "Caddy" sightings. Two miles south of Yachats, Oregon, in 1937, several witnesses (who insisted upon anonymity) saw an animal with "a 15-foot exposed neck and a horse- or camel-like head." The body was described as about 6 feet across, "the size of a steam boiler," and the animal's total length was estimated at 55 feet. In March 1953, Mrs. E. Stout and her sister-in-law were walking along the beach at Dungeness Spit when they spotted a creature with a "large flattish head [and] three humps behind the long neck." Mrs. Stout, a trained marine and freshwater biologist, said, "If it had not been for the humps, we would have said it resembled pictures of the herbivorous, marsh-living dinosaurs. The animal was a rich, deep brown, with large reticulations of a bright burnt orange." In 1959, two commercial fishermen saw an animal "with ten feet of visible neck covered in light brown hair, much like coconut fiber, large red eyes, and short ears." For the magazine article, Maxwell herself interviewed Doris Sinclair, of Grays Harbor, on the Pacific coast of Washington, who saw some sort of a monster in February 1992. Mrs. Sinclair observed a head emerge from the water—of the bay, not the ocean—and said, "It looked like the picture of the Loch Ness monster—I would be more comfortable if I could say it looked different, but it truly was the head I've seen in photographs."

In his 1987 book *Whalers No More*, Capt. W. A. (Bill) Hagelund says that he remembers an old whaling crony's description of the creature: "It had a horselike head with large limpid eyes and a tuft of stiff whiskers off each cheek. Its long slender body was covered by a furlike material, with the exception of its back, where spiked horny plates overlapped each other. It had skin-covered flippers and a spade-shaped tail, like a sperm whale." While searching his files during the preparation of his book, Hagelund found a clipping that had appeared in the Vancouver *Province* on October 16, 1937. It showed a shriveled-up object that had been removed from the stomach of a sperm whale at the Naden Harbour whaling station in the Queen Charlotte Islands. The caption accompanying the photograph reads as follows:

> October 16, 1937. Infant "Caddy" found in whale. The fisheries department's news bulletin today described a strange creature taken from the stomach of a Pacific Coast whale, tallying closely with descriptions of the elusive Cadborosaurus of Southern Vancouver Island waters, but much smaller, possibly an infant. Officials say it was surprising to find such a large creature in a whale's stomach, as the mammals feed usually on squid, octopus, and sometimes shrimp. Discovery of the infant mammal was reported by the Daily Province in July. It was found at Naden Harbour whaling station, and its exact species has never been determined.

The creature was 10 feet long and had a horselike head, a long neck, a snakelike body, and a finned, spiny tail. In 1968, while Captain Hagelund was anchored in a place called Pirate's Cove, he collected an animal that he described (in *Whalers No More*) as "a living representative of the Naden Caddy find." Upon seeing "a small, eel-like creature swimming along with its head held completely out of the water, the undulation of its long, slender body causing portions of its spine to break the surface," he dip-netted it and brought it aboard for closer examination. It was "approximately sixteen inches long, and just over an inch in diameter. His lower jaw had a set of sharp, tiny teeth, and his back was protected by plate-like scales, while his undersides were covered in a sort of yellow fuzz. A pair of small, flipper-like feet protruded from his shoulder area, and a spade-shaped tail proved to be two tiny flipper-like fins that overlapped each other."

Hagelund put the little fellow in a plastic bucket, planning to take it to "the biological people at Departure Bay" the next morning. During the night, he heard the "splashes made by his tail, and the scratching of his little teeth and flippers as he attempted to grasp the smooth surface of the bucket," and when he realized that "such exertion . . . could cause him to perish by morning," Hagelund released it. He wrote that the little sea ser-

*U*ndated postcard showing "Edizgigantus," the Port Angeles (Washington) sea serpent, so named because it was observed near the Ediz Hook Light. In the background is Vancouver Island, the home of Cadborosaurus.

pent "should be allowed to go free, to survive, if possible, and fulfill his purpose. If he were successful, we could possibly see more of his kind, not less."

Until such time as unquestionable hard evidence appears to confirm the existence of *Cadborosaurus*, LeBlond and Bousfield will continue to consider it "enigmatic and technically cryptic." However, an article in *The Economist* in August 1992 ("A Puzzle Unloched") indicated that they intended to introduce *Cadborosaurus* as a genuine animal at the Vancouver meeting of the American Society of Zoologists in December of that year, and indeed, Bousfield has written to me that he did just that.* When I asked LeBlond about this, he answered that "until there is evidence sufficient to convince the most doubting skeptics, there remains some uncertainty." His colleague Bousfield seems to have no such uncertainty, and in one of a series of letters to me, he wrote, "As new sightings continue to come to hand, mainly confirming our developing profile on its morphology, life style, and reproductive behavior, we feel that the acquisition of good recent photographs, video-tapes, and even small specimen(s) for study in a marine aquarium, is just a matter of time."

I admire Bousfield's dedication to the imminent appearance of Caddy, but if I were a betting man, I would bet against it. (I would, however, like nothing better than to lose the bet.) Beyond the mythology and mystery of the sea serpent, there are acknowledged marine monsters whose existence has been documented beyond a shadow of a doubt. In addition to the gigantic cephalopods with arms 40 feet long and eyes as large as dinner plates, there are cetaceans that can reach a length of 100 feet and weigh 150 tons. There are sharks capable of swallowing a whole Newfoundland dog and others with bathtub-sized mouths that feed on plankton at great depths. There are—or were until recently—gigantic sirenians that grazed on kelp off the Commander Islands of Siberia and whose forelegs were mere stumps, devoid of anything resembling the manus of other mammals. And there may even be octopuses with an arm spread of 200 feet.

---

*On December 6, 1992, Clyde Farnsworth reported in the *New York Times* that Bousfield and LeBlond "suggest that large serpentine creatures comprising 'a distinct vertebrate species of presently indeterminate class' are swimming in coastal waters off British Columbia and may even be related to the Loch Ness monster."

MERMAIDS AND
MANATEES

She will hear the winds howling,
She will hear the waves roar.
We shall see, while above us
The waves roar and whirl,
A ceiling of amber,
A pavement of pearl.
Singing "Here came a mortal,
But faithless was she!
And alone dwell for ever
The kings of the sea."

—MATTHEW ARNOLD
"The Forsaken Merman,"
1849

*T*HE MYTH OF A CREATURE that is half human, half fish can be traced as far back as 5000 B.C., to the Babylonian fishtailed god Oannes. The Babylonians believed that Oannes left the sea in the daytime and returned to it at night, which would account for the god's amphibious appearance. (Oannes appears as a sculpted figure found at the palace of Khorsabad, in Mesopotamia, now Iraq.) The feminine counter-part of Oannes—and therefore the first representation of an actual mer-maid—was Atargatis, a goddess who also came from the sea. She was portrayed as a woman with the tail of a fish. The Tritons, sea gods who pulled the chariot of Aphrodite, are also represented as fishtailed entities.

In the thirteenth-century Icelandic manuscript known as *Konungs skuggsja* (*Speculum Regale* in Latin; *King's Mirror* in English), we read this description of the merman:

> The monster is tall and of great size and rises straight out of the water. . . .
> It has shoulders like a man's but no hands. Its body apparently grows nar-
> rower from the shoulders down, so that the lower down it has been
> observed, the more slender it has seemed to be. But no one has ever seen
> how the lower end is shaped. . . . No one has ever observed it closely
> enough to determine whether its body has scales like a fish or skin like a
> man. Whenever the monster has shown itself, men have always been sure
> that a storm would follow.

When Odysseus is cast from his raft by a vengeful Poseidon, he is res-cued by the sea goddess Ino (also known as Leucothea), who gives him her veil to protect him from injury as he swims to shore. She then dives back into the sea, and the dark waters swallow her up. Ino had previously been a Theban mortal, and her other name, "Ino of the Slim Ankles," suggests

*O*dysseus and his men withstand the lure of the songs of the beautiful sirens by stuffing their ears with wax.

some posterior appendage other than a fish's tail, but she is still a woman who lives in the sea and therefore can be incorporated into the myth of the mermaid. Pliny seems to have been a believer in mermaids; in his 1601 translation, the Englishman Edward Topsell quoted Pliny thusly:

> And as for the Meremaids called Nereides, it is no fabulous tale that goeth of them: for looke how painters draw them, so they are indeed: only their bodie is rough and skaled all over, even in those parts where they resemble a woman. For such a Meremaid was seene and beheld plainely upon the same coast neere to the shore: and the inhabitants dwelling neere, heard it farre off when it was a dying, to make pitteous mone, crying and chattering very heavily.

Only a few years after the publication of Topsell's *Historie of Foure-Footed Beasts* (in which the mermaid appears despite its lack of hind legs),

Henry Hudson, sailing in search of the Northwest Passage in 1608, described the sighting of a mermaid near Novaya Zemlya:

> This morning, one of our companie looking over boord saw a Mermaid, and calling up some of the companie to see her, one more came up, and by the time shee was come close to the ship's side, looking earnestly on the men: a little after, a Sea came and overturned her: From the Navill upward, her backe and breasts were like a womans (as they say that saw her) her body as big as one of us; her skin very white; and long haire hanging down of colour blacke; in her going down they saw her tayle, which was like the tayle of a Porpesse, and speckled like a Macrell.

In 1620, when Capt. Sir Richard Whitbourne sailed to Newfoundland to investigate the possibilities of English settlements, he, too, saw a mermaid—or a merman—which he described as being quite beautiful, but instead of hair, it had "many blue streaks." It approached the boat, but one of Sir Richard's sailors clobbered it with an oar, and it sank beneath the sea.

Samuel Fallours, official painter of the Dutch East India Company, included a voluptuous mermaid in a 1718 drawing of the aquatic life of the

*I*n the early eighteenth century, some of the colonials believed that mermaids, along with other exotic sea creatures, lived in the waters of the Dutch East Indies. This drawing by François Valentijn appeared in *A Natural History of Amboina* in 1727.

islands, and thus began a process by which the mermaid would be included in the fauna of the East Indies. François Valentijn was a Dutch colonial chaplain assigned to the East Indies in the early years of the eighteenth century. While stationed on one of the islands, he compiled a *Natural History of Amboina*, which included an entire chapter on *Zee-Menschen* and *Zee-Wyven* and a clear copy of Fallours's mermaid illustration. The caption for Valentijn's picture of the *Zee-Wyf* reads as follows:

> A monster resembling a Siren caught on the coast of Borneo in the administrative district of Amboina. It was 59 inches long and in proportion as an eel. It lived on land for four days, and seven hours in a barrel filled with water. From time to time it uttered little cries like that of a mouse. Although offered small fish, molluscs, crabs, crayfish, etc., it would not eat.

Pontoppidan, the learned bishop of Bergen, was renowned for his interest in sea serpents, but he was also a staunch supporter of mermaids. In his *Natural History of Norway,* he wrote, "Amongst sea-monsters which are in the North Sea, and are often seen, I shall give the first place to the Havmanden, or merman, whose mate is called Hav-fruen, or mermaid." While he dismisses many reports as "idle tales," he tells of hundreds of persons in the diocese of Bergen who saw a merman and, in 1723, of three Danish ferrymen who saw an old man with a short black beard who dived beneath the water showing the pointed tail of a fish.

Unlike most other monsters, which, almost by definition, are very large, "mermaids" are small enough to tempt people to manufacture them. And wherever there is temptation, there will be people available to fall victim to it. So it came to pass in the eighteenth century that all sorts of skeletons, mummies, and *faux sirènes* began to appear on exhibit in European capitals. Scottish waters seemed to be a favored haunt of mermaids and produced a spate of sightings, such as the miniature specimen that was stoned to death and buried at Benbecula in the Hebrides in 1830. Another one was captured in Aspinwall Bay in 1881 and found its way to New Orleans, where it was put on exhibit. According to Peter Dance in *Animal Fakes & Frauds*, the Aspinwall mermaid had the head and face of a woman, pale blond hair, claws on its forelimbs like an eagle's talons, and below the waist, "the body [was] exactly the same as the ordinary mullet of our waters, with its scales, fins and tail perfect."

But, says Dance, a proper mermaid, with the torso of a beautiful woman and the tail of a fish, would have been impossible to fabricate, so the mermaid manufacturers "abandoned the attempt in favor of a grotesque parody of it." Throughout Europe and America, these "grotesque parodies" began to appear at taverns, coffeehouses, and fairs, and one was on exhibit at Reubens Peale's museum in New York during the 1830s. The "mermaids," evidently manufactured in Japan, usually consisted of cleverly conjoined skeletons of little monkeys and dehydrated fishes, and unless we assign to nineteenth-century America an unusual level of gullibility or an extraordinary willingness to believe in obvious fakes, it is difficult to see how anyone could have been fooled by these dwarfed, desiccated pastiches. But fooled they were, and mermaids of all shapes and sizes became surprisingly popular.

If there was ever a "marriage" that was arranged in heaven, it was that of Phineas Taylor Barnum and the mermaid. In 1842, Barnum was told the story of a Boston sea captain who had bought a "mermaid" on a voyage to Calcutta in 1817, and after exhibiting it for a while in Europe (and failing to recover the $6,000 he had paid for it), died and left it to his son. The son sold it, for an undisclosed amount, to Moses Kimball, the proprietor of the Boston Museum, a collection of curiosities and oddities. Evidently Kimball never put the mermaid on exhibit, but he did contact Barnum, his friend and rival in New York.

Barnum immediately realized that it could be a major attraction for his newly opened American Museum, at the corner of Ann Street and Broadway in New York. Instead of simply exhibiting the thing, however, Barnum, who never did anything simply, contrived the most complicated humbug he ever perpetrated. An anonymous letter appeared in a Montgomery, Alabama, newspaper in which it was casually mentioned that "Dr. Griffin, agent of the Lyceum of Natural History in London, recently from Pernambuco, S.A., who had in his possession a most remarkable curiosity, being nothing less than a veritable mermaid taken among the Feejee Islands, and preserved in China, where the Doctor had bought it for a high figure. . . ." Shortly thereafter, similar letters appeared in newspapers of Charleston, South Carolina, and then Washington, D.C. Then a story appeared in a New York newspaper with a Washington dateline in which the anonymous correspondent hoped that "the editors of the Empire City would beg a sight of the extraordinary curiosity before Dr. Griffin took ship for England." The mermaid was getting closer to New York.

In Philadelphia, "Dr. Griffin" permitted several newspaper editors to peek at the mermaid, and they obligingly wrote supportive articles about its authenticity. Finally, Griffin arrived in New York and allowed the New York press to see his treasure. Barnum was not ready to tip his hand, so instead of exhibiting the Feejee Mermaid, as it was now known, he claimed that "Dr. Griffin" (who was, in fact, his accomplice, Levi Lyman) would not

P. T. Barnum managed to convince thousands of "suckers" that this object had actually been a mermaid.

sell him the mermaid, and the woodcuts he had had printed up were of no use. The papers published the story of Barnum's failure—alongside the woodcuts, of course—and well before he actually put the Feejee Mermaid on exhibit, Barnum had half the city waiting to see it. Instead of exhibiting it at his own museum, the master showman had it shown *positively for one week only!* at Concert Hall on Broadway. After that week, during which thousands of visitors saw the Mermaid and heard "Dr. Griffin's" learned discourses, it was moved across the street to Barnum's museum. The exhibition was a great success, pulling in thousands of dollars a week, and in later years, Barnum gleefully told the entire story, including the manipulation of the newspaper articles. (In his autobiography, Barnum described the Feejee Mermaid as an "ugly, dried-up, black-looking specimen about three feet long . . . that looked like it had died in great agony".) A. H. Saxon, the author of a 1989 biography of Barnum, wrote, "If ever there was one humbug more 'shameful' than all the rest of Barnum's manufacture, surely it was the Feejee Mermaid. It might just as well have belonged to him, it became so inextricably woven into the fabric of his career."

It may have been the feminine nature of the name, but over time, "Jenny Hanivers" were associated with mermaids, even though they bore hardly any resemblance to a human being, let alone a beautiful woman. The origin of the name appears to be a complete mystery, and it is not listed in the *Oxford English Dictionary.* Its first published appearance was in a 1928 article by the Australian ichthyologist Gilbert Whitley, who discussed the creatures in an article in the *Australian Museum Magazine.* Whitley wrote, "I have been unable to learn the source of the name Jenny Haniver. Perhaps it belonged to some second-sighted fishwife who long ago imparted lucky

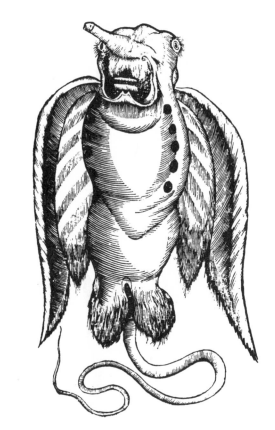

*U*lysses Aldrovandi illustrated a "sea eagle" in *De Piscibus* in 1613. It is obviously a Jenny Haniver with an elongated snout and "wings" that were dried in a drooping position.

*T*he first known illustration of a Jenny Haniver, from Gesner's *Historia Animalium,* 1558

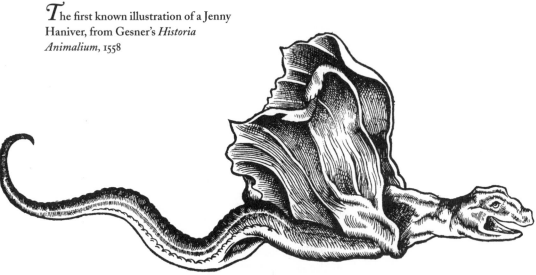

qualities to the little effigies to which her name has now been transferred."
(Probably because they fascinated him—but also because they were manufactured from elasmobranchs—Whitley also included a brief discussion and
several illustrations of these shriveled-up creatures in his 1940 *Fishes of Australia, Part I: The Sharks.*) In another article, E. W. Gudger of the American Museum of Natural History quoted a letter in which his correspondent
wrote, "The name as given to me sounded like Jeanie Hanvers, so maybe it
has something to do with 'Anvers,' the French name for Antwerp, a possible place of their origin." In Spanish—or at least in Puerto Rico—it is
known as a *Garadiavolo*, and the French call it *Diable de Mer*.

To make a Jenny Haniver, first catch a ray (or a skate or a guitarfish).
Cut the fins so they bear a resemblance to wings or tie a string around the
region where the neck would be, thus forming a semblance of a human
head. The nostrils of skates and rays are on the ventral surface, and because

A guitarfish (*Rhinobatus
lentiginosus*) pinned out and ready
to dry in the shape of a Jenny
Haniver. The body of the fish has
been trimmed to form wings, and
the "eyes" are actually the fish's
nostrils.

of their location, they look very much like eyes. (The real eyes are on the top, or dorsal, surface of the animal.) The jaws will protrude as the skin shrinks, and the cartilaginous supports of the fins will appear as crossed "arms." In all elasmobranchs (sharks, skates, rays, and guitarfishes), the males have paired claspers (the intromittent organs), which, when dried, could represent hind legs. Twist the tail to any desired position and allow it to dry in the sun. A coat of varnish will preserve the creature for posterity.

Some of the earliest writers about fishes, such as Belon, Gesner, Rondelet, and Aldrovandi, picture the "monkfish," or "sea bishop," obvious variations on the Jenny Haniver theme but with a human visage. (The eyes of the skates and rays are on the dorsal surface, but the nostrils are on the bottom, lending themselves to a representation of "eyes," and in some species, the mouth can easily be interpreted as a human mouth.) In his 1554 work, Guillaume Rondelet includes a picture of the bishop fish (his caption reads *De pisce Episcopi habitu,* or "the fish dressed as a bishop"), but because he was a professor of medicine at Montpellier, he was somewhat skeptical. To the description he added, "I think that certain details beyond the truth of the matter have been added by the painter to make the thing seem more marvellous."

Even though its form is variable throughout history, the basilisk is another standby of mythological literature and also seems to be a part of mermaid lore. In some later discussions, the basilisk appears as a snake,[*] but by the sixteenth century, the term was being applied to some of the strange apparitions that figured in the early natural histories. In Aldrovandi's *De Piscibus* (1613), there are two illustrations of a *basilicus ex raia,* indicating that the author knew that this was a manufactured creature. (There is another illustration in Aldrovandi, however, that bears the caption *Monstrosi piscus volantis imago,* or "image of a monstrous flying fish," so we ought not to conclude that he doubted all the modified rays.) Although the belief in mermaids and baslisks has diminished, one might still find a Jenny Haniver in a seaside curio shop. They exist not so much to fool people into believing they were monsters but because the underside of a ray resembles a human face and a dried one looks—at least to some people—something like a mermaid.

The Feejee Mermaid was an obvious fiction, and with the exception of the thousands of suckers who paid a quarter to view it, few people actually believed that this shriveled-up grotesque was half woman, half fish. But fic-

---

[*] Nowadays, the term is applied to a genus of tropical American lizards (*Basilicus*) characterized by an elongated lobe on the back of the head and a dorsal crest on the males. These lizards are able to run across the surface of the water on their hind legs.

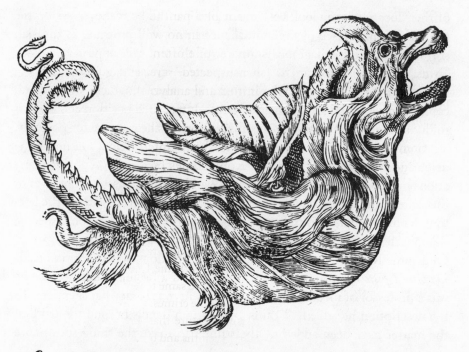

$\mathcal{A}$ldrovandi's *Draco effectus ex raia*, indicating that he knew this "dragon" had been made from a ray

tion comes in many guises. As applied to animals, it can be that environment in which an author consciously invents a creature for a particular literary or symbolic purpose. (Barnum did not invent the Feejee Mermaid; he merely invented the circumstances under which it would be presented to the public, and his "purpose" was purely financial.) Henry Lee, who was affiliated with the Brighton Aquarium, was interested in all sea creatures—he wrote books about the octopus and also the beluga—but he had a particular fondness for sea monsters. In conjunction with the Great International Fisheries Exhibition held in London in 1883, he wrote two "handbooks": *Sea Fables Explained* and *Sea Monsters Unmasked*. In the former, he presented a comprehensive history of mermaids in which he stated, "As his [the reader's] knowledge increases, he learns that the descriptions by ancient writers of so-called 'fabulous creatures' are rather distorted portraits than invented falsehoods, and there is hardly any of the monsters of old which has not its prototype in Nature at the present day."

It is entirely possible to believe in the existence of a mythological animal, even though science later "proves" that it does not exist. As Odell Shepherd wrote in his brilliant study of the unicorn, "No one in mediaeval

Europe ever saw a lion or an elephant or a panther, yet these beasts were accepted without question upon evidence in no way better or worse than that which vouched for the unicorn." Quite often, mythology and reality meld to describe an extant—but unsuspected—creature like the manatee.

Bernard Heuvelmans has identified and analyzed the process by which an animal evolves from one biomythological state to another. In a 1990 article in *Cryptozoology* entitled "The Metamorphosis of Unknown Animals into Fabulous Beasts and of Fabulous Beasts into Known Animals," he wrote: "The mythifying process can sometimes be carried to the point of altering its object beyond recongnition," and as an example presented the manatee:

> Since the manatee has pectoral mammae—like its cousin the elephant and also humans—and a body that tapers to a fishlike tail, it has always been identified, on both sides of the Atlantic, with the fascinating mermaid, despite its (to our eyes) ugly face—and by the same token, considered cannibalistic, and suspected of the most horrible crimes. . . . Now, can anyone imagine a more peaceable, inoffensive creature than this sea-cow, which passes its days lazily browsing water-hyacinths and other succulent plants?

The Greeks were unlikely to have seen manatees; they are found in the Western Hemisphere tropics and in the waters of West Africa, where Greek adventurers are not known to have gone. (The dugongs, close relatives of the manatees, live throughout the Indo-Pacific region, from East Africa to Melanesia, but the Greeks did not venture there, either.)

When Columbus entered the Caribbean, he noticed some strange-looking beasts floating in the aquamarine waters. They were plump, grayish, rough-skinned creatures, obviously mammals, with a body about the size of a small cow, rounded flippers, and a broad, paddle-like tail. For the most part, they kept their heads submerged as they grazed on underwater vegetation, but when they had to breathe, they rose to the surface and exposed a bewhiskered muzzle and a pair of large nostrils. Whatever appellations might be applied to these animals, "beautiful" is not the first one that springs to mind.

Nevertheless, Columbus, and many explorers who followed him to the New World, decided that the manatee was the siren or mermaid of fable. Also included in this romantic-symbolic category is the merman, *homen marinho* in Portuguese. According to Richard Lewisohn,

> Mermen practiced their nefarious calling only in the summertime, and then usually in the vicinity of fresh water. They looked like men, were

quite tall, and had deeply sunken eyes. . . . The mermen grappled to their victims, Negroes and Indians exclusively, then strangled them, after which they crushed them to a pulp. Having murdered, they let out curious sighs, then fled. Often, too, they carried off their victims for cannibalistic purposes, but ate only the eyes, nose, finger and toe tips, and the sexual parts.

Lewisohn attributes this description to "two reputedly sober and dependable observers, the Jesuit father Fernao Cardim and the sugar manufacturer Gabriel Soares de Sousa." Their *homen marinho* sounds something like a manatee, juxtaposed on a description of the damage that might have been done to a drowned seaman by crabs and fishes nibbling on the smaller, exposed parts of the anatomy. In any case, it would be difficult to imagine a creature less like a mermaid (or a merman) than a manatee: A sparsely haired, mustachioed, cleft-lipped, blimplike animal with flippers bears little resemblance to a graceful woman with long hair and a fish's tail or a tall man with deeply sunken eyes.

Columbus described the manatee in his log entry of January 9, 1493, as he sailed along the northern coast of the island of Hispaniola. "I saw three sirens," he wrote, "that came up very high out of the sea. They are not as beautiful as they are painted, since in some ways they have a face like a man." * The original sirens, as discussed in the *Odyssey,* were sea nymphs whose songs could charm all who heard them. (In order to resist the siren's songs, Ulysses stuffed his ears with beeswax.) The manatees (and their cousins the dugongs) were orginally classified with the cetaceans not so much because of their mutual resemblance but because they are the only other mammals that lead a completely aquatic existence. Now they constitute a separate order, but the name persists, for the order is known as Sirenia.

In the twelfth century, the bestiary incorporated the sum of knowledge about the animals of the world, and because of the obvious limitations of the readers (and the authors), there was little attempt or inclination to differentiate fact from fable. Originally based on the *Physiologus,* a second-century Greek work, the medieval bestiary drew moral lessons from monstrous or wondrous animals. A twelfth-century bestiary, translated from the Latin by T. H. White (the author of *The Sword in the Stone,* among other works), includes such fabulous creatures as the phoenix, the unicorn, the griffin, the manticore, and, of course, the siren:

*According to Robert Fuson, who translated and annotated the log of Columbus, "The common manatee [was] known in Spanish as *sirena* until the Taino word *manati* came into use after Columbus, thence into English.

Mermaids and Manatees

The SIRENAE (Sirens), so Physiologus says, are deadly creatures who are made like human beings from the head to the navel, while their lower parts down to the feet are winged. They give forth musical songs in a melodious manner, which songs are very lovely, and thus they charm the ears of sailormen and allure them to themselves. They entice the hearing of these poor chaps by a wonderful sweetness of rhythm, and put them to sleep. At last, when they see that the sailors are deeply slumbering, they pounce upon them and tear them to bits.

The reality of the sirenians differs dramatically from this malicious musicality, and they restrict their vocalizations to snorts and grunts. When the conquistadores encountered these inoffensive animals on their expeditions to the Antilles, Florida, or the coasts of Brazil, Guiana, and Venezuela, the animals acquired many unusual (and totally fictional) characteristics. Off the coast of Martinique in May 1671, two Frenchmen noticed a creature of "very coarse and wild appearance," which Herbert Wendt (in *Out of Noah's Ark*) described thus:

Down to the waist it resembled a man, but below this it was like a fish with a broad, crescent-shaped tail. Its face was round and full, the nose thick and flat; black hair flecked with grey fell over its shoulders and covered its belly. When it rose out of the water it swept the hair out of its face with its hands; and when it dived again, it snuffled like a poodle. One of us threw a fishhook to see if it would bite. Thereupon it dived and disappeared for good.

When Jules Verne wrote *Twenty Thousand Leagues Under the Sea*, which was published in Paris in 1870, he included a dugong among the dangerous denizens of the deep. Verne's Professor Aronnax, author of *Mysteries of the Ocean Depths*, was obviously out of his element when it came to mammals that lived most of their lives at or near the surface. Since most of the adventures in *Twenty Thousand Leagues* occur beneath the surface, we do not meet any of these amphibious creatures until the *Nautilus* comes up for air. Just before their epic journey through the Arabian Tunnel, the keen-eyed Ned Land spots something off in the distance and reports it to Professor Aronnax:

"Look, it's moving! It's diving!" cried Ned Land. "What in God's name is it? It hasn't got the forked tail of a whale, and its fins look like sawed-off legs."

"That means . . ." I said.

"Now it's rolled over on its back," continued the Canadian, "with its mammaries in the air."

"It's a mermaid," cried Conseil, "a real mermaid, begging Monsieur's pardon."

"This word 'mermaid' put me on the right track [says Aronnax], and I realized that this animal belonged to that species from which had sprung the legends about mermaids, creatures which were half woman, half fish."

It turns out, of course, to be a dugong, but as we shall see, a dugong unlike any other. First Aronnax's servant Conseil classifies it: "Order of Sirenia, division of Pisciformae, subclass of monodelphians, class of mammals, subkingdom of vertebrates." "Pisciformae" means simply "fish shaped," and while the taxonomists of the nineteenth century may have classified the dugong this way, it is a classification that has not endured. As far as the dugong being a vertebrate mammal, that is correct.

Having been trapped aboard the *Nautilus* for so long, the Canadian harpooner is anxious to harpoon something, so when Nemo gives him permission to go after the dugong, Ned readily agrees. As if it were some sort of whale, the crew launches a dinghy to pursue it, and armed with his killing iron, Ned Land positions himself in the bow. As they row up close to the dugong, Aronnax gives us a little background:

> The dugong, which is also called the halicore, is somewhat similar to the manatee. It has an oblong body ending in a long tail, and its side fins are tipped with veritable fingers. It differs from the manatee in that its upper jaw is armed with two long and pointed teeth which stick out on each side.
>
> The dugong Ned Land was preparing to attack was enormous; it must have been around twenty-five feet long.

As usual, Verne/Aronnax has got most everything wrong. "Halicore" is another term for the dugong, and because the dugong has a horizontal caudal fin that is indeed like the flukes of a whale, in a profile view it would probably look like a long tail. (How one longs to know what picture book Verne had before him when he wrote this.) It has no fingers, veritable or otherwise, on its side fins, but the males do have teeth sticking out of the sides of their jaws. (We might assume that Verne has the dugong confused with the walrus, but later, when they get to the South Pole, Aronnax carefully describes the resident walruses, tusks and all—even though walruses are to be found nowhere in the Southern Hemisphere.)

Land succeeds in harpooning the dangerous dugong, which tows their dinghy for an hour until it turns on the boat:

> The dugong came within twenty feet of the dinghy, stopped and sniffed the air with its huge nostrils. Then it started moving again, and rushed headlong in our direction.
>
> The dinghy could not avoid the blow. We were almost capsized and the dinghy shipped a ton or two of water which had to be bailed out; we had been saved from actually going over by the coxswain's skill in maneuvering so that we were struck at an angle and not full on the side. Ned Land was clinging to the bow and harpooning the giant animal again and again, as it sunk its teeth into the gunwale and lifted the boat out of the water like a lion attacking a deer. We were thrown on top of one another and things might have ended badly if the Canadian, carrying on the struggle relentlessly, had not finally struck the animal in the heart.

They finally haul in the carcass of this dangerous beast and somehow manage to weigh it. "It weighed," comments the narrator, "eleven thousand pounds."

The average size for a dugong is about 10 feet, and the longest known specimen measured 13 feet. The largest males weigh a little over a ton. If Verne's description of the size and appearance of the dugong is wrong, his account of its behavior is ludicrous. The comparison to "a lion attacking a deer" is fascinating on many counts, not the least of which is that lions usually live in Africa, where there are no deer.* Although the measurements of the dinghy are never stated, earlier it is described as a "splendid little boat; light and unsinkable." It would have to be to take on one or two tons of water. . . .

Jules Verne obviously had a thing about dugongs, because he continued to include these harmless creatures in his novels as dangerous beasts. In *The Mysterious Island* (published in English in 1875), a dugong attacks a dog:

> The dog was already twenty feet off, and Cyrus was calling him back, when an enormous head emerged from the water. . . . It was not a lamantin [manatee], but one of that species of the order of cetaceans, which bear the name "dugong," for its nostrils were at the upper part of its snout. The

---

*Around 1870, when the book was written, however, Paris was captivated by a group of animal sculptors known as *les animaliers*. Foremost among them was Antoine-Louis Barye (1796–1875), who was best known for his bronzes showing combat between various predatory and prey animals, such as tigers attacking snakes, panthers attacking crocodiles, and, in spite of the *animaliers'* knowledge that these encounters did not occur in the wild, lions attacking deer.

enormous animal rushed the dog, who tried to escape by returning towards the shore. His master could do nothing to save him. . . . Top [the dog], seized by the dugong, had disappeared beneath the water.

Instead of killing the dog, the dugong itself is killed:

Doubtless the dugong, attacked by some powerful animal, after having released the dog, was fighting on its own account. But it did not last long. The water became red with blood, and the body of the dugong, emerging from the sheet of scarlet which spread around, soon stranded on a little beach. . . . The dugong was dead. It was an enormous animal, fifteen or sixteen feet long, and must have weighed from three to four thousand pounds. At its neck was a wound, which appeared to have been produced by a sharp blade. What could the amphibious creature have been, who, by this terrible blow, had destroyed the formidable dugong?

Who indeed? It is none other than Captain Nemo, who evidently did not die at the end of *Twenty Thousand Leagues Under the Sea* after the *Nautilus* was caught in the deadly maelstrom. (Professor Aronnax, Conseil, and Ned Land escaped in the nick of time.) It appears that the captain has been cruising the world's oceans alone, using an underwater cavern on Lincoln Island (the name the Union prisoners give to their island) as an occasional sanctuary. Nemo has been keeping an eye on the castaways and anonymously helping them when they need it. But this time Captain Nemo dies, and then, with the proper pyrotechnics, the obligatory volcanic eruption destroys the island.

For the most part, dugongs are shy and inoffensive animals, and one might just as well have been attacked by a goldfish. In assigning an aggressive nature to the dugong, Verne compares it to its cousins and tells us that manatees are "peaceful and inoffensive animals." But he cannot resist exaggerating their size, and when the *Nautilus* encounters "sea cows" living in family groups on the coast of Dutch Guiana, Aronnax tells us that they "grow as long as twenty or twenty-five feet and weigh up to nine thousand pounds." (Manatees are actually somewhat smaller than dugongs.) An illustration in the original French publication shows a pair of manatees, accurately drawn but unrealistically shown resting on rocks out of the water. Like whales—to which they are not related—manatees never leave the water.

ONE OF THE reasons that sirenians have been the subject of such intense scrutiny is the presence of a cryptozoological skeleton in their closet. The manatees and dugongs are indeed shy and inoffensive creatures and do not exceed 13 feet in length. They are all warm-water inhabitants and browse on green plants that they grind with their specially adapted teeth. If someone reported a 30-foot sirenian, with thick, leathery skin and flippers that were cut off at the elbow, living in the icy waters off Siberia, it would be easy to dismiss such a report as a "sea-monster sighting," and yet, two centuries ago, a gigantic sirenian existed that fit this description exactly. It no longer exists, although there are occasional "sightings" around Siberia and Alaska.

When Commander Vitus Bering, sailing in the employ of Czar Peter the Great, was wrecked on a remote island at the western end of the Aleutian chain in 1741, he and his men were starving and needed food, so they were surprised and relieved to discover a herd of these gigantic, slow-moving animals. Bering, who died there, had the islands named for him (they are now known as the Komandorskie, or Commander, Islands), but it was his zoologist, a German named Georg Wilhelm Steller, whose name will forever be affixed to that of the gigantic sea cow.*

Steller's sea cow, known as *Hydrodamalis gigas,* was one of the most unusual mammals that has ever lived. Although it is extinct, there was enough information recorded about its appearance and habits for us to get an idea of what it looked like and how it lived. *Morskaya korova* was an overstuffed sausage of a beast, with a small head, piggy eyes, and skin that was likened to the bark of a tree. It had a forked, horizontal tail like its relative the dugong (the manatee has a rounded, paddle-like tail), and its forelegs were unique in the mammalian kingdom: They had no finger bones, and the animal, which probably could not dive below the surface, pulled itself along the bottom on its stumps as it browsed on kelp. Its mouth had no teeth; instead, there were horny plates that it rubbed together to grind plant matter into a pulp.

Upon Steller's return to Kamchatka on the Russian mainland, the existence of the sea otters, the sea cow, and the islands themselves was made known. The pelt of the sea otter is one of the most luxurious furs in the world, and it was not long before Russian trappers arrived on the islands. It is said that they killed more than eleven thousand foxes and two thousand otters. Russian sealers began to visit Bering and Copper islands for the sea lions that bear Steller's name and also for meat and oil for their voyages. They killed the slow-moving sea cows in such numbers that there were none left by 1768. (We have no way of knowing how many sea cows were on the islands when Bering landed, but Leonhard Stejneger, Steller's biogra-

*Bering, of course, also had a sea and a strait named for him, and Steller's name is affiliated with a jay, an eider, an eagle, and a species of sea lion.

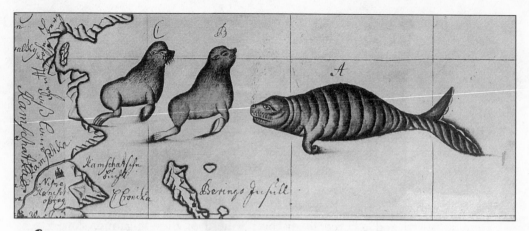

$\mathcal{A}$ sea cow (A), drawn by Sven
Waxell, an officer on Bering's 1741
voyage aboard the *St. Peter*, which was
wrecked on the Commander Islands.
(*B* is a sea lion and *C* is a fur seal.) This
is the only known illustration of a sea
cow by someone who actually saw one.

pher, has estimated that there were some fifteen hundred.) It had taken only twenty-seven years for the Russian adventurers to eliminate the hapless sea cow from the face of the earth, but the sealers had no way of knowing that this was the last of them; they probably assumed that there were similar undiscovered islands with more sea cows.

Although no more sea cows appeared, various explorers continued to report that they had sighted something that bore a marked resemblance to *Hydrodamalis*. Travelers in the western Arctic occasionally claimed to have seen something that was not a seal, sea lion, or walrus, and Heuvelmans, in trying to associate the sea cow with some earlier monster sightings, concocts some behavior that he could only speculate about and writes, "It sometimes lifts its head above water and is not the least shy of approaching man." In July 1962, however, the Soviet whale catcher *Buran* was hunting whales in the area around Cape Navarin, south of the Gulf of Anadyr in the Siberian Arctic, when the crew spotted several large animals that seemed to fit the description of the *morskaya korova*. Soviet biologists A. A. Berzin, E. A. Tikhomirov, and V. I. Troinin reported the sighting in the Soviet journal *Priroda* (Nature) and wrote,

> As far as we know, the sea-cow was completely exterminated in the Komandorski Islands by fur-seal hunters. However, in other areas, where the sea-cow may have lived, if we are to judge from the data we have cited, there was no hunting of this kind, because there were no animals with valuable fur. We may suppose that the sea-cow could have survived there

*S*teller's sea cow, *Hydrodamalis gigas*. Thirty feet long and slow moving, this gigantic relative of the manatee was eliminated in 1768, twenty-seven years after its discovery.

if adequate ecological conditions coincided, but we have no information on the subject. If this is the case, the sea-cow must have been able to remain unnoticed for a long time.

There have been scattered reports of sea cows from various locations in the Arctic, perhaps promulgated by the human hope that we were not really responsible for the extinction of this helpless, lumbering creature. But even if the sea cow is extinct in nature, it lives on in literature, in Rudyard Kipling's "The White Seal." Although it begins in "a place called Novastoshnah, or North East Point, on the Island of St. Paul, away and away in the Bering Sea," the story takes Kotick the white seal all over the Pacific, from the beach where he was born to the Equator. He then swims south to Kerguelen Island deep in the Antarctic, back to the Galápagos ("a horrid dry place on the Equator, where he was almost baked to death"), to the Antarctic islands of South Georgia, the South Orkneys, Bouvet Island, and "even a little speck of an island south of the Cape of Good Hope." Chasing a school of halibut, Kotick finds himself close to the beach on Copper Island, where he "jumped like a cat, for he saw huge things nosing about in the shoal water and browsing on the heavy fringes of the weeds."

*I*n a 1950 edition of Kipling's *Jungle Book,* illustrator Fritz Eichenberg drew Kotick the white seal visiting the last of the sea cows.

"By the Great Combers of Magellan!" he said, beneath his mustache. "Who in the Deep Sea are these people?"

They were like no walrus, sea lion, seal, bear, whale, shark, fish, squid, or scallop that Kotick had ever seen before. They were between twenty and thirty feet long, and they had no hind flippers, but a shovellike tail that looked as if it had been whittled out of wet leather. Their heads were the most foolish things you ever saw, and they balanced on the end of their tails in deep water when they weren't grazing, bowing solemnly to each other and waving their front flippers as a fat man waves his arm.

After trying to engage the great beasts in conversation "in every language that he had picked up in his travels," Kotick discovers that the sea cow cannot talk. ("The sea cows went on schlooping and grazing and chumping on the weed . . . but they did not answer. . . .") The sea cows then began a slow northerly migration, and although the impatient Kotick swoops over and under them, "he could not hurry them up one mile." They sink like stones to an underwater tunnel and emerge at "one of the finest beaches that Kotick had ever seen." After ascertaining that the fishing is good and the beach is protected by bars and shoals "that would never let a ship come within six miles of the beach," Kotick returns to Novastoshnah and convinces the rest of the seals to return with him to the secret beach of the sea cows.

Bering's was also the expedition during which one of the great puzzles

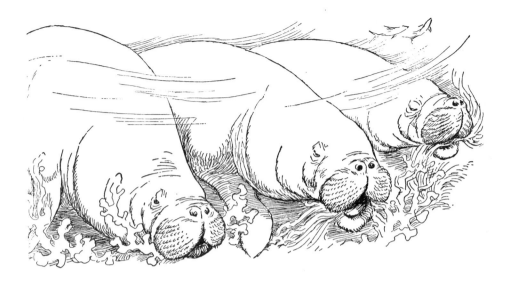

of cryptozoology was raised: In addition to the sea cows, sea otters, and sea lions, Steller described an animal the identity of which has eluded scientists since the account was first published. All Steller's other descriptions are more than adequate to identify the animals in question, and subsequent investigations have demonstrated the existence of all the other creatures he so meticulously cataloged, but what are we to make of this?

> During this time we were near land or surrounded by it we saw large numbers of hair seals, sea otters, fur seals, sea lions, and porpoises. . . . On August 10 [1741] we saw a very unusual and unknown sea animal, of which I am going to give a brief account since I observed it for two whole hours. It was about two Russian ells [six feet] in length; the head was like a dog's, with pointed erect ears. From the upper and lower lips on both sides whiskers hung down which made it look almost like a Chinaman. The eyes were large; the body was longish round and thick, tapering gradually towards the tail. The skin seemed thickly covered with hair, of a grey color on the back, but reddish white on the belly; in the water, however, the whole animal appeared entirely reddish and cow-colored. The tail was divided into two fins, of which the upper, as in the case of sharks, was twice as large as the lower.

Steller went on to say that the only reference he could think of that might help in identifying the creature was Gesner's description (in 1587) of something he called *Simia marina danica*, the Danish sea monkey. The animal cavorted around Steller's boat for hours, playing with strands of kelp,

*O*n August 10, 1741, Georg Wilhelm Steller, the naturalist on Vitus Bering's ship *St. Peter,* spotted a creature he was not able to identify, but he wrote that it "corresponds in all respects to Gesner's *Simia marina Danica*," the "Danish Sea-ape."

and finally, Steller took a shot at it ("in order to get possession of it for a more accurate description"), but he missed. In *Searching for Hidden Animals,* Roy Mackal discounts the suggestion that Steller confused the creature with a sea otter or a seal and writes, "The simplest explanation is that the 'sea-monkey' actually existed, and that Steller saw it for the first and last time before it became extinct."*

The sea cow is gone forever, and the "sea-monkey," if it ever existed at all, is also absent from the zoological record. The sirens are still with us, however, in the form of the manatees and dugongs. They may not have the sex appeal of their namesakes, and they are certainly not as beautiful as the mermaid, but they differ from their historical and literary ancestors in one irrefutable respect: They exist. There are three species of manatees, distinguished by geography and some anatomic details, and a single species of dugong. Like whales and dolphins, the sirenians are completely aquatic and

---

*Along the rocky coasts of Maine and New Brunswick, Canada, until about the end of the nineteenth century, there lived an animal known as the sea mink (*Mustela macrodon*) that might be compared to Steller's sea monkey. Also known as the bull mink or saltwater mink, it was about twice as large as the Eastern mink (*M. vison*) and had coarser, reddish-brown fur. By 1894, the sea mink had been hunted to extinction by trappers, and although there is no reason to assume that a comparable species existed on the West Coast of North America or the East Coast of Asia, there is an Alaskan subspecies of the common mink (*M. vison injens*) and several species of martens, sables, and other mustelids in Siberia. In other words, if Steller had spotted the "sea-monkey" off the East Coast of North America, there would be no problem with its identification.

spend their entire lives in the water. (As mammals, they breathe air and can exist on land, but their forelegs are not designed for terrestrial locomotion, and in place of hind legs, they have only a tail.) The manatees (*Trichechus* sp.) and the dugong (*Dugong dugon*), have large, fusiform (spindle-shaped) bodies; flippers for forelegs; horizontally flattened tails (paddle shaped in the manatees, forked like the flukes of a whale in the dugong); solid, heavy bones; and highly specialized teeth for their herbivorous diet.

In the careful journals of the British explorer and buccaneer William Dampier, we read of his encounters with manatees ("I have seen of the Manatee in the Bay of *Campeachy,* on the coasts of *Bocca del Drago* and *Bocco del Toro,* in the River of *Darien* [all in what is now Panama], and among the South Keys or little islands of *Cuba*"), and his description is as good and accurate today as it was when he wrote it in 1681:

> This Creature is about the Bigness of a Horse, and 10 or 12 Foot long. The Mouth of it is much like the Mouth of a Cow, having great thick Lips. The Eyes are no bigger than a small Pea; the Ears are only two small holes on each side of the Head. The Neck is short and thick, bigger than the Head. The biggest part of this Creature is at the Shoulders, where it has two large Fins, one on each side of its Belly. Under each of these Fins the Female hath a small Dug to suckle her young. From the Shoulders towards the Tail it retains its bigness for about a Foot, then groweth smaller and smaller to the very Tail, which is flat, and about 14 Inches broad and 20 Inches long, and in the Middle 4 or 5 Inches thick. From the Head to the Tail it is round and smooth without any Fin but those two before-mentioned.

Dampier witnessed the harpooning of manatees by the Miskito Indians ("Their Flesh is white, both the Fat and the Lean, and extraordinary wholesome Meat. The Tail of a young Cow is most esteem'd. . . .") and noted that the "Skin of the Manatee is of great use to Privateers," since they made oarlocks and horsewhips from it. From historical records, it would appear that people hunted manatees almost from the time they discovered them. Despite Jules Verne's preposterous accounts, manatees are inoffensive, slow-moving creatures, and the amount of meat per animal, plus the manatee's almost complete inability to escape from hunters, made it an ideal target. The Mayas of Central America and Mexico evidently hunted them with obsidian-tipped spears and dragged them ashore to die of their wounds. The Miskitos struck them with harpoons with a float attached and clubbed the wounded animal on the head when it surfaced. Archaeological evidence in Florida indicates that manatees have been hunted there for at

*T*he Florida manatee,   least eight thousand years. After the elimination of Florida's
Trichechus manatus   aboriginal Indian population around A.D. 1700, northern
                          Indians (collectively known as Seminoles) moved in, and
they harpooned the manatee for food.

Manatees are strictly vegetarians, browsing mostly on floating plants.
Every day they consume about one pound of vegetation for each pound of
body weight, and a full-grown manatee can weigh over a ton. They do not
use their flippers to guide the leaves into their mouths; rather, they turn
their lip pads inside out and use the bristles to tuck the food in. When they
are not feeding, manatees are likely to be resting either at the bottom or just
at the surface, with only the nostrils exposed. (It is assumed that the manatee's sense of smell is rudimentary or absent; they keep their nostrils closed
while they are submerged and only open them briefly to inhale at the surface.) They never go very fast—top speed is about fifteen miles per hour—
but they usually mosey along at between two and six miles per hour.
Manatees spend a lot of time under water; in the wild, they spend six to
eight hours a day feeding.

Manatee skin is dark gray, but its coloration may be affected by various
algae that grow on it. The flippers of the Florida and Caribbean species
have fingernails but no fingers. Because manatees are designed to move

smoothly—but not swiftly—through the water, all unnecessary protuberances have been eliminated. The ears are just pinholes, and the genitalia are internal. Gestation is about thirteen months, after which a 60-pound calf is born. The female nurses her calf from a teat located under the flipper. (The "breast" location of the manatees' mammaries may be responsible for some of the earliest "mermaid" rumors.)

Manatees used to live as far north as the Carolinas and all the way around Florida into the Gulf of Mexico. Although they can exist in salt or fresh water, they never wander far from shore, and they are restricted now to the inland and coastal waters of southern Florida. They favor warm waters, and in the winter they migrate to the warm springs (such as Florida's Crystal River) or the warm-water effluents of power plants. Threatened by development in its restricted habitat, by pollution, and by powerboaters who don't see the submerged mammals and run over them, the Florida manatee is officially considered an endangered species. Its

A Florida manatee, photographed in the Crystal River. Notice the scars on the tail, probably inflicted by a motorboat's propeller.

reproduction rate is low—one calf per adult female every three years—and there are thought to be no more than one thousand of the ponderous, blimplike creatures left.*

Science now accepts the Florida manatee (*Trichechus manatus latirostris*) as a valid subspecies of the West Indian manatee. (The other subspecies is the Antillean manatee, *Trichechus manatus manatus*.) The differences between the two are mostly skeletal, and the layperson viewing either one in, say, a captive situation would not be able to tell one from the other. But in the wild, the problem is more easily resolved, because the Florida subspecies is found in the state's waters year-round and during the warmer months may range north to Virginia or west to Louisiana. In Florida, the harvesting of manatees for food has ended, but the danger has not. Because of their desire to inhabit coastal waterways, they are in constant danger from powerboats: The boats run over the manatees, and the spinning propeller slices the animal's back, often fatally.

While the Florida and Caribbean manatees have fingernails, the Amazonian variety has none. Its specific name, *inunguis*, means "no nails." (The Latin word for nail or claw is *unguis*, and it also appears in the name for the hoofed animals, the ungulates.) The Amazonian manatee is somewhat smaller than its northern relatives and can be differentiated by the presence of an irregular white patch on the belly. This species is also the only manatee that is confined to a river system and does not venture into salt water. Its range includes the Amazon River basin in Brazil (where it is known in Portuguese as *peixe-boi*, or "ox-fish") and also into Peru and Ecuador, where its Spanish name is *vaca marina*, the familiar "sea cow."

South American aborigines have hunted the manatee for food, but when Brazilian authorities realized that the animals had been reduced to dangerously low numbers, they banned manatee hunting. As might be imagined, enforcement of such a ban is difficult, if not impossible, in the vast reaches of the Amazon jungle, so the numbers continue to drop, and of course, the mass destruction of their habitat cannot help but contribute to their imperiled state. (The same factors that make policing the hunt so difficult contribute to the lack of information on the status of the Amazonian manatee: too much acreage, not enough policemen.)

Across the Atlantic, another manatee swims slowly in the coastal waters of West Africa, a virtual carbon copy of its American relative. ("It has been

---

*In 1982, nearly fifty manatees died mysteriously in the waters off Fort Myers, on the Gulf Coast of Florida. The exact cause was never found, but it is believed to be related to a toxic red tide, which was ingested by sea squirts (also known as tunicates, minute creatures that live in the plants eaten by the manatees) that eventually worked their way into the systems of the manatees.

$\mathcal{E}$arl Herald, director of the Steinhart Aquarium in San Francisco, with "Butterball," the baby Amazonian manatee

said," wrote sirenologists John Reynolds and Daniel Odell, "that if a West Indian manatee and a West African manatee lay side by side, even an expert would be hard pressed to distinguish between the two animals.") Their behavior, too, is similar, as is their habitat—the only difference being that *Trichechus senegalensis* is found (not surprisingly) in Senegal and also in the littoral and riverine waters of Gambia, Liberia, Guinea-Bissau, Sierra Leone, the Ivory Coast, Ghana, Chad, Nigeria, Cameroon, Gabon, Zaire, and Angola. Like all of its relatives, the West African manatee feeds on floating vegetation and may occasionally eat clams.

Manatees breathe air, so they must surface to inhale, and they can therefore be observed regularly. They also live in regions that are in proximity to those inhabited by people—a situation that often proves their undoing. The manatee (and the dugong, although less is known of the Indo-Pacific sirenians) has passed through various stages that are paradigmatic for all the monsters discussed here: first the unknown creature of the seas, given names in various languages, undescribed and unnamed, fearsome because we don't know what it is. It then emerges from the mists of mythology and assumes a corporeality that enables man to identify and categorize it. When that has been accomplished, we can then hunt it—for food, for sport, for glory.

The first of the "monsters" to experience the acceleration of this process was the sea cow. Discovered in 1741, it was identified by no less an identifier than Georg Wilhelm Steller, then almost immediately hunted to extinction. Its smaller relatives, the manatee and the dugong, graze, blow, and float like giant, bewhiskered sausages, unaware that they, like their extinct cousin, are hovering on the brink of eternity. Now come the conservationists, who fall in love with the face only another sirenian could love, and elevate the hapless manatee into a realm of adoration and putative protection designed to preserve the species for the enjoyment of our grandchildren. It is no longer the chubby, slow-moving, slightly dim relic of another age but a lovable creature whose visage now appears on T-shirts, mugs, posters, and bumper stickers. There is a "Save the Manatees" organization dedicated to the preservation of their endangered numbers, educating the public to their plight and their cuddly character.

Florida manatees share their habitat with some of the most avaricious land grabbers in the history of the United States, and worse, the people want to use the very waterways that the manatees call home. According to Reynolds and Odell, "In Florida, 90% of the human population occupies areas within 10 miles of the coast. That population is growing by at least 800–1,000 new residents each day." When the time came to marshal the environmental forces for the preservation of the whales, one thing was clear: Living as they did in the open ocean, the whales threatened nobody's way of life. In that sense—and that sense only—it was a relatively easy battle, because there was virtually no opposition. With the exception of the remaining whalers, nobody was going to campaign for an *increase* in whale killing. Nobody wanted to live in the middle of the North Pacific or on the Antarctic ice pack, but a lot of people want to live in coastal south Florida. The existence of the hapless manatee is therefore in direct conflict with the existence of the developer, and given the history of both species, it is not difficult to guess which will prevail.

"Endangered species" has become the buzzword for the mythology of our times; no sooner does an animal find itself in trouble than someone or some organization comes riding to the rescue. There are now organizations (and individuals—some animals are not yet popular enough to require an entire organization) dedicated to the preservation of seals, birds, whales, dolphins, sea otters, rain forests, owls, trees, sharks, snakes, shorelines, bays, forests, and even bats.

Protecting the manatees (and at the same time collecting a little environmental publicity), the Tampa Electric Company in 1986 dedicated the discharge canal of the Big Bend Power Station as a permanent winter refuge for manatees and built an observation deck. Since the opening of the sanctuary, the Manatee Viewing Center has received more than 200,000 visitors. When I wrote to Florida Power & Light in Tampa, asking what they were doing to protect the manatee, they sent me a fat envelope crammed with fact sheets, press releases, newspaper articles, and brochures. In the interest of manatee preservation, I could "adopt a manatee," view manatees at Tampa Electric's Manatee Viewing Center, color "Molly the Manatee," and from the "Save the Manatee Club," I could buy a manatee T-shirt, cap, cuddly stuffed manatee, poster, bumper sticker, or hand puppet.

And, of course, the apotheosis of the manatee will continue, even if there are no more left. For there is no greater glory for an animal in our times than to go the way of the passenger pigeon, the great auk, the Carolina parakeet, or Steller's sea cow: They are in that special place in wildlife heaven reserved for those creatures that we, in our infinite wisdom, managed to remove from the earth forever. Like the gods of old, we hold them sacred for the lessons they never taught us.

Halfway around the world, a similar problem exists with the dugong, the manatee's only living relative. Whereas the manatee's mouth is on the front of its face, that of the dugong is on the bottom of its muzzle, for the dugong is strictly a bottom feeder. It has the same fusiform shape as the manatee (although dugongs are slimmer than their cousins); and whereas the tail fin of the manatee is rounded, that of the dugong looks more like the flukes of a whale. Dugongs have different dentition from the manatees in that they have incisors (which manatees lack), which, in the males, develop into short tusks. The remainder of their teeth consists of molars that are used for the grinding of plant matter.

The single species of dugong is found in the territorial waters of forty-three countries along the Indian and western Pacific oceans. It ranges from Mozambique and Madagascar on the East African coast, up through the Arabian Sea and Persian Gulf, the west coast of India, through Southeast Asia and Indonesia, all along the coast of northern Australia, and around New Guinea, Melanesia, and the Philippines. With this wide a distribution, through some of the most densely populated areas of the world, the problems of the dugong are as wide and diversified as its range. Stated simply, however, the problem is this: Dugong meat is said to taste like veal or pork, and throughout its range, it is hunted for food.

In most of its range, it is considered endangered, but along the mostly uninhabited coasts of northern Australia, a large proportion of the world's remaining dugongs can be found. There may be seventeen thousand in the Gulf of Carpentaria and as many as seventy thousand throughout Australian waters. The meat is prized by aboriginals, who are permitted to hunt dugongs in their territorial waters, but hunting is otherwise prohibited. Nevertheless, many of these slow-moving creatures are injured by boats, and many are lost or drowned in shark nets. An adult dugong will yield five to eight gallons of a high-quality oil, and this oil, used for medicinal purposes, formed the basis of a cottage industry in Queensland from the middle of the nineteenth century to the middle of the twentieth. (Dugongs were declared protected in Australia in 1960.) The dugong's skin is used for leather, the oil for cooking and ointments, and the bones and tusks for carving and ornaments. In Sri Lanka, India, Kenya, and Papua New Guinea, a major cause of dugong mortality is fishnets: Dugongs have poor eyesight, and they frequently blunder into the nets by accident. The dugong is listed as vulnerable to extinction, and trade in dugong products is monitored by CITES, the Convention on International Trade in Endangered Species. As with the other sirenians, however, it is difficult to keep watch on small aboriginal villages where dugongs are still being speared and netted for food.

In Reynolds and Odell's 1991 book *Manatees and Dugongs*, Daryl Domning, a sirenian specialist, wrote an essay he called "Why Save the Manatee?" We ought to save them, he wrote, because they are fascinating animals, because they eat canal-choking aquatic weeds, and because they

The Dugong, *Dugon dugon*

have been a part of our estuary and near-shore environments for thousands of years. They are an integral part of our lives and, like every other living thing, part of our responsibility as stewards of the planet: "A planet with no space for wild manatees will also not have space enough for what human beings were meant to be." Domning asks, "Is there any reason for *not* doing it?" No. "Like Al Capp's shmoo, a more harmless and accommodating animal could not be imagined. What excuse could we give for its extinction? If, as citizens of the United States, we cannot save the manatees in Florida, we cannot expect anyone to save any species anywhere."

EVEN IF THE manatee/mermaid is in trouble in nature, it is flourishing—in a somewhat modified form—in modern literature and movies. One of its earliest and best-loved appearances is in Hans Christian Andersen's poignant fairy tale "The Little Mermaid." The story was first published in 1835 (Andersen was born in 1805 and died in 1875) and contains many of the elements that moviemakers would later incorporate into their mermaid stories, from *Mr. Peabody and the Mermaid* to *Splash,* and, of course, the Disney animated version of Andersen's tale.

The little mermaid is one of six mermaid sisters who live under water but are able to rise to the surface, "sit in the moonlight on the rocks, and watch the great ships sailing past. . . ." On her visit to the surface, the youngest sees a ship capsize in a storm and saves a handsome prince from drowning by carrying him to shore. She falls in love with the prince, and because she cannot go to him as a mermaid, she asks for help from the sea witch, who changes her fish's tail into legs and removes her power of speech. Out of love for her prince, the little mermaid agrees to these harsh conditions, but because she is mute, she cannot tell the prince that she was the one who saved him or of her love for him. On the evening of his marriage to the princess from a neighboring kingdom, the mermaids bring their littlest sister a knife with which to kill him and by so doing save her own life. She cannot and throws herself into the sea. But because of her suffering, instead of being turned into foam, she ascends to the heavenly kingdom, where she and her sisters must do good deeds for three hundred years, after which they will receive an immortal soul.

Hans Christian Andersen is the favorite son of Copenhagen (even

*A*t the entrance to Copenhagen harbor stands Edvard Eriksen's famous bronze statue of Hans Christian Andersen's little mermaid.

though he was born in Odense), and in 1913 the city fathers erected a bronze statue of the wistful Little Mermaid sitting on a rock at Langelinie Pier overlooking the harbor. (According to the Danish Tourist Board, the statue is the largest tourist attraction in Denmark and is the most photographed statue in the world.) "*Den Lille Havefrue*" is considered one of Andersen's most enduring stories and paved the way for many others in which the mermaid almost always falls in love with a mortal and is more or less mute.*

Take *Mr. Peabody and the Mermaid,* for example. A Hollywood film made in 1948, it stars William Powell as Peabody and Ann Blyth as the mermaid. On a vacation to a Caribbean island, Mr. Peabody, a proper Bostonian, hooks a mermaid while fishing and brings her home to his hotel—which just happens to have a gigantic swimming pool complete with underwater caves and what appear to be trees growing in it. Peabody immediately falls in love with the mermaid and she with him, although she can communicate her feelings only through an adoring gaze, since she cannot talk. (She seems to be able to sing, however, and throughout the film, we hear her haunting refrains, which sound not unlike those of the singer Yma Sumac.) Nobody else ever sees the mermaid, but we know she is not a hallucination because there is a moment when she bites the other woman who is swimming in the same pool. (The mermaid also eats all the goldfish in the pool, neatly lining up the skeletons alongside.) Because Mrs. Peabody does not believe in the mermaid, she suspects her husband of dallying with another woman, and she (Mrs. Peabody) runs away, which naturally results in her husband's being accused of murdering her. To escape from the police, Peabody sails off to a neighboring island, where the mermaid tries to teach him to remain under water so they can live happily ever after. Although he loves her dearly, this action—which he later describes as "trying to drown me"—turns him off mermaids, and he returns to snowy Boston to become reunited with his wife. Peabody tells his tale to a psychiatrist, who informs him that it was only a hallucinatory mid-life crisis.

Ann Blyth's mermaid is a peculiar combination of 1940s bathing beauty and traditional mermaid. Outfitted in a fashionable bathing-suit top, she sings the siren's songs, smiles fetchingly, and bats her eyes at Peabody, but she also has a habit of snarling unattractively at any other woman who vies

---

*Andersen's story appears as one of the references in Karl Banse's 1990 spoof of scientific articles "Mermaids—Their Biology, Culture, and Demise," in which Banse, a professor of oceanography at the University of Washington, presents the details of the establishment of the mermaid as a legitimate genus (*Siren*), with three species, *S. sirena, S. indica,* and *S. erythraea.* He suggests that even though they were capable of underwater agriculture, they became extinct when land-based fishermen reduced the finfish predators, leaving the oceans populated with "dangerously poisonous" jellyfish, to which the defenseless mermaids succumbed.

for his attention. For most of the film, those who see the mermaid see only her tail, so they derogatorily refer to her as a fish, but there are other references to her as a "sea cow," or a "manatee," revealing that the producers were aware of the mermaid's true lineage. One curious element in this and future mermaid movies is the arrangement of the tail fin. In order for a human in a mermaid outfit to swim, she must move her "tail" up and down, for that is the only way human legs can move. (Of the aquatic vertebrates, only the whales, dolphins, and the sirenians use a horizontal tail motion.) But mermaids in the movies are not supposed to be bound by those restraints that affect mortals, so despite the cetological orientation of the empennage, the tail structure is usually shown with the scales of a fish.

Just as it is in *Splash,* a 1984 version of the mermaid-and-mortal love story. In this installment, the mermaid at age eight first encounters Allan Bauer (Tom Hanks) when he—also age eight—inexplicably jumps overboard while riding on a ferry at Cape Cod. She immediately falls in love with him (note the parallels to the fairy tale, although Andersen gets no screen credit), and when he ends up in Cape Cod some twenty years later (again inexplicably), we are meant to believe that he does so because of some mysterious force calling him there. And there she is, peeking over the bushes. She has grown up to be Daryl Hannah and has legs to prove it (but no clothes), so she runs into the ocean. He is smitten and returns to New York, only to read that a naked woman has appeared at the Statue of Liberty. It is guess who, having swum from Cape Cod to seek her one true love. Unfortunately (and inexplicably), she can stay only for six days, but they fall into a torrid romance, and while she could not talk at all when they met (like all descendants of Andersen's mermaid), she learns English in an afternoon by watching television at Bloomingdale's. It is at this point that Bauer names her "Madison," because they have been strolling on Madison Avenue.

The somewhat mad scientist Dr. Walter Kornbluth (Eugene Levy) realizes that she is a mermaid, and because he knows that her tail will only appear when she is wet, he follows her around trying to throw water on her from buckets or spray her with a hose. He eventually succeeds, and as soon as her true identity is revealed, the evil scientists of the government imprison her in order to conduct some tests. (She is placed in a giant fish tank at the American Museum of Natural History, where we see her scales and her horizontal tail.) Bauer, Allan's brother (John Candy), and Dr. Kornbluth rescue her from the infamous mermaid-testing laboratories of the museum, escape the military, who chase them through the streets of New York, and fetch up at a pier at the South Street Seaport. As the army closes in, Madison leaps into the East River, and her handsome prince follows. Madison the mermaid kisses Allan, which imparts to him the ability to remain under water, and the happy couple swim off into the equivalent of an underwater sunset, which appears (inexplicably) to be in the Bahamas, if the water clarity and coral reefs are any indication.

In 1989, in the contemporary apotheosis of the mermaid, she appears in a Walt Disney animated film. (*Splash* was made by Buena Vista films, a subsidiary of the Disney company.) In *The Little Mermaid*, Hans Christian Andersen gets a credit ("based on a story by . . ."), and except for some new material tacked on to provide a more pleasing ending, the Disney film adheres fairly closely to the original fairy tale. Of course, there are the obligatory cute characters to guide and advise "Ariel" (a better name than "Madison," surely) in the form of a chubby little fish called "Flounder," a calypso crab named "Sebastian," and a screechy seagull named "Scuttle." The Little Mermaid has the requisite complement of sisters, and in this version, her father is Triton, King of the Sea. Just as Andersen wrote it, the mermaid falls in love with handsome Prince Eric, and because she is not allowed to visit mortals, she strikes a deal with Ursula the Sea Witch, a marvelous character who has the upper body of a garish woman and an evening dress that terminates in the tentacles of an octopus. In exchange for giving her legs, Ursula takes the mermaid's voice and will take her soul if she cannot get the prince to kiss her by sunset of the third day.

With the exception of *Twenty Thousand Leagues Under the Sea* (and books specifically about sea monsters), few works incorporate more than one monster at a time. As interpreted by the Disney animators, however, *The Little Mermaid* can serve as a general introduction to the remaining assembly of sea monsters. In addition to the mermaid, who appears as a graceful, long-haired teenager with a beautiful voice, we see the evil shark, which chases her in a sunken wreck. Cephalopods are represented by the bad queen Ursula, half woman, half octopus; in the climax of the film, as a manifestation of her frustration and anger, she emits a great cloud of ink. No squid appear, but early in the movie a couple of benign whales cruise by.

In the original story, the prince falls in love with a neighboring princess, but here the Sea Witch transforms herself into a beautiful young thing and charms the prince into marrying her. Her deception is revealed (by the fish, crab, and seagull), and she begins to revert to her true form, but just as the prince is about to kiss the mermaid, the sun dips below the horizon, and the witch triumphs. At this point, the Disney people improvise a completely new ending, designed to get audiences to leave the theater singing some of the songs written by Howard Ashman and Alan Menken, one of which

("Under the Sea") won an Academy Award. In a series of rapid reversals, King Triton offers to trade his soul for his daughter's, which makes the Witch the Queen of the Sea; Prince Eric commandeers a ship and drives it into the nasty Queen Ursula, which kills her, reverses all her evil spells, and turns everyone back into what they were supposed to be. King Triton, now reestablished as the Ruler of the Sea, recognizes that his opposition to his daughter's marrying a mortal is futile, so he gives her legs, and she comes out of the ocean and is reunited with her prince. (In a subtle tribute to the author of the original story, when the mermaid awaits the prince, she adopts the pose of the Copenhagen statue.) Not surprisingly, everybody lives happily ever after, rainbow and all.

THE KRAKEN

Below the thunders of the upper deep,
Far, far beneath the abysmal sea,
His ancient, dreamless, uninvaded sleep
The Kraken sleepeth; faintest sunlights flee
Above his shadowy sides: above him swell
Huge sponges of millennial growth and height;
And far away into the sickly light,
From many a wondrous grot and secret cell
Unnumber'd and enormous polypi
Winnow with giant fins the slumbering green.
There hath he lain for ages and will lie
Battening upon huge seaworms in his sleep,
Until the latter fire shall heat the deep;
Then once by man and angels to be seen,
In roaring he shall rise and on the surface die.

—ALFRED, LORD TENNYSON
"The Kraken"
Poems, Chiefly Lyrical,
1830

$\mathcal{P}$ROBABLY THE BEST-KNOWN SCENE in *Twenty Thousand Leagues Under the Sea* is the attack on the submarine *Nautilus* by a giant squid. (If it is not the most celebrated episode in the book, it is certainly the scene most people remember from the 1954 movie.) In this scene, after a characteristic discussion of the immediate perils that might await them (and some historical references as well), Aronnax, Conseil, and Ned Land espy "a terrible monster worthy of all the legends about such creatures":

> It was a giant squid twenty-five feet long. It was heading toward the *Nautilus*, swimming backward very fast. Its huge immobile eyes were of a blue-green color. The eight arms, or rather legs, coming out of its head— it is this which earned it the name of "cephalopod"—were twice as long as its body and were twisting like the hair of a Greek fury. We could clearly make out the 250 suckers lining the inside of its tentacles, some of which fastened onto the glass panel of the lounge. The monster's mouth—a horny beak like that of a parakeet—opened and closed vertically. Its tongue, also made of a hornlike substance and armed with several rows of sharp teeth, would come out and shake what seemed like veritable cutlery. What a whim of nature! A bird's beak in a mollusk! Its elongated body, with a slight swelling in the middle, formed a fleshy mass that must have weighed between forty and fifty thousand pounds. Its color, which could change very fast according to the animal's mood, would vary from a ghastly gray to reddish brown.

From the number of arms (or legs) to the eye color, body color, and the nature of the tongue, Verne/Aronnax has almost everything wrong about

*A*n illustration from the original edition of *Twenty Thousand Leagues Under the Sea*. The illustrator, identified only as "De Neuville," drew the animal as a gigantic squid.

the giant squid. (It is beyond merely "wrong" to attribute a weight of "forty or fifty thousand pounds" to an animal that is 25 feet long and mostly tentacles; to weigh this much it would have to have been made of iron. A 25-foot minke whale, which is all meat and muscle and has no long, skinny arms, weighs about ten tons.) Later, as the squid tries (and fails) to hold on to the submarine with its suckers, Aronnax exclaims, "What vitality the Creator has given them, and what vigor of movement! And to think they possess three hearts!"

Giant squid are far more interesting than Jules Verne could have imagined. Even now, so little is known about the giant squid that Verne's intentional exaggerations are more than likely to be underestimates, and his fanciful interpretations of their biology are probably far too limited. While he gets the weight wrong by an order of magnitude, he gets the length wrong by making it far too short. Regardless of what his 25-footer would weigh, the largest known specimens of the genus *Architeuthis* have been measured at 60 feet, from the tip of the mantle (the body) to the ends of the two long tentacles—which, incidentally, gives it a total of ten arms, not eight. A squid of this size would weigh about a ton. (Squid do indeed possess three hearts, and their tongues, which are relatively small, are equipped with teeth.)

In *Twenty Thousand Leagues Under the Sea*, the squid attacks the submarine, presumably to get at the people, and because Nemo's electric bullets do not affect the cephalopods ("their soft flesh doesn't offer enough resistance to make them explode"), the crew takes after them with axes and Ned Land's harpoon. As the submarine surfaces and the hatches are

The *poulpe* "brandishes its victim like a feather" as stalwart crewmen of the *Nautilus* hack away at it. In the lower left, one of the arms is correctly shown as the clublike tentacle of a squid.

opened, one of the squid's arms snakes down the hatchway, where Nemo lops it off with a blow of his boarding ax. With seven of its eight arms cut off, the monster still manages to capture one of the sailors. The poor wretch is dragged off in a cloud of ink, and the crew attacks the remaining ten or twelve squid that "had invaded the platform and sides of the *Nautilus*." As brave Ned Land harpoons one of the monsters, he becomes trapped, and as a squid is about to chomp down on him with its huge beak—unaccountably likened to that of a *parakeet* (the original reads "*comme le bec d'un perroquet*")—Nemo saves him and buries his ax between the two mandibles. Land then plunges his harpoon deep into the creature's triple heart, and the episode draws to a merciful conclusion.

Aboard the *Nautilus*, the following exchange takes place between Conseil and Land:

> "I myself can remember," said Conseil with the most serious tone of voice in the world, "having seen a large boat dragged down by the arms of a squid."
>
> "You've seen that?" asked the Canadian.
>
> "Yes, Ned."
>
> "With your own eyes?"
>
> "With my own eyes."
>
> "Where, if you don't mind telling me?"
>
> "At St.-Malo," replied Conseil imperturbably.
>
> "In the harbor?" asked Ned Land sarcastically.
>
> "No, in a church," answered Conseil.

The French naturalist Pierre Denys de Montfort published a *Histoire naturelle des Mollusques* in 1802, which, in one form or another, was probably responsible for much of Verne's information about the *poulpe*. Off the coast of Angola, goes the story, a sailing ship was seized by a monster with arms that reached to the top of the masts. The terrified sailors vowed to St. Thomas that they would make a pilgrimage if he would save them, and with axes and cutlasses—and the support of the good St. Thomas—they broke free. Therefore (according to Denys de Montfort), in St. Thomas's chapel at St. Malo there is a votive picture of a ship in the embrace of a monster, which picture—if it really existed—might have been consulted by Verne, but there is hardly any question that Verne read de Montfort's study. The original illustrator of *Vingt mille lieues sous les mers*, identified only as "de Neuville," also must have seen the reproduction in de Montfort, but whereas de Montfort depicts an eight-armed animal that could be a squid, de Neuville's version has obvious

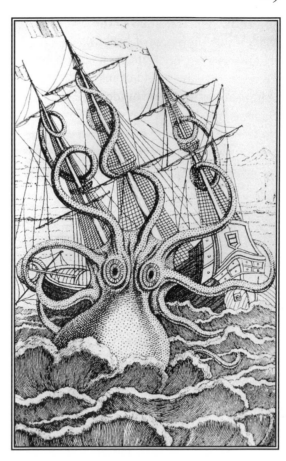

𝒟enys de Montfort's illustration of some sort of giant cephalopod attacking a ship. Count the arms emanating from the head.

octopus overtones.* (It is known that an octopus was displayed at the aquarium at Boulogne as early as 1867, so either the author, the artist, or both could have seen it.) In the chapter on "Gigantic Cuttle-fishes" in *The Octopus* (published in 1875), Henry Lee calls the de Montfort illustration "fitter to decorate the outside of a showman's caravan at a fair than seriously to illustrate a work of natural history." (A. S. Packard, writing in the *American Naturalist* in 1873, refers to "the well-known hoax of Denys Montfort.")

---

*All cephalopods have suckers on their arms, but the structure of these suckers is a differentiating factor between octopuses and squid. In octopuses, the suckers are smooth-like suction cups and are attached directly to the tentacle, but those of the squids are on short stalks and are often equipped with a ring of horny teeth. (In some species, the suckers of the tentacular clubs are armed with claws as well.) Although they share some fundamental cephalopod characteristics, the body plan of the squid is quite different from that of the octopus. Both have a horny beak at the center of the corona of arms, and both have well-developed eyes. Octopus and squid have a funnel (also called a siphon) that is used to eject water taken in through the mantle opening and can propel the animal through the water. Octopuses often "walk" along the bottom, but squid, which are equipped with a pair of flexible fins at the posterior end of the mantle, rarely establish contact with the ocean floor.

Verne probably knew of the published material on giant squid that was available before he wrote his own book. In fact, he incorporates much of it into his own book. He refers by name to Olaus Magnus and Bishop Pontoppidan and then delivers a brief discourse on events involving the ship *Alecton*. A giant squid was encountered at sea, and "Commander Bouguer"

had the creature harpooned and shot, but without much success, for the bullets and the harpoons went through its soft flesh as if it were loose jelly. After several unsuccessful attempts, the crew managed to pass a slipknot around the creature's body. The loop slid back to the caudal fins and there it stopped. They then tried hauling the monster on board, but it weighed

In November 1861, off Tenerife in the Canary Islands, the crew of the French corvette *Alecton* harpooned a giant squid, but all they could get aboard was the tail. It would be another twelve years before the first complete specimen of *Architeuthis* would be examined.

so much that the tail merely broke off and the squid itself, separated from this part of its body, disappeared beneath the surface.

Verne's abbreviated version of the *Alecton*'s story is true as far as he takes it. It actually occurred on November 30, 1861, off the island of Tenerife in the Canaries, and the captain's name was Bouyer, not Bouguer. After the loss of the tail, the crew of the *Alecton* noticed a strong scent of musk. (This *violente odeur de musc* appears somewhat later in the story, when the crew of the *Nautilus* kills the attacking monster.) The report gave the actual measurements of the squid's body at 18 feet, with the arms adding another 5 to 6 feet, for a total of 24 feet, very close indeed to the *poulpe* of Verne/Aronnax. Lieutenant Bouyer filed a report at Tenerife, which was forwarded to Sabin Berthelot, the French consul, who presented the paper at the December meeting of the French Academy of Sciences. From the similarity of the details, it appears obvious that Verne saw the Bouyer report and adapted it for his own designs.

According to Henry Lee, it was de Montfort's purpose to "cajole the public," and he is reported as saying, "If my entangled ship is accepted, I will make my 'colossal poulpe' overthrow a whole fleet." Both events seem to have occurred, for soon de Montfort was putting forth the story that six French men-of-war and the four British ships that captured them were attacked and sunk by a colossal cuttlefish. Lee concludes his discussion of de Montfort by saying, "I have been told, but cannot vouch for the truth of the report, that de Montfort's propensity to write that which was not true, culminated in his committing forgery, and that he died in prison."

New England sperm whalers often noticed that the whales vomited up some sort of "arms" while in their death throes, and while their biology was often less than reliable, there was no question that they were indeed seeing pieces of the kraken. Here is whaleman Charles Nordhoff (the grandfather of the Charles Nordhoff who co-wrote *Mutiny on the Bounty*) describing the animal in his *Whaling and Fishing*, published in 1856:

Sperm whales feed on an animal known among whalemen as "squid," but which is, I believe, a monster species of cuttle fish. These, like their smaller congeners, cling to the rocks, the larger species, of course, having their haunts at the bottom of the sea, while the smaller frequent only the shores of bays.

Very few men have ever seen an entire squid or a sperm whale cuttle fish, and I incline to the belief that most of the few instances on record of their appearance at the surface are apocryphal. Whalemen believe them to be much larger than the largest whale, even exceeding in size the hull of a large vessel; and those who pretend to have been favored with a sight of the body, describe it as a huge, shapeless, jelly-like mass, of a dirty yellow, and having on all sides of it long arms, or feelers, precisely like the common rock-squid.

Aside from the whalers' experiences, most of our information about giant squid is known from dead animals washed ashore or sightings at sea, and there are few authenticated records of an attack on a ship, let alone a man. In one account, printed in the *Times* (London) on July 4, 1874, the master of the steamer *Strathowen,* bound from Mauritius to Rangoon, sighted a small schooner (later identified as the *Pearl*) and next to it, "a long, low swelling on the sea, which from its colour and shape I took to be a bank of seaweed." The "seaweed" reached up and dragged the schooner under, and several members of the crew escaped and were picked up by the *Strathowen.* The incident—if it occurred—took place after the publication of *Twenty Thousand Leagues Under the Sea,* and it is included here only as an ex post facto demonstration of the possibility of the squid's attacking a ship.* Bernard Heuvelmans, who wanted very much to believe in sea monsters, questions the veracity of the account, writing, "This tale has never been confirmed and it may well have been an opportune hoax, for the *Strathowen* is not to be found in *Lloyd's Register* for that year." Frank Lane also investigated the story but could find no confirmation in Britain— "from Lloyd's, the National Maritime Museum, the General Register of Shipping and Seamen, shipping lines and other likely sources." Nevertheless, he chooses to accept it and writes, "The most *reasonable* explanation seems to be that the account was a report of an actual incident, including the presence on the *Pearl* of a man from the one place [Newfoundland] where, at that time, giant squids and their behavior were reasonably well-known."

Architeuthis, the giant squid, is the quintessential sea monster, probably responsible for more myths, fables, fantasies, and fictions than all other marine monsters combined. In the *Odyssey* we read of Scylla, a horrible monster:

---

*One of the few recent incidents of a giant squid "attacking" a ship occurred in the Pacific between 1930 and 1933 and was reported in 1946 by Arne Gronningsaeter, master of the fifteen thousand-ton freighter *Brunswick,* sailing between Hawaii and Samoa. Although short on details (he never even estimates the size of the squid), Gronningsaeter's account describes the squid swimming alongside the ship at a speed of twenty to twenty-five knots and then turning toward the vessel, "hitting the hull approximately 150 feet from the stern at a depth of 12–15 feet." Since it could not get a grip on the hull, it "skidded along until it ended up in the propeller, where it was ground to pieces."

Her legs—and there are twelve—
are like great tentacles,
unjointed, and upon her serpent necks
are borne six heads like nightmares of ferocity
and triple serried rows of fangs and deep
gullets of black death. Half her length she sways
her heads in the air, outside her horrid cleft,
hunting the sea around that promontory
for dolphins, dogfish, or what bigger game
thundering Amphitrite feeds in thousands.
And no ship's company can claim
to have passed her without loss and grief; she takes
from every ship, one man for every gullet.

Also known as the kraken, the polyp (*poulpe* in the French of *Vingt mille lieues sous les mers*), and the sea serpent, the giant squid is, next to the shark, perhaps the most infamous animal in the sea. Aristotle introduced us to the *teuthos,* the giant squid (as differentiated from *teuthis,* the smaller variety), and somewhat later, in his *Naturalis Historia,* Pliny discusses a "polyp" that plucked salted fish from the fish ponds of Carteia (now Rocadillo in Spain) and "brought on itself the wrath of the keepers, which owing to the persistence of the theft was beyond all bounds." The guards that surrounded the polyp were

astounded by its strangeness: in the first place its size was unheard of and so was its color as well, and it was smeared with brine and had a terrible smell; who would have expected to find a polyp there, or who would recognize it in such circumstances? They felt they were pitted against something uncanny, for by its awful breath it also tormented the dogs, which it now scourged with the ends of its tentacles and now struck with its longer arms, which it used as clubs, and with difficulty they succeeded in dispatching it with a number of three-pronged harpoons.

The head was as big as a cask and held 90 gallons; its arms ("knotted like clubs") were 30 feet long, with suckers like basins holding three gallons and teeth corresponding to its size. Its remains weighed 700 pounds. The longer tentacles identify the polyp as a squid rather than an octopus, but whatever it was, this would appear to be the only record of a squid's coming ashore for any reason except to die. (Pliny tells us that it was "getting into the uncovered tanks from the open sea," so perhaps these were somehow accessible to a deep-water inhabitant. That the tanks held "salted fish" indicates that they were not holding tanks at sea, however. Pliny, of course,

*I*maginary View of a Kraken Seizing a Ship

depended on the reports of others for his *Naturalis Historia,* but if we assume that something like this actually happened in antiquity [even allowing for exaggeration], it is the only such occurrence in all the literature.)

The many-armed sea beast lay relatively dormant, however, until it was resurrected by Olaus Magnus, a veritable fount of information on sea monsters. In his 1555 *Historia de Gentibus Septentrionalibus,* he describes and illustrates several "monstrous fish," as follows:

> Their forms are horrible, their Heads square, all set with prickles, and they have long sharp horns round about like a Tree rooted up by the Roots: They are ten or twelve Cubits* long, very black, with huge eyes . . . the Apple of the Eye is of one Cubit, and is red and fiery coloured, which in the dark night appears to Fisher-men afar off under Waters, as a burning fire, having hairs like goose feathers, thick and long, like a beard hanging down; and the rest of the body, for the greatness of the head, which is square, is very small, not being above 14 or 15 Cubits long; one of these

*A cubit is a linear measure based on the distance from the elbow to the tip of the middle finger, or from seventeen to twenty-two inches. Noah's Ark, therefore, at three hundred cubits was about five hundred feet long.

Sea-Monsters will drown easily many great ships provided with many strong Marriners.

This would appear to be history's first description of a giant cuttlefish. Two centuries after Olaus Magnus, Bishop Pontoppidan referred to this beast as "the largest and most surprising of all the animal creation" and "incontestibly the largest Sea-monster in the world." The bishop wrote:

> It is called *Kraken* or *Kraxen*, or, as some name it, *Krabben*. . . . He shows himself sufficiently, although his whole body does not appear, which in all likelihood no human eye ever beheld (excepting the young of this species) its back or upper part, which seems to be in appearance an English mile and a half in circumference (some say more, but I choose the least for greater certainty), looks at first like a number of small islands, surrounded with something that floats and fluctuates like sea weeds . . . at last several bright points or horns appear, which grow thicker and thicker the higher they rise above the surface of the water, and sometimes they stand as high and large as the masts of middle-siz'd vessels.

The kraken never appeared, but somewhat reduced in size, it assumed a biological reality as *Architeuthis*. The earliest record seems to be of a carcass that washed ashore at Thingøre Sand, in Iceland, in 1639. It was introduced by Prof. Japetus Steenstrup, a lecturer in geology, botany, and zoology at Copenhagen University. In a paper read in 1849, he quoted the original description in *Annalar Björns á Skardsa* (in Danish) for 1639, which was translated as follows:

*B*ishop Pontoppidan's sea serpent, which has been explained as a giant squid

In the autumn on Thingøresand in Hunevandsyssel a peculiar creature or sea monster was stranded with *length and thickness like those of a man; it had 7 tails and each of these measured approximately two ells.* These tails were densely covered with a type of button, and the buttons looked as if there was an eye ball in each button, and round the eye ball an eyelid; these eyelids looked as if they were gilded. On this sea monster there was in addition *a single tail* which had grown out above those 7 tails; *it was extremely long, 4–5 fms* [7.50–9.40 m]; *no bone or cartilage were found in its body* but the whole to the sight and to the touch was like the soft body of the female lumpfish (Cyclopterus lumpus). No trace was seen of the head, except the one aperture, or two, which were found behind the tails or at a short distance from them.

Even though the annalist managed to read the animal upside down, confusing the head with the tail(s), it is quite obvious that the "monster" was a giant squid that had lost one of its arms and one of its tentacles.

In 1673, a 19-footer was found on the beach of Dingle Bay, County Kerry, Ireland. It was displayed for all to see, and a broadsheet was printed up in Dublin that announced the exhibition of "A Wonderful Fish or Beast that was lately killed . . . which had two heads and Ten horns, and upon Eight of the said Horns about 800 Buttons or the resemblance of little Coronets; and in each of them a set of Teeth, the said Body was bigger than a Horse and was 19 Foot Long Horns and all, the great Head thereof Carried only the ten Horns and two very large Eyes." The broadside also described the "Wonderful Fish" as being reddish in color, with another "little head" with "a wonderful strange mouth and two Tongues in it."

The broadside is one of a number of documents that are included in an 1875 study by A. G. More, who takes the description and the accompanying drawing almost literally and says: "I do not see why the extensible proboscis should not be accepted as correct, though the little eyes may have been added as ornaments by an enterprising showman." He then proposes to name the Kerry "monster" *Dinoteuthis proboscideus,* which can be roughly translated as "terrible squid with a big nose." W. J. Rees, a biologist with the British Museum of Natural History, quoted this broadsheet in an article about giant squid that appeared in the *Illustrated London News* in 1949 and explained, "The 'little head,' of course, refers to the siphon through which water is pumped out to propel the squid through the water."

At irregular intervals, squid carcasses in various stages of decomposition appeared on beaches around the world, and by 1735, Linnaeus was ready to include *Sepia microcosmos* in the first edition of his *Systema naturae.* (Perhaps because he doubted its existence, Linnaeus dropped *S. microcosmos* from subsequent editions, and it does not appear at all in the definitive tenth edition.) Denys de Montfort then enters the story with his six-volume *Histoire Naturelle générale et particulière des mollusques,* and although his *poulpe colossal* was a wild mixture of fact and fantasy, it encouraged other people to investigate cephalopod stories. Returning via the Cape of Good Hope from the first voyage in 1771, Capt. James Cook's naturalists, Drs. Banks and Solander, reported a giant *Sepia* carcass floating on the surface, surrounded by dense flocks of feeding seabirds. (But because Banks described it as having arms "furnished with a double row of very sharp talons," we know it was not *Architeuthis.*) Steenstrup found another early record of a giant squid in Iceland; in the winter of 1790, a creature that the people called *Kolkrabbe* drifted ashore at Arnaraesvik. This one seems to have been considerably larger than its predecessor, with a total length of 39 feet.

In December 1853, a gigantic cephalopod washed ashore at Raabjerg beach, on the Jutland peninsula of Denmark. It was cut up for fish bait, but the beak, which measured approximately 3 by 4 inches, was the basis for Steenstrup's designation of a new species, *Architeuthis monachus.* His description of the Raabjerg specimen, based on eyewitness accounts and the impressive beak, was published in 1857 and marked the official transition of the giant squid from the realm of fable into the scientific literature. Three years later, Steenstrup described another new species of giant squid, *A. dux,* from the remains of another carcass that a Captain Hygom had brought from the Bahamas to Denmark. Another North Atlantic stranding took place in 1860, when a 23-footer with a 7-foot-long head and mantle was stranded on the Scottish coast between Hillswick and Scalloway. Captain Bouyer returned from Tenerife in 1861 with the *Alecton*'s tale of the giant squid whose tail was detached while the crew was trying to bring it aboard. Its body was 18 feet long.

Like almost all the pelagic squids, *Architeuthis* is a creature whose very existence is shrouded in mystery. We know virtually nothing about the natural history of the giant squid except that it occasionally washes ashore—and when that happens, we don't even know why. Its feeding habits, breeding habits, vertical and geographic distribution, life span, and habitat are all unknown. Furthermore, there are some areas in which the nature of the animal itself almost precludes our obtaining any but the most rudimentary information. Take size, for example. While the mantle is a tough, muscular structure that cannot be easily deformed, the tentacles can be stretched like gigantic rubber bands, allowing for great exaggerations of the animal's total length. Therefore, "mantle length" is usually considered the most reliable length measurement, but since the tentacle length of different species varies greatly—and may even be diagnostic—it must also be taken into consideration.

The maximum size of the giant squid has long been a subject of speculation among scientists, seamen, whalers, authors, and almost anyone else with an interest in the sea's larger inhabitants. On Arthur C. Clarke's 1988 video series *Mysterious World,* Frederick Aldrich of Memorial University of Newfoundland examined a 20-foot-long immature specimen of *Architeuthis* and said, "I believe the giant squid reach an approximate maximum size of something like 150 feet." Aldrich was one of the world's foremost authorities on the giant squid, and it is difficult to imagine why he would have made such an irresponsible statement unless it had to do with being on camera. From the physical evidence, it would appear that the largest known specimen was the 55-footer that washed ashore in New Zealand in 1887. But because *Architeuthis* is such a spectacular animal, those who would include it in their catalogs of monsters often increase its length substantially and frequently its weight as well. In a Time-Life book on *Dangerous Sea Creatures,* for example, Thomas Dozier introduces his discussion of octopuses and squids by saying that "two 42-foot tentacles were vomited by a captive whale in an aquarium, and experts calculated that these had to belong to a monster measuring at least 66 feet and weighing better than 85,000 pounds." * Later, Dozier calls a 50-footer "ordinary" and says that there have been sperm whales captured with "tentacle marks 18 inches across, which would have to have been inflicted by a gargantuan squid of at least 200 feet long."

Then there is the question of color. Certainly it is helpful in identifying a particular animal if we know what color it is. Although we must infer this from our limited knowledge of other large teuthids, we assume that *Architeuthis* can change color more or less at will, so there can be no definite identification based on color. Most of the dead or dying specimens showed some traces of reddish coloration, and in their 1982 article in *Scientific American,* Clyde Roper and Kenneth Boss wrote: "The multilayered integument that envelops the body, the head and the arms is a dark purplish red to maroon dorsally and slightly lighter ventrally." In her 1948 description of a giant squid that was found at Victoria, Australia, Joyce Allan wrote of the animal's coloration: "The living animal must be simply amazing to witness.

---

*It is this sort of wild exaggeration and these undocumented "facts" that have given *Architeuthis* such a bad name. Aside from the obvious impossibility of the weight, no cetacean larger than a 30-foot killer whale has ever been maintained in captivity. It seems unlikely that an orca was the putative swallower, and no sperm whale—of any size—has ever been kept in an aquarium.

Remains of the outer skin (underneath this the flesh was firm, smooth, and blanc-mange white) was brilliant carmine red, due to a minute speckling of that colour. . . ." When fishermen in Trinity Bay, Newfoundland, encountered a live giant squid at the surface, they saw that it displayed "vivid color changes" before it dived and disappeared. (The wording comes from Aldrich's 1991 summary of giant squids in Newfoundland and appears in the description of a dead squid—which may or may not have been the same animal—that was found in Trinity Bay three days after the above sighting.)

Squid can also utilize an ink strategy as one of their defense mechanisms. The squid's mantle contains a specially developed sac that contains a dark brown fluid that the animal can eject at will. (The ink of the cuttlefish is still used to produce the ink known as sepia.) Many observers have noted that the discharge often takes the approximate form of the squid itself, which means that it does not so much blind the incipient predator or even hide the escaping squid; rather, it serves as a decoy. While the giant squid does have an ink sac, it is quite small and suggests that the animal does not eject clouds of ink that are commensurate with its size. In the lightless depths of the ocean the giant squid has no known predators except the sperm whale, and the whale, an animal that hunts by sound in total darkness, is not going to be deterred by a cloud of ink or a change of color.

The stomachs of most stranded giant squid have been empty, so we have little idea of what they eat, but from fishing experiences, it has been observed that other species, such as the 12-foot Humboldt squid, *Dosidicus gigas,* are cannibalistic. (Because of the radular "teeth" on the tongue and on the pharynx, chunks of food bitten off by the powerful beaks are ground to a pulp before entering the alimentary canal. This is one of the reasons why the food items of squid are so difficult to identify.)

Deep-water animals, whether fishes or cephalopods, usually have larger eyes than their shallow-water counterparts. Since *Architeuthis* has the largest eyes of any animal on earth, it follows that it must use them to see where there is limited light. It does not follow, however, that the eyes are large simply because the squid is large. The sperm whale, which can reach approximately the same length as the giant squid and at least on some occasions frequents the same depths, has an eye about 2.5 inches long, not much larger than the eye of a cow.

The eyes of a squid are almost as complex as those of a human, with an adjustable lens, a dark iris, and an eyelid, but no cornea. "Sight, more than any other sense, dominates the squid's life," wrote Harry Thurston. The eyes of a giant squid can be as much as 15 inches in diameter, larger than an automobile hubcap. (The eye of a blue whale, the largest *animal* in history, gets to be about 7 inches across.) A giant squid is rubbery and heavy out of the water, but because its muscles are filled with vacuoles containing a solution of ammonium chloride, which is lighter than water, it has a neutral buoyancy in water, which probably explains why dead or dying squid float to the surface. The ammoniacal squids, of which *Architeuthis* is but one, are, according to the Russian teuthologist Kir Nesis, "not edible to humans, though they might satisfy the taste of the sperm whale."*

THE FIRST giant squid ever taken in American waters was collected in 1871 by a Gloucester fisherman on the Grand Banks. Its body was 15 feet long, and the arms, which were badly mutilated, were estimated to be 9 to 10 feet long. Named *Architeuthis princeps* (*princeps* means "first"), this specimen was estimated to weigh 2,000 pounds. In the fall of the following year, an even larger specimen washed ashore at Coombs' Cove, Fortune Bay, Newfoundland, where it was secured by local fishermen. One arm was about the diameter of a man's wrist and was 42 feet long. The body was 10 feet long (and "nearly as large round as a hogshead"), so the total length was 52 feet.

In October 1873, off Portugal Cove, Newfoundland, herring fishermen Daniel Squires and Theophilus Piccot rowed over to what they thought was a piece of wreckage, but when they tried to draw it near with a boat hook, it struck the gunwale of the dory with its beak and threw a tentacle around the boat. Twelve-year-old Tom Piccot hacked off the tentacle (undoubtedly saving his life and the lives of the other fishermen) and brought it to the Reverend Moses Harvey, an amateur naturalist in St. John's.† The tentacle, some 19 feet long, appears to have been the first conclusive evidence of the body of a giant squid. (Professor Steenstrup's 1857 description was based only on a beak.) In an article written for *Wide World Magazine* in 1899, Harvey recalled his reaction upon being presented with the tentacle: "I was now the possessor of one of the rarest curiosities in the whole animal kingdom—

---

*Upon the completion of his doctoral dissertation (on the *Bathyteuthidae*), Clyde Roper celebrated by cooking a piece of giant squid for himself and two other teuthologists, but it proved to be inedible because of the "strong, bitter taste of ammonia."

† This event was fictionalized in a children's story by Norman Duncan entitled "The Adventure of the Giant Squid of Chain Tickle." In Newfoundland waters, Billy Topsail and Bobby Lot battle a giant squid, which they eventually subdue, and present the carcass to "Dr. Marvey" (Moses Harvey); it is described in a monograph by Prof. John Adams Wright (Verrill). In the *Anthology of Children's Literature,* N. C. Wyeth illustrated the story with the painting that appears as the frontispiece of this book.

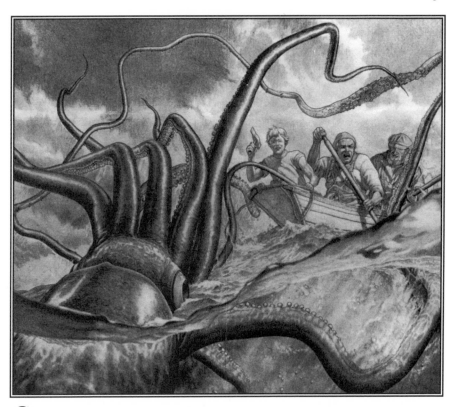

Glen Loates's re-creation of the 1873 incident at Conception Bay, Newfoundland, in which twelve-year-old Tom Piccot hacked off a 19-foot tentacle of a giant squid that attacked the boat. Except for a beak that had been described in 1853, this tentacle represented the first physical evidence of the existence of *Architeuthis*.

the veritable tentacle of the hitherto mythical devilfish, about whose existence naturalists had been disputing for centuries. I knew that I held in my hand the key of the great mystery, and that a new chapter would now be added to Natural History."

Wisely recognizing his limitations as a biologist, Moses Harvey contacted Addison Emery Verrill, professor of zoology at Yale University, an expert on the phylum mollusca. Verrill began publishing papers on these specimens almost as fast as they came in. (In the bibliography of M. R. Clarke's *Review of the Systematics and Ecology of Oceanic Squids* [1966], Verrill is listed as the author of no fewer than twenty-nine papers, almost all of which refer to the specimens that appeared in Newfoundland between 1871 and 1881.)

Also in Newfoundland, in December 1873—only a month after the incident at Portugal Cove—four fishermen were hauling in their herring

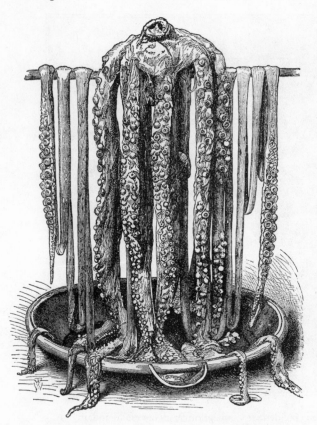

A drawing made from Moses Harvey's 1873 photograph of the head and tentacles of the first giant squid ever examined. It has been hung over the Reverend Harvey's sponge bath to allow the tentacles to show to best advantage.

net in Logy Bay when they realized that the heavy, writhing net contained more than herring. A giant squid was trapped in the net, and the fishermen managed to kill it with their knives. They, too, brought the carcass to Reverend Harvey, who would later write, "I remember to this day how I stood on the shore of Logy Bay, gazing on the dead giant, 'and rolling as a sweet morsel under my tongue' the thought of how I would astonish the savants, and confound the naturalists and startle the world at large, I resolved that only the interests of science should be considered. I speedily completed my bargain with the fishermen, whom I astonished by offering 10 dollars to deliver the beast carefully to my house." To enable the steady stream of curious visitors to see the carcass, Harvey draped the head and arms over a wooden frame called a sponge bath. The tentacles were 24 feet long, and the entire animal was 32 feet long. When Verrill saw this specimen (it is not clear from his description if he went to Newfoundland or if Harvey sent the pieces to New Haven), he described it in great detail in the steady torrent of articles he was producing. As a tribute to his friend, correspondent, and squid supplier, Verrill named the species *Architeuthis harveyi*.

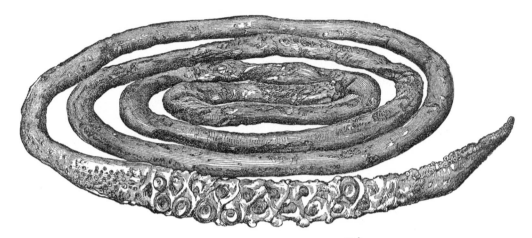

The 19-foot tentacle of the first *Architeuthis* ever examined on land. It was hacked off a living animal in October 1873 by a young Newfoundland fishermen, who brought it to the attention of Rev. Moses Harvey.

During the 1870s in Newfoundland—for reasons that probably had to do with some unexplained climactic or oceanographic changes—dozens of giant squid washed ashore or were seen floating at the surface. According to Verrill's analysis, some fifty or sixty were collected by fishing vessels on the Grand Banks and used as bait for cod. Another twenty-three were the subjects of Dr. Verrill's meticulous examination.

In a paper entitled "The Cephalopods of the North-eastern Coast of America. Part I. The Giant Squids (Architeuthis) and their Allies; with Observations on Similar Large Species from Foreign Localities," Verrill listed every specimen of *Architeuthis* known at the time of publication. That such a thing was possible is a direct function of the rarity of this animal; few other large creatures are known from such a small number of individuals.* (Since Verrill's day, of course, the total has increased, but each giant squid that washes up or is taken from the stomach of a sperm whale is still an occasion for a teuthological celebration.) Many of Verrill's specimens are discussed in some detail in this book, but others are mentioned only in passing. A few selections from Verrill's article are included to round out the list of what surely is the most remarkable unscheduled arrival in the history of zoology, crypto or otherwise. An

*Only the beaked whales of the family Ziphiidae are rarer. Of the nineteen known species, only Baird's beaked whale (*Berardius bairdii*), the northern bottlenose whale (*Hyperoodon ampullatus*), and the goose-beaked whale (*Ziphius cavirostris*) are known from more than a couple of specimens. The rarest known large animal in the world is probably the Indo-Pacific beaked whale (*Indopacetus pacificus*), which has never been seen in the flesh and is known only from two skeletons that were found on the beach, one in Somalia and the other in Queensland.

animal that was believed by many to be mythological verified its corporeal existence by appearing all over the beaches and shallows of Newfoundland from 1871 to 1881.

In 1872, Reverend Harvey wrote to Verrill that he had been apprised of
a large specimen that was cast ashore at Bonavista Bay. Only the jaws and
tentacular suckers were measured—the largest ones were 2.5 inches in
diameter—but Harvey's informant, a fellow clergyman named Munn,
remembered that the short arms, about 10 feet in length, were "thicker
than a man's thigh." The Logy Bay animal filled the quota for 1873, and in
1874 another giant came ashore in Newfoundland, this one at Grand Bank,
Fortune Bay. The magistrate of Grand Bank, a Mr. George Simms, had
examined the carcass before it was cut up for dog meat and had recorded
that the longest tentacles were 26 feet long and 16 inches in circumference. The body length was 10 feet, making the Fortune Bay specimen
a 36-footer.

*B*eached alive at Trinity Bay, Newfoundland, this giant squid was exhibited first at
St. John's, and after it died, it was taken to New York, where a cast was made of it for the
American Museum of Natural History.

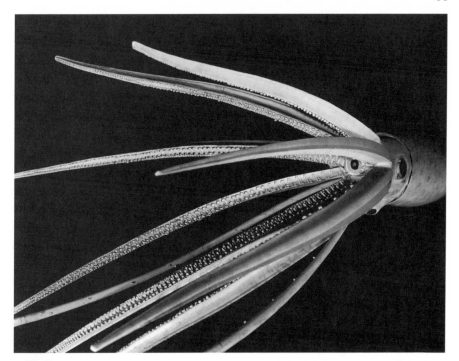

Model of *Architeuthis*, cast from a 47-foot specimen that washed ashore in Newfoundland in 1877, shown in the old Hall of Ocean Life at the American Museum of Natural History in New York

Another animal washed ashore at Harbor Grace during the winter of 1874–75, but, reports Verrill, "it was destroyed before its value was known, and no measurements were taken." In September 1877, however, a "nearly perfect specimen" came ashore at Catalina, Trinity Bay, during a severe gale. It was living when found, so it was exhibited for two or three days in St. John's and then packed in brine and exhibited at the New York Aquarium. Based on an examination of the suckers (which were sent to him by the proprietors of the aquarium), Verrill identified it as *Architeuthis princeps.* As of that time, it was "the largest and best specimen ever preserved." The body was 9.5 feet long, and the longest tentacle was 30 feet long. The eyes were 8 inches in diameter.*

Although neither Verrill nor his informant saw it, Verrill quotes the report of a Dr. D. Honeyman of Halifax, Nova Scotia, who recorded the statement of a gentleman who was present at the capture in the Straits of Belle Isle. (No date is given.) This giant squid, which was 52 feet long,

*A full-sized cast of this specimen is now the centerpiece of the invertebrate display at the American Museum of Natural History in New York.

including the body and longest arms, was disturbed with an oar as it lay peacefully in the water, but Verrill writes that it was "probably disabled [because] animals of this sort probably never float or lie quietly at the surface when in good health." In 1876 a specimen was discovered at Hammer Cove, on the southwest arm of Green Bay, in Notre Dame Bay, Newfoundland. By the time it could be examined, it had been partially devoured by foxes and birds, so only a five-foot hunk of the body remained, with two-foot stumps attached to it. In 1877, Harvey wrote to Verrill describing a specimen that was stranded at Lance Cove, Trinity Bay, some twenty miles up the bay from the location of the Catalina stranding. This animal was alive and thrashing when it was found, and in its struggles to get back into the water, "it ploughed up a trench or furrow about thirty feet long and of considerable depth by the stream of water that it ejected with great force from its siphon. When the tide receded it died."

In a letter to the Boston *Traveller* dated January 30, 1879, Reverend Harvey described a huge squid that had been sighted off Thimble Tickle the previous November. Three fishermen spied

> some bulky object, and, supposing it might be part of a wreck, they rowed toward it, and, to their horror, found themselves close to a huge fish, having large glassy eyes, which was making desperate efforts to escape, and churning the water into foam by the motion of its immense arms and tail. It was aground and the tide was ebbing. From the funnel at the back of its head it was ejecting large volumes of water, this being its method of moving backward, the force of the stream, by the reaction of the surrounding medium, driving it in the required direction. At times the water from the siphon was as black as ink.

The intrepid fishermen threw a grapnel at it, dragged it to shore, and tied the line to a tree. The squid died and was cut up for dog food, but Dr. Harvey, the coordinator of all this information, estimated that the Thimble Tickle squid was 55 feet long.

Several more giants appeared on Newfoundland beaches before the fabulous decade came to a close: In November 1878, "a fine and complete specimen" was captured at James Cove, Bonavista Bay. The fishermen, "as usual, indulged immediately in their propensity to cut and destroy," so none of it was preserved. In a later letter from an observer, however, its capture was described: "One of the men struck at it with an oar, and it immediately struck for shore and went quite upon the beach." The body was 9 feet long, and the tentacles were 29 feet each. On December 2, 1878, after a heavy gale, a specimen identified as *A. princeps** came ashore at Three Arms; its body was measured at 15 feet from the beak to the end of the tail.

The decade closed with no more strandings in Newfoundland, but in 1881, at Portugal Cove, one last specimen was found floating at the surface. It was packed in ice and shipped to New York by steamer, where the indefatigable Professor Verrill examined it at the museum of E. M. Worth, at 101 Bowery. It was too damaged for accurate measurements, but Verrill believed that the total length was about 20 feet. He wrote, "The color, which is partially preserved, especially on the arms and on the ventral surface of the body . . . consisting of small purplish-brown chromatophores more or less thickly scattered over the surface."

In April 1875, three fishermen were at sea in a curragh near Boffin Island, off the Connemara coast of Ireland. Upon noticing a large, shapeless mass floating at the surface, they rowed over to investigate and were more than a little surprised to find that the mass was a giant squid. They grabbed one of the tentacles and lopped it off, causing the creature to erupt in a violent flurry of foam and ink. They amputated one arm at a time—always trying to keep out of range of the remaining flailing appendages—until they had a feebly thrashing, moribund, almost armless squid that they towed to shore. From the remains they calculated that the tentacles were 30 feet long, the beaklike mandibles were 4 inches across, and the eye was 15 inches in diameter. An estimate of its total length was 47 feet.

Something must have been happening in the oceans during the years 1870–90 that caused giant squid to appear at the surface and on certain beaches, but unless there is a repeat of this inexplicable phenomenon, we will never know what it was.[†] The favorite location was Newfoundland, but what are we to make of a similar, albeit smaller, invasion of *Architeuthis*, halfway around the world in New Zealand, during the same years?

*Because almost every known specimen of the genus *Architeuthis* is a little different from every other—and many of them were described from only a beak or a piece of tentacle—almost every description resulted in a new species. Thus *A. harveyi* for the Logy Bay animal, *A. bouyeri* for the one caught off Tenerife in 1862, *A. princeps* for one caught by the Gloucester fishermen in 1871, *A. japonica* for one found off Japan, and so on. But in a 1982 article, Clyde Roper suggested that "the 19 nominal species can in fact be encompassed by only three: *Architeuthis sanctipauli* in the Southern Hemisphere, *A. japonica* in the northern Pacific, and *A. dux* in the northern Atlantic." And in 1991, refining it even further, Frederick Aldrich wrote, "I reject the concept of 20 separate species, and until that issue is resolved, I choose to place them all in synonymy with *Architeuthis dux* Steenstrup."

†Frederick Aldrich suggested that fluctuations in the Labrador Current were responsible for the appearance of giant squid off Newfoundland every ninety years or so. When the cold portion known as the Avalon Branch hits northeastern Newfoundland, the squid, following the cold mass of water, come close to shore. He predicted that the next period of *Architeuthis* strandings would occur around 1960, and he was proven correct when six specimens stranded between 1964 and 1966.

In May 1879, a specimen was stranded at Lyall Bay, Cook Strait, New Zealand, and described by T. W. Kirk to the Wellington Philosophical Society. It took three years before the specimen was examined by scientists, and by that time, all that remained was the beak, radula, and a few suckers. A year later, another giant squid stranded at Island Bay (also in Cook Strait), and again Kirk described it, naming it *A. verrilli.* In their 1982 article in *Scientific American,* Clyde Roper and Kenneth Boss call the 1880 specimen from Island Bay, at 55 feet long, "the largest specimen recorded in the scientific literature." In 1886, a specimen was found on the beach at Cape Campbell, and the author, a lighthouse keeper named C. W. Robson (not to be confused with G. C. Robson, teuthologist of the British Museum), named it *A. kirki,* for T. W. Kirk. Then, in 1887, another squid came ashore at Lyall Bay, and Kirk wrote, "And now we have another of these highly interesting, but very objectionable, visitors." Kirk proceeded to the beach, made a careful examination, took notes, measurements, and also "obtained a sketch, which, although the terribly heavy rain and driving southerly wind rendered it impossible to do justice to the subject, will, I trust, convey to you some idea of the general outline of this most recently arrived Devil-fish." Kirk named this new species *A. longimanus* for the enormous length of its arms: a local fisherman named Smith had paced it off at 62 feet, but Kirk measured it at 55 feet 2 inches, "or more than half as long again as the largest species yet recorded from these seas."

Of these nineteenth-century New Zealand strandings, R. K. Dell wrote (in 1970), "Most specimens have been in poor condition or have not been examined by competent workers. Strandings of these squids on uninhabited stretches of our coasts and sightings of dead bodies at sea are probably much more common than the published records would indicate." When a giant squid washed ashore at Makara in 1956, it gave Dell the opportunity to examine a "perfectly fresh" specimen. The tentacular arms had been sheared off obliquely about a meter from the head (possibly by a sperm whale), but the body was in good condition. Where the color had not been abraded, it was described as being somewhere between madder brown and brick red.

Although the predominant large teuthids off the California coast are thought to be *Dosidicus,* a 10-footer, and *Moroteuthis,* a species that may reach 16 feet in length, Architeuthids are also known to occur offshore in the eastern North Pacific. In 1911, fishermen found a 30-foot squid—"most certainly not *Dosidicus gigas,*" according to Stanford University teuthologist Stillman Berry—floating dead on the surface of Monterey Bay, and two years later some Italian fishermen "encountered and captured" an immense

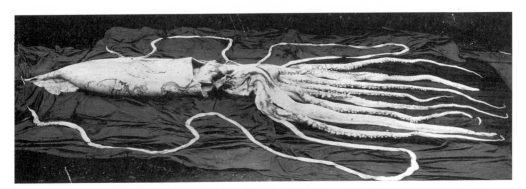

squid and brought it to shore. It was not measured, but its weight was estimated at close to 500 pounds, and when a Mr. Hovden of the Booth Canning Company attempted to purchase the carcass for five dollars, his offer was refused by the fishermen, "who devoured the prize raw."

*M*easuring 32 feet from tentacle tip to tail, this specimen of *Architeuthis* was collected in 1896 at Hevne, outside the Trondheimfjord in Norway.

Norway, a country that is almost all west coast, has also been a fertile location for observing dead or dying giant squid. In a 1916 discussion of the animals the Norwegians refer to as *Kjaempebleblekkspruten*, August Brinkmann lists some of the strandings prior to the year of his publication, which is primarily devoted to an animal that was found swimming at the surface just north of Bergen in November 1915:

> Joakim Lerøen . . . discovered the animal swimming on the surface of the water, criss-crossing its way towards the neck of the bay, with its rear-end in front. He ran into the boat-house and grabbed a gaff with which he cut into the eye of the squid when it resurfaced at the breath of the bay. Up to this point, the animal appeared to be light colored but when the gaff cut into its eye, it turned deep purple. It simultaneously released its ink bag, thus darkening the surrounding water, and threw one of its giant tentacles above the surface, attempting twice to clasp the man. Meanwhile, the fisherman's neighbor had come to help, and the two men managed to pull the animal up and fasten it in the shallow water.

When a giant squid drifted ashore in Vike Bay, Romsdalfjord, in September 1946, Bjorn Myklebust, a teacher from the Technical College of Fisheries at Aukra, went out to measure and photograph it. It measured 30 feet overall, with the longest tentacle at 23.5 feet. In the Norwegian journal *Naturen*, Myklebust wrote that "within the last month, the sea serpent had reportedly been seen twice in Romsdal." Eyewitnesses reported seeing something with a large head that pierced the waterline, followed by several "backward curves" that arched high enough so that water could be seen beneath them. "In one case," wrote Myklebust, "the monster had trailed a rowing boat, and the man in the boat, who became a bit frightened, hurriedly scrambled to shore."

In another Norwegian discussion of a stranded individual (this one at Ranheim in 1954), Erling Sivertsen includes a map of Norway, showing the locations and dates of eighteen strandings that occurred from 1874 to 1954.* One might envision a central location in the North Atlantic with lines radiating outward toward Newfoundland in the west and Norway in the east, whence the giant squid disperse, but such a concept would require far more information about the distribution and habits of *Architeuthis* than is actually available. (Although several of the Norwegian records occurred during the decade from 1870 to 1880, the greater proportion occurred afterward, showing what would appear to be an irregular chronology, with a couple of records during every decade from 1900 to 1950.)

In recent years, more giant squid have washed ashore or have been found floating at the surface. In addition to the Ranheim 30-footer described by Sivertsen, a 405-pound *Architeuthis* was recovered from the stomach of a sperm whale harpooned off the Azores in 1955. (If nothing else, this item from the stomach of a cachalot demonstrates that a sperm whale is fully capable of swallowing a man.) At his laboratory at the University of Miami, Gilbert Voss was the recipient of a 47-footer that had been picked up floating on the surface in the Bahamas in 1958. As predicted by Frederick Aldrich, fifteen specimens were recorded from Newfoundland between 1964 and 1982, some of which were in such poor condition that the animal could not be preserved.† In February 1980, a 12-foot specimen (its long feeding tentacles had broken off) with 10-inch-diameter eyes washed ashore at Plum Island on the Massachusetts coast. Scientists estimated that this half-grown individual would have measured about 30 feet with its tentacles intact. And then, in August 1982, fisherman Rune Ystebo looked out the window of his home near Bergen, Norway, and saw what he thought was a group of divers. He launched his little fishing boat to investigate, and when he realized that it was a live giant squid, he speared it. He dragged it to shore, where it expired, and weighed it at 485 pounds and measured it at 33 feet total length. Upon examining the specimen, Dr. Ole Brix, director

---

*See Appendix B for a listing of the known records of *Architeuthis* sightings and strandings.

† One of these specimens, found floating at the surface in White Bay, Newfoundland, in 1964, had tentacular clubs that were so different in size and configuration that Frederick Aldrich and his wife Margueritte published a paper on the hitherto unsuspected ability of the giant squid to regenerate lost tentacles.

*I*n order to get a sense of what *Architeuthis* actually looks like, it has to be arranged on the ground. This 30-foot specimen washed ashore at Ranheim, Norway, on October 2, 1954.

*P*lum Island, Massachusetts, February 1980: The first giant squid (*Architeuthis*) found on a U.S. beach in twenty years. It was considered half-grown at a length of 30 feet, including tentacles.

of the zoological laboratory at the University of Bergen, ran a blood analysis and concluded that the oxygen capacity of the giant squid's blood was severely limited, which led him to conclude that the animal is indeed a slow swimmer and perhaps even a passive predator.

In January 1982, an Australian research vessel was trawling in two-thousand-meter-deep water off Sydney and hauled in a juvenile female *Architeuthis* with a mantle length of 16.5 inches. A more recent specimen washed ashore at Cove Bay, south of Aberdeen, Scotland, on January 8, 1984. As described by P. R. Boyle of the University of Aberdeen, it was 4.23 meters (13.28 feet) overall, with a mantle length of 1.75 meters (5.74 feet). Both tentacles were missing. Its total weight was 168.4 kilograms (370 pounds), and because of freezing temperatures and snowstorms, it proved to be difficult to lift out of the water. It was a female, with well-developed nidamental glands and three detached egg strands, with approximately three thousand eggs attached. Where Ole Brix had suggested that giant squid suffocate near the surface because the hemocyanin content of the blood requires the cold-water temperatures associated with the depths, Boyle wrote that "the low water temperature associated with the Scottish stranding does not support the proposal that mortality of *Architeuthis* at the surface is due to asphyxia caused by the low temperature of oxygen affinity of the hemocyanin."

Even if it is true that the kraken is a flaccid blob that couldn't catch a sea cucumber, legends die hard, and when the country's foremost natural-history mythmaker chose *Architeuthis* as the protagonist of his 1991 novel, he was virtually guaranteeing the resurrection of the animal's fearsome reputation. In 1975, Peter Benchley had already raised the great white shark to superstar level in *Jaws*, and he now turned his attention to the giant squid. His "beast" is the kraken incarnate, 100 feet of pure, predatory malice, with an appetite for anything it could get, including human beings. As was its predecessor in *Jaws*, the animal is introduced in the opening paragraph:

> It hovered in the ink dark water, waiting.
>
> It was not a fish, had no air bladder to give it buoyancy, but because of the special chemistry of its flesh, it did not sink into the abyss.
>
> It was not a mammal, did not breathe air, so it felt no impulse to move to the surface.
>
> It hovered.
>
> It was not asleep, for it did not know sleep, sleep was not among its natural rhythms. It rested, nourishing itself with oxygen absorbed from the water pumped through the caverns of its bullet-shaped body.
>
> Its eight sinuous arms floated on the current; its two long tentacles

were coiled tight against its body. When it was threatened or in the frenzy of a kill, the tentacles would spring forward, like tooth-studded whips. . . .

It existed to survive. And to kill.

For, peculiarly—if not uniquely—in the world of living things, it often killed without need, as if Nature, in a fit of perverse malevolence, had programmed it to that end.

As with all novels of this genre—and Benchley is the master—the predatory protagonist picks off various members of the human cast until someone (or something) finally eliminates it. (We have not heard the last of the conflict between sperm whale and giant squid.) *Beast* was a best-seller during the summer of 1991, and of course, if and when it is produced, it will make a marvelous film. But no subject can compare with the star of *Jaws*, for Benchley had the absolute genius to choose a creature that was already known to attack swimmers and divers. Giant squid are awesome creatures that may or may not be swift and powerful killers, but with the exception of those eighteenth- and nineteenth-century tales of the kraken sinking ships or the seamen being plucked from the *Alecton* (or the *Nautilus*), there are no substantiated records of giant squid attacking people.*

In *Beast,* Benchley's fisher-

*T*he cover of Peter Benchley's 1991 novel. Each of the suckers on the arm is drawn with a single claw in the middle—nothing like the real thing.

---

*In *Kingdom of the Octopus,* Frank Lane recounts the tale of the *Britannia,* a World War II troopship sunk in the Atlantic by a German raider in 1941. Twelve crew members, including Lt. R. E. G. Cox, clung to a raft that did not have room for all of them, since it was "no bigger than a hearthrug." Cox told Lane that a sailor was plucked from the raft by a large squid, and later the same night, Cox himself was attacked. A tentacle twisted around his leg but released him almost immediately. The story might very well be true, but we have no way of identifying the attacking squid—if indeed it was a squid.

men encounter a "gelatinous doughnut, an oblong measuring six or eight feet by two or three feet, undulating, with a hole in its center"—the egg mass of the giant squid. In the final chapter of the novel, one of these "doughnuts" hatches: "At last, ripe, it broke apart and scattered into the sea thousands of little sacs, each containing a complete creature." That no one has ever seen the egg mass of *Architeuthis* was not—and should not be—an impediment to the novelist; even if the novel is about animals, the writer need not be inhibited by the limitations of biological knowledge. If Benchley wants to make up egg masses (or man-eating squid, for that matter), he has every right to do so. (His squid, however, manifest emotions such as hatred, anger, and vengeance, feelings that may not be in their emotional repertoire.)

There is only one instance where the egg case of the giant squid has been seen, but the evidence is anecdotal. (The story is repeated in Lane's *Kingdom of the Octopus*.) It seems that some children on holiday in Jamaica around the turn of the century encountered a 6-foot-long "great big sausage" with a diameter as great as that of a galvanized iron pail. Their zoologist father identified it as the egg case of the giant squid. There are also a couple of records of juvenile *Architeuthis* in the literature. A baby giant squid is almost a contradiction in terms; we have been so conditioned to think of these creatures as formidable monsters that it is almost impossible to envision a baby. Of course, before the giant reaches its full size, it has to pass through normal—but so far, unknown—growth stages. Two juveniles have been examined, both in the collection of the Institute of Marine Sciences at the University of Miami. (Neither was collected by Miami scientists; both were found in the stomach contents of fishes in the ichthyological collections.)

The larger of the two was 56 millimeters (22 inches) in mantle length and had been taken from the stomach of a long-nose lancetfish (*Alepisaurus ferox*) captured off Madeira. The second specimen was taken from the stomach of a fish—also probably *Alepisaurus*—in the eastern Pacific off Chile, and was 45 millimeters (17.7 inches) in mantle length. (Frank Lane quotes teuthologist Gilbert Voss as saying, "Stripping the stomachs of these fish is one of the approved methods of collecting deep-sea squid and octopods.") As Roper and Young put it, "They are an order of magnitude smaller than the smallest previously reported specimen," which was a 460-millimeter (15-foot) specimen of *A. physeteris*.

We do not know how large *Architeuthis* is at birth (or anything else about the spawning process), but in their discussion of the two juveniles, Roper and Young suggest that "the small size of the present specimens suggests they were spawned in the nearby region of their localities of capture in tropical or warm temperate waters." The lancetfishes that swallowed these two juveniles are known to hunt primarily in the upper three hundred meters of the open ocean around the world, so this gives us a fleeting clue about the vertical distribution of these otherwise enigmatic decapods.

When a blue shark (*Prionace glauca*) was caught in the eastern equatorial Atlantic off Africa, portions of a large squid, identified by the Russian teuthologist C. M. Nigmatullin as *Architeuthis*, were found in its stomach. With a mantle length of 76 centimeters (30 inches), this specimen was hardly in the 50-foot class, but it was a large squid indeed. Using the figures employed by Nesis et al. (1985), where total length of some specimens was shown to be some 440 percent of its mantle length, this specimen's total length can be estimated at 11 feet. More interesting than its appearance in the stomach of a shark, however, is the location in which the shark—and therefore the squid—was captured. From the limited records, it was believed that *Architeuthis* bred in subtropical waters and headed for the higher, colder latitudes to feed. With the exception of the juvenile specimen taken from the stomach of a lancetfish off Chile, no architeuthid has been found in tropical waters, but this might have more to do with limited sampling than absence of squid. Giant squid are known primarily from specimens that have been cast ashore or found in the stomach contents of sperm whales, and although nineteenth-century whalers often hunted their quarry "on the line," more recent sperm whaling has occurred in the colder waters of the North Pacific and the Antarctic. There may be juvenile squids in equatorial waters; as Nigmatullin wrote in his discussion of this specimen, "Possibly, in the future, when the mid-depth tropical fauna is better known, *Architeuthis* individuals will be found to be typical representatives."

Often overlooked in discussions of monster squid are occasional mentions of "miniature" or "pygmy" *Architeuthis*.* A miniature adult, with a mantle length of 7 inches, was found in the stomach of a 6.5-foot swordfish caught in Florida waters. According to Toll and Hess, who described it, "This specimen . . . is the smallest functionally mature *Architeuthis* known. Its size and state of maturity raise several questions regarding the life history of the 'giant squid.' " In his overview of the cephalopods of the world,

---

*In 1952, Japanese scientists examined two specimens that had been found in the digestive canal of sperm whales caught off the Bonin Islands. The larger of the two measured 8 inches in total length, mantle *and* tentacles, and the second specimen was smaller. Eiji Awai, one of the scientists, identified the specimens as "oegopsiden squid belonging to the genus *Architeuthis*." In a subsequent discussion, however, Roper and Young wrote that there is "no doubt that the identification is incorrect" and suggested that "the specimens appear to be members of the Psychroteuthidae, a little known family of oceanic squid, previously known only from Antarctic waters."

Kir Nesis wrote that "the pygmy giant squid may be an undescribed species."

In addition to the toothed rings that surround the suckers on some of the larger species of squid, some have individual claws—the ones Bullen said were "the size and shape of a tiger's"—at the ends of their tentacles.* The best known of these is *Galiteuthis armata* (*armata* means "armed with weapons"), a 2-foot-long species that is distributed almost worldwide in temperate waters. Although it is a lovely (or terrifying) conceit to imagine such claws as part of the armament of *Architeuthis*, the club ends of the tentacles of the giant squid have no such talons. (In *Beast*, the giant squid keeps leaving claws described as "crescent-shaped, two inches long, and sharp as a razor" as proof of its existence.)

With the dramatic exception of the collective appearance of giant squid during the decade 1870–80, *Architeuthis* has hardly ever been seen at the surface. Some scientists have suggested that the squid can only exist at great depths because they require the pressure to function, that they thrive in the cold of the abyssal depths, and that the warmer, deoxygenated waters nearer the surface may debilitate or even kill them. As an indication of how poorly known *Architeuthis* really is, there are teuthologists who hold a diametrically opposite view: that cold winter currents incapacitate the animals to the point where they become helpless and wash ashore. In fact, many teuthologists believe that the giant squid, despite its great size and fearsome reputation, is actually a relatively weak, slow-swimming animal that feeds at great depths and therefore has no reason to approach the surface unless it is sick or dying and cannot remain below.

Japetus Steenstrup believed that *Architeuthis* lived on the bottom in dark, deep water. In a 1959 magazine article, Gilbert Voss wrote, "In the giant squids ... these organs [the mantle-locking cartilages, funnel valve, and so on] are very poorly developed; the funnel is flabby, the valve is weak, and the locking cartilages are mere shallow grooves and ridges." And in a 1933 description of a specimen that had washed ashore at Scarborough, Yorkshire, G. C. Robson, a British cephalopod specialist, said,

> I am inclined on the whole to think that *Architeuthis* is rather a sluggish animal, living near the upper stretches of the continental slope in water between 100–200 fathoms, or deeper where the water temperature is high.

*When the navy frigate USS *Stein* put in for repairs in San Diego in 1977, the rubber coating of her underwater sonar dome was found to be shredded by what appeared to be claws, some of which had been left in the rubber. In the *U.S. Naval Institute Proceedings*, biologist Scott Johnson wrote: "If a squid was indeed responsible for the damage (and there seems to be no other likely explanation), then it must have been extremely large and of a species still unknown to science."

The structure of the suckers suggests that it does not deal with large prey. The remarkable small size of the fins suggests an inactive life, so that it may keep near the bottom and feed on sedentary invertebrates and carrion.

J. Z. Young, who would later identify the neurological importance of the giant nerve fibers of squid, examined the same Scarborough specimen in 1933 and did not find that the giant squid had giant fibers. From this, he concluded that "*Architeuthis* is not an especially fast-moving animal. This would agree with evidence that it is neutrally buoyant with a high concentration of ammonium ions in the mantle and arms." In defense of the giant squid's reputation, Malcolm Clarke wrote, "Stomachs [of stranded specimens] are almost invariably empty, but the suggestion that squid are probably poor swimmers and ill adapted for catching active prey (Robson, 1933; Voss, 1956) seems incompatible with the many hundred large suckers up to 3 cm diameter, the very powerful buccal muscles, the short, thick jaws giving maximum leverage, and the thick mantle wall."*

The opposite approach is taken by Kir Nesis, who believes that "giant squids are not the powerful animals depicted in the popular stories." In a 1974 discussion of *Architeuthus* in the Soviet journal *Gidrobiologiia* (Hydrobiology), he wrote that they have poorly developed muscles, their tentacles are long and thin, and their fins are very small and weak. He stated: "Architeuthids are comparatively slow and passive predators, which do not actively pursue their prey, but ambush or trap it. Their very long arms and tentacles compensate for their slowness, but they certainly are able to capture and overcome living prey."

Frederick Aldrich, who died in July 1991, was probably the giant squid's most enthusiastic advocate. He claimed to have seen fifteen of them, more than any other person in history. In his comprehensive 1991 discussion of *Architeuthis* in Newfoundland, Aldrich reviewed the earlier hypotheses about the behavior of the giant squid, and wrote:

My thesis is that those who consider *Architeuthis* to be a feeble swimmer perhaps tend to confuse rapid swimming with flexibility. The mantle

---

*In a study of the "Energetic Limits on Squid Distributions," O'Dor wrote that "*Architeuthis* could go around the world in 80 days (under the North Pole?). Why it would want to is unclear, but traveling from the northern bloom to the southern bloom [of plankton] is energetically feasible for some whales and could take *Architeuthis* less than a month. Such a pattern is consistent with its distribution. It is now popular to say that *Architeuthis* is not a strong swimmer, but the evidence is only that it is ammoniacal and not as muscular, relatively, as the smaller squids. . . . At cruising speeds, squids use only 10% of the power (and presumably 10% of the muscle) available for an escape jet. Perhaps *Architeuthis* needs only cruising muscle, since there cannot be too many things it needs to escape from."

locking apparatus is indeed poorly developed . . . and one can easily envision that, if an architeuthid were to "turn on a dime," it could well turn itself inside out. This is not to be confused with rapid swimming, but rather is indicative of a lack both of maneuverability and facility in changing direction with rapidity.

Moreover, wrote Aldrich, since *Architeuthis* is known to be one of the chief dietary items of sperm whales, they have to be able to escape: "The classical report on the speed of architeuthid swimming is that of Grønningsaeter (1946) . . . he clocked an architeuthid's speed at between 20–25 kn[ots]. If this observation is valid, and I believe it is, then the morphological apparatus with which the squid has been provided is clearly capable of speed sufficient to evade whales." (Sperm whales are capable of speeds of ten to twelve knots.)

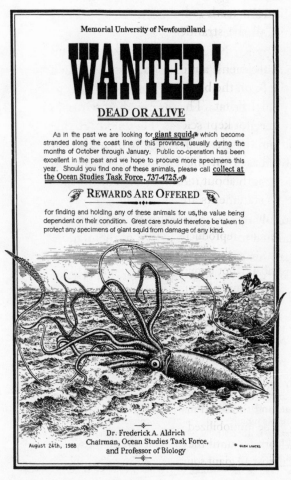

Memorial University of Newfoundland

WANTED!

DEAD OR ALIVE

As in the past we are looking for **giant squid** which become stranded along the coast line of this province, usually during the months of October through January. Public co-operation has been excellent in the past and we hope to procure more specimens this year. Should you find one of these animals, please call **collect at the Ocean Studies Task Force, 737-4725.**

REWARDS ARE OFFERED

for finding and holding any of these animals for us, the value being dependent on their condition. Great care should therefore be taken to protect any specimens of giant squid from damage of any kind.

Dr. Frederick A. Aldrich
August 24th, 1988   Chairman, Ocean Studies Task Force,
and Professor of Biology

No one has seen a giant squid feeding—in fact, no one has ever seen a healthy giant squid doing anything at all—so until someone observes *Architeuthis* chasing something, the debate about its speed and strength will remain unresolved. Aldrich assumed that *Architeuthis* is a powerful, aggressive animal, which, at least in one instance, was able to plow a great furrow in beach gravel before it expired. Precisely how the giant squid hunts—or what it eats, for that matter—is not known, but Aldrich believed that its prey consists mostly of sharks, skates, and rays, not the diet of a weak hunter.

Surely we ought to be able to ascertain something about the life of *Architeuthis* by examining it, and we might even speculate about what sort of life it might lead in the deepest oceans. (In

A 50-foot giant squid shown in the same scale as a 6-foot man. These monsters live at great depths, and healthy ones have never been seen at or near the surface.

their study of the vertical distribution of squid species, Roper and Young wrote, "Although the giant squid has received a great deal of attention in the literature, very little is known of its vertical distribution or any other aspect of its biology.") We don't know what it feeds on—its radular teeth reduce the prey to mush—and besides, as Nesis has written, "all the stranded specimens that were examined had empty stomachs."

With the exception of trawled specimens, almost all known specimens have been seen at or near the surface or on the beach, locations that are certainly far from the animal's normal habitat. The scarcity of hard data regarding the habits of *Architeuthis* has not kept scientists from speculating, and because of its size and reputation, the giant squid has been the subject of many learned discussions, often based on the scantiest evidence. For example, Nesis has written at some length about its distribution and natural history, with little to suggest that his statements are speculative:

They are probably subtropical animals, reproducing in the subtropical waters of both hemispheres. But because the subtropics are the areas of the lowest productivity, there is probably not enough food for such large predators. Therefore, when the giant squids become bigger, they move into the more productive waters of the World Ocean; those of the Northern Hemisphere migrate into the boreal zone, and those of the Southern Hemisphere to the subantarctic zone. Giant squids are passive swimmers, and are carried by the warm summer currents which transport them to the rich areas where warm and cold currents mix. There is a plenitude of food in these areas, but there is also the danger of the water temperature dropping with the approach of winter, and the squid may become trapped by cold water masses. Giant squid can be immobilized by cold, and they surface and drift with the winds or currents until they strand on the shore. Because of these circumstances, almost all giant squid have been found on shore in the colder half of the year; in the Northern Hemisphere from September to March, and in the Southern from May to October. Most often they are found where warm and cold waters mix (e.g., Newfoundland), or where warm currents run parallel to the shore, slowly becoming colder (Ireland, Norway, the Japan Sea coast of Honshu); or where waters of great depths are close to the shore, such as Eastern Florida, the Azores, Madeira, Southern Japan, Cook Strait (New Zealand). No architeuthids have been found on the seashores which are next to cold currents, such as the Northeast U.S., Northwest and Southwest Africa, Russia, California, Chile, because these animals instinctively avoid seashores.

In their examination of three South African specimens of *Architeuthis*, Roeleveld and Lipinski found that the statocysts were proportionally large—no surprise there—but also that they were oriented obliquely, which suggests "that the natural position of *Architeuthis* may be at an oblique angle to the horizontal plane, with the head and arms, generally the heaviest part of the body, hanging downward." If this is the case, say the authors (following Nesis), then the giant squid may hunt by using "some system of ambush, using the large tentacles to capture the prey." (Since every teuthologist has an opinion about the swimming and hunting capabilities of *Architeuthis*, Roeleveld and Lipinski weigh in with "the suggestion that *Architeuthis* is a poor swimmer and a passive and sluggish predator.")

ON THOSE occasions when the giant squid appears in literature, it fulfills, or often exceeds, its reputation. When H. G. Wells wrote "The Sea Raiders" in 1905, it had only been twenty-odd years since a large number of giant squid had washed ashore in Newfoundland. In this story, Wells changes the locale to Sidmouth, on the coast of Devonshire. He invents *Haploteuthis ferox* (which can be translated as "one fierce squid"), and then he has them attacking a Mr. Fison, who has spotted some of them feeding on the carcass of a man. When Fison goes to investigate, he sees that

> the rounded bodies were new and ghastly-looking creatures, in shape somewhat resembling an octopus, and with huge and very long and flexible tentacles, coiled copiously on the ground. The skin had a glistening texture, unpleasant to see, like shiny leather. The downward bend of the tentacle-surrounded mouth, the curious excrescence at the bend, the tentacles, and the large intelligent eyes, gave the creatures a grotesque suggestion of a face. They were the size of fair-sized swine about the body,

and the tentacles seemed to him to be many feet in length. There were, he thinks, seven or eight at least of the creatures.

Fison tries to drive them off by shouting, but when he makes the mistake of throwing a rock at them, they chase him up the beach: "And then, slowly uncoiling their tentacles, they all began moving towards him—creeping at first deliberately, and making a soft purring sound to each other."

The hapless Fison escapes the amphibious squid by climbing a cliff ("At one point he could hear the creatures splashing in the pools not a dozen feet behind him . . ."), but when the cephalopods return to the water, people in boats do not fare so well. The squid congregate just offshore ("Then these things, growing larger, until at last the bottom was hidden by their inter-coiling forms, and the tips of their tentacles rose darkly here and there into the air above the swell of the waters"), pulling fishermen overboard and then eating all the occupants of an excursion boat: three women, a child, a boatman, and "a little man in a pink-ribboned straw hat." The image of swarms of giant, noisy squid in shallow off-shore waters is the stuff of nightmares, and if they should ever come *ashore* . . .

The fearsome reputation of the giant squid also makes it a natural for inclusion in movies, but because of its poorly understood morphology and habits, it is rather difficult to replicate. Unlike the scientists, the moviemakers never had a problem with its reputation; they knew it was a killer. In 1942, Cecil B. De Mille directed *Reap the Wild Wind,* a lavish extravaganza of sailing ships in the early nineteenth century. (The cast includes John

Wayne, Ray Milland, Susan Hayward, Paulette Goddard, Raymond Massey, and Robert Preston.) In the big underwater denouement, two hard-hat divers (Wayne and Milland), rivals for the hand of Goddard, descend to the depth of "ten fathoms" to investigate a wreck that will either exonerate or implicate Wayne of complicity in the wreck of the *Southern Cross*. Enter the villain, a giant squid that has taken up residence in the wreck.

As shown here, the squid is an orange sponge-rubber creature that emerges from the fo'c'sle and throws a tentacle around Milland. John Wayne, whose career depends on his rival not finding certain evidence, watches passively as Milland struggles with the squid, but eventually his better nature takes over, and he enters the battle. Of course, since Wayne was actually guilty, he manages to free Milland, but he has to go down with the squid. In this film, *Architeuthis* probably fulfilled the public's expectations of what this beast was supposed to do: It lurks in drowned ships, awaiting luckless divers. From the vantage point of hindsight, the squid in *Reap the Wild Wind* is not very accurate, and its habits are ludicrous, but it

*T*he giant squid attacks the submarine *Nautilus* in Disney's production of Jules Verne's fantasy *Twenty Thousand Leagues Under the Sea.*

was such a unique addition to the lexicon of the cinema that the film was awarded an Oscar for special effects.

It took the genius of Walt Disney Studios to bring the giant squid to life in the movies. In the 1954 production of *20,000 Leagues Under the Sea***** the animal is portrayed as an aggressive, deep-water predator (before the attack, Captain Nemo announces that the *Nautilus* is "deeper than man has ever gone before") that attacks the submarine. When the approaching squid is first sighted through a porthole of the *Nautilus,* a crewman shouts, "Giant squid astern, sir!," and the battle is joined. The squid grasps the rudder of the submarine but is dissuaded by a jolt of electricity. Captain Nemo (played by James Mason) brings the *Nautilus* to the surface—in a howling gale, naturally—and the squid follows. It envelops the submarine in its tentacles, and Nemo arms his men with axes, halberds, flensing knives, and harpoons. As he prepares to lead his men into battle, Nemo announces, "You'll be fighting at close quarters with the most tenacious of all sea beasts. Take care of the tentacles; they'll seize anything within reach and hang on to the death!" In a tangled welter of writhing arms and driving rain, men fall overboard, the tentacles probe the open hatchways of the submarine looking for suitable victims, and Nemo shouts that the only way to kill the beast is by striking it right between the eyes. Before Nemo can administer this coup de grace, his assailant pulls him under water with a snakelike tentacle and draws him toward its ominously clicking jaws. Ned Land (Kirk Douglas), who had been imprisoned below, breaks free in time to climb on deck and harpoon the squid right between the eyes and then dives in to rescue Captain Nemo.

When it was made, this film was considered a marvel of spectacular special effects, especially the manufacture and deployment of the giant squid. For the battle scenes on deck, a two-ton model squid was designed requiring sixteen men to operate the electronics, hydraulics, and remote controls and another fifty in the rafters to handle the wires that moved the individual tentacles. The kapok-bodied squid was the creation of sculptor Chris Mueller and mechanical-effects expert Bob Mattey, who would go on to design the white shark in *Jaws.* At first, the battle scene was shot against a placid sea with a red sunset sky, but all the wires showed, so the decision was made to change the weather to a storm and film it again. In his mem-

---

*When the Disney organization decided to film Verne's novel, instead of spelling out the distance, they used the number "20,000." Ernest Williamson's 1916 version was officially titled: *The First Submarine Photoplay Ever Filmed. Based on Jules Verne's "Twenty Thousand Leagues Under the Sea."*

*S*ixty-six technicians were required to manipulate the electronics, hydraulics, remote controls, and wires that activated the 2-ton model squid in the Walt Disney production of *20,000 Leagues Under the Sea.*

oirs, Richard Fleischer, the director, described the events that led to the reshoot:

> Lighting the set for day not only exposed every wire that was used to manipulate the squid but also showed every fault in its construction, and there were many. The deck of the *Nautilus* looked like a concrete slab. With all the sailors and the huge squid, it should have canted a little, or rocked. It didn't. Then there was the squid itself. The stuff it was made of started to deteriorate. Big hunks of the tentacles would drop off when the sailors were wrestling with it. Sometimes whole tentacles would come off and we'd have to stop to glue them back on again.

For the underwater shots, a two-foot-long model squid was used, along with a corresponding scaled miniature submarine. (In the scene where the squid first attacks the *Nautilus,* the model squid was positioned with its tentacles wrapped around the rudder and then pulled off. When the film was reversed, it looked as if the squid were approaching and then grabbing the submarine.) It would appear that the inclusion of a giant squid is a sure road to an Oscar; like *Reap the Wild Wind,* this film won an Academy Award for best special effects.

Because the giant squid is still inadequately known, most of the discussions of this creature have been either fantasies about its attacking ships and dragging people from the shrouds or detailed scientific descriptions of the carcasses that have washed ashore. There have been few attempts to speculate on its abundance (assuming there is a single species) or its habits. In his 1933 discussion of *A. clarkei,* G. C. Robson of the British Museum of Natural History included a section he called "General Characteristics and Presumed Mode of Life of the Group" in which he notes that the fins are small in relation to the total size of the body; the locking apparatus of the funnel mechanism is weak; the suckers are small and feeble; and the lateral and dorsal membranes of the arms are poorly developed when compared to other species. (Other teuthologists have commented on the predatory inadequacies of *Architeuthis*—see pp. 146–48—but Robson was probably the first to try to extrapolate a "way of life" for the animal, based on his observations of its structure.) He believed the giant squid was ill equipped to hunt large prey; it was probably an inactive scavenger, lurking close to the bottom and waiting for invertebrates and carrion to come its way.

In contrast, Peter Benchley imagined his "beast" as a powerful, vengeful hunter and despite all evidence to the contrary made it 100 feet long. In the novel, various scientists and fishermen try to lure the killer squid to their boat so that they can dispatch it, and they attract it by using a dummy squid armed with hundreds of stainless-steel hooks and emitting what a scientist describes as "a spoor that will travel for miles. . . . One of its kind is ready for breeding, and it will be a call of nature that the beast won't be able to resist." This device fails to capture the beast, but it does make him very angry, and he responds by displaying a range of emotions that few, if any, invertebrates have ever been accused of demonstrating before:

> Its chemistry was agitated, and its colors changed many times as its senses struggled to decipher conflicting messages. First there had been the irresistible impulse to breed, then perplexity when it had tried to mate and been unable to; then confusion when the alien thing had continued to emit breeding spoor; then anxiety as it had tried to shed the thing and could not, for the thing had attached itself like a parasite; then rage as it had perceived a threat from the thing and proceeded, with its tentacles and beak, to destroy the threatener.

*H*ungry? Try Nissin Noodles," says the announcer in a Japanese television commercial in which a *giant* giant squid is shown chasing prehistoric hunters on the beach. The commercial was the Grand Prize Winner at the Cannes International Advertising Festival in 1993.

In fiction, a giant squid can be 100 feet long; it can weigh a dozen tons; it can have hooks on its tentacles; and it can even feel anxiety. Real ones are not so cooperative in revealing anything but their gross morphology—and then so inadequately that we still don't know how many species there are, where they live (we only know where they die), what they eat, how they breed, how big they get, or whether they are aggressive hunters or passive eaters of carrion.

Regardless of how little we know about it, the frightening appearance of the kraken has encouraged people throughout the ages, from Pliny the Elder to Peter Benchley, to speculate on its nature, often in exaggerated, terrifying, and repulsive terms. For example, here is Frank Bullen introducing the giant squid in a compilation of fact and fantasy he entitled *Denizens of the Deep:*

> He does not pursue his prey; he waits like some unimaginable spider in the centre of his web of far reaching tentacles, with his huge eyes piercing the surrounding sepia-stained waters until a quiver from one of the outly-

ing arms sets the abyssal mouth agape, the mighty parrot-like mandibles clashing as the struggling victim is conveyed inwards.

In 1992, Arthur C. Clarke wrote an article for *Omni* magazine entitled "Squid! A Noble Creature Defended." Clarke doesn't so much defend the squid as discuss his literary affiliations with it, and he opens the article by announcing that he had just heard Peter Benchley promoting his *Beast* on the radio and then writing, "Good for you, Peter—but why did it take you so long? After all, it's a pretty obvious idea. *I* should know." Evidently, the producers of *Jaws* had asked Clarke to write the screenplay for *Jaws 2*, but he countered with an outline for a story in which *Architeuthis* would be the protagonist. He based this proposal on a short story he had written in 1965 called "The Shining Ones." In the *Omni* article, he wrote, "I couldn't resist calling it [the screenplay] *Tentacles*," although I realized that this would provoke lewd sniggers at the box office." (Clarke was right about the "lewd sniggers"; see pp. 278–80 for a discussion of the real *Tentacles*.)

Clarke's literary involvement with *Architeuthis* began in his 1953 novel *Childhood's End*. It is a story of alien "Overlords" that oversee the end of the world, a subject that one might assume has very little to do with giant squid. But even here we can see the beginning of his fascination with this creature, as he has two of the characters prepare a tableau for the "museum" of the Overlords. Although it sounds as if it ought to be a description of a real undersea encounter, it is actually a description of a diorama:

> The long, saw-toothed lower jaw of the whale was gaping wide, preparing to fasten upon its prey. The creature's head was almost concealed beneath the writhing network of white, pulpy arms with which the giant squid was fighting desperately for life. Livid sucker-marks, twenty centimeters or more in diameter, had mottled the whale's skin where those arms had fastened. One tentacle was already a truncated stump, and there could be no doubt as to the ultimate outcome of the battle. When the two greatest beasts on earth engaged in combat, the whale was always the winner. For all the vast strength of its forest of tentacles, the squid's only hope lay in escaping before that patiently grinding jaw had sawn it to pieces. Its great expressionless eyes, half a meter across, stared at its destroyer—though, in all probability, neither creature could see the other in the darkness of the abyss.

"The Shining Ones" is a remarkable story containing technological and teuthological elements that would not actually be discovered for many years to come. Briefly, it concerns an underwater engineering consultant who is summoned by the Russians to repair a mammoth hydrothermal generator that has somehow been damaged at a depth of five hundred fathoms off Sri Lanka. The engineer, a Swiss named Klaus Muller, descends in his minisub and sees that a great chunk of the heating element has been ripped away. He repairs the damage, surfaces, and reports that he can think of nothing that could possibly have wreaked such havoc with the grid, which resembles a gigantic automobile radiator. On his next dive, however, he spots two 20-foot giant squid, obviously too small to have damaged the grid. As he watches them, however, he realizes that they are flashing their photophores in recognizable patterns. First he sees a flashing pattern that resembles his submarine, and then they create patterns that look like squid. He grasps that *the squids were talking to each other* (Clarke's italics).* They then flash a "picture" that Muller recognizes as an enormous squid, and he says, "My God! They feel they can't handle me. They've gone to fetch Big Brother." The story is written as a transcript of a tape recording, and it ends with Muller's words: " 'Joe! You were right about Melville! The thing is absolutely gigan—' "

The quotation from Herman Melville that "Joe" alluded to in "The Shining Ones" is as follows: "A vast pulpy mass, furlongs in length, of a glancing cream-colour, lay floating in the water, innumerable long arms radiating from its centre, curling and twisting like a nest of anacondas, as if blindly to catch at any hapless object within reach." It appears again in Clarke's story called "Big Game Hunt." In "The Shining Ones," Clarke defines a furlong, which is, in fact, an eighth of a mile, somewhat large for giant squid as we know them, but he writes that Melville "was a man who met sperm whales every day, groping for a unit of length to describe something a lot bigger . . . so he automatically jumped from fathoms to furlongs."

"Big Game Hunt" is only a six-page story. It concerns a biologist who has devised a method for electrically affecting the behavior of various invertebrates, so he goes to sea to try his device on our old friend *Architeuthis*—here called *Bathyteuthis* by Clarke. It works. The squid is summoned to the surface by electrical impulses, and they even film the "monstrous beast that no human being had ever before seen under such ideal conditions." Unfortunately, the squid is more powerful than the device, and a blown fuse results. As soon as the squid realizes that it is "its own master," it reacts violently, and although the end of the story is largely left to the reader's imag-

---

*Giant squid do not have photophores and therefore cannot flash messages to each other with lights. But all squids—*Architeuthis* included—can change color rapidly, and it is now believed that these color changes are employed, among other functions, for purposes of communication.

ination, we have to assume that the film and the professor were victims of a very angry, very large squid.

Clarke's love affair with *Architeuthis* continues in *The Deep Range,* but for some reason he refers to the animal as "*Bathyteuthis maximus,*"* although he certainly knew its proper scientific name. Set in the future, when men are farming whales for profit, this novel concerns one of the whale rangers who discovers that sperm-whale casualties are unusually high in a particular sector. (One whale, found badly mauled and dead at the surface, was covered with sucker marks six inches in diameter.) The scientists and rangers realize that the only creature capable of inflicting such damage on a sperm whale is a giant squid that they suggest "may be a hundred and fifty feet long." But instead of merely killing the monster, they decide to capture him. Using a light-studded submarine as a lure, they descend to a depth of six hundred fathoms:

> A forest was walking across the sea bed—a forest of writhing, serpentine trunks. The great squid froze for a moment as if impaled by the searchlights; probably it could see them, though they were invisible to human eyes. Then it gathered up its tentacles with incredible swiftness, folding itself into a compact, streamlined mass—and shot straight upward toward the sub under the full power of its own jet propulsion.

They manage to implant a sonar beacon in the mantle of the giant squid—nicknamed "Percy"—so they can return to capture him. They have been offered $50,000 by Marineland for the delivery of a healthy giant squid ("a giant squid would be the biggest attraction Marineland ever had"), and they plan to use the money to further their research. (At this point in the story, Clarke quotes the entire giant-squid passage from *Moby-Dick.*) Percy measures "a hundred and thirty feet from his flukes to the tips of his feelers," and they manage to anesthetize him with narcotic bombs, which enable them to bring him to the surface, draped like a limp dishrag over one of the subs. They install him in a specially built pen, and the first giant squid ever brought to the surface is now in captivity:

> First it swam slowly from end to end of the rectangular concrete box, exploring the sides with its tentacles. Then the two immense palps started to climb into the air, waving towards the breathless watchers gathered around the edge of the dock. They touched the electrified netting—and

---

Bathyteuthis means "deep-water squid," from the Greek *bathos* for "deep," and while this might be a nice name for a giant that lives at great depths, the name, as the taxonomists say, is "preoccupied" by a genus of small, chubby little squids that reach a maximum length of about a foot.

flicked away with a speed that almost eluded the eye. Twice again Percy
repeated the experiment before he had convinced himself that there was
no way out in this direction, all the while staring up at the puny spectators
with a gaze that seemed to betoken an intelligence every whit as great as
theirs.

Would that Clarke had followed up on Percy's captivity. Did they get
him to Marineland? What did they feed him? Did he live happily ever
after? Unfortunately, *The Deep Range* abandons Percy in his pen and goes
on to the conclusion of the story, in which the leader of the Buddhist world
wants to eliminate whale farming altogether and the man who actually captured Percy has to contend with bigger issues than a squid in a concrete box.
But in 1992, at the conclusion of his *Omni* article, Clarke hopes that Benchley's *Beast* "does not trigger another ocean pogrom, aimed at the giant
squid." (Clarke holds Benchley responsible for the massive destruction of
white sharks following the publication of *Jaws*.)

Clarke's giant squid are a far cry from the malevolent monsters envisioned by Jules Verne, H. G. Wells, and Peter Benchley. The animal he calls
Bathyteuthis in one story is larger than anyone else's giant squid (even
Benchley's "beast" is only 100 feet long), but instead of attacking and eating
people, it only wants to be left alone in the depths to light up and avoid
sperm whales. Even though the only specimens we have seen outside of
fantasy have been dead or dying and have given no clue as to their normal
behavior, Clarke persists in his ardent admiration. He writes, "This century
has seen a complete transformation in our attitude towards other animals,
including many once considered implacably hostile. . . . The giant squid is
almost certainly a highly intelligent animal; given the opportunity, it might
be as playful as its cousin—that charming mollusk, the octopus." Then
again, it might not.

ON OCTOBER 31, 1983, road workers near Stinson Beach, north of
San Francisco, spotted an "unidentified animal" swimming offshore. As
reported in the San Francisco *Chronicle*, the animal was being followed by a
flock of birds and about two dozen sea lions. One of the workers interviewed said, "There were three bends, like humps, and they rose straight
up. Then the head came up to look around." On November 2, surfers
reported a "sea-serpent" near Costa Mesa, which they described as resembling "a long black eel." One of the surfers (quoted in the Costa Mesa *Daily
Pilot*) said, "There were no dorsal fins. The skin texture wasn't the same as
a whale, and when it broke water, it wasn't like a whale at all. I didn't see the

head or the tail." From this sketchy information (first appearing in the ISC *Newsletter* and then in a Time-Life book called *Mysterious Creatures*) it is difficult to form an opinion about the nature of this beast—assuming it was the same in both cases—but it is not unreasonable to visualize the elements that were described as being parts of a large squid. And recently giant squid have been documented off the California coast.

While most known specimens—particularly those from the prime sources, Norway and Newfoundland—have been collected dead or dying on the beach, there is only one recorded stranding on the entire Alaskan, Vancouver, Washington, Oregon, California, or Mexican coast, and that appears to be an anecdotal record. Hochberg and Fields (1980) wrote, "Recently, a specimen of *Architeuthis japonica* was found washed ashore on a beach in Oregon." Further evidence that *Architeuthis* exists in the eastern North Pacific is manifest in the occasional appearance of its mandibles in the stomachs of sperm whales caught in California waters (Fiscus and Rice, 1974), but more specimens have begun to appear, suggesting that this region might be quite densely populated with giant squid whose existence was heretofore unsuspected. In 1980, 150 miles off the coast of Southern California, an oceanographic sampling trawl was brought up with a twelve-foot section of a giant squid tentacle attached. According to Robison (1989): "The tentacle had been wrenched from a living squid; the tissue was still elastic, the suckers contracted and gripped when they were touched, and the chromatophores contracted when rubbed." The squid lost its tentacle at between five hundred and six hundred meters, and since it could only have become entangled when the trawl was open—and since we know that depth—we have a faint clue about the depth range of the giant squid. As the author says, however, "The present data set is based on only a portion of a single *Architeuthis,* and it should not be extrapolated to represent whole body composition or species-wide depth habits. Unfortunately, much of what we know about this genus is based on such bits and pieces."

Perhaps the shroud of mystery is lifting. In a study published in 1985, Soviet (now Russian) teuthologists Nesis, Amelekhina, Boltachev, and Shevtsov described a whole new crop of *Architeuthis* specimens that had been collected by "large-scale variable-depth trawlers, capable of capturing giant squid and verifying evidence as to the location and depth of the habitat." The first of these was captured in September 1976 by the Spanish trawler *Yeyo* in South African waters at a depth of 375 meters (1,230 feet). (It was described in a 1978 paper by Spanish teuthologists Pérez-Gándaras and Guerra.) In 1980 and 1981, G. A. Shevtsov collected squid of various species from the Soviet research vessel *Novoulianosk* in the North Pacific. The largest specimen was found in the open ocean, some fifteen hundred miles off Oregon, at a depth of only fifteen meters (about fifty feet) in water that was almost three miles deep. The mantle was 5.33 feet in length. The *Novoulianosk* collected an astonishing eighteen more specimens, in late March and early April 1980, some 250 miles off Los Angeles. Although they were considerably smaller than the monsters found in Newfoundland, Norway, or New Zealand—the mantles averaged only 2 feet in length— they were genuine giant squid of the heretofore gigantic (and formidable) genus *Architeuthis*.

In the southeastern Atlantic, A. P. Boltachev captured two more specimens. Working in waters some four hundred meters deep off Zaire, the research vessel *Novoukrania* collected a giant squid at a depth of about four hundred meters, but the body was separated from the tentacles during the unloading process and fell overboard, leaving only the tentacles, which measured some 13 feet in length. A couple of months later, *Novoukrania*, now farther south off Namibia, presented Boltachev with another *Architeuthis*, this one complete and measuring 14.46 feet in total length. Nesis, Amelekhina, Boltachev, and Shevtsov analyzed the existing data and for the first time have been able to ascribe a distribution pattern to *Architeuthis*.

The Russian scientists consider *Architeuthis* a "subtropical animal" that spawns and spends the first stages of its life in warmer waters and migrates in adolescence to feed in richer, colder waters near the polar fronts or where there are significant upwellings. With the advent of accurately calibrated mid-water trawling devices, the vertical distribution of *Architeuthis* can now be postulated; of course, the more specimens that are examined, the more we are able to learn about the life-style and distribution of this heretofore enigmatic creature. "It is conjectured," wrote Nesis and his colleagues, "that their youth is spent at depths of 100–300 meters, whereas the adults live in mid-water and at the bottom, from 100–200 to approximately 500 meters. . . . At least during the warm part of the day, they seem to inhabit the epi- and mesopelagic zones, from subsurface levels to depths of at least 500–600 meters and probably deeper." The larger specimens—those with a mantle length of 3 to 5 meters—have been found only at the extreme boundaries of their known range, in the cold waters off Newfoundland, New Zealand, and Norway, but "the absolute majority of known types of *Architeuthis* had a mantle length of not more than 2–2.5 meters," suggesting that the mature individuals inhabit colder waters. (In those cases where the sex could be determined, the larger specimens were usually females.)

Even with an abundance (relatively speaking) of new material, the Russians do not resolve the problem of how many species of giant squid there are. They wrote, "More than a century of research concerning giant squid has thus not established with any certainty the number of species, not to mention any differences between species." There might be one species in each of the three isolated regions, for example, *Architeuthis dux* in the North Atlantic, *A. martensi* in the North Pacific, and *A. sanctipauli* in the Southern Hemisphere. Or they might all be considered subspecies of *A. dux,* and therefore *A. dux martensi* and *A. dux sanctipauli.* But since so many of the specimens were small and possibly immature, we cannot discuss the taxonomy of the group with any degree of certainty. It is also possible that there is a pygmy or dwarf version, exemplified by the miniature, mature male with a mantle length of 7 inches, recovered from the stomach of a swordfish in Florida waters in 1978 (Toll and Hess, 1981).

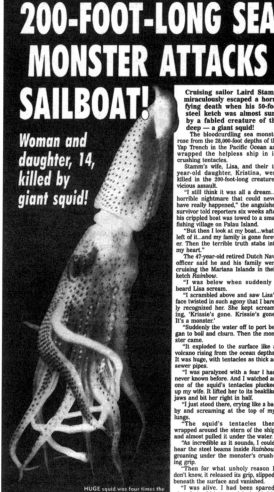

*I*n the tabloids, the giant squid continues to pose a threat to sailors. The picture, however, shows the 6-inch-long *Histioteuthis.*

200-FOOT-LONG SEA MONSTER ATTACKS SAILBOAT!

Woman and daughter, 14, killed by giant squid!

Cruising sailor Laird Stamm miraculously escaped a horrifying death when his 50-foot steel ketch was almost sunk by a fabled creature of the deep — a giant squid!

The bloodcurdling sea monster rose from the 28,000-foot depths of the Yap Trench in the Pacific Ocean and wrapped the helpless ship in its crushing tentacles.

Stamm's wife, Lisa, and their 14-year-old daughter, Kristina, were killed in the 200-foot-long creature's vicious assault.

"I still think it was all a dream...a horrible nightmare that could never have really happened," the anguished survivor told reporters six weeks after his crippled boat was towed to a small fishing village on Palau Island.

"But then I look at my boat...what's left of it...and my family is gone forever. Then the terrible truth stabs into my heart."

The 47-year-old retired Dutch Navy officer said he and his family were cruising the Mariana Islands in their ketch *Rainbow.*

"I was below when suddenly I heard Lisa scream.

"I scrambled above and saw Lisa's face twisted in such agony that I barely recognized her. She kept screaming, 'Krissie's gone. Krissie's gone. It's a monster.'

"Suddenly the water off to port began to boil and churn. Then the monster came.

"It exploded to the surface like a volcano rising from the ocean depths. It was huge, with tentacles as thick as sewer pipes.

"I was paralyzed with a fear I had never known before. And I watched as one of the squid's tentacles plucked up my wife. It lifted her to its beaklike jaws and bit her right in half.

"I just stood there, crying like a baby and screaming at the top of my lungs.

"The squid's tentacles then wrapped around the stern of the ship and almost pulled it under the water.

"As incredible as it sounds, I could hear the steel beams inside *Rainbow* groaning under the monster's crushing grip.

"Then for what unholy reason I don't know, it released its grip, slipped beneath the surface and vanished.

"I was alive. I had been spared when I should have perished with Li-

HUGE squid was four times the size of the Stamms' ketch.

* * *

OF THE MONSTERS in this book, the cephalopods still retain almost all of their mystery. They exist in great profusion and variety, and we think we have a pretty good idea of their habits and maximum sizes. But still, almost out of the range and scope of field research, at depths we can only imagine, there might be squid or octopuses greater than those we know. (There are surely species remaining to be discovered.) It is difficult enough to envision a giant squid 55 feet long, and given the traditional reluctance of these animals to show themselves, who can say that no larger ones remain undiscovered? All we can state with certainty about the maximum size is that none larger than 55 feet long has ever washed ashore. Moreover, the presence of smaller, mature individuals casts the whole issue of *Architeuthis*-as-monster into question. Even with the new information and the new hypotheses, the giant squid continues to be a giant enigma. In her keynote address to the American Institute of Biological Sciences in February 1991, Sylvia Earle said:

> And what of that never-never creature, that squid of all squids, *Architeuthis dux*, the giant squid? There are many sea stories, numerous possible glimpses, and fragments of animals taken from the stomachs of sperm whales or washed up on various beaches. But no one has recorded certain, direct observations of these creatures in their own realm. It would not be likely that an animal eighteen meters long would escape notice in any terrestrial habitat on land, but it has been possible thus far for giant squids to elude even highly motivated ocean scientists.

And *Architeuthis* has indeed eluded marine zoologists, ocean scientists of every stripe, and even underwater filmmakers. Outside of re-creations in the movies, no one has ever seen a healthy giant squid. Even those spotted struggling with sperm whales at the surface were probably more than a little debilitated by the crushing jaws of the cachalot. Many of the sea's heretofore hidden monsters have been tracked to their subaqueous lairs; cinematographers chased the great white shark around the world until 1971, when Peter Gimbel finally nailed one off South Australia. The sperm whale itself was first filmed under water off Sri Lanka in 1984, and Victor Hugo notwithstanding, when the habitat of the giant Pacific octopus was revealed, divers were eager to enter the world of a cephalopod with a 20-foot arm span. But the giant squid remains tantalizingly out of range. A film of one (or more) of these 60-footers, propelling itself (at whatever speed it affects) through the murky deep, remains the last uncaptured image.

THE BIOLOGY OF
SQUID, GIANT AND
OTHERWISE

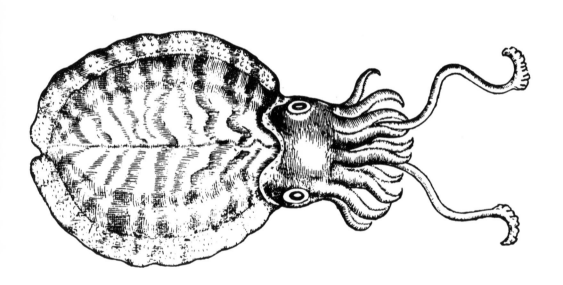

*I*N A BOOK about monsters, we expect to find revelations about large, intimidating animals, real or imaginary. For information on the biology of the "real" animals—whales, sharks, octopuses, and manatees—we can look to their relatives, or even to themselves, since most of our "monsters" have been shown to be living, breathing creatures. (For the imaginary creatures, like the sea serpents, the Loch Ness monster, or the 200-foot-long octopus, we are perforce limited to speculation or fiction.) In recent years, scientists have discovered that squids—usually the California squid, *Loligo opalescens;* the Eastern squid, *Illex illecebrosus;* or the most accessible of all, *Loligo pealei*—make excellent laboratory subjects; therefore, we can learn a great deal about the biology and biomechanics of these fascinating creatures by observing them in captivity. But even though the giant squid shares many characteristics with its smaller relatives, it is not simply a larger version of the smaller species. It is a subject unto itself, still keeping its secrets hidden from prying eyes by its mysterious habits and impenetrable habitat. Even so, we cannot discuss the radula or the tentacular clubs of *Architeuthis* without establishing some sort of a teuthological framework; before we can understand how the giant squid works, we must have some background information on its smaller, better-known relatives. (It is no more accurate to compare the information garnered from the study of an 8-inch *Loligo* to the 60-foot *Architeuthis* than it would be to equate a mouse with a hippopotamus on the grounds that both of them are mammals, but because we obviously cannot study *Architeuthis* in captivity and since most of the specimens we have seen have been dead or dying, we must make these comparisons—even if some of them are forced or perhaps totally inapplicable.)

*P*ortrait of the Caribbean reef squid, *Sepioteuthis sepioidea*

Squids* come in a dazzling array of sizes and shapes; some are equipped with claws, hooks, suckers, giant axons, eyes as complex as those of the "higher" vertebrates, beaks like parrots, or a bioluminescent ability unmatched in the animal kingdom. Some are tough and muscular, while others are as flabby as jellyfish. Some species can soar through the air; others can descend to abyssal depths. Some live in uncountable congregations; others are solitary hunters, prowling the abyssal depths in search of food. They are the most numerous and varied of all the cephalopods, officially classified as mollusks, even though their shell (known as the *gladius*, or "pen") is found inside the body. In the smaller species, the pen is less than half an inch long, while in *Architeuthis* it can be 4 feet in length. (The familiar chalky material used in bird cages is the pen of the cuttlefish.) The size range for the various squids is enormous, ranging from the tiny *Idiosepia* (smaller than its name printed here) to the giant squid, the largest of all

---

* "It should be noted," wrote W. C. Summers, "that squid is both singular and plural. The language allows gatherers (hunters and fishermen) the option to refer to any number of the same sort by the singular term—squid. Where one species is concerned and there is a large-scale operation, we have no trouble with the exception—squid is plural. But the option is based on the perception of the reporter and how narrow a distinction that person wishes to make. *Squids* implies a collection of more than one kind, though it should be considered that the apparent plural may refer to species, numbers of one species, or even sizes (if these have a different market value). Scientific literature in English will usually reserve the plural term squids for multiple species; both words are used for several examples of the same species."

invertebrates. There are many species under a foot in length, a few between 1 and 10 feet (*Dosidicus* reaches a total length of 12 feet, including tentacles), and several species not quite as large as *Architeuthis* but also considered giants.

Although smaller than *Architeuthis*, there is a teuthid known as the "Pacific giant squid" (*Moroteuthis robusta*) that has been reported from the West Coast of North America. As far as we know, its range is limited to the North Pacific, and according to the 1989 study by Fiscus, Rice, and Wolman, it is the most common species of squid in the diets of sperm whales taken off the coast of California. (There must be something about ammonium that appeals to sperm whales, since *Moroteuthis*—like *Architeuthis*—has ammonium ions in its tissues, which makes it inedible to humans but attractive to sperm whales.) *Moroteuthis* has also been recorded in trawls and beachings from Alaska to Oregon and California. A. G. Smith published a list of the specimens recorded from Alaska and California from 1872 to 1963 and wrote that "one Alaskan specimen was probably well over 14 feet long when alive." (The Japanese version, *M. japonica*, is believed to grow even larger.) The Pacific giant squid also differs from *Architeuthis* in that it *does* have hooks on its tentacular clubs.

Although many squid species have been examined, we have no idea how many more remain to be discovered, and there are still many others that are known from only a few examples. (Roper, Young, and Voss identified twenty-five distinct families of the order Teuthoidea.) In his 1966 "Review of the Systematics and Ecology of Oceanic Squids," Malcolm R. Clarke identified 181 species and wrote, "Work on oceanic squids . . . hovers between the basic data gathering and the revision stages. While a large number of species have been described, revisionists have been struggling to clarify the taxonomic situation for well over half a century. The taxonomic tangle prevents any but the most limited analysis of the ecological data. . . ."

All squid have ten arms, which makes them decapods (as contrasted with octopuses, which are octopods), but the arrangement and proportion of the arms differs from species to species. In most squids, there are eight shorter arms and two longer tentacles, but some (such as *Chiroteuthis*) have six arms of varying length, two heavier, longer arms, and two tentacles that are as much as ten times as long as the body. For most species, the tentacles have developed into long, slender appendages with expanded, clublike ends, but in some cases the tentacles are the same length as the arms, differentiated only by the flattened manus at the end. In some species there are lateral expansions, or "swimming keels," on the outer surface of the third pair of arms, while in others the arms are joined by a web. Although the pattern varies, species are identifiable by the arrangement of the suckers on the arms and the tentacles, some of which have retractable claws and most of which are equipped with toothed rings. The arms have suckers for their entire length, but the tentacles have suckers only on the flattened ends.

Squid catch their prey by shooting out their tentacles, which can be partially retracted into a pouch when not in use. They draw the victim in toward the center of the circle of arms, where the powerful, parrotlike beak and radula are located. Most species of squid are equipped with paired poison glands that release powerful neurotoxins as a prey animal is bitten. They are extremely efficient predators, and from hatching onward, they can capture and consume a variety of prey, often of their own size or even larger.

The eight arms are thicker than the tentacles and are equipped with a double row of suckers that decrease in size toward the tips. (Because of the location of the mouth, the inner, sucker-bearing surface of the arm is referred to as the *oral* surface; the outer side, the *aboral*.) The tentacles are positioned between the third and fourth arms, known as the ventrolateral and ventral arms. (The other two pairs are the dorsal and dorsolateral.) In cross section, the tentacles are round, while the arms are roughly triangular, with the suckers on the flattened oral surface. In some teuthids—*Architeuthis*, for example—the arms and tentacles are equipped with a "locking apparatus" consisting of tubercles and suckers that fit together like snaps, allowing the tentacles to be held tightly together when extended. J. B. Phillips (1933) characterizes this apparatus as "enabling the hooked clubs to be brought into play as though man had adhesive organs on the inner surface of his wrists, allowing his hands and fingers full play." The tentacles are longer and much smaller in circumference at the base than the arms and function like a pair of tongs or pliers, grabbing the prey and pulling it into the crown of arms, where it is then transferred to the mouth. Unlike those of the octopods, the suckers of squid are on stalks and can be moved independently.

All the suckers on the arms and the tentacles are equipped with a ring of chitinous "teeth" that help the squid keep a grip on its often slippery prey. (It is these "teeth" on the suckers of the larger squid that leave the circular scars on the skin of sperm whales.) In the popular literature, from *Twenty Thousand Leagues Under the Sea* to *Beast*, the tentacles of the squid are used like those of an octopus; that is, they twine around the prey—usually luckless sailors—and often constrict, like a python. It seems more likely that the muscular arms are used to grapple with prey items and that the tentacles entrap the prey and transfer it to the arms, which in turn bring it to the mouth. The beak of the squid is located at the center of the corona of arms

*T*he formidable teeth on the suckers of *Dosidicus gigas*. Alex Kerstitch, who took this photograph, was attacked by one of these terrifying animals while diving in the Sea of Cortez.

and consists of an upper and lower mandible, set into a muscular configuration known as the "buccal mass." Using the buccal musculature, the squid can rotate and protrude its beak. The beak is hard, but unlike a parrot's beak, the lower mandible is larger than the upper, and the upper fits inside the lower. (In the film *20,000 Leagues Under the Sea,* the giant squid's beak is shown upside down.) Inside the mouth, there is a rasping tongue, known as the radula, the surface of which is covered with minute, backward-pointing teeth, which help move the food down the gullet and grind it down. The teeth of the radula are different enough that they can be used for species identification.

A squid moves through the water—in whatever direction it chooses—by various forms of "jet propulsion." By ejecting water from its mantle cavity and by shooting water from its funnel, the squid can move either head- or tailward. The funnel is a short, hoselike organ that projects from the mantle below the head and can be rotated in any direction. (The animal's head is that part that extends from the mantle, on which the eyes are located and from which the arms and tentacles radiate.) Squids maneuver by a combination of funnel jet and fins. There is no "forward" or "backward" for the squid (anatomically, the tail is the anterior, but functionally,

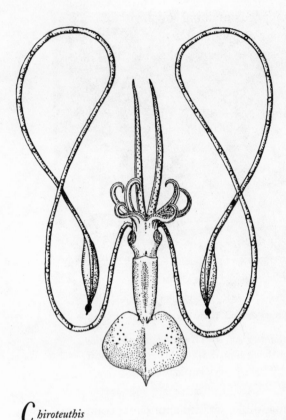

C hiroteuthis

the tail is the posterior), but disdaining such confusing terrestrial distinctions, it can move powerfully through the water in whichever direction is most convenient.

All squid have a pair of fins at the tail end of the mantle that are used for steering or slow locomotion; when a squid jets backward, the fins act as rudders. In some genera, such as *Dosidicus* and *Ommastrephes*, these fins are large and powerful, indicating that the squid uses them for propulsion. In many others, however, the fins are relatively small, which would suggest that these species depend on other forms of power. (*Architeuthis* has very small fins for its size.) Although it looks as if it ought to be a horizontal animal, the natural attitude for a squid at rest is at an angle, usually about forty-five degrees, with the tentacles pointing down.

In 1931, Paul Bartsch, then curator of marine invertebrates at the Smithsonian, wrote: "Inch for inch, the squids will compete in swimming power with any other creature that lives in the sea." More recently, at Dalhousie University in Halifax, Nova Scotia, Ron O'Dor has been studying the smaller squid and has come up with some remarkable observations. O'Dor refers to the squid as "invertebrate athletes" and "the elite cadre of the most athletic class of molluscs." In a 1989 study (with R. E. Shadwick) called "Squid, the Olympian Cephalopods," O'Dor wrote that "the inherent inefficiency of jet propulsion . . . forced squid to develop their remarkable athletic prowess. Squid not only migrate actively over thousands of kilometers, but their power outputs and oxygen consumptions are higher than anything else in the sea." Squids are drag racers compared to fishes, which cannot accelerate as fast but can sustain a pace for a much longer time. Inhaling also moves more water over the gills, enabling the squid to extract oxygen from the water more effectively than fishes. To transport oxygen, squid blood uses the copper-containing pigment hemocyanin rather than the hemoglobin used by vertebrates, but it is less viscous and therefore easier to pump. (Hemocyanin means "blue blood," and oxygenated squid blood has a bluish cast.)

In squid, as in all cephalopods, the circulatory system is enhanced by the presence of two branchial hearts that contract rhythmically to force blood into the two gills, which are attached to the inner wall of the mantle by a thin membrane. The blood goes to the branchial hearts through the gills to the ventricle heart and then to the body. Breathing consists of "inhaling" water into the mantle cavity, where the gills extract the oxygen, and then passing the water out through the funnel. The oxygen content of the water in which they live is very important to cephalopods; if it is low, they quickly lose their strength, become flaccid, and die.

Squid specialize in a high reproductive rate and a short life cycle, as contrasted with fishes, which typically have long-lived adults that invest only as much in reproduction as they can afford while ensuring their own survival. (In almost all squid species, death follows breeding.) Although there is no hard data to support such an assumption, some teuthologists believe that *Architeuthis* grows quickly and lives only a short time. If the giant squid is not an apex predator, it must pass rapidly through the stages where it could be easily consumed by other predators. Clyde Roper, who believes that the giant squid is not a powerful swimmer, is quoted (in Abrahamson, 1992) as saying, "The more rapidly you can grow, the quicker you can reduce the number and kinds of other animals that can prey on you. With its growth rate, by the time it reaches adolescence, it is already too large to be eaten by anything other than toothed whales." In a 1990 study, Arnold and O'Dor point out that oceanic squid probably develop to swimming forms faster than any other complex animal; in laboratory-raised *Abraliopsis,* the time from fertilization to free swimming was sixty-eight hours.

Bartsch wrote that "the mollusca rank of all invertebrate life in complexity of organization and intelligence, as they certainly do in size, ferocity, and speed of movement." Clams and oysters do not have prominent eyes (scallops do), but the eyes of the cephalopods are among their most remarkable organs. Squid have huge optic lobes for the processing of information. The biological principle of convergence, where similar characteristics have evolved in totally dissimilar animals, is marvelously demonstrated by comparing the eye of the squid and that of the higher vertebrates. Both have an eyelid (although there are some species of squid that do not); behind the cornea in both cases there is a chamber filled with aqueous humor that contains a pupil that can expand or contract; both have an iris diaphragm and a lens set in a muscular ring. The eyes of vertebrates and teuthids have dark pigments that act as light screens, and both have fibrous coats to retain the eye's shape. Squid retinas, like those of humans, have rods and cones, suggesting that they see detail—and possibly even color. Except for those species with eyes on stalks, the squid's eyes are not binocular; each one sees what is on its side of the head.*

When a squid is simply "looking around," its pupil is U-shaped, with an adjustable flap in the middle of the "U." In low light, the pupil expands almost to a filled circle, but when it wants to see forward and backward, the "U" becomes exaggerated, narrowing at the base and widening at the ends, essentially creating two pupils in each eye. It is therefore possible for a squid to see forward and backward with each eye simultaneously. "Whereas the human eye has a point of focus on the retina," wrote Harry Thurston (in an article about Fred Aldrich), "the squid eye has an equatorial band where it is able to focus, thus making the squid's vision, theoretically, twice as good as a human's."

In addition to their highly developed eyes, all cephalopods are equipped with light-sensitive organs, known as "extraocular photoreceptors," that enable them to respond to ambient light in the water, even at depths where very little light penetrates. The actual function of these photoreceptors is not clear, but since they are found in all octopuses and all squids, they must be a part of the animals' modus operandi. Richard Young of the University of Hawaii has studied these photosensitive vesicles in various cephalopod species, from the deep-water squid *Bathyteuthis* to the mysterious *Vampyroteuthis infernalis,* an ink-black, soft-bodied creature that is not exactly a squid and not exactly an octopus. Hardly anything about *Vampyroteuthis* conforms to the cephalopod norm—if there is one—and its photoreceptors are designed to read its own bioluminescence, in what Young suggests is a device to respond to the glowing of the prey it is consuming, to ensure that the vampire squid does not emit any light that would attract predators. (See pp. 284–86 for a discussion of the "vampire squid from Hell.")

In the other teuthids, the light-sensitive photoreceptors, usually located near the optic lobe, transmit information to the brain via the optic nerves. Translucent "windows" in the skin enable the dorsal and ventral surface receptors to "see" daylight from above or luminescent organisms—

---

*Some of the deep-water species have their eyes on stalks; some have eyes with built-in lights; and in some, the right one is completely different from the left. In the genera *Histioteuthis* and *Calliteuthis*, individuals have a relatively gigantic left eye and a right eye that is only a quarter as large. To date, no one has come up with an explanation for this development, although the larger eye might be used for seeing in reduced light.

including themselves—from below, in order to adjust their own luminescence accordingly. In his discussion of these receptors, Kir Nesis (1987) has written:

> There is no doubt that the functions of the light-sensitive vesicles in cephalopods are diverse and probably differ in different species, but it is most probable that their main function is to give the animal an idea of the general level of illumination in the surrounding water and of long-term changes (seasonal, for example) of illumination.

Throughout the course of their evolution, squid have developed various adaptations to enable them to compete with fishes. "There are too many things that fish do well that squid either do poorly or cannot do at all," wrote O'Dor and Webber. "On the other hand, there appear to be some things that squid can do better." The squids devote a greater portion of their body weight to the nervous system than any other cold-blooded vertebrate (approaching some reptiles in that regard), and the neural control of the circulatory system probably accounts for the incredible athletic feats they can perform. The large and complex brains of some cephalopods enable them to control a process that fish lack entirely: the direct nervous control of color and pattern. Squid use color for defense, and they have evolved a pattern-based "language" that affects their social organization. ("One certainly has the impression," wrote O'Dor and Webber, "that there is more going on than a simple random association of equal individuals as is found in most squid schools.") They also use arm signals. The most common gesture is the upraised middle arms, which can be translated as "go away."

In *Kingdom of the Octopus,* Frank Lane wrote, "Cephalopods are not generally considered to be colorful animals. It is therefore all the more surprising to find that they surpass even the famed chameleon in the speed and variety of their color changes." The skin of most species is equipped with a dense field of round, elastic-walled cells known as chromatophores that can be expanded or contracted all at once or in sequence, producing a dazzling variety of spots, stripes, or most spectacularly, a moving wash or ripple of changing hues. The individual pigment cells come in various colors, including red, orange, yellow, brown, and black. Squids can also match their color to their background if necessary, but whereas it might take a fish hours to perform such a feat, a squid can do it instantly.

Squid employ their ability to change color in a variety of ways. Their primary defense mechanism is flight, but they can also camouflage themselves to blend in with their environment. They can be light-colored in shallow water or in bright sunlight; darker in deep water or at night. If this defense does not work, an individual will flee, but this flight may also be accompanied by a lightning-fast color shift. Another defense mechanism is "dymantic behavior," which involves rapid change of what Roger Hanlon prefers to call "body patterns" (as opposed to "color change") in order to bluff, frighten, or startle the predator. If the squid can interrupt the normal attack sequence of a predator—even for a millisecond—it might be able to gain enough time to make its escape. (Because of its extraordinarily efficient neurological capabilities, the squid can react much faster than any fish.) In this process, a squid might change color several times, adopt a pattern of prominent eye spots or stripes, or even alter its texture by erecting bumps or nodules on its skin.

Since squid have no mechanisms for making sounds, it is assumed that communication among individuals and groups is conducted—at least in part—by color or pattern changing. Perhaps the most unusual use of changing body patterns is in the sex display of the males. In competition for the attention of a female, males will run through a repertoire of color changes that are exclusive to males—"dueling" with color for the hand(s) of a mate. The female also uses body patterns to signal her choice or perhaps to induce more flashing by the competing males.

Many species of squid are also equipped with light-producing organs known as photophores. These are "special photogenic cells, often equipped with a reflector that can point the light in one direction, redirect it to an area remote from the source, or spread it out over a surface. Sometimes the light passes through filters that change the wavelength of the emitted light, and sometimes it escapes through half-silvered tubes to increase its angle of emission. These devices can impart a variety of effects, from an overall dull glow or a bright woolly, ethereal effect, to sharp pinpoints of light or a torch-like beam" (Clarke, 1988). Among the primary uses of the photophores is counterillumination. To prevent a predator from picking out the squid silhouetted against a sunlit surface, it can illuminate its underside, effectively "downlighting" itself and eliminating its shadow. (Some species can also emit a cloud of luminescent bacteria as a flashing pseudomorph, designed to seriously confuse a potential predator.)

Depending on the species, the photophores can range in size from tiny pinpoints of light to a glowing disc the size of a quarter. Sometimes the photophores are simple structures, but in other cases they are almost unbelievably complex. (There are more than fifty different kinds of photophores.) According to Frank Lane, "Some have reflector mechanisms, pigment cups, lenses, mirrors, and color screens," and there is at least one species (*Histioteuthis*) that has mirrored searchlights. Photophores appear

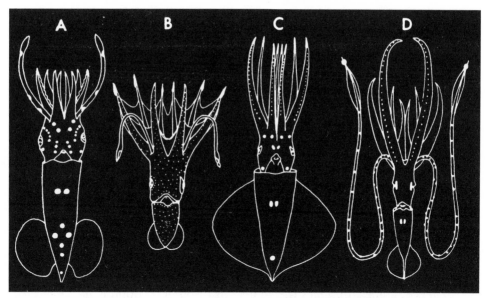

in every imaginable location, sometimes distributed all over the mantle and arms, sometimes
appearing only on the ends of the tentacles.
Some species have eyes that light up, and in
the transparent squid *Megalocranchia*, the photophores are on the liver. There are other species

*V*arious squid species showing
the different arrangement of
photophores, shown as white
dots. A: *Pterigioteuthis*,
B: *Histioteuthis*, C: *Octopoteuthis*,
D: *Chiroteuthis*

in which the eyes, gonads, and ink sacs are equipped with light organs. It
has been suggested that since these organs obviously cannot be transparent,
they have photophores that they can coordinate with the downwelling
light, which eliminates the shadows and contributes to the squid's overall
transparency.

Animals with lights are truly extraordinary. On the *Valdivia* expedition
in 1899, the German teuthologist Carl Chun (who published some of the
most important and comprehensive studies of squid ever written, including
the first description of *Vampyroteuthis*) was observing some individuals of
the small squid *Lycoteuthis diadema* in a container on deck:

> Among the marvels of coloration which the animals of the deep sea
> exhibited to us nothing can be even distantly compared with the hues of
> these organs. One would think that the body was adorned with a diadem
> of brilliant gems. The middle organs of the eyes shone with ultramarine
> blue, the lateral ones with a pearly sheen. Those towards the front of the
> lower surface of the body gave off a ruby-red light, while those behind
> were snow-white or pearly, except the median one, which was sky-blue. It
> was indeed a glorious spectacle.

However, as with so many aspects of teuthid biology, luminescence is still poorly understood. In a 1977 essay on this subject, Peter J. Herring of the Institute of Oceanographic Services in Surrey, England, wrote:

So much of the information on luminescence in cephalopods and fish is still purely anatomical, and so bewildering in its variety, that functional interpretations almost certainly err on the side of conservatism, an inevitable consequence of our restricted concepts of our understanding of the normal lives of these remarkable animals. Any purpose that is fulfilled by colour or pattern in the illuminated terrestrial or coastal environment can also be achieved by luminescence in the dark of the deep sea. The cephalopod inhabitants of this environment almost certainly make far more extensive and varied use of their impressive luminescent abilities than we can presently envisage.

In any discussion of these wonderful strategies, the question of "intelligence" comes up. Does the squid run through its options in the face of a particular predator, or is it pure reflex? Certainly the squid has a most sophisticated analysis system, which enables it to assess the size, speed, and type of predator and produce the appropriate response within fractions of a second. With its giant nerve axons, squid can react faster than most other animals, and its rapid-fire neurological responses enable it to dart through the water, often in such erratic patterns (called "protean behavior") that a predator cannot focus on an individual or predict where it might be next. In his 1990 study of the intelligence and evolution of squid, John Arnold wrote, "There is a vast literature on the behavior and learning ability of the cephalopods and with the possible exception of the primitive and seemingly unintelligent Nautilus, all cephalopods tested have displayed some level of intelligent behavior. . . . This is not surprising, since their brain size in relation to body weight is higher than most fishes and ranks mid-way among the birds and mammals." Of the Caribbean reef squid (*Sepioteuthis sepioidea*), Moynihan and Rodaniche wrote,

Reef squid and other cephalopods are forced to make choices constantly. . . . The elegant experimental studies of the brains of *Octopus vulgaris* and *Sepia officinalis* have been focused upon decision-making, usually the decision between attacking and not attacking a possible prey, a crab or a shrimp, under controlled conditions in the laboratory. Doubtless the experimental animals take this problem seriously, especially when mistakes are negatively enforced by electric shocks. Yet for most cephalopods . . . selection of prey is neither the most frequent nor the most difficult of problems with which they must attempt to cope under natural conditions in the wild. . . . Sometimes the choices seem to be calculated on deliberate and rational grounds. Rational or not, they must be crucial to the survival of individuals and the species.

One of the most remarkable athletic feats of some squids is their ability to take to the air. This is most often done to escape from predators that cannot leave the aquatic environment and probably do not expect their prey to disappear suddenly. They do not actually fly, of course, but like some of the "flying" fishes, they are able to build up enough speed under water to escape the restrictions of their native element and launch themselves through the air. Some observers have noted that a squid in flight ejects water from its siphon, which would liken it to a rocket in the air. Many sailors have been surprised to find squid on their decks in the morning, but there have been occasions when this seemingly contradictory behavior has been observed in daylight. When Thor Heyerdahl and his companions were sailing the *Kon-Tiki* across the Pacific in 1947, they first thought that squid had come on deck by climbing aboard the raft, but when they found one on the thatched roof of the deckhouse, they began to wonder. Finally, the mystery was solved:

> One sunny morning we all saw a glittering shoal of something which shot out of the water and flew through the air like large rain drops, while the sea boiled with pursuing dolphins. At first we took it for a shoal of flying fish, for we had already had three different kinds of these on board. But when they came near, and some of them sailed over the raft at a height of four or five feet, one ran straight into Bengt's chest and fell slap on deck. It was a small squid. Our astonishment was great.*

As if flying squid were not unusual enough, there is another characteristic of their aerial behavior that is almost as unusual as the flight itself: Whereas flying fish leap out of the water and glide more or less as individuals, squid fly in formation, entering and leaving the water in unison. There have not—thank God—been any reports of flying *giant* squid, but *Dosidicus*, a 10-foot-long hunk of armed muscle that can weigh over 200 pounds, has been known to leap out of the water. In 1964, off the coast of Chile,

---

*Their astonishment would have been lessened if they had read Thomas Beale on the subject. In 1835, he wrote, "I have myself seen, very frequently while in the north and south Pacific, tens of thousands of these animals dart simultaneously out of the water when pursued by albacore, or dolphins, and propel themselves *head first,* in a horizontal direction for eighty or a hundred yards, assisting their progression, probably, by a rotary or *screwing* motion of their arms and tentacles, and which they have the power of thus moving with singular velocity."

D. L. Gilbert shot a movie of a 4-foot *Dosidicus* becoming airborne. Stills from the film are reproduced in his 1970 paper (with K. S. Cole) on "Jet Propulsion in Squid."

The examination of stranded specimens of *Architeuthis* has provided some of the requisite anatomic data; otherwise, very little is known about the reproduction of giant squids. Most of our information—with the exception of the description of the physical elements—has been taken from accounts of other, more accessible species and should therefore be considered conjectural for *Architeuthis*. Mature male squids (and octopuses) have one or more of their arms modified to form a hectocotylus,* a sex organ used to transfer spermatophores (long tubes filled with sperm) to the female. Males, which can be easily differentiated from females by these two arms with flattened tips and no suckers, store the spermatophores in an organ known as Needham's sac (because it was discovered by John Needham) and then, using their specialized arms, transfer them to the oviduct of the female, where they can be stored alive, sometimes for months, until they are needed in the spawning process. The spermatophores of *Architeuthis* are tightly coiled and between 4 and 8 inches long, which seems more than large enough, but the Pacific octopus (*Octopus dofleini*) has spermatophores that may measure nearly 4 *feet* in length when unrolled.

Architeuthis is probably a solitary animal, but there has to be a time, however fleeting, when two of them get together. As with most aspects of the biology of the giant squid, we can only speculate on what transpires at those times, but there are some smaller species of squid whose mating activities have been closely observed. Off the coast of Southern California in the spring, the market squid, *Loligo opalescens,* gathers for its annual spawning and mating rituals. In recent years, diving into and filming the mating frenzy of the squid has become a popular activity, so there is no shortage of images, still and moving, of mating squid. They congregate in enormous numbers: "We were in the middle of an almost solid layer," wrote Cousteau and Diolé, describing their dive, "several yards thick, of writhing squirming

---

* The word *hectocotylus*, which means "a hundred suckers" (*hecto* = hundred, *cotyla* = cup), has a fascinating history. In 1829, Baron Cuvier examined several argonauts (primitive octopuses also known as paper nautiluses because of their fragile shell) and found what he believed to be a parasitic worm. Because the worm *resembled* the arm of a cephalopod, he called it *Hectocotylus*. It was not until 1853 that the German zoologist Heinrich Müller recognized that this "worm" was the sex organ of the tiny male argonaut—which breaks off after fertilization. The male himself is only an inch long compared to the females' 18-inch bulk (including tentacles), and he consists almost entirely of reproductive organs; he has no heart, does not eat or breathe, and is often carried around in the shell of the female. Thus, hectocotylus and its adverbial form hectocotylized have come to describe the specially adapted arms of all cephalopods.

creatures who darted to and fro by expelling water from their funnels, like a vast fleet of miniature jets."

As observed and described by Arnold (1990a), the mating behavior of *Loligo peali* goes like this:

> Before copulation . . . the male swims beside and slightly below his poten-
> tial mate and flashes his chromatophores. He grasps the female from
> slightly below about the mid-mantle region and positions himself so that
> his arms are close to the opening of her mantle. He then reaches into his
> mantle with his hectocotylus and picks up several spermatophores from
> his penis. In one quick motion, the spermatophores are ejaculated and
> cemented to the inside of the mantle near the opening of the oviduct or
> upon it. The male then releases the female and they return to paired
> swimming.

Fertilization of the eggs is the trigger for their being laid, and depending on the species, the egg masses are deposited in various forms. Some
oceanic squids shed their eggs directly into the ocean, surrounded by only a
thin layer of egg jelly, and the eggs float individually in midwater. In other
species, the females attach the egg cases to the ocean floor with an adhesive
stalk. Many species lay eggs that number in the millions. The Cousteau
team described the clusters of egg cases as "looking like dahlias." (In other
species, such as the common European squid *Loligo vulgaris,* so many eggs
are laid that the egg mass looks not unlike the head of a mop. In the eighteenth century, a certain Professor Bohadsch laboriously counted the eggs
in a single *L. vulgaris* egg mass at 39,766.) After the frenzied copulation and
egg laying, the squid are substantially weakened, and those that do not die
outright are easy prey for the sea lions, sharks, and dolphins that hungrily
attend the annual spawning. While many invertebrates pass through a larval stage, squids hatch as miniature adults, capable of escaping and feeding.
While the egg masses are distasteful to most animals and therefore not subject to predation, the embryonic squid certainly are and provide sustenance
for any animal that can catch them.

Giant squid must perform a more cumbersome version of the mating
death dance of *Loligo,* but we must strain our imaginations to conjure up a
picture of two of these apparitions locked in a spectacular embrace in
which, if the animals were to face each other, the tail fins of the female
would be sixty feet from those of her mate. (If we are to judge by the observations of the smaller species, all the tentacles are not interwoven, and all
but a few pairs of arms are curled back, allowing for the uncomplicated
transfer of the spermatophores by the hectocotylus.) Do they flush an

unseen crimson in the blackness of the abyss? Are some of the dead or dying giants that have washed ashore casualties of this titanic battle of the sexes?

A 1988 article on squids by Malcolm Clarke opens with these words: "To many biologists the squid conjures up a vision of an unusually large nerve fibre with graphs issuing from one end while electrodes are applied to the other." (Some neurobiologists refer to the squid as "a support system for the axons.") The "unusually large nerve fibre" is another wonder of squid biology, for it can be 0.1 inch in diameter, as compared with the largest human axon, which is 0.001 inch. The size of these giant axons enables the squid to transmit messages to its muscles substantially faster than any other creature; therefore, the squid's ability to respond to a particular stimulus can be almost instantaneous. That can be seen in the speed which which some species can turn or attack. (One of the advantages of having no forward or reverse gear is that squid can change direction without turning around.) For human neurological research, these giant axons are much easier to study than those of most other animals, and almost all we have learned in recent years about nervous conduction is from research on *Loligo peali.*

In the entire world of invertebrates, only the cephalopods have what might be referred to as a brain. It actually consists of a concentration of nerve ganglia, and it is enclosed in a cartilaginous "skull." The brain encircles the squid's esophagus and lies between the eyes. Although only a few species of squid have been examined in detail, many have been observed to have sensory papillae near the eyes, which may function as organs of taste. (Smell and taste are the same in the water.) Some even have sensory cells all over their bodies that are thought to be sensitive to changes in temperature. Because of their more sedentary nature, octopuses do far better in captivity than squid, so much more work has been done in testing their capabilities (see pp. 287–88), but if we could figure out what questions to ask and how to ask them, we might find the squid the intellectual equal of its eight-armed relative.

As the German (now Texas) zoologist Bernd-Ulrich Budelmann has put it, "Whereas other stimuli, such as odor, taste, light, and sound, may change or even be absent during periods of time, the gravitational field has a unique feature: during the life span of an organism, it is constant in magnitude and direction." Although we rarely think about it, we (and all other vertebrates) have developed a sophisticated system of orientation to keep us aware of our position in three-dimensional space. In mammals the equilibrium system consists of the vestibular apparatus of the inner ear, but cephalopods, having no ears, inner or outer, have had to develop an alternative system. In the octopus, cuttlefish, and squid, the equilibrium receptor system consists of fluid-filled vesicles called statocysts that have calcareous particles called statoliths suspended within them. The paired statocysts are embedded in the cartilaginous brain capsule and orient the animal with regard to gravity and movement, providing the mysterious sense we call balance.

In many areas, the cephalopods have developed characteristics that enable them to compete with the bony fishes: Advanced locomotion (i.e., jet propulsion), efficient energy consumption, and superior vision are among these. Their ability to change color instantly is a defensive adaptation that may be more effective than flight and is certainly superior to the slow camouflage technique of fishes such as flounders. In some species of cephalopods, the statocyst system closely resembles the inner ear and lateral line system of the bony fishes,* and the statoliths of the octopus and squid correspond to the otoliths of fishes.

Although we have come a long way from what Jacques Cousteau called "The Silent World" in 1953, we still do not automatically associate the undersea environment with noise. (For cetaceans, particularly the odontocetes, sound is the primary means of navigation, communication, prey location, and even prey debilitation. [See pp. 247–50 for a discussion of the sperm whale's reliance on sound.]) There are fishes that make noises, shrimp that snap their claws, and even some squids that have been recorded making crunching noises while eating. But do the cephalopods, with no known structures for hearing, respond to sound? And if so, with what?

In 1985, Martin Moynihan wrote an article for the *American Naturalist* entitled "Why Are Cephalopods Deaf?" in which he suggested that "it might be an adaptation to cope with, or adjust to, odontocete attacks." Because they are susceptible to the "bombing" of toothed whales, deafness might have been selected as a way of avoiding the whales' predation. He also writes that they probably don't need hearing as a protective device because their vision is so good and therefore "the animals are effectively deaf." Moynihan concludes his article with "The argument presented here may or may not be convincing," and it certainly did not convince Roger Hanlon and Bernd-Ulrich Budelmann.

In a 1987 issue of the same journal, they wrote "Why Cephalopods Are

---

*It has recently been shown that some cephalopods also have a "lateral line" system. Examining parallel lines of epidermal cells in embryonic cuttlefish, Budelmann, Riese, and Bleckmann (1991) wrote, "We have now demonstrated that these lines of cells serve to detect small water movements and thus are a further example of convergent evolution between a sophisticated cephalopod and a vertebrate sensory system."

Probably Not 'Deaf,' " in which they said, "Surprisingly, Moynihan did not consider the available morphological and physiological data." Among these data: Blind octopuses have been observed to respond to vibrations caused by tapping on a tank, and in one set of experiments, when a hidden experimenter knocked on a tank containing small squids, they instantly changed color and jetted backward. Hatchling squids, examined under scanning electron microscopes, were observed to have ciliated cells on the head and mantle, and a 1963 study of the common octopus by Maturana and Sperling showed that the statocysts contain hair cells that are sensitive to low-frequency vibrations.

To justify the existence of an auditory capability, Hanlon and Budelmann postulated the ecological necessity for such a system:

> Much predation by cephalopods occurs at night or in mesopelagic or bathypelagic zones, where light is greatly limited or lacking. Many cephalopods also live in murky water. Vision, therefore, is a restricted resource that may not allow detection of a fast-moving predator until it is too late. Hearing is a far better distance receptor, and it does not depend greatly on the time of day, depth (i.e., light intensity), or water clarity. It seems likely from an evolutionary standpoint that, rather than being deaf, cephalopods have developed a sensory system for underwater wave perception that is not only capable of detecting the approach of prey items or predators at such distances that appropriate behavioral responses can be implemented. . . .

According to Hanlon and Budelmann, "Hearing is nearly impossible to define for aquatic animals, because sound and vibrational stimuli are essentially equivalent in an aquatic medium," so until more detailed information on the hearing capabilities of octopuses and squid appears, we can assume that they are not deaf. In 1990, Packard, Karlsen, and Sand wrote that "cephalopods seem to be well equipped for detection of water-borne vibrations. Ciliated sensory cells that look like mechanoreceptors have been found in epidermal lines on the head and arms of squids and cuttlefish, and Budelmann and Bleckmann (1988) have recently demonstrated that local water movements evoke microphonic potentials in the head lines of these animals." They also wrote, "In the infrasound [low-frequency] range, cephalopods can hear quite well."

Even though squid are active and voracious predators, they also serve as prey for almost every vertebrate animal in the sea. Ranging in size from the sperm whale, the largest predatory animal in history, at a known maximum length of 60 feet, to any fishes large enough to capture the smaller varieties of squid, the predators depend on the squid populations for the basis of their diet. Included in the list of squid predators—which would also include almost every fish in the sea—are dolphins, porpoises, seals (especially the deep-diving elephant seals, which seem to feed almost exclusively on squid), sea lions, sharks, and other squid. Some species are known to cannibalize their own kind, and there is no question that a larger, more powerful species will prey upon a smaller one. Because they are difficult to capture—they easily evade most nets—we do not have much of a sense of their numbers, but collectively, they must be among the most numerous animals in the world.

Despite the mystery attending the giant squid, its lesser relatives play an important role in the study of human physiology. The smaller squid, such as the foot-long *Loligo*, have comparatively huge nerve fibers, which are extremely important in neurological studies. In 1909, L. W. Williams of Harvard University noted the size of these fibers, but he did not recognize their potential for human studies. He wrote, "The very size of the nerve processes had prevented their discovery, since it is well-nigh impossible to believe that such a large structure can be a nerve fiber." (The fiber of *Loligo* can be about the size of a small pencil lead, and that of *Architeuthis* has been shown to be even larger than that.) It was in 1933 that J. Z. Young rediscovered the giant nerve fibers in *Loligo* and revolutionized the study of neurophysiology. For the squid, larger fibers translate into faster conduction of impulses, accounting for the meteoric reaction time of the smaller species and also their rapid-fire color changes, but these axons are also critical to humans. In *Scientific American* in 1951, H. B. Steinbach wrote:

> All man's thoughts and actions, his neuroses and psychoses, depend upon the functioning of the nervous system. Fundamental advances in treating nervous disorders and in understanding normal functions will depend upon what we can find out about the processes that occur within a few thousandths of a second in the confines of the axone membrane. Thus squid are important to human welfare. Their nerves may eventually tell us a great deal about our behavior.

ALTHOUGH *Architeuthis* remains a giant enigma, there is another teuthid that would appear to embody all of its most terrifying—if not apocryphal—aspects on a somewhat smaller scale. One of the earliest references to the "giant" squid of the Pacific appears in William Beebe's *Arcturus Adventure*, published in 1926. The *Arcturus*, a research vessel sponsored by the New York Zoological Society, was sailing down the west coast of South America, with a seventeen-member scientific staff in attendance. As the ship cruised the Humboldt Current off Peru, observers sitting on the fantail one evening spotted a large ghostly shape rising from the depths and assumed it was a shark. When it shot right out of the water, "his wriggling tentacles seeming to reach for the row of legs that dangled from the ladder," they realized it was a squid:

> He was different from the other lesser squids, not only in size and shape, but in color, being a pale pinkish tan, wholly unlike what any of the others could achieve by whatsoever combination of their chromatophores. Hardly had we gasped out our joy, when in exactly the same spot he appeared again, and went through the same maneuvers, springing from the water as though propelled by a submarine cannon. . . . None of us will ever forget the spectacle of that long, torpedo body shooting out of the froth of the rip, the snaky, outreaching arms beaded with big vacuum cups, and above all, the huge disks of eyes which glowed like silver plates in the tan flesh.

In 1940, also off the coast of Peru, a group of big-game fishermen had the opportunity to observe *Dosidicus gigas,* known as the jumbo or Humboldt squid. As reported in the *National Geographic* by author/photographer David Duncan, they were fishing at night, and the water was phosphorescent:

> Even as we watched, meteorlike streaks of light shot in from all sides; the blackness below glimmered. Then the very foundation of the ocean seemed to burst in the blinding flash of a terrific, but soundless explosion. . . .
> Every scrap thrown overside sank from sight accompanied by a trailing streamer of fire, and no sooner did the most insignificant morsel fall sparkling through the water than legions of squid rushed in from all directions to pounce upon it. Small wonder that the place was so feared by the native fishermen. Suppose a man should fall overboard!
> Only then did we realize how grotesque and truly fearsome were these creatures we had been fighting. The first squid caught on rod and reel was a terrible thing. Stretched on the stern of the boat, it measured nearly 9 feet in length and weighed more than 100 pounds. One end supported ten armlike tentacles which were frightening to behold.
> Nested at the apex of these tentacles was a glistening beak, against the slashing attack of which few living things could survive. As if not suffi-

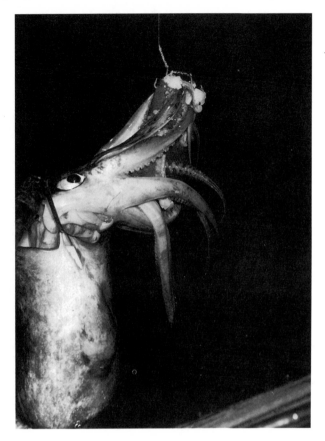

$\mathcal{F}$ishermen of the 1940 Lerner Expedition to the Humboldt Current off Peru intended to catch swordfish and marlin, but they found an added attraction in the jumbo squid, *Dosidicus gigas*. Here a 6-foot squid has grabbed a chunk of bait with its tentacles and been brought to the surface and gaffed.

ciently ghastly, the creature was endowed with two baleful, unblinking eyes, laterally placed behind the head.

When Thor Heyerdahl and his crew were preparing to sail *Kon-Tiki* across the Pacific in 1947, they asked the editors of the *National Geographic* what they ought to look out for, and obviously based on the article quoted above, this is what they were told:

The National Geographic Society in Washington had shown us reports and dramatic magnesium photographs from an area in the Humboldt Current where monstrous octopuses had their favorite resort and came up to the surface at night. They were so voracious that if one of them fastened on to a piece of meat and remained on the hook, another came and began to eat its captured kinsman. They had arms which could make an end of a big shark and set ugly marks on great whales and a devilish beak like an eagle's hidden among their tentacles. We were reminded that they

*S*pearfishing off the coast of Chile in 1967, Argentine champion skindiver Ricardo Mandojana shot an aggressive Humboldt squid (*Dosidicus gigas*).

A diver confronts and photographs the Humboldt squid off the coast of Baja California. These powerful creatures can reach a length of 10 feet and weigh over 200 pounds.

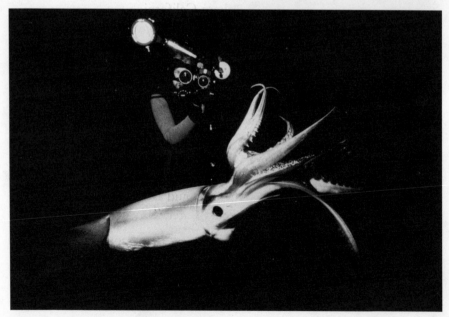

lay floating in the darkness with phosphorescent eyes, and that their arms were long enough to feel about in every small corner of the raft, if they did not care to come right on board.*

The Humboldt squid is an extremely gregarious creature, and there is one record of *thousands* of them washing up on the beach at Talcahuano Bay, Chile. But because *Architeuthis* usually appears singly—at least on the beach—we assume that it is a solitary predator, not a pack hunter. According to Gilbert Voss (who believed that *Architeuthis* is a weak creature), it is the heavily muscled *Dosidicus* that is the true terror of the seas: "Possible near relatives would be the smaller giant squids of the Humboldt Current, which attain a length of 8–12 feet and 150 pounds. Their bullet-shaped bodies are heavy and strong, with powerful jet funnels and large fins. Their arms and tentacles are massive and strong and with their beaks they can bite oars and boat hooks in two and eat giant tunas to the bone in minutes."

For reasons that may go forever unexplained, in July 1976, California inshore waters were graced by an invasion of what the Los Angeles *Times* called "Mating Giant Japanese Squid." They weren't mating; they weren't Japanese; and while they weren't actually giants, they were certainly large: They ranged in length from 22 inches to 6 feet. The invaders were Humboldt squid, usually found off Peru and Chile. (The species has been reported from the west coast of southern South America, Queensland, New Zealand, and Baja California.) Southern California squid fishermen, used to catching the foot-long "market squid" (*Loligo opalescens*), had a field day with what they called "jumbo squid." In *Oceans* magazine in 1977, Karen Straus wrote that "*Dosidicus* was first sighted off the coast of California thirty-five years ago. The run lasted four consecutive years, with the largest masses appearing during the summer nights."

In fact, the first reported runs of *Dosidicus* in California waters was in 1934–35, but the first specimens were only 2–2.5 feet long and weighed about 5 pounds. By 1937, however, 20-pounders had begun to appear, much to the consternation of local fishermen. The squid ripped the baits from the hooks of albacore trollers, and worse, when a squid is hooked, "it proceeds to shower boat and fishermen with ink and water, and then delights in biting

---

*Obviously, Heyerdahl et al. took some liberties with the information given to them by the *National Geographic*. Humboldt *squid* (not octopuses) are probably not given to feeling about in rafts—or climbing aboard, for that matter. In the film of these animals shot by Howard Hall in the Sea of Cortez, *Dosidicus* can be seen grabbing small fishes by enveloping them in its arms and then swimming away with its broad tail fins undulating.

its captor with its parrot-like beak. Several fishermen have been seriously bitten this year" (Croker, 1937).

When cinematographer Howard Hall was filming in the Sea of Cortez in 1991, he decided to dive at night to see if he could film the Humboldt squid that the fishermen said sometimes followed a hooked fish to the surface. ("Not a good idea," said one of the Mexican fishermen.) As a 14-foot thresher shark was being reeled in, Hall, hanging about thirty feet down, noticed flashing lights—"rapid-fire strobes going off about five times a second"—and then saw the squid ascending. They were 5 feet long and "flashing from bright red to ivory white." As Hall watched, they dashed in and attacked the shark, a 4-foot needlefish, and then Hall's fellow photographer, Alex Kerstitch. Hall wrote:

> Alex was behind me in the darkness. He had no movie lights to ward off the squid. A group ascended from the depths below, frenzied by the smell of blood in the water. Three large squid grabbed Alex at the same time. Suddenly, he felt himself rushing backward and down. A tentacle reached around his neck and ripped off his pre-Columbian gold pendant and chain, tearing the skin on his neck. Another squid ripped his decompression computer off his pressure gauge. Tentacles tore his dive light from his wrist and his collection bag off his waist. Then, as suddenly as they had grabbed him, the squid were gone.

When Kerstitch came back on board the dive boat, he went directly to bed. In an article in the magazine *Baja Explorer,* Kerstitch wrote, "As I fell asleep, I thought about the squid's icy tentacles wrapped around my head and understood Victor Hugo's description of the squid's close relative, the octopus, as a nightmarish sea-vampire: '. . . The tiger can only devour you; the octopus inhales you; to be eaten alive is terrible, to be drunk alive is inexpressible.' "

LEVIATHAN, OR,
THE WHALE

*O*NE OF THE FIRST adventurers we know by name who actually encountered the threatening fauna of the ocean was St. Brendan, an Irish cleric who lived during the sixth century A.D. His story—which Samuel Eliot Morison insists is true but "enhanced by the Celtic imagination"—details the adventures of an intrepid Irishman and eighteen other monks who sailed in a curragh from Ireland across the ocean, landing on a black treeless island along the way. As described in the *Navigatio Sancti Brendanis Abbatis:*

> At last they went upon an island weening to them that they had been safe, and made thereon a fire for to dress their dinner, but S. Brandon abode still in the ship, and when the fire was right hot and the meat nigh sodden, then this island began to move, whereof the monks were afeard, and fled anon to ship and left the fire and meat behind them, and marvelled sore of the moving. And S. Brandon comforted them and said it was a great fish named Jasconius, which laboreth night and day to put his tail in his mouth, but for greatness he may not.

Later on the voyage, Brendan and his crew were threatened by an enormous monster that was dispatched by an even larger one that Brendan had summoned up through prayer, reminding God of the manner in which He had saved Jonah. Some seven years later, Brendan landed again on the whale, but according to Morison, this time he instructed his crew to light no fires, and they "enjoyed a cold picnic on board Jasconius the whale, who considerately returned the iron pot in which they had started to cook a meal years before."

If the very body of the ocean presented a fearsome aspect, with its dark, roiling waters, its threatening visage, and its intimidating vistas, its occupants were the quintessence of terror. The landlubbers' only contact with the large creatures of the sea was at best sporadic and often completely incomprehensible. Imagine the response of the first aboriginals who encountered a dead sperm whale washed up on the beach.* The cachalot is like no other animal on earth, not only because of its vast size (a full-grown bull can be 60 feet long and weigh as many tons) but also because it is constructed so strangely that the term *sui generis* seems to have been coined with *Physeter macrocephalus* in mind.

Whereas the more familiar terrestrial mammals have teeth in both jaws, the sperm whale has a set of ivory pegs only in its lower jaw. This jaw, a narrow, pincerlike affair, seems poorly designed to do any sort of eating as we understand the term. Then there is the nose, a titanic organ with a single, S-shaped nostril that may be 20 feet long—the largest nose in the animal kingdom, past or present. Cut open this proboscis and you find, in addition to a bewildering array of tubes, sacs, and other unfamiliar nasal elements, a reservoir of clear amber oil that, to this day, has defied interpretation.

A GREAT, DARK, wrinkled carcass has washed ashore, and the observers are baffled. It looks like no other animal on earth and suggests nothing less than an ocean populated by other, even more frightening monsters. (Of course, the ocean *is* populated by other, even larger "monsters," but the sperm whale, with its mysterious habit of stranding on shallow beaches, was probably responsible for many of the legends and myths of sea monsters— at least until men ventured out onto the ocean and saw for themselves.) And if a single sperm whale was cause for such consternation, what would those early whale watchers have made of a whole herd of cachalots thrashing and blowing in the shallows, all eventually to expire?

In a 1959 study of sperm-whale strandings, Raymond Gilmore listed the more spectacular events in this long and mysterious history. In 1723, seventeen whales came ashore at the mouth of the Elbe River in Germany, and in 1784, thirty-one washed up on the shores of Brittany. Across the Atlantic in 1888, residents of Cape Canaveral, Florida, saw sixteen sperm whales on their beaches, and in 1911, thirty-seven of these bluff-headed

---

* It was one of these aboriginals—or perhaps a Neolithic European—whose anatomic confusion was probably responsible for the sperm whale's unusual name in English. (In other languages, the problem was neatly avoided by giving the animal a name—*potvisch* in Dutch; *pottwal* in German—that refers only to the bulbous aspect of its nose; or, utilizing the Basque name *cachalote*, resulting in the Spanish and French *cachalot*, and even the Russian *kashalot*.) The oil in the whale's nose was thought to be the whale's seminal fluid (admittedly in a somewhat unusual location); thus *spermaceti*, or "seed of the whale." Yankee whalers sometimes referred to their prey as the "spermacetty" whale, eventually shortened to "sperm whale."

monsters appeared on a beach in Tasmania. In 1954, in the little fishing village of La Paz, Baja California, twenty-two cachalots washed ashore and died. The coasts of New Zealand are particularly attractive to sperm whales in trouble, and these islands have the dubious distinction of hosting the largest sperm-whale strandings on record: fifty-nine animals in 1970 and an incredible seventy-two in 1974. In 1979, fifty-six animals surfaced at Rancho San Bruno, again in Baja California, and later that year, another forty-one stranded at Florence, Oregon.*

Three Beached Whales, a 1577 engraving by the Dutch artist Jan Wierix. While these are obviously sperm whales, they have been drawn with two blowholes. There are at least nine more whales in the surf waiting to strand.

Single sperm whales have been known to strand all over the world, but they seem to have a particular affinity for the coast of the Netherlands. In 1992, a book called *Op het strand gesmeten: Vijf eeuwen potvisstrandigen aan de Nederlandse kust* (Thrown on the beach: Five centuries of sperm whale strandings on the Netherlands coast) was published listing fifty-five strandings from 1255 to 1990. (The four strandings from 1255 to 1334 are docu-

---

*The post-1959 information comes from Peter Bryant's 1979 discussion "The Baja Sperm Whale Mass-Stranding."

*E*laborately costumed gentlefolk visit a stranded whale at Katwijk in Holland in 1598. Not even the dogs want to get too close.

mented in various medieval manuscripts, and the actual records begin in 1402.) Many of the Dutch strandings were documented by contemporaneous drawings and etchings, so the records leave no doubt as to the species. The British coasts are also a favored spot for sperm whales to come ashore, but the records are not quite as comprehensive or as well illustrated as those of the Dutch. Nevertheless, Sheldrick's synopsis of British stranding records shows that a total of twenty-three sperm whales washed ashore on the coasts of England, Ireland, Scotland, and Wales during the sixty-four years from 1913 to 1977.

At one time or another, almost every sort of cetacean has fetched up on the beach. The largest of them—indeed, the largest animal ever to have lived on earth—is the blue whale, which, while not a common strander, has come ashore.* One of the first blue whales ever seen stranded was at the Firth of Forth in Scotland, where it was described by Sir Robert Sibbald in 1692. So influential was Sibbald's description of the animal that came to be

---

*Although the blue whale has long held the title of "largest animal ever to have lived on earth," recent discoveries are producing pretenders to that throne. In the 1970s in Colorado, bones of two gigantic sauropod dinosaurs (named *Supersaurus* and *Ultrasaurus*) were found, and in 1986, the bones of an even larger dinosaur were found in New Mexico: *Seismosaurus* may have exceeded 100 feet in length, and while it would not have been as heavy because of its long neck and tail, it might have been longer than any blue whale.

known as *Balaenoptera musculus* that for a long time it was known as "Sib-bald's rorqual," or even *Sibbaldus sulfureus.*

In 1827 a 95-foot blue whale was found floating in the sea off Ostend, Holland. (Until 1831, Belgium was part of the Netherlands.) In Ostend it was reduced to its articulated skeletal components, and its journey began. For the next seven years, the "Ostend Whale" made the rounds of England, France, and Holland. It was one of the most popular attractions of the day, and numerous descriptions and illustrations have survived. (At a length of 95 feet it had to have been a blue whale; no other living animal in the world is that large.) "To whatever species the individual specimen in question belongs," wrote William Dewhurst, "it is doubtless the largest animal that has ever been captured, and I do not hesitate to say that the skeleton is the most perfect in Europe."

Throughout the world, other whale carcasses were placed on exhibition, further enhancing the image of the whale as gigantic monster. In 1838, under the dual sponsorship of Oxford and Cambridge universities, the skeleton of a blue whale that had been found off Plymouth was trucked through England in a caravan of carriages. In the accompanying broadside, it was described as "the biggest born, hugest of all living creatures. . . ." A fin whale had washed ashore near the Swedish city of Malmö in 1866, and when it was exhibited in Stockholm, the mouth was propped open so wide that spectators could wander in and out. In British Columbia in 1835, the Pacific Whaling Company toured a 55-foot, 66-ton fin whale on a railroad flatcar, calling it "A Mystery of This Age" and a "Playmate of Dinosaurs and Mastodons, Last of a Race of Towering Giants."

Because such gigantic blue whales were being killed in the Antarctic by the turn of the century, museums competed to exhibit a model of this species—as long as they had the space to house an object that was nearly a hundred feet long.* Early in the twentieth century, the American Museum of Natural History in New York erected a full-sized model of a blue whale, fabricated of wood, iron pipe, chicken-wire lath, and plaster of paris. The British Museum of Natural History responded with a plaster-covered whale with wooden "ribs," like a ship. The Smithsonian Institution in Washington added a life-sized blue-whale model to its exhibit of ocean mammals in 1964, and in 1968 the American Museum updated its exhibit

---

*It is easy to measure a whale; you just stretch a tape from the tip of the rostrum to the tip of the tail. According to Gerald Wood's *Guinness Book of Animal Facts and Feats*, the longest blue whale was a female that measured 110 feet 2.5 inches and was taken off South Georgia in the Antarctic. Weighing such a creature is somewhat more difficult, since few scales are calibrated in hundreds of tons. Nevertheless, a blue whale processed aboard the Soviet Antarctic factory ship *Slava* in 1947 was weighed piecemeal at 190 tons, or 380,000 pounds.

with a 94-foot-long representative, supported by steel I-beams and crafted of Styrofoam and fiberglass.

Even with these models in place, however, enterprising showmen continued to take advantage of the public's fascination with real whales, and as recently as 1954, an embalmed specimen was the subject of an exhibition in Europe and America. Harpooned by a Danish whaler off the Norwegian island of Harøy, the 70-ton female finback made a tour of 165 European cities and then crossed the Atlantic on a freighter. To prevent—or more accurately, postpone—decomposition, "Mrs. Harøy" was injected with eight thousand quarts of formaldehyde, but at Coney Island in New York, when the carcass began to stink, the health authorities complained, and Mrs. Harøy was burned.

When whales strand in literature, it is usually to the benefit of people, and often those people have been without other resources. For example, in *The Swiss Family Robinson,* written by Johann Wyss in 1813, the family, shipwrecked on an uninhabited island, finds a stranded whale. The whale is a great boon; they boil down the blubber for the oil and use the skin for leather. Between the publication of *The Swiss Family Robinson* and *The Mysterious Island,* which appeared in 1875, a worldwide whale fishery had risen, so it is not surprising that Jules Verne would incorporate a whale into his story. It is also not surprising that Verne got almost everything wrong, since he had already demonstrated such an inclination in *Twenty Thousand Leagues Under the Sea,* published in 1870.* After gazing longingly at the whale that is swimming tantalizingly offshore, the castaways find that the whale has obligingly stranded itself. Verne describes their good fortune:

> It was a southern whale, eighty feet long, a giant of the species, probably not weighing less than a hundred fifty thousand pounds! . . . The whale was a female, and a large quantity of milk was taken from it, which according to the opinion of the naturalist Duffenbach, might pass for cow's milk, and indeed, it differs from it neither in taste, color, nor density. [They boil the whale down and] the tongue alone yielded six thousand pounds of oil, the lower lip four thousand.

From this description, it is difficult, if not impossible, to make out what sort of whale Verne intended this to be, but since they are very much in the

---

*In *Twenty Thousand Leagues Under the Sea,* Verne's skewed cetology includes a gigantic narwhal that is accused of sinking all the ships that were eventually shown to have been sunk by Captain Nemo and the submarine *Nautilus,* and in a whaling scene, he describes sperm whales as "cruel and destructive whales . . . ferocious whales [that are] all mouth and teeth!" Because they are such nasty creatures, Nemo kills them with the *Nautilus's* sharp prow and condones the slaughter by saying that "it was a massacre of harmful animals."

Southern Hemisphere (somewhere between South America and New Zealand), it is probably supposed to be a right whale, which he contrasts with the "northern whale" (the bowhead?), "whose head is not so depressed." The right whale actually reaches a maximum length of 55 feet, and whale milk is a glutinous, cheesy substance that is said to taste very fishy.

Shallow, shelving beaches are eminently suitable for the stranding of whales. As we shall see, there are any number of "explanations" for stranding, and one of the most popular concerns the failure of the whale's navigational system, which means that the echolocating pulses emitted by the whales do not encounter any recognizable obstacles and the whales, believing they are still in open water, swim onto the beach. While part of this explanation is correct—shallow beaches do not reflect pulsed sounds very well—the other part is virtually useless. Of course, whales are going to strand on shallow beaches; they obviously can't be expected to climb steep rock walls or other inclines to get to terra firma, whatever the reason for this urge. Whale strandings have been recorded from practically every country with a shoreline, but nowhere have such meticulous records been kept as the British Isles.

Since 1913, the British Museum of Natural History has maintained detailed records of every whale, dolphin, and porpoise that has been reported on any beach in England, Scotland, Ireland, or Wales. For a student of whale (and dolphin) strandings, these reports are a virtual gold mine of information. They include the date, time (if known), precise location, weather conditions (if recorded), any other data reported, and, of course, the type and number of stranded cetaceans. (Many whale strandings involve numbers of whales of the same species, but most reported incidents are of individual animals.) In a 1979 report on the stranding phenomenon edited by J. B. Geraci and D. J. St. Aubin, an article by M. C. Sheldrick summarizes the history of the British cetacean strandings. The most frequent strander on British coasts is the harbor porpoise (*Phocoena phocoena*), followed by the common dolphin (*Delphinus delphis*), and the pilot whale (*Globicephala melaena*). Then we have the bottlenose dolphin, *Tursiops truncatus*, followed by the minke whale, *Balaenoptera acutorostrata*. In fifth place, the minke is a somewhat unexpected entry, since it is a baleen whale. The toothed whales, such as the sperm whale and the various dolphins and porpoises, are the superior echolocators, and most strandings are thought to be somehow related to the acoustic capabilities (or failures) of the various whales. (We will discuss this at greater length when we reach the problem of why whales strand.) It goes almost without saying that the most frequent stranders are going to come from the most numerous whales, and what the number of stranded harbor porpoises and pilot whales probably tells us is that these are the most plentiful cetaceans in British waters.

Other countries will probably prove to have a slightly different emphasis, but the predominant species will always be the ones that are most numerous in local waters. This may sound almost tautological—the more whales, the more strandings—but if strandings are caused by an outside force, the equation would not be so neat. Another important consideration is the way in which they strand, either singly or in groups. Since some of the cetaceans—such as the pilot whales, common dolphins, and sperm whales—are highly gregarious animals, it stands to reason that these would be the species given to mass strandings.

As to the question of why cetaceans throw themselves upon the beach, often to die there, we are no closer to the answer than we were some two thousand years ago, when Aristotle wrote, "It is not known for what reason they run themselves aground on dry land; at all events, it is said that they do so at times, and for no obvious reason." Pliny the Elder associated strandings with storms and wrote, "There are rushing whirlwinds and rain-storms and tempests hurtling down from the mountain ridges that upturn the seas from their bottom, and roll with their waves monsters forced up from the depths in such a multitude, like shoals of tunnies in other places. . . ."

Some odontocete species strand with great and disarming regularity, while certain mysticetes do it rarely. Depending on the species, the number of individuals in a stranding varies enormously. Certain species, such as pilot whales and false killer whales (which, despite their names, are really large dolphins), have been known to strand in enormous numbers, with the record being 835 false killers that came ashore and died on the beach at Mar del Plata, Argentina, in 1946. Pilot whales are also gregarious stranders, but the record for them is probably in the 200 to 300 range. Sperm whales, the largest of the toothed whales, also show a predilection for stranding in groups, and there are Atlantic records of 17 *pottfisch* (pilot whales) stranding at the mouth of the Elbe in 1723, and 31 on the coast of Brittany in 1784. Many of the early Dutch illustrations of sperm whales were drawn from stranded specimens, but these lowland stranders often came in as singletons.*

The most notorious stranding location on the Atlantic seaboard is

---

*Probably the most famous sperm whale since Moby Dick was "Physty," who came ashore at Fire Island, New York, in April 1981. This young male was kept in captivity in a boat basin for eight days, during which time he was fed (unsuccessfully), medicated (probably unsuccessfully), and televised (very successfully). He was released after a week's rest—probably the best thing to do for a stranded whale with pneumonia—and swam off into the Atlantic, never to be seen again.

*T*he tail flukes of two of the forty-one sperm whales that stranded and died at Florence, Oregon, in June 1979

Cape Cod, Massachusetts. In the early years of this country, businessmen took advantage of this situation by encouraging pilot whales to strand, often driving them toward the beach from boats and then killing them in the shallows. These little whales (which are also large dolphins), had a high-quality oil in their heads that was used for the lubrication of fine machinery, especially watches. (Farther south, off New Jersey and North Carolina, late-nineteenth-century hunters also initiated a fishery for bottlenose dolphins, the object of which was the "jaw oil.") In recent times, the invasion of Cape Cod beaches by pilot whales has not stopped; if anything, it seems to have increased. The New England Aquarium, in Boston, has established a rescue network. Upon hearing of a stranding, trained workers rush to the scene and attempt to rescue the whales. In most cases, the stranded cetaceans have been pilot whales, but there have also been recent records of white-sided dolphins, a Risso's dolphin, and even a humpback whale.

Regardless of the success of the Good Samaritans who try to return stranded whales to the ocean, most whales that strand end up dead. Therefore, the question of why they strand has to be raised. There is no shortage of theories, including the following:

1. That they are being chased by predators and run up onto the beach to escape. (This suggestion is rendered inoperative by the inclination of killer whales and sperm whales to strand, animals that have no natural enemies except man.)

2. That their echolocation signals are diminished or ineffective because of the shallow slope of the beach. (This might work in a few isolated instances, but it has nothing to do with mass strandings, nor does it explain why some of the baleen whales, which do not, as far as we know, echolocate, can also be found stranded on the beach.)

3. That their brains (or inner ears) are infested with parasitic worms that interfere with the whales' navigation. (A good idea except when the brains or inner ears of nonstranded whales are examined—for example, under whaling circumstances—and the same parasites are found in whales that are nowhere close to stranding.)

4. That the whales are committing suicide in a protest to the whaling industry. Other suggestions have included entrapment by a receding tide, pregnant females seeking safety from predators in the shallows, phases of the moon, red tides, and many other possibilities, but to date none of these arguments has proven to be any more persuasive than any others.

An intriguing new theory is that single strandings might be a function of a mental malaise, something like a painful migraine headache, that causes the whale to throw itself onto the beach, but this theory is ultimately unprovable, because there would be no physical manifestation of such a condition presented in a necropsy.

In many cases—except those where live cetaceans are seen to throw themselves on the beach—we do not know if the whale was alive when it came onto the beach and then died there or if it was dead in the water and the carcass washed ashore. (This distinction is particularly important in an attempt to ascertain why live animals come ashore.) Some of the more recent attempts to resolve this biological mystery come from unsuspected quarters. Biologist F. G. Wood proposes that since cetaceans are descended from land animals, "the need to seek safety on land may become ingrained in its subcortical structure as a stress-induced 'drive,' which drive, operating at an instinctive level, causes stressed cataceans to seek the safety of the land of the ancestors." This may indeed be true, but as Wood himself says, "The hypothesis is not readily susceptible to experimental confirmation or refutation, nor does it seem likely that future observations could bring about any significant revisions of this explanation for strandings."

It is, of course, possible to postulate a simple survival function for a single stranding (even though the hypothesis doesn't work nearly as well for mass strandings): Since breathing in cetaceans is a conscious act, not an autonomous one, as it is for terrestrial mammals, an individual has to think about where it is when it inhales. If an animal is stressed, it might take itself into shallow water where it can get its blowhole out of the water so that no matter what else happens to it, it will not drown. There have been many strandings where at least one of the members of the pod was seen to be injured and the others followed it onto shore. This speaks to the gregariousness of certain cetaceans: There may be a strong urge to follow a leader even if that leader is leading the whales to shore or to their death. (Such a hypothesis is particularly applicable to pilot whales, false killer whales, sperm whales, and certain dolphins.)

Using some of the same species, Canadian biologist David Sergeant has suggested that some toothed whales strand en masse when their population is at a high density. In a careful analysis of the available data on the pilot whale in the North Atlantic, the Atlantic white-sided dolphin, and the sperm whale in New Zealand, Sergeant has found that once intensive whaling had ceased, the various species began to mass-strand more frequently. All three species of cetaceans are known to be numerous in the study areas, and Sergeant points out that most mass strandings occur within the "core" of the range but not at its periphery. Once again, the suggestion is speculative at best, but Sergeant makes a convincing argument for the possibility of stranding as a population control. Writing of the Orcininae (killer whales, pilot whales, false killer whales, etc.), he says, "Since most mortality in these latter species is mass mortality, mass mortality must regulate their populations. Psychological mechanisms leading to mass strandings remain to be investigated, but could include stress."

If European artists depicted the cachalot (and other whale species) with a certain degree of accuracy, it was because the beached animal was visible in the round and also because it is relatively easy to draw something that is immobile and lying there in front of you. But under those circumstances, it was difficult, if not impossible, to capture the image of the living whale. The problem of deducing what the living animal looked like from its dessicated carcass was elucidated by Herman Melville, who had a lot to say about whales, dead and alive, real and imaginary, in and out of the water:

> Consider! Most of the scientific drawings have been taken from the stranded fish; and these are about as correct as a drawing of a wrecked ship, with broken back, would correctly represent the animal itself in all its undashed pride of hull and spars. Though elephants have stood for their full-lengths, the living Leviathan has never yet fairly floated himself for

his portrait. The living whale, in his full majesty and significance, is only to be seen at sea in unfathomable waters; and afloat the vast bulk of him is out of sight, like a launched line-of-battle ship; and out of that element it is a thing eternally impossible for mortal man to hoist him bodily into the air, so as to preserve all the mighty swells and undulations.

BY THE SEVENTEENTH century, British, Dutch, and German explorers, searching for a passage to India, had encountered the polar whales (now known as bowheads) that inhabited the high Arctic. Not only did these whales prove to be harmless to men and ships; they proved to be eminently susceptible to a major fishery. Although this whaling was difficult and dangerous, it was more because of the weather and the uncertain ice conditions than because of the whales. The whales of Spitsbergen and Jan Mayen Island did not endanger the men (except in rare and unusual instances), but the men were so threatening to the whales that they virtually hunted them out of existence. (How quickly do men overcome their fears where commerce is involved.) This fishery—and the whalers knew full well that their prey were mammals, not fishes—was conducted partly in Dame Fashion's name, since the whales provided, among other commodities, the baleen that was so important for milady's corset stays and skirt hoops.

As whalemen, seamen, and navigators became more familiar with the ocean, some of the mysteries began to diminish. If they saw whales at sea and realized that these gigantic creatures were quite harmless, the fear of ship-sinking leviathans was also lessened. There were, of course, regions still to be explored—and with them, new animals to be discovered. And who was to say that these new regions would not contain unexpected monsters? Regardless of how many of the myths were dispelled, there were still those who believed that unknown creatures—usually gigantic and probably dangerous—still lurked just outside the immediate view of the contemporaneous scientists.

The early whalers saw their quarry as dangerous not only because the whales were huge creatures but also because they tended to react badly to having a lance plunged into them. And if you are in a small boat and you anger an animal that weighs as much as sixty tons, the results might prove harmful to you and your boat. It was not, therefore, the aggressive behavior of the whales that resulted in those upended whaleboats with hapless sailors trying desperately to escape the whale's crushing jaws, but the aggressive behavior of the men themselves, men who had the temerity (and the consummate arrogance) to assume that they could kill an animal that weighed

$\mathcal{A}$rctic whaling, as practiced in the eighteenth century. The whales are bowheads, the ships are Dutch, and the mountain in the background is Beerenburg on Jan Mayen Land.

a thousand times more than they did, from a fragile boat, with a slender spear, in the middle of the ocean.

After the Basques, the first major commercial whale fishery was that conducted by the Dutch and English Arctic adventurers of the seventeenth century. They hunted the bowhead whale,* a huge, blubbery beast, renowned for its cooperation in participating in its own demise—and eventually in its own extinction. The first pictures of this endeavor show men at work killing and processing these smooth-backed, placid whales in the ice-choked Arctic. The image of this whale as a harmless giant was enhanced by its nature; the bowhead was a toothless creature whose only defense was its size (bowheads can reach a length of 60 feet and a weight of 70 tons), since its baleen plates are dangerous only to plankton.

In the earliest depictions of Arctic whaling, we see dangerous polar bears and walruses, but the whales themselves are shown mostly as possessing smooth black backs or a pair of raised flukes as the animal dives in its

---

*The whale we now refer to as the bowhead was known to the whalers as the Polar Whale, the Greenland Whale, the Mysticetus (from its scientific name, *Balaena mysticetus*), or simply, the Whale. The Dutch called it *Walvis*.

*T*he whale portrayed as the embodiment of danger. In Elton Cowen's painting, the whale—painfully harpooned, but never mind—overturns a boat and endangers the lives of the hapless whalemen.

attempt to escape. Occasionally, a whaleboat was upset as a harpooned whale surfaced, but for the most part, the danger in this enterprise came not from the prey but from the circumstances in which it was hunted. (The frontispiece of William Scoresby's 1820 *Northern Whale Fishery* shows a somewhat unlikely tableau of a harpooned bowhead with a whaleboat flying over its back, with one man stuck upside down in the boat and the others swimming for safety.) In these prints, ice floes rise out of the cold gray seas, often towering over the fragile wooden sailing ships that sailed from Hull and Rotterdam. It would be another century before the whale would be perceived as a menace, when the whalers would be hunting the mighty sperm whale, an animal that not only strongly resented being stabbed in the vitals but had the equipment to retaliate.

In art as well as literature, the sperm whale was celebrated as a dangerous monster. Off the beach and in its own element, it assumed malevolent characteristics directly proportional to its size. For men involved in pursuit of the cachalot, the business of whaling was considered potentially life threatening, and although there are indeed illustrations of the whale being expeditiously dispatched, the most popular pictures of the fishery involved the retaliation of the hunted whale, with the whale portrayed as a threat to life, limb, and vessel. When Louis Garneray painted one of a pair of pictures of the *South Sea Whale Fishery*, in 1835, he depicted a right whale (a close relative of the bowhead's) spouting blood alongside a whaleboat as the harpooner prepares to drive home the killing lance. In the companion illustration, the prey is a sperm whale, and it has upended and broken the back of a whaleboat as the crew leaps into the sea to avoid being crushed in the enraged whale's jaws.

It would be beyond the scope of this study to investigate all the illustrations of angry sperm whales attacking or upsetting their pursuers. Indeed, several published collections of whaling prints and paintings have already performed that function, albeit unintentionally. There are, of course, pictures of whalemen rowing up upon unsuspecting whales and illustrations of ships in exotic anchorages, such as Tahiti or Kamchatka, but by far the most dramatic aspect of the whale fishery was the bloody battle to the death between the whalemen and the whale, and it was this that most artists chose to illustrate.

The Yankee sperm whale fishery was under way around 1750, some thirty-five years after the (perhaps apocryphal) voyage of Nantucket captain Christopher Hussey, who was blown offshore in a storm while chasing right whales and found himself in the midst of a school of forward-blowing, bluff-headed black whales. He killed one, so the story goes, and towed it back to shore, thus initiating the worldwide hunt for the whales that provided the clear amber oil from which the best candles were made. The first whales hunted from New England ports had been right whales, but these animals were quickly fished out, and the Nantucketers turned their attention and their harpoons to the sperm whale. Before the nineteenth century had begun, whalers from Nantucket, New Bedford, Providence, Mystic, Sag Harbor, and other Yankee towns were roaming the world in search of the cachalot.

When Britain shipped her convicts to Australia in 1788, the captains of the ships transporting this "live lumber" saw that the waters of New Holland were thick with whales. Across the Tasman Sea, sperm whales were observed spouting and diving in the waters of New Zealand. The whaler *Emilia* rounded Cape Horn in 1789 and discovered the plentiful stocks of the eastern South Pacific. The "Japan Grounds" were discovered in 1820 by Capt. Joseph Allen in the Nantucket whaler *Maro*, and to the north the whales of the North Pacific and the Sea of Okhotsk began to fall to the whalers' harpoons. (In most locations, the first whales hunted were the rights, but because the whalers often killed off the females and calves first, these hapless creatures—whose name comes from their "rightness" as prey for the whalers—were quickly reduced to such low numbers that it became uneconomical to hunt them.) Whaling literature, which first consisted of logbooks and journals kept by the captains or the occasional literate seaman, soon evolved into a genre of whaling books in which the author would chronicle his travels, with special attention paid to the whales and the techniques of whaling.

Capt. William Scoresby of Whitby was one of the first whalemen to set down his experiences and observations in the northern bowhead fishery; his 1820 *Account of the Arctic Regions with a History and Description of the Northern Whale-Fishery* is the benchmark for everything that followed. (The twentieth-century whaling historian Sidney Harmer called it "one of the most remarkable books in the English Language.") In 1835 a British surgeon named Thomas Beale wrote *A Few Observations on the Natural History of the Sperm Whale,* which did for the *Physeter* what Scoresby had done for the *Mysticetus.* Another sperm-whale voyage followed in the wake of Beale's; Frederick Debbell Bennett wrote his *Narrative of a Whaling Voyage . . . with an Account of Southern Whales, the Sperm Whale Fishery, and the Natural History of the Climates Visited* in 1840, and in 1846, J. Ross Browne's *Etchings of a Whaling Cruise . . .* was published. All of these works contributed to the public knowledge of the sperm whale, but more significantly for our literary discussion, all of the aforementioned works were known to Herman Melville and employed in the creation of what Howard Vincent calls "the cetological center" of *Moby-Dick.*

Because Melville so obviously believed that the sperm whale was God's most divine creature, he unabashedly devoted chapter and verse to its glorification. There are entire chapters about the whale's head, the case, the skin, the spout, the tail, and the animal's social life. When he compares the sperm whale to any other whale—the bowhead, for example—the sperm whale emerges triumphant from the comparison. Here, for instance, is what Melville has to say about Captain Scoresby and his whale:

> But Scoresby knew nothing and says nothing of the great sperm whale, compared with which the Greenland whale is almost unworthy mentioning. And here be it said, that the Greenland whale is an usurper upon the throne of the seas. Yet, owing to the long priority of his claims, and the profound ignorance which, till some seventy years back, invested the then fabulous or utterly unknown sperm whale, and which ignorance to this present day still reigns in all but some few scientific retreats and

whale-ports, this usurpation has been in every way complete. . . . This is Charing Cross; hear ye! good people all,—the Greenland whale is deposed,—the great sperm whale now reigneth!

Even though one member of the species achieved a mythological status, the remainder of the tribe was presented as living, breathing creatures. One of the surprising aspects of *Moby-Dick* is the amplitude of the natural history it includes. In the chapter called "Cetology," many other species are discussed, but using Beale, Bennett, and other contemporaneous authorities, Melville incorporates—in an emotional, biased, hyperbolic style, not at all the way we expect natural history to be written—almost everything that was known of the sperm whale. It is surprising that this novel, written in eighteen months, could not only emerge as one of the greatest works of fiction ever written in America but could summarize the biology of one of the world's least-known large animals. Then as now, as Melville wrote, ". . . the sperm whale, scientific or poetic, lives not complete in any literature. Far above all the other hunted whales, his is an unwritten life."

In a book of 135 chapters, most of which include at least a passing mention of the sperm whale (and some of which are completely devoted to some anatomic, physiological, or philosophical aspect of the animal), it is not a little difficult to summarize the extent of Melville's knowlege of the whale he chose to celebrate. In the "Cetology" chapter, in which he

*R*ockwell Kent's illustration of Moby Dick from the 1930 edition

categorizes various whale species according to size, he introduces the sperm whale thusly:

> This whale, among the English of old vaguely known as the Trumpa whale, and the Physeter whale, and the Anvil Headed whale, is the present Cachalot of the French, and the Pottfisch of the Germans, and the Macrocephalus of the Long Words. He is, without doubt, the largest inhabitant of the globe; the most formidable of all whales to encounter; the most majestic in aspect; and lastly, by far the most valuable in commerce; he being the only creature from which that valuable substance, spermaceti, is obtained. . . . Some centuries ago, when the sperm whale was almost wholly unknown in his own proper individuality, and when his oil was accidentally obtained from the stranded fish; in those days spermaceti, it would seem, was popularly supposed to be derived from a creature identical with the one then known in England as the Greenland or Right Whale. It was the idea also, that this same spermaceti was the quickening humor of the Greenland Whale with which the first syllable of the word literally expresses. In those times, also, spermaceti was extremely scarce, not being used for light, but only as an ointment and medicament.

Once it had been established that Leviathan was a real creature, the next stage in its apotheosis was accomplished through literature, then the only available medium for popular aggrandizement. The earliest, and certainly the most successful, example of the animal-made-myth can be found in *Moby-Dick,* the story of the whale that triumphs over the puny efforts of man to kill it.*

The white whale is *monstrum horrendum,* the quintessence of evil, the literary paradigm of malevolence. Who better to describe the monstrous qualities of his creation than the author himself? In the chapter in which he introduces the white whale, Melville says that he did "in the end incorporate with themselves all manner of morbid hints, and half-formed foetal suggestions of supernatural agencies, which eventually invested Moby Dick with new terrors unborrowed from anything that visibly appears." And

---

*The whale Moby Dick did not spring fully formed from the mind of Herman Melville. In 1835, there was a whale known as "Mocha Dick," named for the island of Mocha off the Chilean coast, that terrorized and sank whale ships and was introduced in J. N. Reynolds's May 1839 article in the *Knickerbocker Magazine.* The whale ship *Essex* was stove and sunk by a sperm whale in the Pacific in 1820, and Melville is known to have spoken to the mate, Owen Chase, about the incident. In 1851, another whaler, the *Ann Alexander,* was sunk by a sperm whale, but that was too late for Melville, since *Moby-Dick* was published in that year.

although whiteness is usually perceived as representing goodness, Melville sees the absence of color as "the intensifying agent in things the most appalling to mankind":

> This elusive quality it is, which causes the thought of whiteness, when divorced from more kindly associations, and coupled with an object terrible in itself, to heighten the terror to the furthest bounds. Witness the white bear of the poles, and the white shark of the tropics; what but their smooth, flaky whiteness makes them the transcendent horrors they are? That ghastly whiteness it is which imparts such an abhorrent mildness, even more loathsome than terrific, to the dumb gloating of their aspect.

Moby Dick is not actually white; he is described as having "a peculiar snow-white wrinkled forehead, and a high, pyramidical white hump. . . . The rest of his body was so streaked, and spotted, and marbled with that same shrouded hue, that, in the end, he had gained the distinctive appellation of the White Whale. . . ." In chapter 42 ("The Whiteness of the Whale"), Melville lists those things that, while white, are inherently evil, including such diverse creatures as the polar bear, the white shark, the albatross, the albino man, and travelers in Lapland "who refuse to wear colored and coloring glasses upon their eyes." Melville writes, "And of all these things, the Albino whale was the symbol. Wonder ye at the fiery hunt?"

The supernatural nature of the whale can be found throughout Melville's stirring narrative. "Some whalemen," he wrote, "should still go further in their superstitions; declaring Moby Dick not only ubiquitous but immortal (for immortality is but ubiquity in time); that though groves of spears should be planted in his flanks, he would still swim away unharmed; or if indeed he should ever be made to spout thick blood, such a sight would be a ghastly deception; for again in unensanguined bellows hundreds of leagues away, his unsullied jet would once more be seen."

Moby Dick is not only a myth and a monster; he is also the materialization of everything depraved and villainous. Even the crazy Captain Ahab, his would-be conqueror, cannot compete with the power of the whale and the whale's black heart. In *The Trying-Out of Moby-Dick*, Howard Vincent's 1949 study of the creation of the novel, Vincent identifies the quintessentially evil nature of the whale by equating it with the greatest evil ever known: "Through Melville, Moby Dick has been absolved of mortality. Readers of *Moby-Dick* know that he swims the world unconquered, that he is ubiquitous in time and place. Yesterday he sank the *Pequod;* within the past few years he has breached five times, from a New

Mexico desert, over Hiroshima and Nagasaki, and most recently, at Bikini Atoll."*

Vincent points out that it is primarily to Ahab that the whale is the personification of evil: "Ahab's reaction [to the whale] is not the normal sort of response; it is that of one scarred and maimed by life. It is the monomania of the paranoid. To Mankind in general, the White Whale in *Moby-Dick* must symbolize something else," and that is, according to Vincent, "life itself with its Good and its Evil; it is the final Mystery which no man may know and no man should pursue unrelentingly."

Although square-rigged sperm whaling ended with the end of the nineteenth century, the sperm whales were not spared. Mechanized whalers aboard diesel-powered catcher boats, armed with exploding grenade harpoons, exponentially escalated the hunt for *Physeter macrocephalus*. First in the Antarctic, then off the coasts of South America, South Africa, Australia, and New Zealand, the whalers pursued the spermaceti whales for their oil-rich blubber. (The oil of their heads was no longer needed for the manufacture of high-quality smokeless candles.) The high point of sperm-whaling history was not, as many people might assume, during Melville's time (1819–91) but in the 1960s. Soviet and Japanese catcher boats attached to gigantic factory ships killed the whales of the North Pacific—a population totally unknown to Yankee whalers—in numbers that could only have been accomplished by state-supported, technological whaling juggernauts. In 1959, for the first time, the annual kill of sperm whales throughout the world's oceans, including the Antarctic, rose to over twenty thousand, and by 1964, it was over twenty-eight thousand.[†]

While the natural history of the sperm whale does not concern us here, its perception in the popular mind is of considerable importance, since the whale has quite obviously metamorphosed from a monster to a real animal and at the hands of Melville the novelist, again into a mythological beast of supernatural proportions and qualifications. The story of Moby Dick's rise to fame does not end with the resurgence of interest in the novel. (When it was first published, *Moby-Dick* was far from a critical or financial success.) As alternative devices for publicity evolved, they were used (sometimes inadvertently) in the exaltation of Moby Dick. And where there is an area of *Moby-Dick* or Melville scholarship to be investigated, there will certainly appear an investigator. In the case of *Moby-Dick* in the popular culture, it is

*The name of the novel *Moby-Dick* is written with a hyphen, but following Melville's example, its eponymous protagonist is deprived of that punctuative device.

† For a complete discussion of the intermingled destinies of men and sperm whales, see *Men and Whales*, Knopf, 1991.

*J*oan Bennett, the love interest of Captain Ahab (John Barrymore) in the 1930 Hollywood interpretation of *Moby-Dick*. In this version, the whale loses.

M. Thomas Inge. In *A Companion to Melville Studies* (1986), edited by John Bryant, Inge has contributed a chapter entitled "Melville in Popular Culture" in which he discusses film, comics, radio, television, recordings, children's literature, and adult fiction; that is, "popular novels that employ [Melville] and his work."

Moby-Dick first appeared in movie houses in 1926, but it had hardly anything to do with Melville's novel. It was a silent film called *The Sea Beast*, with John Barrymore as Ahab. In this version, as well as the next, Ahab has a last name ("Ceely"), a half brother Derek, and a girlfriend, played here by Barrymore's wife-to-be, Dolores Costello. The moguls at Warner Brothers obviously believed that Melville's story was too tame as written, so they decided to provide an assortment of ancillary characters, a ridiculous papier-mâché whale, and a plot that emphasizes Ahab's love life (and Barrymore's famous profile) more than his pursuit of the white whale. Barrymore was known as "the World's Greatest Actor" and was so popular that audiences obviously would not stand for his being killed off, so the poor whale dies instead. Playing at the Warner Theater in New York, the movie was an enormous success and took in $20,000 a week as thousands of people a day were turned away.

Barrymore made another version of *Moby-Dick*, and although the story was no closer to the original than *The Sea Beast*, Melville's title was employed. Once again Ahab Ceely woos a starlet, but Dolores Costello, now married to Barrymore and pregnant, was replaced by Joan Bennett. Brother Derek also appears in the 1930 version, as do other characters who have less than nothing to do with Melville's novel, such as "Whale Oil Rosie." Once again Barrymore flashes his profile, the whale loses, and peg-legged Ahab returns to New Bedford to his true love. In her biography of the Barrymores, Margot Peters wrote:

> Compared to his appearance in *The Sea Beast* only four years before, Jack is shockingly older, something which his opening acrobatics up in the crow's nest only emphasize. This Ahab is more a caricature of John Barrymore as a drunk and a make-out artist; Jack seems drunk from beginning to end. . . . Early sound was notoriously poor, but that does not explain why Ahab talks like an old cowhand: "Beg pardon, ma'am. . . . Aint'cha friends anuf ta intraduce me?"

Almost lost in the shuffle is the eponymous whale, which appears in the distance as a humpback and in the leg-chomping and whale-stabbing scenes as an oversized, soggy potato. (Despite several references to "the white whale," this whale is always black.) Probably having more to do with Barrymore's popularity than Melville's, this version, too, was an enormous success, and a reviewer for *Theatre Magazine* (displaying a certain unfamiliarity with literature) wrote, "Altogether *Moby-Dick* is a highly creditable, moving record of Melville's stunning tale."

It was not until 1956 that Melville's great novel was properly brought to the screen. Produced again by Warner Brothers, this *Moby Dick* was directed by John Huston, with a screenplay written by Huston and Ray Bradbury, the science-fiction writer. (Bradbury has recently written a "novel" called *Green Shadows, White Whale* in which he circuitously discusses his volatile relationship with Huston but sheds little light on the making of the film.) The first unit worked in Ireland, and the actual whaling scenes were shot in Madeira and the Azores, while the models of the white whale (there were three in all, one of which was lost at sea) appeared in an eighty-thousand-gallon tank at Elstree Studios outside London.

The cast consisted of Gregory Peck as Ahab, Richard Basehart as Ishmael, Leo Genn as Starbuck, Dublin drama critic Seamus Kelley as Flask, and Harry Andrews as Stubb. Friederich Ledebur, an Austrian sportsman,

*I*n the 1956 version of *Moby-Dick*, Captain Ahab (Gregory Peck) is taken to his death by the vindictive white whale. (With all those harpoons stuck in him, it's easy to see why the whale is so angry.)

was made up as the cannibal harpooner Queequeg; Edric Connor, a Trinidadian calypso singer, was Daggoo; and Orson Welles played Father Mapple. There are no women in this version except those of the Irish village of Youghal (got up to look like New Bedford by removing all power lines and modern signage and refurbishing the quay) who silently watch the *Pequod* set sail in the film's opening. The whale ship was a rebuilt schooner that Alan Villiers, who supervised the seafaring aspects of the film, called "small, strained, and decrepit." She was decked over with a false deck, under which the actual crew sailed her, while the actors played their roles, often in genuinely foul weather. In his biography of Huston, Alex Madsen tells the story of the filming of the typhoon scenes during an actual storm, and when Gregory Peck informed Huston that such a thing was impossible, he is quoted as saying, "It's a mistake to tell John that something is impossible."

When Carlo Lorenzini (1826–90) wrote *The Adventures of Pinocchio* in 1882, he could hardly have suspected that the story, first published in Italy, would become one of the most popular children's stories of all times. Lorenzini—who wrote under the name of Carlo Collodi—created the talk-

When Walt Disney Studios made *Pinocchio* in 1940, Monstro the whale (seen at the bottom of the poster) was the most frightening character in the film.

ing wooden puppet who endures a series of dangerous adventures before being transformed into a real boy. Late in the original story, Pinocchio has been turned into a donkey, but when he comes up lame, he is sold to a man who wants to make a drum of his skin and throws him into the sea. But the salt water turns him back into a wooden puppet, and he swims away, only to be swallowed by a sea monster with a wide-open, cavernous mouth and three rows of enormous teeth. The monster, known as the Dogfish, has also swallowed Geppetto, the puppeteer who made Pinocchio in the first place, and they escape by walking out of the Dogfish's mouth as he sleeps.

If Collodi's Pinocchio had simply strolled out of the mouth of the Dogfish, he would not find himself in this discussion of whales as monsters. Indeed, were it not for the Walt Disney Studios, the little marionette might have vanished altogether, but in 1940, after the astonishing success of *Snow White* (in 1937), *Pinocchio* was released as the second of Disney's animated, feature-length films. Again, the puppet is almost turned into a donkey, but he escapes and returns home to discover that Geppetto, who had gone looking for him, was swallowed by Monstro the whale, and is now at the bottom of the ocean. Pinocchio ties a rock to his tail for ballast, and, accompanied by his "conscience" Jiminy Cricket, leaps into the sea. Pinocchio tries to locate the whale, but the mere mention of his name causes all the other fishes to flee in terror, and the only way for Pinocchio to find Geppetto is to get himself swallowed by Monstro. As envisioned by the Disney artists, the whale is a thoroughly terrifying creature with the belly pleats of a baleen whale, the approximate square-headed shape of a sperm whale, lips for sneering, and the upper and lower teeth of no known animal on land or sea. In the cavernous belly of the whale, Pinocchio and Geppetto build a fire to make the whale sneeze, and he obligingly spews them out. But unlike Collodi's version, the story does not end with their ejection from the whale; rather, there ensues a chase that must have terrified every viewer under the age of ten and many who were older. Monstro is a roaring, raging, fire-breathing monster that chases poor Pinocchio all over the ocean until it crashes into a rock wall and the puppet escapes, to be turned into a real boy by the Blue Fairy. The film was an enormous success; and while it did wonders for Disney, it did so at the expense of the whale. Until people got a better idea of what real whales looked like or how they behaved, Monstro was the reason that generation after generation perceived the whale as a malevolent monster—a threat to life, limb, and beloved marionette.

OF ALL THE transformations from myth to monster and back to myth, none has been so emphatic as that of the whale. First perceived as a threat to sailors, then as a bonanza of meat, oil, and bone, the whale soon became an object of a worldwide commercial fishery, which itself was transformed by technology into a business. The whales died in direct proportion to the success of this industry. It required an extraordinary combination of circumstances to turn the tide, and in the process, the whale was remythified, turned almost into an object of worship.

Although whales have, so to speak, always been with us, for most of the past thousand years they have been perceived as objects of commerce or sources of "products." Illustrated books of natural history always showed drawings of whales—free-swimming whales were not photographed under water until 1975—accompanied by tales of the bravery of the men who hunted them or by statistical calculations of how much oil could be obtained from a single animal. Somewhere around 1970, however, there began to develop a different awareness of whales. Articles appeared in popular magazines with titles like "The Last of the Great Whales" (Scott McVay) and "Vanishing Giants" (David Hill). These articles—in *Scientific American* and *Audubon*, respectively—were prompted by the realization that somebody was killing off the great whales and hardly anyone, except the members and delegates of the International Whaling Commission (IWC), was aware of it. In 1971, Roger and Katy Payne recorded the haunting "songs" of the humpback whale and produced a record that is still selling today. In 1972, at the UN Conference on the Human Environment at Stockholm, a unanimous resolution was passed calling for a moratorium on all commercial whaling. "Save the Whale" became the rallying cry for the entire conservation movement, and organizations dedicated to this goal sprang up all over the country. The American Cetacean Society, founded in Southern California in 1967, was the first of these. Then came the Whale Center in Oakland, Project Jonah, and the Connecticut Cetacean Society in Hartford. Soon the major conservation organizations—National Audubon Society, the Cousteau Society, Sierra Club, the National Wildlife Federation, the Humane Society, and the World Wildlife Fund—joined the fray, and millions of Americans became righteously incensed about the massive and insensitive slaughter of whales on the high seas.

At approximately the same time that people were beginning to worry about the killing of the great whales, various researchers were recognizing that dolphins—for all intents and purposes, miniature whales—also possessed some very special characteristics. As early as 1954, F. G. Wood had identified the sounds made by captive dolphins at Marineland in Florida as "some form of communication." Then other researchers realized that dolphins had a language of their own, composed of whistles, squeaks, and barks. It was only a short step before someone decided to speak to the dolphins. The neurophysicist John Lilly experimented with trained bottlenose dolphins, eventually conducting his research at a full-scale research facility he had commissioned in the Virgin Islands. He never achieved the "interspecies communication" he hoped for—that is, he never got the dolphins to talk to him—but he did serve as "scientific adviser" to the 1973 movie *Flipper*, which in turn led to the enormously popular television series. Later, Lilly's research inspired the novelist Robert Merle to write *The Day of the Dolphin*, in which the dolphins are able to mimic human speech.

Prior to 1965, killer whales were considered by most people to be seagoing homicidal maniacs that killed anything and everything in the ocean. But in that year, "Namu," a young male orca, was trapped in a salmon net off the British Columbia town of the same name, brought down to the Seattle Aquarium by director Ted Griffin, and proceeded to change everyone's preconceptions of the killer whale. To the astonishment of visitors, Griffin swam with the 10-ton whale, hand-fed him salmon, and rode around on his back as if he were a big pool toy. The following year, a new marine "theme park" called Sea World put a killer whale named "Shamu" on display, and it became clear that not only did killer whales not live up to their name, they were amenable to training, just like their smaller cousins. (Despite their unfortunate name, killer whales are actually the largest of the dolphins.)

Victor Scheffer was a biologist with the U.S. Fish and Wildlife Service, specializing in marine mammals. He had published many technical studies of the pinnipeds and cetaceans of the northwest coast of North America,

*T*he first killer whale successfully raised in captivity. Born at Sea World in Orlando in 1984, "Baby Shamu" now performs as part of the show in San Diego.

but when he decided to turn his hand to fiction, he almost single-handedly created a nationwide awareness of the plight of the endangered whales. *The Year of the Whale* was published in 1969 to enormous acclaim (it won the prestigious Burroughs Medal for nature writing) and unprecedented popularity. Alternating chapters of narrative exposition with scientific observations, it is the story of the first twelve months in the life of "Little Calf," a newborn sperm whale. The calf and its mother roam the Pacific and experience all sorts of adventures with other sea creatures as well as those creatures that ply the seas in ships, such as Japanese whalers. "Little Calf" survives his first year, and Scheffer's book—still in print—became an instant classic. Loren Eiseley, writing for the *New York Times,* said, "The author's knowledge is great, his prose poetic and sensitive . . . a volume to be treasured."

By the early 1970s, people were killing whales in staggering numbers—the quota for sperm whales in the North Pacific for 1973 was 10,703—and for the first time, the public knew about it. (It had never actually been a secret; it was just that the IWC had no interest in publicizing its actions.) Greenpeace bravadoes put themselves between the harpoon cannons of a Soviet whaler and the whales in 1975, and in 1979, the pirate whaler *Sierra* was rammed and sunk in a Portuguese harbor by a conservation commando named Paul Watson. The battle lines were drawn: It was the whale killers against the whale lovers. The whales sang haunting, mysterious songs; they were photographed swimming gracefully underwater (Jim Hudnall's photographs of Hawaiian humpbacks, the first free-swimming great whales ever photographed, appeared in *Audubon* in 1977); their little cousins the bottlenose dolphins were leaping through hoops from New England to Hawaii; killer whales were wearing funny hats and allowing trainers to brush their teeth; and because we loved them so, we wanted to *watch* them—not only in oceanariums* but also in the wild.

Whale watching, which had previously been restricted to a few whale lovers who gathered at various locations around San Diego to watch the gray whales on their southward migrations to the lagoons of Baja, suddenly became a big business. From Provincetown, the boats headed for Stellwagen Bank to watch the feeding humpbacks; from Lahaina on the Hawaiian island of Maui they looked for the breeding humpbacks (the Hawaiian whales are the same ones that feed in Alaskan waters, and cruise ships were also plying the waters of Glacier Bay, so that people could see the humpbacks there, too); charter boats all along the coast of Southern California, from Los Angeles to San Diego, would observe the gray whales' migration; in Puget Sound there were killer-whale families; and almost anywhere else along the Atlantic and Pacific coasts of the United States, boats would take people whale or dolphin watching. It is a happy accident of cetacean evolution that so many types of whales frequent American inshore waters. In Europe, by contrast, the only whales that might be seen that close to shore were right whales, but they were eliminated five hundred years ago. It is therefore no coincidence that the whale conservation movement was so strongly supported by Americans—they had more whales to watch in their front yards.

Where one might expect proximity to breed familiarity, the opposite has been the result. The "friendly" whales of Magdalena Bay and San Ignacio Lagoon in Baja, California, have engendered only more mystery, and in other regions, whale watchers have interpreted ordinary sightings of whales as events of profound significance. A breach is often seen as an expression of "joy"—even though we have no idea why whales lunge out of the water and certainly no way of knowing if they experience emotions like joy—and

---

*From March 1971 to March 1972, "Gigi," the only great whale ever maintained in captivity, was on display at Sea World in San Diego. The juvenile gray whale, captured as a calf in Scammon's Lagoon, Baja California, was 18 feet 2 inches long when she was captured and weighed 4,300 pounds. A year later, she weighed 8,500 pounds and was 24 feet long. She was tagged with a radio beacon and released into the Pacific five miles off San Diego, where she was supposed to join her migrating relatives. Later reports indicate that the return to the wild was successful and that she produced a calf.

One of the "friendly" gray whales surfaces amid the whale watchers at San Ignacio Lagoon, Baja California.

the willingness of whales to be watched has been interpreted as a desire on their part to initiate interspecies contact.

Gray whales also pass Monterey Bay en route to Baja, and they sometimes hang a left and enter the bay, much to the delight of the whale watchers there. In 1955, according to Gordon and Baldridge's study, there was only one boat out of San Diego to take people to look at the passing parade. By 1991, over three hundred vessels were active, and what began as an activity of eccentric, curious nature lovers had become a major industry. In California in 1990, the total revenues for whale watching exceeded $6 million, and this does not take into account the ancillary sales of T-shirts, posters, and guidebooks.

As this "whale consciousness" grew, people discovered that they could do something to help the whales. A massive boycott was directed at the Japanese and the Soviets in an attempt to influence their governments by affecting them where it hurt—in their pocketbooks. Millions of signatures were collected on petitions that were submitted to our embassies and theirs. There was also the realization that the IWC was not sacrosanct and that nongovernmental observers (NGOs) were entitled to observe the workings of a group that seemed to have decided that the world's whales were theirs to parcel out.

It was nowhere written that membership in the IWC required a current or past involvement with whaling (or even a coastline, as it turned out), so nations whose interest was only in stopping whaling joined the commission. As their numbers increased, the possibility of a solid antiwhaling faction within the IWC increased accordingly. Countries such as India, Finland, the Seychelles, Switzerland, Oman, and Kenya voted "yea" on the antiwhaling motions. Like ex-smokers, the former whaling nations were also fervent opponents of whaling. Paramount among the "reformed" were Britain, Australia, and New Zealand—countries with a long and bloody whaling history.

Influenced by the grass-roots conservation movement, governments found themselves under increasing pressure to instruct their delegates to join the ranks of the antiwhaling faction of the IWC. The whaling nations, led by Japan, the U.S.S.R., and Norway (but including Iceland, Spain, Brazil, Peru, and South Korea) continued to oppose any attempts to put their whalers out of business, and although the quotas were reduced annually, they still had enough votes to defeat any moratorium motion. But in 1982, at the IWC meeting held at the Metropole Hotel in Brighton, England, the motion to ban all commercial whaling was passed, with twenty-seven nations voting for, seven against, and five abstentions. The ban was scheduled to take effect in the 1985–86 season, ostensibly to allow the whalers to phase out their operations.

After a thousand years of merciless slaughter, it looked as if commercial whaling had finally ended. The whale ships were retired, and the whaling stations in Japan, the Soviet Union, Norway, and Iceland were shut down. There was some confusion about the terms of the moratorium, and the Japanese struck some bilateral deals with the United States about a limited number of sperm whales, but by 1990, it appeared as if whaling were over. Sadly, however, because of economics, tradition, or just plain stubbornness, some nations refused to give up the battle, even in the face of massive world disapproval. By 1991, Norway and Iceland were threatening to quit the IWC and go back to commercial whaling, and in 1992, Iceland withdrew, and Norway announced her intention to resume whaling regardless of what the IWC said about it.* But with Japan and Russia *hors de combat*, the major whalers were sidelined, perhaps permanently. There was still some "research whaling" going on, but the number of whales killed was compar-

---

* Norway had never withdrawn her objection to the moratorium, so in a legal sense she had every right to go whaling. According to the IWC's bylaws, if a nation files an objection to a resolution, that resolution is not binding on the objecting country.

atively insignificant. With whale killing almost a thing of the past, the apotheosis of the whale could begin.

An animal that can get to be 100 feet long and weigh 150 tons is something very special indeed. And there is something special about an animal that can go for seven or eight months without eating and then gorge itself for four months, eating day and night. There are whales that sing and whales that can hold their breath for an hour and a half and dive to depths of a mile or more. There are whales that are restricted to narrow Arctic habitats and whales that are found from pole to pole and in almost all the oceans in between. There are whales that feed on organisms thousands of times smaller than they are and whales that feed (occasionally) on organisms that are larger than they are. But most important, there is something special about an animal that was hunted relentlessly for centuries and has only now been rescued from the precipice of extinction.

There are those who would argue that whales are not particularly special; they do the same things as other mammals, and it is only their size that

Ninety-four feet long and weighing more than 10 tons, the blue whale model dominates the Hall of Ocean Life at the American Museum of Natural History in New York.

distinguishes them. But it is not the uniqueness of the whale's situation that differentiates it from other imperiled creatures; if it were, we would be as concerned with manatees, condors, snail darters, and golden toads, for each species is unique in its own way. In fact, it is the very concept of uniqueness that defines the species. The generic "whale" (there are actually some thirty-three species, ranging in size from the 100-foot blue whale to the 12-foot pygmy sperm whale) has achieved a unique degree of veneration; it has become more than a biological entity, more than a hunted creature. It has become a symbol.

Although whaling was ostensibly the subject of *Moby-Dick,* the novel is arguably about much more than a whaling voyage undertaken by a crazed and vindictive master. Literary historians refer to *Moby-Dick* as a "transcendental" work in which the whaling narrative is used as a substructure for a far more profound theme, the battle between good and evil. The white whale is no ordinary whale; he is "not only ubiquitous, but immortal (for immortality is but ubiquity in time)."

As early as the mid-nineteenth century, the whale had regained some of the mystery of its earlier incarnations; to Herman Melville, anyway, it had become a creature whose significance transcended its reality. By the twentieth century, however, when mechanized whaling would reduce the whales to oil, meat, and fertilizer, they would sacrifice their mysterious qualities to commerce. Recently, they have been exalted once again as creatures that are, literally and figuratively, larger than life.

One example of this can be found in D. H. Lawrence's poem entitled "Whales Weep Not." Lawrence was writing about the sensuality of whales, but there seems to be no question that he was aware of the totemic significance of his subject, as demonstrated in this excerpt:

> And they rock, and they rock, through the sensual
> Ageless ages in the depths of the seven seas.
> And through the salt they reel with drunk delight
> And in the tropics they tremble and love
> And roll with massive strong desire, like gods.

Most early writers on whales and whaling described the quarry or the process. The whaling literature is rich with journals of captains describing their voyages, the number of barrels of oil yielded by each whale, or the tribulations endured on the voyage. But even during the heyday of the New England whale fishery there were those who pondered the fate of the whale. In 1851, Herman Melville, usually associated with the killing of whales and not their salvation, wrote:

Comparing the humped herds of whales with the humped herds of buffalo, which, not forty years ago, overspread by tens of thousands the prairies of Illinois and Missouri, and shook their iron manes and scowled with their thunder-clotted brows upon the sites of populous river-capitals, where now a polite broker sells you land at a dollar an inch; in such a comparison an irresistible argument would seem furnished, to show that the hunted whale cannot escape a speedy extinction.

Soon after the publication of *Moby-Dick,* the New England whaling industry collapsed, not necessarily because of a decline in the number of whales—although that was certainly a factor—but also because of the discovery of petroleum in Pennsylvania in 1859, the gold rush (young men who would seek their fortunes on a whaler headed instead for the gold fields of California), and, of course, the looming Civil War, which preoccupied most of the nation by 1860. There was a brief respite during the latter half of the century with the discovery of the last remaining population of bowhead whales north of the Bering Straits. The Arctic fishery came to an abrupt halt in 1871 when almost the entire whaling fleet was trapped in the closing ice pack and most of the ships were lost. (Miraculously, not a single seaman perished in this disaster; the whalers crossed the ice on foot and were rescued by the few ships that had been standing offshore and were therefore not entrapped.) Also around this time, Captain C. M. Scammon discovered the breeding grounds of the gray whales in the protected lagoons of Baja California and led the slaughter there until they ran out of whales.

Even during the early decades of the twentieth century, with whalers taking an unprecedented number of whales in the Antarctic, the chroniclers of the industry continued to record numbers and sizes of whales, and barrels of oil. Having discovered the feeding grounds of the last of the great whales, it must have seemed to the whalers as if the resource were limitless. (In the 1930–31 season alone, 29,410 blue whales were killed in the Antarctic.) The same could be said of the sperm whales of the North Pacific, the targets of the Soviet and Japanese harpoon cannons of the 1960s.

Because of the persistent imagery of square-rigged sailing ships, "Nantucket sleigh rides," and whalers being dumped into the water by enraged sperm whales, most people, if they thought about it at all, would probably think that the nineteenth century was the zenith of the whale fishery. In fact, more sperm whales were killed during the decades 1950–70 than in the entire history of the Yankee whaling industry. In a 1935 study of the logbooks of nineteenth-century American whalers, zoologist C. H. Townsend tabulated the numbers of whales of various species that had been killed. He had access to the logbooks of 744 vessels, many others having been lost or destroyed. His study is certainly incomplete, but one can get a sense of the magnitude of the Yankee sperm-whale fishery from it. For the hundred years under study, he was able to find records of 36,908 sperm whales killed, and he wrote, "At its best period [that] great fleet probably captured less than 10,000 whales a year." For the period 1950–70, North Pacific sperm whalers killed a total of 337,604 sperm whales (McHugh, 1974).

When figures like this were encountered, Americans began to "Save the Whale"—an avalanche of a movement that succeeded faster and more efficiently than anyone could have possibly imagined. In 1974, when the "movement" was building up steam, David Hill wrote the following gloomy prognosis in *Audubon* magazine:

> The whale crisis has never been more acute. Each year the cost of killing whales goes up while the number of animals goes down. The economic squeeze has pushed most whaling nations out of the business. Two countries with sizable whaling fleets, Japan and the Soviet Union, stubbornly hang on. An industry historically plagued by greedy mismanagement of the resource does not have to give thought to the future of the industry because there is no future. But two critical questions remain: Will whaling cease of its own accord before or after species become extinct? Will the great majority of nations that no longer hunt whales sit idly by and allow the animals to become extinct?

We now know the answers: None of the species have become extinct, and the "great majority of nations" did not sit idly by. They voted to end the slaughter that had been going on for a thousand years. When people learned that whales sang mysterious songs, that they had the largest, most convoluted brains of any animal that has ever lived, or that they had been hunted almost to extinction, they adopted an attitude that consisted of equal parts of awe, wonder, reverence, and guilt. These factors contributed substantially to the foundation of a religion, with the whale as godhead. Listen to the words of Loren Eiseley, the anthropologist-poet:

> If man had sacrificed his hands for flukes, he would still be a philosopher, but there would have been taken from him the power to wreak his thought upon the world. Instead, he would have wandered, like the dolphin, homeless across currents and winds and oceans, intelligent, but forever the curious observer of unknown wreckage falling through the blue light of eternity. This role would now be a deserved penitence for man. Perhaps such a transformation would bring him once more into the mood of child-like innocence in which he talked successfully to all things living but had

no power and no urge to harm. It is worth a wistful thought that someday the whale might talk to us and us to him. It would break, perhaps, the long loneliness that has made man a frequent terror and abomination even to himself.

It was this sentiment that has glorified and enshrined the whale. By now the realities and technicalities of whale biology mattered only to the scientists. In the lagoons of Baja California, whale watchers were exposed to a most unusual phenomenon: The gray whales, which had heretofore kept their distance from the little boats, now approached them and allowed themselves to be touched and petted. Some zealots described these encounters with the "friendly whales" as an attempt by the whales to communicate with us, to express their forgiveness for the havoc we wreaked upon their brethren.

Like us, whales breathe air, and also like us, they have large brains. They communicate with one another "vocally," but we have yet to decode what the vocalizations mean. They form complex social groups that differ from one species to the next. Sperm whales, with perhaps the most complex social structure of any mammal other than man, seem to live in matriarchal societies, like elephants. In elephant and sperm whale societies, the big bulls do not dominate or even lead the herds; rather, they isolate themselves from the group except for breeding purposes. Moreover, female and juvenile sperm whales form "nursery schools," "bachelor groups," and other affiliations, still poorly understood by cetologists. Other species have other social structures: The migration of gray whales is led by the pregnant females; the eerie songs of the humpbacks are believed to be a function of the male-dominance hierarchy, and so on. Like the diverse societies of man, each species has apparently developed its own "culture."

One overzealous cetophile suggested that the songs of humpbacks represented the transmission of their "oral history": Lacking hands or tools with which to write, they passed along the history of their race in song, transmitting their wisdom and traditions from generation to generation. That the songs changed from year to year was interpreted as evidence of their "intelligence," for which read: "similarity to humans." After all, the songs of birds and the howls of wolves are more or less constant over time, while the songs of humpbacks are modified annually, a sort of cetacean hit parade. Moreover, every singing whale sings the same phrases—in the same sequence—which further enhanced the notion of a superior intelligence. If they were this clever, the argument went, surely they should be ranked above the other "dumb" animals. Whales were different, and through this difference we brought them closer and closer to human equivalency—and beyond.

They were, we believed, caring, sensitive, social animals. How easy it was to elevate them to a higher plane than humans, who often used their capabilities for less than benign purposes. The whales swam serenely in their eternal, peaceful, aquatic world. (Wasn't there something about mammals originating in water? Or blood being remarkably similar to sea water?) At the same time, the whales seemed more fundamental and more advanced than humans. They were, wrote the Apostles of the Whale, above and beyond mankind. In their ageless wisdom they had surpassed us, and because of their elevation to a higher plane, we conferred upon them the status of superior beings.

We have now emerged from the dark ages of whale killing into the light of whale reverence. The mechanisms have long been in place for a new religion, admittedly restricted to those who are prepared to accept cetaceans as godlike creatures. We have all the necessary clergy, the icons, and even the litany—sung by the whales. If Herman Melville is the high priest—or at least the author of the Bible—and D. H. Lawrence the author of the Book of Cetacean Prayer, the leaders of the "Save the Whale" organizations are the evangelists. I have attended many meetings of these groups that resembled revival meetings in virtually all particulars. It seems not altogether unreasonable to consider the whale a superior being: It is larger than life, literally and figuratively; endowed with "extensions of senses that we have lost or never attained, living by voices we shall never hear," as Henry Beston wrote in *The Outermost House.* Farther along in the same paragraph, he said, ". . . they are other nations, caught with ourselves in the net of life and time, fellow prisoners of the splendour and travail of the earth." (Beston was writing of animals in general, but this sentence seems particularly applicable to cetaceans.) One whale researcher has suggested that we are wasting time and money trying to make contact with extraterrestrials in outer space. If we could only figure out how to talk to the whales, he says, we would find another intelligence right here on our own planet.

Since we do not even have an effective definition of intelligence for humans, how can we expect to find one that works for creatures that are so different in almost all particulars and live in a different medium? Nevertheless, one of the foundation blocks of the "Save the Whale" movement was the admiration of cetacean intellect, and a critical element in that attitude was a book called *Mind in the Waters.* Edited by Joan McIntyre and published in 1974, the book claimed to be "a celebration of the consciousness of whales and dolphins," and on the jacket appeared these words: "We are beginning to discern the outline of another mind on the planet—a mind anatomically like ours, but profoundly different."* The book contains poems, drawings (some of them by me), and essays on such subjects as "The Evolution of Whale Intelligence" (Sterling Bunnell), "The Whale Brain: Input and Behavior" (Myron Jacobs), and "A Feeling of Weirdness" (John Lilly).

In *Mind in the Waters,* Joan McIntyre wrote:

This is the mind that I have always believed existed somewhere. The deep calm mind of the ocean, connected to body, living *in* the world, not looking out at it. Surrounded by the gentle clicking of each other's sound, these creatures drift and dive, carve shining bubbled circles in the still water, move like dream ghosts out of the seas' unchanging past. Not changing the world around them—only listening, touching, eating, being. It seems enough.

Given the abundance and variety of religions on earth, it is not surprising that a "whale religion" has arisen. Certainly the salvation of a fellow mammalian species is a laudable objective, religious or otherwise. Better this, it might be argued, than a religion that calls for the death of infidels or the ostracism of nonbelievers. (Unfortunately, there is some of this in the whale religion: The evangelists refer to those who kill whales for profit as "pagans" or "barbarians.") It is not surprising that the whale has been chosen for the symbol of the environmental movement; to the faithful it represents purity, goodness, and hope for the future.

Not everyone manifests their "whale worship" in the same fashion. The Japanese began commercial whaling somewhere around the middle of the seventeenth century, but even though they have had a long and bloody whaling history, their attitudes toward cetaceans have not always been consumer oriented. As with so many things Japanese, there is a paradox in their approach: At the same time that they have been slaughtering whales by the thousands, they have been making them the objects of religious veneration. According to Paul Ryan, "The Japanese attribute souls to both animals and objects—specifically, to those that have been of some use, have been

---

* There are some heretics who do not believe that whales are particularly intelligent. In a 1989 article entitled "How Brainy Are Cetaceans?" the British researcher Margaret Klinowska wrote, "In many respects, then, the cetacean brain is actually quite primitive. It retains all the structures found in primitive mammals, such as hedgehogs or bats. It shows none of the structural differences from area to area typical of advanced brains like those of primates. . . . What of the much-vaunted learning ability of cetaceans? Not all species have it, even though the ones that don't perform such tricks have brains as large as those that do. And many other animals—for example, sheep dogs, sea lions, and parrots—perform equally impressive feats without being granted a special order of intelligence."

*O*ne of the more surprising developments in the convoluted history of men and whales has been the introduction of Japanese whale watching. Shown here is a diving humpback off the Ogasawara (Bonin) Islands in April 1992.

harmed, or have come to the end of their usefulness." At various temples and whaling stations throughout Japan, one can find memorial tablets to whalers that have been lost, but there are also stones erected to the souls of the whales.

According to the material distributed by the Japanese Whaling Association (JWA) during the battle to fend off the moratorium, the Japanese *love* whales. They worship their departed souls at Buddhist shrines; simultaneously, they eat whale sashimi, whale bacon, whale steak, and whale sausage. From a 1980 JWA publication:

> The Japanese started hunting whales about 1,000 years ago along Japanese coasts. In the 17th century, they developed a unique method called the netting system that employed sculls to catch whales. Catches were completely used—meat, skin, and all, since the Japanese had a religious belief that hunted whales could enter Nirvana only when complete use was made of them. The Japanese often built tombstones for hunted whales, or treated them as gods of the ocean.

To the Judeo-Christian mind, preparing your gods as steak or bacon might appear somewhat disrespectful, but there are many aspects of the

Japanese culture that the *gaijin* does not understand. In the same leaflet (called "Living with Whales"), we can read the following:

> ... Whale meat continues to play an important role as a protein source even now that whale catches have been curtailed considerably, and whale meat is used in many sectors, including school feeding. Apart from being important in Japanese eating customs, whale meat is an important source of animal protein with a cholesterol count less than half that of beef or pork, and less than that of fish in general.*

The whale has come full circle; it began as a mythical monster and metamorphosed into a commercial object. Precursing the twentieth-century beatification of the whale was Herman Melville, whose white whale was the first literary monster. When the commercialism became too crass and the whales were threatened, the new religion of conservation embraced the whales and dolphins, elevating them through the use of science and emotion to a higher level than they had ever achieved before. The transition took them from monster to commodity, from literary icon to religious icon.

In 1986, as if to validate the whale's status as sacred monster, a film was made in which the whales actually save the world. In *Star Trek IV: The Voyage Home,* an alien space probe arrives at planet Earth in the twenty-third century, vaporizing the oceans and ionizing the atmosphere. Mr. Spock suggests that the transmissions may not be meant for humans, since there is—or *was,* by the twenty-third century—another intelligent life form on earth. They deduce that the probe is trying to communicate with humpback whales, but unfortunately, by this time all the whales have been eliminated. The intrepid crew of the starship *Enterprise* travels back in time to San Francisco in the 1980s to collect the whales needed to talk the aliens out of blowing up the earth. To familiarize themselves with these creatures from the past, they pay a visit to the Cetacean Institute (actually the Monterey Bay Aquarium), where there are humpbacks in captivity. (The filming of captive humpbacks involved some very effective model making, since it was obviously impossible to maintain a full-grown whale in a tank.) The whales are released from the aquarium because it is too expensive to feed them, but Kirk, Spock, et al. locate them in Alaskan waters and beam them aboard just before they would have been shot by a whaler's harpoon. In

---

*In January 1993, the Japanese government announced its intention to encourage people to eat more whale meat. According to David Sanger in the *New York Times,* "The campaigns, including television advertisements, newsletters and thousands of pamphlets to be distributed in the schools, are part of Japan's effort to build support for the resumption of commercial whaling after the International Whaling Commission meets in Kyoto in May."

whale-sized tanks aboard the *Enterprise* they are whisked forward to the
year 2315, to the relief and salvation of the entire planet.

In 1993, a movie was made that unequivocally celebrated the whale—
and vilified its would-be captors and jailers. *Free Willy* is the story of a killer
whale held captive in a Seattle oceanarium, where he is befriended by a
young orphan boy. When the villainous owners of the park decide to kill
Willy so they can collect the insurance ("the whale is worth more dead than
alive"), the boy (with the help of his foster father and an Indian named
Randolph) frees Willy by loading him on a truck and delivering him to a
place where he can rejoin his family in the wild. The message of *Free Willy*
is that whales are so special that they should not be maintained in captivity—certainly not by people who would exploit them—and the argument
against keeping cetaceans in captivity is simplistically resolved not only by
the film but by its very title.

The right whale, the first species to be hunted commercially, lives only
in scattered populations around the world, putting in appearances, as if to
confirm its existence, at places where it used to be plentiful: Australia,
South Africa, New England. (But in the Bay of Biscay and other European
locations where they were first hunted, there are no survivors.) The vast
herds of rorquals—the blue, fin, and sei whales—that drew the factory
whalers to the Antarctic are no more, and it has been suggested that the
blue whale, the largest and grandest creature ever to have lived on earth,
will become extinct in our lifetime or that of our children. Thirty-foot
minkes, long ignored by the whalers in favor of larger prey, are now coming
under the gun—because their larger cousins are so reduced in number as to
make them commercially extinct. The trusting humpbacks, always among
the first whales to be killed when the whalers arrived, carol into the abyssal
thermoclines from their isolated breeding grounds (Hawaii, the Caribbean,
Australia) or breach lustily with the "gay foam" that so entranced Melville
on the feeding grounds of southeast Alaska, New England, and the Antarctic. The bowheads of Spitzbergen, Greenland, and the Canadian high Arctic were slaughtered to extinction by the Dutch and British whalers of
Rotterdam and Hull, and when the California steam whalers found another
population north of the Bering Straits, they killed them, too. The barnacled
gray whales of Baja California were threatened twice, first by the California
whalers and then in the 1920s, when the Norwegians who found them offshore during their migrations reduced the populations to dangerously low
levels. The gray whale has come back to what we believe are "pre-exploita-
tion" numbers, not necessarily because it was protected (which it was) but
also because there was no rival species to supplant it when its numbers were

reduced. Gray whales are bottom feeders, and with no competition for the amphipods they scoop up from the muddy bottom of the Bering Sea, their resurrection went unchallenged by other whale species. (In the Antarctic, by contrast, when the blue and fin whales were hunted out, minke whales, which feed on the same organisms, proliferated, making it difficult for the larger species to recover.) Only the sperm whale, the enigmatic lord of the deep, exists today in substantial numbers.

We know now that the monsters are threatened, not only because we are more sophisticated about their mythology but also because their actual numbers are being drastically reduced. The various species of "great" whales (those that were hunted for commerce) are almost all seriously depleted. No species has actually been exterminated, but some populations have completely disappeared. Whereas there used to be an Atlantic population of gray whales, it was gone by the seventeenth century, and the western Pacific gray whale, once the object of Japanese and Korean fisheries, is also gone.* Now the only representatives of the genus *Eschrichtius* are found along the western coast of North America. Dutch and British whalers of the seventeenth and eighteenth centuries completely eliminated the bowhead (which they called the Polar Whale, the Greenland Whale, or the Mysticetus) from the waters of the eastern Arctic, leaving only the Bering Sea stock, which was not discovered until 1848. Commercial whalers took after this population with their customary zeal, and now the only remnants of a species once so plentiful that it supported a European fishery for two centuries are found along the North Slope of Alaska, where they can be hunted—for traditional and subsistence reasons—only by the Alaskan eskimos.

Why do we need whales? As monsters they are obsolete, and as commercial objects, they seem to have outlived their usefulness. As endangered species, however, they serve to remind us of our frailty, which may be, in this crucial time of our planet's peril, their most important function.

---

*In 1993, underwater photographer Koji Nakamura was diving off the island of Izu (south of Tokyo Bay) when he saw (and videotaped) feeding gray whales. He reported it to Jim Darling, a gray whale researcher in Vancouver, who wrote in *Ocean Realm* that "perhaps this is a sign of recovery of gray whales . . . or perhaps this is just another haunting of the Japanese shores, once home to thousands of gray whales."

LEVIATHAN VERSUS KRAKEN

The sperm whale is found in all climates, and in every sea; he feeds upon an inanimate animal substance called a squid, which grows upon the bottom of the sea, and is never seen upon the surface, except when torn up by the whale. I have seen a dying whale vomit it up. I have opened the stomach of a whale and seen it there in pieces, which convinces me that the animal is very large also, as well as small; and that the sperm whale almost always when in want of food goes to the ocean bed.

—From a letter from
Capt. Thomas W. Roys (whaler) to
Lt. Matthew Fontaine Maury (oceanographer),
January 19, 1851

*W*HILE SCIENTISTS WERE debating the existence of the kraken, another group of men knew that there was certainly something that fit the early descriptions; in fact, many of them had actually seen it. Yankee sperm whalers, plying the world's oceans in pursuit of the cachalot, often saw their prey, in its death throes, regurgitate large pieces of *something,* and they sometimes hooked one of the pieces to get a closer look at it. In 1856, Charles Nordhoff wrote a book called *Whaling and Fishing* in which he described what the whalemen called "squid," which he believed to be "a monster species of cuttle fish":

> The animal seldom exhibits itself to man; but pieces of the feelers are often seen afloat, on good whaling ground. I have examined such from the boats, and found them to consist of a dirty yellow surface, beneath which appeared a slimy, jelly-like flesh. Of several pieces which we fell in with at various times when in the boats, most had on them portions of the "sucker," or air exchanger with which the common cuttle-fish is furnished, to enable him to hold the prey about which he has slung his snake-like arms. These floating pieces are supposed to have been bitten off or torn by the whales, while feeding on the bottom. Many of those we saw were the circumference of a flour barrel. If this be the size of the arms, of which they probably have hundreds, each furnished with air exhausters the size of a dinner plate, what must be the magnitude of a body which supports such an array?

Of all the monsters mentioned in this book, only two of them are intimately and regularly associated. The sperm whale has been described as feeding on squid, giant and otherwise, and the giant squid has often been accused of causing the circular scars on the head of the whale either in an attempt to eat the whale or in the struggle not to be eaten. Because there are other species of whales—the bottlenose whales (*Hyperoodon*), for example, which can and do dive as deeply as *Physeter*—if the squid was the attacker and not the victim, some of these other whales might also show sucker scars on their skin. Since there are no records of any other whale species with sucker marks, the argument could be made that the sperm whales are the aggressors. (Interviewed for a 1989 article in *Equinox*, teuthologist Frederick A. Aldrich was quoted to the effect that in a battle with a sperm whale, the giant squid always loses.)

Some believe that *Architeuthis* is a sluggish animal, neither powerful nor aggressive, but suppositions like that are never going to interfere with the creature's enduring reputation as a man-eating, ship-grabbing, whale-wrestling monster. It has long been a part of sperm-whale lore that it has to dive to prodigious depths to seek out its favorite prey. The size and alleged ferocity of *Architeuthis* provide more than enough ammunition for the creative writer or overimaginative naturalist, and titanic battles between the squid and its (perhaps apocryphal) archenemy, the sperm whale, will continue to appear in the popular literature. (In the Hall of Ocean Life of New York's American Museum of Natural History, there is a diorama that purports to show this very action; unfortunately, it is too poorly lit to see what is going on.)

There are very few contemporary accounts of a battle between a giant squid and a sperm whale, but just before the outbreak of World War II, J. W. Wray was sailing off the Kermadec Islands (north of New Zealand) when he spotted a disturbance in the water. As he tells the story in *South Sea Vagabonds*, he sailed over to investigate, "when, to our amazement, a giant tentacle, easily twenty-five feet long, came out of the water, waved around for a second, and crashed back into the water again. A few seconds later our hearts stood still as the fore part of a large whale shot out of the water barely thirty yards away and, encircling its head, its enormous tentacles thrashing the water, was a truly villainous giant octopus. . . . Two more giant tentacles emerged, making a terrific commotion on the water." Although Wray calls the animal an octopus, the length of the tentacles makes the case for a giant squid, and the battle with the whale (unidentified but occurring in an area well known for sperm whales) certainly suggests the traditional antagonists.

In *Moby-Dick*, as the *Pequod* sails northeast of Java, the harpooner Daggoo sees a "strange spectre" from his perch on the main masthead. They lowered the boats and "gazed at the most wondrous phenomenon which the secret seas have hitherto revealed to mankind":

In the distance, a great white mass lazily rose, and rising higher and higher, and disentangling itself from the azure, at last gleamed before our prow like a snow-slide, new slid from the hills. Thus glistening for a moment, as slowly it subsided, and sank. Then once more arose, and silently gleamed.

It turns out to be "the great live squid." No "battle of the giants" there, but Frank Bullen, another whaleman turned author, had no compunctions about describing a clash between a squid and a whale. Bullen's narrative, *The Cruise of the "Cachalot,"* is replete with improbably theatrical episodes of courage—usually his—and wildly unlikely behavior on the part of various animals, and most historians are inclined to dismiss his book as more fiction than fact. Nevertheless, the book does contain a vivid description of a battle between the two gigantic predators:

> A very large sperm whale was locked in deadly conflict with a cuttle-fish, or squid, almost as large as himself, whose interminable tentacles seemed to enlace the whole of his great body. The head of the whale especially seemed a perfect net-work of writhing arms—naturally, I suppose, for it appeared as if the whale had the tail part of the mollusc in his jaws, and, in a businesslike, methodical way, was sawing through it. By the side of the black columnar head of the whale appeared the head of the great squid, as awful an object as one could well imagine even in a fevered dream. Judging as carefully as possible, I estimated it to be at least as large as one of our pipes, which contained three hundred and fifty gallons; but it may have been, and probably was, a good deal larger. The eyes were very remarkable from their size and blackness, which, contrasted with the livid whiteness of the head, made their appearance all the more striking. They were, at least, a foot in diameter, and seen under such conditions, looked decidedly eerie and hobgoblinlike.

Bullen's narrative (which was published in 1898) appears to owe something to Melville's, especially as concerns the coloration of the squid.* The amount of salt required to season Bullen's story is evident from his setting: The cuttlefish and the whale staged their epic battle by moonlight.

Bullen and Melville may have embellished their observations with a

---

*In Melville's novel, the living squid is a ghostly white color, and Daggoo actually mistakes it for Moby Dick, crying out, "There! there again! there she breaches! right ahead! The White Whale, the White Whale!" Most squid that have been examined were washed ashore or taken from the stomachs of sperm whales, which would account for their bleached appearance. Since very few healthy giant squid have ever been observed, their color—which they can change at will—is not well documented, but in those instances where some of the color was preserved, it was seen to be a dark brick red.

*I*n 1875, viewers aboard the bark *Pauline* off Brazil saw what some described as a fight between a sea serpent and a sperm whale. Except for the "eye," it is quite easy to see the "serpent" as the tentacle of a giant squid.

helping of fictional exaggeration, or they may have completely fabricated their descriptions of giant squid, but there seems to be no question that the crew and officers of the bark *Pauline* saw a battle between a sperm whale and another creature on July 8, 1875. As later reported in the *Illustrated London News*, Capt. George Drevar was some twenty miles off Cape San Roque (Brazil) when the *Pauline* came upon "a monstrous sea serpent coiled twice round a large sperm whale." The "sea serpent" conquers the whale in Drevar's narration, pulling the hapless cetacean below the surface, "where no doubt it was gorged at the serpent's leisure." A week later, Captain Drevar was still in the same latitude, now eighty miles from shore, when he "was astonished to see the same or a similar monster. It was throwing its head and about 40 feet of its body in a horizontal position as it passed onwards by the stern of our vessel." Drevar described the serpent's mouth as "always being open," but with this exception, the creature sounds suspiciously like a giant squid. (Heuvelmans, ever on the lookout for verifiable serpents, concludes that the open mouth and the coloration cannot be reconciled with a squid and writes that it was a snake or, more likely, a giant eel, which, he writes, "are immensely powerful constrictors"—which they certainly are not.)

Sperm whales are known to feed on cephalopods, and because these whales have been hunted commercially for almost three centuries, we have had more than ample opportunity to examine the stomach contents. (In the early days of the fishery, however, when the blubber was stripped off along-side the ship, the carcass, along with the stomach contents, was discarded. It was only when the whales were hauled up on the decks of the great factory ships that the stomach contents were spilled out on deck.) But even before the days of mechanized whaling, whalers observed their quarry, in its death throes, vomiting up great hunks of what could only have been giant squid. As one might expect, Melville discusses this phenomenon in *Moby-Dick*:

> For although other species of whales find their food above water and may be seen by man in the act of feeding, the spermaceti whale obtains his food in unknown zones below the surface; and only by inference is it that anyone can tell of what, precisely, that food consists. At times, when closely pursued, he will disgorge what are supposed to be the detached arms of the squid; some of them thus exhibited exceeding twenty or thirty feet in length. They fancy that the monster to which these arms belonged ordinarily clings by them to the bed of the ocean; and that the sperm whale, unlike other species, is supplied with teeth in order to attack and tear it.*

Some fifty years later (in *Denizens of the Deep*), Frank Bullen wrote much the same thing:

> Every officer, to say nothing of the men, must have known of the very real existence of the great Squid, since scarcely a sperm whale can be killed without first ejecting from his stomach huge fragments of this popularly believed by seamen to be the largest of all God's creatures. Not only so, but in every book which has been written about the sperm whale fishery some allusion to the great Cuttle-fish will surely be found, although it must be admitted that so much superstitiously childish matter is usually mixed up with the facts as to make the latter difficult of belief.

Aboard the fictional *Cachalot*, Bullen espies "great masses of white, semi-transparent-looking substance floating about, of huge size and irregular shape," and asks the mate to tell him what they could be. "When dying," the mate explains, "the cachalot always ejected the contents of his

---

*Melville turned out to be wrong about both the squid *and* the whale. Squid—giant or otherwise—do not cling to the seabed with their arms; and the teeth of sperm whales, located in only the lower jaw, are probably used only to capture the squid, pincer fashion, not to tear them. For the most part, squid that have been examined from the stomachs of sperm whales exhibit no tooth marks or punctures, and it is now assumed that the sperm whale captures its prey by emitting focused sound beams of such intensity that they can stun or even kill their prey.

stomach, which were invariably composed of such masses as we saw before us; he believed the stuff to be portions of a big cuttle-fish, bitten off by the whale for the purpose of swallowing. . . ." Bullen hooks one of the lumps, and draws it alongside:

> It was at once evident that it was a massive fragment of cuttle-fish—tentacle or arm—as thick as a stout man's body, and with six or seven sucking discs or *acetabula* on it. These were about as large as a saucer, and on their inner edge were thickly set with hooks and claws all round the rim, sharp as needles, and almost the size and shape of a tiger's.

Prince Albert I of Monaco seems to have developed a unique method of studying fast-moving creatures that could not easily be caught in nets or trawls. He collected those animals that might themselves have captured mid-water speedsters such as squid, and upon opening their stomachs, *voilà!* the elusive cephalopods. While sailing *Princesse Alice* through the Azores in 1895, Albert approached some Azorean whalers who had harpooned a 40-foot sperm whale and observed that the dying whale was vom-

*A*s in almost all illustrations of the sperm whale versus the giant squid, it is not clear who is attacking whom.

iting up large pieces of squid. His crew collected the "precious regurgita-tions" and upon analysis recognized that they had the tentacles of a giant squid. This technique so intrigued the prince that he promptly went into the whaling business and commissioned two boats to collect various cetaceans and report to him with the stomach contents.

In one instance, the crew collected two large cephalopods that were previously unknown to science. One of them (according to an 1896 article in *Nature* by J. Y. Buchanan) was "covered with large, solid, rhomboidal scales, arranged spirally like those of a pine cone." A squid with scales was highly unusual, and later examinations revealed that these were actually nipple-like projections called papillae, which only *looked* like scales. (The species was named *Lepidoteuthis grimaldii; lepidos* is Greek for "scale," *teuthis* is "squid," and Grimaldi is the family name of the reigning house of Monaco.) Buchanan concluded his discussion of Prince Albert's unusual way of catching squid with these words: "Their great agility enables them to avoid every attempt to take them by nets; and it would appear that, for the present, the only means of capturing these interesting and gigantic ani-mals is to commission a bigger giant to undertake the task, and to kill him in his turn when he has performed the service."

In his comprehensive study of the sperm whales captured from the Durban, South Africa, fishery between 1926 and 1931, L. Harrison Matthews examined the stomachs of eighty-one whales. The stomachs of nearly all of them contained the remains of cephalopods, among other things.* Most of them were small, averaging about a meter in length, but the "very large cephalopods were represented only by beaks in the stomachs and scars on the skin." There is no question, however, that sperm whales occasionally battle and ingest monster squid: According to Rees and Maul, one was even regurgitated in a state where it still showed signs of life. A whale harpooned off Madeira in 1952 had vomited up a 34-footer that weighed about 330 pounds and writhed on the flensing deck until it expired. Biologist Robert Clarke was present at the whaling station at Porto Pim on the Azorean island of Fayal in 1955 when a squid was discovered in the stomach of a 47-foot-long whale. It weighed 405 pounds and measured 34 feet 5 inches from the tip of the tail to the tip of the longest tentacle.

The digestive juices of sperm whales are strong, and the remains of

---

*The diet of sperm whales is not restricted to cephalopods. In a study of the stomach contents of 174 North Pacific sperm whales, Soviet scientist M. N. Tarasevich discovered sixteen species of squid, two species of octopus, and five species of fish. According to this study, because male *Kashalots* are larger and more powerful—and can therefore dive deeper—their diet differs substan-tially from that of the females. In other regions of the world ocean, sperm whales are recorded as eating numerous species of fish, sharks, rays, and an occasional crustacean.

their food items are often corroded beyond recognition. Squid beaks, however, are composed of a tough, chitinous material and resist digestion much more successfully than the soft parts.* A branch of teuthology involves the identification of squid beaks as a way of identifying the species (it is fairly easy to identify the beak of *Architeuthis;* it can be 6 inches long). That sperm whales do indeed capture and eat giant squid can be seen in Fiscus and Rice's examination of the stomach contents of sperm whales that were collected off the coast of California from 1959 to 1970: Twelve of the 552 whales examined had mandibles of giant squid in their stomachs. But, wrote the authors, "sperm whales may eat *Architeuthis* more often than our records indicate. . . . *Architeuthis* mandibles could be overlooked among remains of *Moroteuthis robusta,* another "giant" species (although smaller than *Architeuthis*) that is the predominant food of sperm whales off California."

The analysis of sperm whales' stomach contents can also be used to distinguish the various components of their diet. Moreover, the relative numbers of squid, which would otherwise be totally unavailable to science, can be estimated by the number of beaks in the stomachs of captured sperm whales. Finds of 5,000 to 7,000 beaks per whale are not uncommon, and Berzin mentions one Soviet scientist who counted 28,000 beaks in the stomach of a single whale, indicating a feeding frenzy in which 14,000 squid were consumed. It would appear that such consumption would require a dense concentration of squid; indeed, squid may be the most numerous large animals in the ocean.

Malcolm Clarke, a British scientist who specializes in sperm whales and squid, commented on the complex interaction of the two in a 1977 study:

> Man's awareness of the existence of large squid came, not from what he caught in his nets, but from monsters floating dead or moribund at the sea surface and from the tales of whalers who had seen, with unbelieving eyes, whales vomit complete or dismembered kraken of immense proportions. Such doubtful tales hardened into drawings and recorded measurements over one century ago, and ever since, man has tried desperately to catch by net and line, these will-o'-the-wisps of the sea. Though our nets have become larger and larger and faster and faster, very little progress, and most of that in the last decade, has been made towards catching any deep

---

*Although the actual process of its formation is unknown, the material known as ambergris occurs in the intestinal tract of sperm whales and can be found in the whale or vomited up and floating on the surface of the ocean. It is a grayish, crumbly material, often compared to peat moss, that somehow forms around a squid beak. In the past it was worth more than its weight in gold and was used as a fixative for perfumes. The largest lump ever recorded weighed 983 pounds.

sea squids greater than half a meter or so in length. In a century, many tantalising glimpses of the deep sea squids have come from strandings on the coast and from the stomachs of toothed whales, particularly the commercially exploited Sperm Whale.

Clarke estimated the amount of food required to feed the enormous world population of sperm whales. (Recognizing the difficulties of estimating whale populations, he wrote, "Estimates of the whale population are, unhappily, notoriously questionable, but a 1973 estimate placed this at 1¼ million.") Using a mean weight of 15 tons for males and 5 tons for females, Clarke arrived at a total weight of the world's sperm whales of 10 million tons, which would require *100 million tons of squid per year*. This is larger than the biomass of the annual world catch of fish by fishermen "and probably approaches the total biomass of mankind." In other words, the weight of squid eaten every year by sperm whales is greater than the weight of the entire human race.

From the examination of the stomach contents, it was obvious that sperm whales consumed large numbers of squid, but how the squid were transformed from fast, free-swimming animals to stomach contents was a mystery. Like all odontocetes (toothed whales), sperm whales are known to echolocate. From an apparatus in the head, sperm whales and most dolphins can broadcast high-frequency sounds directionally into the water and then read the returning echoes for information on the identity (and perhaps the condition, speed, texture, etc.) of the object. The echolocation of dolphins has been long recognized, but the mechanics by which the animals actually *caught* their prey were more problematic. It is one thing to locate, say, a school of small squid, but quite another to catch enough of them to make a meal. After all, the squid don't have to surface to breathe, but the whales have to do their food-locating and food-catching while holding their breath, often in the darkness of the depths.

Even when the echolocating capabilities of odontocetes were understood, there was a piece missing from the puzzle, since the first cetological acousticians simply assumed that the whales found the squid by listening to their echoes and then dashed around gobbling them up. Upon reflection, this did not appear to be a terribly efficient method of hunting, especially considering the speed and maneuverability of the prey as well as its obvious unwillingness to be eaten. The sperm whale has massive peglike teeth in its lower jaw, so if the whale chased down its prey and snagged it in its jaws, the squid ought to have shown some evidence of having been bitten, but they didn't. One of the first to notice this was the Soviet cetologist

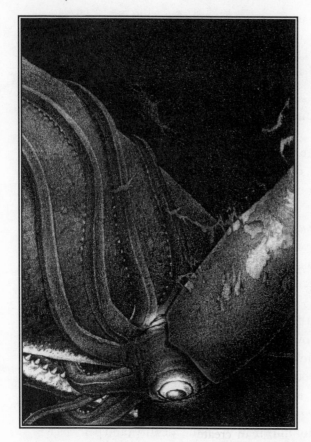

*W*rapped in the arms of a giant squid, a sperm whale dives for the depths. The squid is probably better adapted to continue the battle under water, since—unlike the whale—it does not have to surface for air. Notice the gigantic, bioluminescent eyes of the squid and the way its delicate skin is shredded during the struggle.

A. A. Berzin, who published an exhaustive study of the sperm whale in 1972. After examining the stomach contents of a large number of sperm whales, he wrote:

> But the mystery of how this whale feeds deepened in view of the follow-ing circumstances. . . . Beale gives an example of a capture of sperm whales in normal condition, one of which was blind while two others had deformed jaws. Up to 10 sperms with badly deformed jaws were recorded in our materials. They were in the same condition as all the other animals and had well-filled stomachs, the contents of which did not differ qualita-tively from those of other sperm whales caught the same day. . . . All the above suggests that neither the teeth nor the lower jaw need to participate in obtaining food and in the digestive process.

If the sperm whale does not use its jaws and teeth to capture its food, what does it use? In his study, Berzin reviewed the earlier theories, one of which had been propounded by our old friend Thomas Beale (he of the octopus "attack" on pp. 261–63). Like most sperm whalers, Beale could not imagine how "such a large and unwieldy animal as this whale could ever catch a sufficient quantity of such small animals, if he had to pursue them individually for his food" and suggested that the whale descends to a certain depth, where he "remains in as quiet a state as possible, opening his narrow elongated mouth until the lower jaw hangs down perpendicularly. . . ." The jaws and teeth, wrote Beale, "being of a bright glistening white colour . . . seem to be the incitement by which the prey are attracted, and when a sufficient number are in his mouth, he rapidly closes the jaw and swallows the contents."

Berzin noted that "at a depth of some 100 meters, both prey and hunter are invisible to each other. Moreover, squid are known to be much more mobile than sperm whales . . . even small squid can develop speeds of up to 40 km an hour, and larger specimens still higher speeds, far outdistancing sperms." Obviously, there had to be some device whereby the whale could stop or at least slow down the squid to capture them, and indeed there was. Even earlier than Berzin, another pair of Soviet cetologists, Vladimir Bel'kovich and Alexei Yablokov, had calculated the sound intensity that might be developed in the sperm whale's nose, and in 1963 they collaborated on a short article entitled "The Whale—an Ultrasonic Projector" in which they suggested that the whale might somehow use its nose to project sounds loud enough to stun its prey. Berzin wrote that by concentrating its sound beam on a selected object, "the animal can create a short-term pressure which must act as an ultrasonic blow capable, even if briefly, of halting, stunning, and paralyzing the object."*

In 1983, Kenneth S. Norris of the University of California at Santa Cruz and Bertel Møhl of Aarhus University in Denmark published their hypothesis that odontocetes could indeed debilitate their prey with sound. Other theories (such as Beale's, above, or Clarke's), according to which the whale maintains a position of neutral buoyancy and waits for a school of squid to swim within range, did not explain the uninjured state of the squid in the sperm whale's stomach, nor did these other theories explain how a large animal like the sperm whale could obtain the one to two thousand kilograms of food per day that would be required to sustain it. The "sonic boom" hypothesis not only explains how the cumbersome sperm whale

*According to V. A. Kozak, another Soviet cetologist, in order to be able to hunt in complete darkness, the sperm whale has developed "a unique video-receptor system in the process of evolutionary transformation, which lets the animal obtain the image of objects in the acoustic flow of reflected energy even in complete darkness." In other words, the sperm whale has a sort of audiovisual system that transforms sound into "images," employing the "blisters" on the rear wall of the whale's nasofrontal sac, located in the hollowed-out cradle of the skull.

hunts and captures the swift cephalopods; it also answers many other questions that had heretofore been as problematic as the feeding technique.

If the sperm whale debilitated or killed its prey with sound, it would go a long way toward explaining the unusual construction of the jaws; the whale could use its tooth-studded lower jaw pincer fashion to pluck the floating squid out of the water or off the bottom—which would then account for the lack of tooth marks on the prey. If the squid floated to the bottom, the sperm whale might plow its lower jaw through the sediment to pick them up, which would explain the occasional strange items found in sperm-whale stomachs: shoes, rocks, logs, sand. It would also account for the occasional entrapment—and subsequent drowning—of sperm whales by undersea telegraph cables; plowing along the bottom, the whale might accidentally become entangled in a loop of cable; or it might even mistake the cable for the tentacle of a giant squid. In a 1957 study entitled "Whales Entangled in Deep Sea Cables," oceanographer Bruce Heezen listed fourteen instances of sperm whales trapped and drowned in cables and wrote, "It is possible that the whales attack tangled masses of slack cable mistaking them for items of food." The deepest recorded entanglement was 620 fathoms, or 3,720 feet.

Even though its components are still a mystery, the gigantic nose of the sperm whale, with its sacs, tubes, valves, and above all, its gigantic reservoir of oil, would make a very effective resonating chamber. In their summary, Norris and Møhl wrote, "We find the dimensions and structure of the spermaceti organ complex not to be in conflict with the functions of a high power sound generator, possibly with focussing abilities."

Not everyone agrees that the nose of the sperm whale is a sound resonator. Malcolm Clarke, who has devoted a professional lifetime to the study of sperm whales, squid, and the interaction of the two, believes that the function of the oil in the spermaceti organ in the whale's nose is "to provide a system by which the whale can be near neutral buoyancy at the surface and at great depth, and can, by temperature control of the wax, rise to the surface from great depth with no physical effort." Of Norris's hypothesis, Clarke wrote, ". . . It is hard to accept the suggestion of one worker that such focussing can concentrate sound intensely enough to stun the squids that are the sperm whale's main prey." And Norris (1972) strenuously disagrees with Clarke, calling some of his ideas "incorrect," "misleading," and "inconceivable." It is possible, of course, for the sperm whale's nose—like the noses of other mammals (the elephant, for example)—to serve more than one purpose, unless those purposes are somehow mutually exclusive.

And what of the squid in all of this? One observation becomes clear

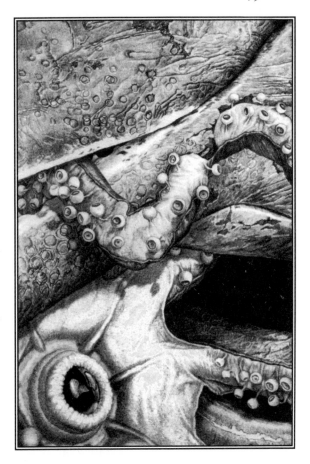

*I*n this drawing by Glen Loates, a sperm whale chomps down on the tentacle of a giant squid. (You are looking at the underside of the lower jaw of the whale, which is facing to the left.) The squid's beak is at the lower left, ready to be brought into play by the powerful muscles of its buccal mass.

immediately: If the sperm whale is going to debilitate its prey with sound, the prey has to be debilitatable; that is, it has to have some mechanism on which the sonic booms can act. In other words, the squid has to be able to hear, or at least respond to, underwater vibrations, a subject that has been debated for years (see pp. 183–84). Norris and Møhl experimented with small (4 centimeter mantle length) specimens of *Alloteuthis,* and larger (18 to 27 centimeters) *Loligo,* and discovered that certain underwater sound values could fatally injure the squid. (The process is not unlike fishing with dynamite, in which the sudden explosion ruptures the viscera, swim bladders, kidneys, or gonads of the fishes and kills them.) But, wrote the authors, "the lowest pressure that will debilitate the largest squid remains unknown."

The question of the squid's response to the whales' sound bursts is a complex one. One of the more persuasive arguments against squid "hearing" was forwarded by Michael Taylor in an essay in *Nature* in 1986. (It was a comment on Moynihan's 1985 article on why cephalopods are deaf.) Taylor observed that since the whale has to locate the squid by sending out bursts of sound energy and then waiting for the echoes to tell it where the prey actually is, a squid that can hear would recognize these sounds even before the echoes returned to their sender and be warned well in advance of an impending attack. Even if the squid *could* hear the echolating sounds of the whale, it probably could not ascertain the direction from which the sounds were coming and could not, therefore, take the necessary evasive action. There is no question about the acuteness and directionality of odontocete hearing (mostly observed in captive bottlenose dolphins), so the whale still holds a significant auditory advantage.

One thing that we cannot learn from the examination of sperm whales' stomach contents is where in the water column *Architeuthis* lives or hunts. (Other species of squid have been caught in nets and trawls at certain depths—Roper and Young produced an extensive study on "Vertical Distribution of Pelagic Cephalopods" in 1975—but of *Architeuthis*, they wrote, "Very little is known of its vertical distribution or any other aspect of its biology.") Sperm whales are the deep-diving champions of the mammalian world, able to dive to known depths of ten thousand feet and hold their breath for an hour and a half. They would therefore be able to capture giant squid at any level that they can reach. Two juvenile giant squids were obtained from fish stomachs, but most of what we know about their distribution—vertical or otherwise—comes from the squid appearing on the beach, at the surface, or spilled out of a dead whale's stomach. These specimens are obviously related to where the whalers caught their prey, and just as the whalers hunted where the whales were supposed to be, so might the whales have gone to those locations where the squid were present.

Captured sperm whales are often scarred with round marks that look very much like those that would have been left by the suckers on the arms of giant squid. Since it is known that these whales eat squid of all sizes (but mostly smaller ones), it is not an unreasonable assumption that the scars are caused by squid unwilling to be eaten.* In *Depths of the Ocean* (1912), Johann Hjort made one of the most often quoted—and misquoted—remarks ever made about the giant squid. In 1902, Hjort was aboard the research vessel *Michael Sars* in the North Atlantic when the ship came across a small giant

---

*The durability of these scars might be a function of the depth at which the squid attached itself to the whale. Jacques Piccard, writing in his discussion of the submersible *Trieste*, says, "Suction is a formidable force in the atmosphere but it is truly enormous under the sea, doubling in force at 33 feet, tripling at 66 feet, and so on. Witness the severe lacerations imposed on the snouts of sperm whales by the suckers of the giant deep-sea squid *Architeuthis!*"

*A*lthough this scene has never been witnessed by man, it is known that giant squid engage in titanic battles with sperm whales.

squid floating dead at the surface north of the Faroes. Nothing spectacular about this sighting, but then Hjort wrote, ". . . In 1903 in Iceland I had the opportunity of making an interesting observation, showing the gigantic dimensions of these squids." The ship visited the whaling station at Mofjord, where there was a freshly killed sperm whale and a right whale. Hjort wrote:

> Inspecting the cachalot, I saw around its enormous jaw several long parallel stripes, consisting, as closer scrutiny revealed, of great numbers of circular scars or wounds about 27mm in diameter. . . . It occurred to me that these scars must have been left by the suckers of giant squid, and following up this idea I found in the whale's mouth a piece of squid tentacle 17cm in maximum diameter.

In Hjort's book there is a picture of the "skin of the cachalot with marks from the struggle with *Architeuthis*. Nat. size." The scars that Hjort measured at twenty-seven millimeters were a little over an inch in diameter, and

*A*t its maximum known size, *Mesonychoteuthis hamiltoni* has been measured at well over 20 feet in total length. In this photograph the long tentacles are out of the picture, and the ruler is 18" long.

in the photograph the largest one measures one inch across. The picture has been reproduced in almost every discussion of sperm whales and squid, but somehow the diameter of the circular scars has increased to ludicrous proportions, perhaps through a confusion of the 27-millimeter scars and the 17-centimeter-diameter *tentacle*, which equals 6.63 inches.*

There is another species of squid that figures prominently in the diet of Antarctic sperm whales, and that is *Mesonychoteuthis*. (The name can be translated as "middle-hooked squid" and refers to the location of the hooks

*A few of the more egregious examples follow: In the Time-Life book *Dangerous Sea Creatures*, we read that "an ordinary giant squid of 50 feet leaves teeth-ringed sucker marks measuring between three and four inches across on a whale, but sperm whales have been captured with tentacle marks 18 inches across. . . ." In *The Guinness Book of Animal Facts and Feats*, Gerald Wood wrote that scars "measuring up to 5 in. in diameter have been found on the skins of sperm whales captured in the North Atlantic," and Willy Ley—who should have known better—wrote (in *Exotic Zoology*): "Another claim goes for marks on the skin of such a whale of a sucking disk over 2 feet in diameter."

on the middle of each arm, between the basal and terminal ringed suckers.) According to G. C. Robson's 1925 description of the type specimen (based on fragments of two specimens collected off the South Shetland Islands), the longest arm was 46.3 inches (118 centimeters) long, and its "hand" was equipped with a series of swivel-based hooks that could be rotated in any direction. *Mesonychoteuthis* has a body that may be as large as or larger than that of *Architeuthis*, but its tentacles are much shorter. The single specimen that has been examined had a body length of 1 meter, but Nesis refers to it as a "giant," with a mantle length of 200–225 centimeters (7–7.5 feet.) It is believed to have a circumpolar Antarctic distribution.*

Because many of the known squid species live at unknown depths and cannot be effectively sampled by the use of nets, much of what we know about squid has come from the examination of the stomachs of sperm whales. In fact, some of the major studies of the distribution and systematics of squid use sperm-whale specimens as the basis. For example, Fiscus, Rice, and Wolman are the authors of a 1989 paper entitled "Cephalopods from the Stomachs of Sperm Whales Taken off California." Malcolm Clarke has published papers on cephalopod remains from sperm whales caught off western Canada, in the Tasman Sea, off Peru and Chile, and elsewhere in the Southern Hemisphere and has written the definitive guide on the subject, *A Handbook for the Identification of Squid Beaks*. The Japanese and the Russians, in recent years the world's leading whalers, centered their sperm whale fishery in the North Pacific, roughly between Hawaii and the Aleutians, and the factory ships often listed on their manifest a teuthologist—or at least a scientist other than a cetologist. Many species, such as *Mesonychoteuthis*, are known *only* from the stomachs of whales.

---

*When an adult male sperm whale was captured and examined at the Richmond (California) whaling station in 1970, several large squid beaks were discovered and, primarily because of their size, were assigned to *Architeuthis*. Malcolm Clarke subsequently identified them as *Mesonychoteuthis* in spite of the locality of the collection. When I wrote to Clarke to ask him about the presence of an Antarctic squid in the stomach of a California whale, he wrote, "I have examined numerous predators' stomachs and net catches from all over the world, and I have only collected flesh of this genus from south of the South Subtropical Convergence. Such specimens, including flesh, number many hundred and extend over a large sector of the Antarctic. My conclusion that *Mesonychoteuthis hamiltoni* is highly unlikely to occur off California seems reasonable to me."

THE OCTOPUS AS MONSTER

*I*N *Kingdom of the Octopus,* a book that is unabashedly pro-octopus, Frank W. Lane wrote that "their strangely repulsive appearance, and the fictional stories of their attacks, have built up in the popular mind a picture of the 'devil fish' which no amount of accurate description is ever likely to cut down to authentic size." And James Atz, of the American Museum of Natural History, wrote, "Ever since people started writing about such things—and probably when they only talked about them—they have never been content simply to name and describe the octopus, but have insisted upon passing judgment upon it." Even the *National Geographic,* dedicated to the dissemination of accurate scientific information, could not resist a description that includes much wild exaggeration and frightening rhetoric. In a 1919 article called "Devil-Fishing in the Gulf Stream," John Oliver La Gorce wrote:

> In appearance the octopus is most repulsive, having a large, ugly head, a fierce-looking mouth, armed with a pair of powerful horny jaws, shaped much like a parrot's beak, topped with two diabolical eyes set close together, which are positively capable of sending forth a demonic glare when angered. The grotesque head is mounted on a somewhat oval body, from which radiate eight arms, usually united at the base by a membrane. The arms or tentacles are provided with rows of suckers, with which it clasps and clings to its prey with uncanny strength and quickness. As a rule, it will not give battle to a man unless angered or injured, but when challenged will fight to the last, doing its best to pull the object of its wrath beneath the surface of the waters.

Things hadn't improved for the poor octopus by 1935. In another *National Geographic* article, this one by Roy Waldo Miner, the octopus is described as

> ... one of the most gruesome marauders of the sea. Hiding in rocky crevices on the bottom, or squatting in the midst of a nestlike lair of boulders, which it has dragged together, the repulsive creature lies in wait for its prey, the eight tapering arms sprawling in all directions, extending and contracting, clinging to the rocks with their powerful sucking disks, or undulating through crevices as they explore everything within reach. The large, coldly staring eyes are elevated on round protuberances enabling it to see in all directions. . . . Should an unwary fish or crustacean venture within reach, a long tapering tentacle darts forth, the slender tip encircles the prey, which struggles desperately to escape the adherent suckers, but without success, and the hapless creature is dragged down to the cruel jaws to be torn apart by the parrotlike beak.

By 1971, the *National Geographic* had tempered its approach, helped by the author of the article "Shy Monster: The Octopus," Gilbert Voss of the University of Miami, who wrote, "Over the years I have spent studying octopuses, [their] behavior has never failed to fill me with admiration and appreciation of their varied talents." Despite his admiration, Voss's article includes this negative introduction:

> With its writhing arms, big staring eyes, and bulbous body, the octopus arouses distaste in many people. Lacking a rigid skeleton, its seems a ghostly monstrosity as it flows stealthily along.

But then the author openly confesses his admiration for the octopus:

> Students of the octopus recognize it, however, as perhaps the most marvellous of all marine creatures. Possessing a highly sophisticated nervous system, it is endowed with intelligence superior to any other seadweller—except, of course, the marine mammals.

If the octopus has a problem, it is surely with language. Virtually every discussion of octopus behavior until quite recently has been couched in monstrously pejorative terms. For example, in Arthur Grimble's *A Pattern of Islands,* the "autobiographical" chronicle of a young British diplomat's posting to the Gilbert and Ellice Islands in the South Pacific, we read of his encounters with the local octopus hunters of Tarawa, which naturally causes him to recollect his preoccupation with Victor Hugo's *Toilers of the*

Sea (about which more later). He calls the octopus of Hugo's book "a giant so strong and loathsome" and then introduces the "atrocious monster that inhabits the seas between Samoa and the Ellice Islands: it is a "foul fiend; . . . a wicked looking piece of work, even in death, with those disgusting suckers studding its arms and those bulging filmed eyes staring out of the mottled gorgon face." Grimble eventually finds himself intimately entwined with one of these "flabby, moving horrors," but it is a little difficult to believe his description—which we will recount when we discuss encounters with the monsters.

There is no single creature known as "the octopus"; rather, some 150 varieties, ranging in size from the 2-inch *Octopus arborescens* to the giant *Octopus dofleini,* found in the cold waters of the North Pacific, which has been measured at 31 feet from arm tip to arm tip. The most common species is *Octopus vulgaris,* which feeds on lobsters and crabs and inhabits tropical and temperate waters around the world. Although this species can reach an arm spread of 10 feet, most specimens are smaller. Octopuses were probably confused with squid until fairly recently, but there are some historical instances where there is no question that the animal was an octopus. Even

A stylized octopus (with only six arms) appears on this cup from Rhodes.

*O*n this oil jar (*lekuthos*) Hercules battles the Hydra, here shown as a ten-armed, snake-headed monster.

though we may doubt the existence of Hercules and relegate his exploits to the realm of mythology, there is a marble tablet in the Vatican that shows him killing the Hydra (his second labor), which appears as a most octopus-like animal. The Hydra was usually described as having nine heads, and every time one was cut off, two new ones appeared in its place. (An octopus can regenerate a lost arm.) Hercules knocked off eight of the nine heads with his club and buried the ninth under a rock.

In *Naturalis Historia*, Pliny the Elder lumps squid and octopus together under the heading of polyp, but the descriptions are different enough to enable us to separate them easily. The octopus is introduced with a description of its feeding habits, as accurate today as it was when it was written: "They feed on the flesh of shellfish, the shells of which they break open by enfolding them with their tentacles, and consequently their lair can be detected by the shells lying in front of it." Pliny's fish-eating squid is described earlier, but his octopus also warrants inclusion here, chiefly for the vicious nature he ascribes to it:

No animal is more savage in causing the death of a man in the water; for it struggles with him by coiling round him and it swallows him with its sucker-cups and drags him asunder by its multiple suction, when it attacks men who have been shipwrecked or are diving. But should it be turned over, its strength gets feebler; for when polyps are lying on their backs they stretch themselves out.

The octopus is, in fact, a gentle, curious creature with a surprising "intelligence"—if that is the right word for an invertebrate. In numerous experiments, octopuses have demonstrated an ability to learn from experience and can solve problems and puzzles with a proficiency that belies their lowly position on the cognizance scale. Despite their peaceful nature and nonaggressive behavior (to everything except shellfish), octopuses are generally considered evil, dangerous animals, and because of the multitude of arms, replete with suckers, the soft, bubbly skin, and the bulbous, baglike head, they do not conform at all to our idea of comeliness.

Thomas Beale was a British surgeon who shipped aboard the British whaler *Kent* in 1831–32. Upon the conclusion of the voyage, he wrote up his observations of the sperm whale and later appended an account of his "South-Sea whaling voyage." Beale's *A Few Observations on the Natural History of the Sperm Whale,* published in 1835, is considered one of the primary sources for the cetology incorporated into *Moby-Dick,* and Melville himself owned a copy of Beale's book, referring to Beale as an "exact and reliable man." While in the Bonin Islands (southeast of Japan), he had this encounter with an octopus:

> . . . I was much astonished at seeing at my feet a most extraordinary looking animal, crawling towards the surf, which had only just left it. I had never seen one like it under such circumstances before; it therefore appeared the more remarkable. It was creeping on its eight legs, which from their soft and flexible nature, bent considerably under the weight of its body, so that it was lifted by the efforts of its tentacula only, a small distance from the rocks. It appeared much alarmed at seeing me, and made every effort to escape, while I was not much in the humour to endeavor to capture so ugly a customer, whose appearance excited a feeling of disgust, not unmixed with fear. I however endeavored to prevent its career, by pressing on one of its legs with my foot, but although I made use of considerable force for that purpose, its strength was so great that it several times quickly liberated its member, in spite of all the efforts I could employ in this way on the wet and slippery rocks. I now laid hold of one of the tentacles with my hand, and held it firmly, so that the limb appeared as if it would be torn asunder by our united strength. I soon gave

it a powerful jerk, wishing to disengage it from the rocks to which it clung so forcibly by its suckers, which it effectually resisted; but the moment after, the apparently engaged animal lifted its head with its large eyes projecting from the middle of its body, and letting go of its hold on the rocks, suddenly sprang upon my arm, which I had previously bared to my shoulder, for the purpose of thrusting it into holes in the rocks to discover shells, and clung with its suckers to it with great power, endeavoring to get its beak, which I could now see, between the roots of its arms, in a position to bite!

A sensation of horror pervaded my whole frame when I found this monstrous animal had affixed itself so firmly upon my arm. Its cold slimy grip was extremely sickening, and I immediately called aloud to the captain, who was also searching for shells at some distance, to come and release me from my disgusting assailant—he quickly arrived, and taking me down to the boat, during which time I was employed in keeping the beak away from my hand, quickly released me by destroying my tormentor with the boat knife, when I disengaged it by portions at a time. This

*T*homas Beale, surgeon on a British whaling voyage in 1835, told the story of being attacked by a very large octopus while taking a walk on the beach on the Bonin Islands, south of Japan.

animal must have measured across its expanded arms, about four feet, while its body was not larger than a clenched hand.

Everything else in Beale's book checks out; if anything, he was a conservative chronicler of the whale fishery. It would therefore appear that his story is a true account of a surfside skirmish with a sizable octopus. Most of the "horror," of course, was in the eye of the beholder, since it is obvious that the animal only wanted to escape, while Dr. Beale kept his foot on one of its tentacles. It was only when he picked it up that it "attacked." Regardless of the reality, such an account, replete with terms like "sensation of horror," "cold slimy grip," and "disgusting assailant," could only contribute to the octopus's already unfavorable reputation.

Arthur Grimble learned that the Gilbert Islanders capture the octopus by using themselves as bait. One man swims in front of the octopus's lair until the animal attacks, and then the other diver closes in and bites it between the eyes, killing it instantly. ("Any two boys of seventeen," he says, "will get you half a dozen octopus like that for the mere fun of it.") Grimble allows himself to be talked into becoming the bait and dives into the lagoon:

I do not suppose it is really true that the eyes of an octopus shine in the dark; besides, it was clear daylight only six feet down in the limpid water; but I could have sworn the brute's eyes burned at me as I turned towards his cranny. That dark glow—whatever might have been its origin—was the last thing I saw as I . . . rose into his clutches. Then I remember chiefly a dreadful sliminess with a herculean power behind it. Something whipped around my left forearm and the back of my neck, binding the two together. In the same flash, another something slapped itself high on my forehead, and I felt it crawling down the back of my singlet. My impulse was to tear at it with my right hand, but I felt the whole of that arm pinioned to my ribs. But my boyhood's nightmare was upon me. When I felt the swift constriction of those disgusting arms jerk my head and shoulders in towards the reef, my mind went blank of every thought save the beastliness of that squat head. A mouth began to nuzzle below my throat, at the junction of the collar bones. . . . I was awakened from my cowardly trance by a quick strong pull on my shoulders back from the cranny. The cables around me tightened painfully, but I knew I was adrift from the reef. I gave a kick, rose to the surface and turned on my back with the brute sticking out of my chest like a tumor. My mouth was smothered by some flabby moving horror. The suckers felt like hot rings pulling at my skin. . . .

*W*hen Arthur Grimble was
stationed in the Gilbert Islands of
the South Pacific, he told of being
attacked and nearly drowned by
an octopus that leaped on him
from a cave.

Grimble is saved, of course, by his companion, who "pounced, pulled, bit
down, and the thing was over." One might suspect that Grimble's account
was not absolutely factual, but it was not the first time that someone had
fabricated an adventure with an octopus.

Denys de Montfort, who rarely bothered to differentiate between
cephalopods (or between truth and fiction, for that matter), tells a tale of a
battle between a "cuttlefish"—which, from its actions, would appear to be
an octopus—and a dog. As told in his *Histoire naturelle générale et particulière des mollusques,* De Montfort was out for a stroll on the beach when he
heard the excited barking of his mastiff—"an animal of immense size and
strength and undaunted courage, which had already once saved my life
when attacked by a wolf." The dog had happened upon a cuttle out of the
water and charged in to attack it:

Instantly four arms were drawn up and twined rigidly around the dog, who struggled vainly to free himself, and, for once losing his courage, uttered piteous howls and cries for help. Meantime the cuttle, whose huge protruding eyes actually seemed to flash fire, and whose body had turned many colors, from dark violet to bright scarlet, was drawing itself with considerable speed toward the water, dragging with little effort the heavy body of my struggling dog. The rough rocky ground helped him to drag the weight along, by giving his arms secure holds.

De Montfort rushes in to join the fray and succeeds in pulling two of the cuttle's arms off. (Not off the dog; *off.*) Heartened by his master's example, the pooch tears off a couple of arms himself, and together they overpower the disabled monster. "I determined," says De Montfort, "never again to attack an animal of this kind unarmed, or to venture to close quarters with it."

These episodes are mere trivia compared to literature's most sensational and perverse account of the "devil-fish": Victor Hugo's *Toilers of the Sea.* The scene where Gilliat fights an octopus to the death in a cave rivals anything that Jules Verne ever wrote for ignorance of biology, hysterical fantasy, and unmitigated malice. *Les travailleurs de la mer,* published in Paris in 1866, is a tale of unrequited love and redemption; of rivalry for the hand of

*A*n octopuslike *poulpe* attacks a ship, according to Denys de Montfort. The caption reads: "The Kraken Supposed a Sepia or Cuttlefish," covering almost all cephalopod possibilities.

a maiden; and, of course, of money. Unlike contemporary thrillers in which the animal is the protagonist and the story depends on the human hero's ability to conquer it, in *Les Travailleurs de la mer* the plot turns on the octopus's killing of one man and the near success of its attack on another. It is during the death struggle with Gilliat that the *pieuvre* is described in such extraordinarily pejorative terms.

Our hero, Gilliat, has managed to get himself shipwrecked and stranded on a rock, and because he is starving, he chases a crab into a cave. He reaches into a crevice, and "suddenly he felt himself seized by the arm. A strange indescribable horror thrilled through him." It may be indescribable, but Victor Hugo gives it a good try. If he was writing a manifesto dedicated to the eradication of the octopus, he could not have done a better job. During the struggle, Hugo devotes an entire chapter to a teleological discussion of the devilfish; why such a slimy, awful, disgusting, monstrous, scabrous, glutinous, malignant, repulsive, loathsome, hideous apparition should exist at all. A sample:

> The philosopher determines their characteristics in dread. They are the concrete forms of evil. What attitude can he take toward this treason of creation against herself? To whom can he look for the solution of these riddles? The possible is a terrible matrix. Monsters are mysteries in their concrete form. Portions of shade issue from the mass, and something within detaches itself, rolls, floats, condenses, borrows elements from the ambient darkness, becomes subject to unknown polarizations, assumes a kind of life, furnishes itself with some unimagined form from the obscurity, and with some terrible spirit from the miasma, and wanders ghostlike among living things. It is as if night itself assumed the forms of animals. But for what good? With what object?
>
> Every malignant creature, like every perverted intelligence, is a sphinx. A terrible sphinx propounding a terrible riddle; the riddle of the existence of Evil.

Meanwhile, back at the cave, Gilliat is being wrapped by five of the creature's eight arms, which are "encircling [his] whole body, cutting into his ribs like cord . . . forming a ligature around his stomach . . . enfolding and constricting his diaphragm like straps, producing such compression that he could hardly breathe. . . ." Never mind that the octopus doesn't use its arms for constriction but only for grasping its prey; Hugo has obviously decided that the *pieuvre* is an animal made up of pythons, but pythons that have suckers on them, with needles at their tips, the better to pierce the

Gilliat battles the giant octopus
in Victor Hugo's *Toilers of
the Sea.*

flesh of their hapless victims. "It has no blood, no bones, no flesh," writes
Hugo. "It is soft and flabby, a skin with nothing inside. . . .

> It is with the sucking apparatus that it attacks. The victim is oppressed by
> a vacuum drawing at numberless points; it is not a clawing or a biting, but
> an indescribable scarification. A tearing of the flesh is terrible, but less ter-
> rible than a sucking of the blood. Claws are harmless compared with the
> horrible action of these natural air-cups. The talons of the wild beast will
> enter into your flesh; but with the cephaloptera it is you who enter into the
> creature. The muscles swell, the fibres of the body are contorted, the skin
> cracks under the loathsome oppression; the blood spurts out and mingles
> horribly with the lymph of the monster, which clings to its victim by
> innumerable hideous mouths. The hydra incorporates itself with the man;
> the man becomes one with the hydra. The spectre lies upon you: the tiger
> can only devour you; the devil-fish, horrible, sucks your life blood away.

He draws you to him, and into himself; while bound down, glued to the ground, powerless, you feel yourself gradually emptied into this horrible pouch, which is the monster itself.

No wonder Gilliat is trying so hard to get away. Luckily for him, he brought a knife with him into the grotto, and because he knows that the cephaloptera* are only vulnerable through the head, and then only "at a certain moment in the conflict which must be seized," he chops off its head. "He had plunged the blade of the knife into the flat slimy substance, and by a rapid movement, like a flourish of a whip in the air, describing a circle around the two eyes, he wrenched the head off as a man would draw a tooth."

Hugo's description of the octopus is so misguided that Henry Lee, naturalist of the Brighton Aquarium in England, devoted two chapters of his 1875 book *The Octopus* to *Toilers of the Sea*. In one, he retells the entire story, and in the second, he endeavors "to compare 'the devilfish' of the author with the octopus of nature, and to indicate the points in which M. Hugo's representation of his 'monster' is substantially correct, partly true, or entirely unreal." In a footnote to his 1879 discussion of the "Cephalopods of the North-eastern Coast of America," Addison Verrill wrote, "The description of the 'Poulpe' or devil-fish by Victor Hugo, in 'The Toilers of the Sea,' with which so many readers have recently become familiar, is quite as fabulous and unreal as any of the earlier accounts, and even more bizarre. His description represents no real animal whatever." And in 1904, Frank Bullen wrote, "If high art in fiction be to clothe the utterly impossible as well as improbable in such fascinating language that the reader shall be crammed for the rest of his life with absurdities, then Victor Hugo was indeed the greatest fictional artist that ever lived." (The demimonde of Paris, however, took to Hugo's fictionalized octopus with a passion, and according to a 1991 *National Geographic* article, "Newspapers debated the dangers of this 'devil fish.' Restaurants featured octopus entrees. Milliners created an octopus hat for ladies to show off at seaside resorts.")

Like any rational scientist, Henry Lee dismisses most of Hugo's description of the octopus, and of the philosophical ruminations, he writes, "The language is sententious, and would, no doubt, be impressive if it was not incomprehensible." As for the rest of it, it would be inconsequential nonsense if it didn't make such a negative contribution to the reputation of the octopus. Frank Lane, writing of Hugo's novel, says, "Because of the

---

*Hugo has evidently decided against the accepted term *cephalopod*, which means "head-foot," and substituted *cephaloptera*, which means "head-wing."

lurid atmosphere which has been engendered, quite harmless encounters between octopuses and humans are often written up as unprovoked and deadly attacks." Both Henry Lee and Frank Lane—the authors of octopus books written ninety-nine years apart—discuss the interactions of octopuses and men that have resulted in injury or, infrequently, death to the humans, but these are considered accidental by both authors and should not impugn the already damaged reputation of the octopus.

The monster octopus that attacked Gilliat in *Toilers of the Sea* must have come from somewhere; even Victor Hugo could not have postulated such a fearsome beast on the basis of the small cephalopods that live in the Mediterranean. The scene actually takes place on the English Channel island of Guernsey, a location well known for small octopuses. There are indeed very large octopuses, but they live very far from Guernsey. The biggest is *Octopus dofleini*,* found in the inshore waters of the Pacific Northwest, including southeast Alaska, Vancouver Island, Seattle, and the San Juan Islands of Puget Sound.

The Cousteaus' love affair with the octopus is evident throughout their book *Octopus and Squid.* They admire the grace and beauty of these eight-armed animals, the way they hunt, the way they move, and even the way they think. (Their book is subtitled *The Soft Intelligence.*) Contrast the following paean to the octopus to the ridiculous description by Victor Hugo:

> One must have lived in the water with octopuses for months, swum in the same waters, brushed past the same rocks and the same algae in order to be able to appreciate the beauty of the octopus. In the water, the octopus looks like a silken scarf floating, swirling, and settling gently as a leaf on a rock, the color of which it immediately assumes. Then it disappears into a crack which appears to be hardly large enough to accommodate one of its arms, let alone its entire body. The whole process is reminiscent of a ballet. It is somehow ethereal and, at the same time, elaborate, elegant, and slightly mischievous.

Frank Lane never actually identifies the largest octopus, but he writes of "the Pacific octopus (*Octopus hongkongensis*), a large specimen of which from Alaskan waters spanned 32 feet." Many of these giants have not been measured, and in a popular article about diving in British Columbia waters, Neil McDaniel speaks of "the legendary 600-pound monster, the largest on

---

*The species encountered by the Cousteau team is identified as *O. appolyon,* and Frank Lane employs an earlier synonym, *O. hongkongensis,* but in 1964, Grace Pickford of Yale University published a paper in which she not only established the proper common name ("Giant Octopus"), but also concluded—with some exceptions that should only concern the cephalopod taxonomist—that the very large octopus of the Pacific Northwest should be known as *O. dofleini.*

$\mathcal{T}$he giant Pacific octopus, *O. dofleini*, on exhibit in a tank at the Steinhart Aquarium, San Francisco

record" and then mentions "rumors of commercial divers having spotted one hulking monster some 50 feet in diameter in deep water off the coast of Japan." The last word on record-sized animals is usually Gerald Wood's *Guinness Book of Animal Facts and Feats*. In the 1982 edition, he lists one that was trapped in a fisherman's net in Monterey, California, that weighed 110 pounds and had a radial spread of 20 feet. When divers were "wrestling" giant octopuses in Puget Sound, a man named Donald Hagen brought up one with a radial spread of 23 feet. Finally, Wood quotes Cousteau and Diolé, who heard a story about a 30-footer; and Bernard Heuvelmans, who discusses 32-footers ("some say 38 feet") that weigh 275 pounds. In the *National Geographic* (March 1991), Fred Bavendam wrote, "No one knows how big the giant octopus gets. Mature males average about 23 kilograms (50 pounds), females about 15 kilograms (33 pounds). Arm spans average 2.5 meters (about eight feet). One octopus found off western Canada in 1957 was estimated to weigh 272 kilograms (nearly 600 pounds) and have an arm span of 9.6 meters (just over 31 feet), setting a widely acknowledged world record for the Pacific giant, which inhabits an area from California northward along the coast to Alaska and off eastern Asia as far south as Japan."*

In the making of their cephalopod film (of which their book was a by-product), the Cousteau team visited Elliot Bay (near Seattle), Tacoma, and the San Juan Islands. They dived with the giant Pacific octopuses, and although underwater measurements were obviously impossible—especially for creatures that can change their shape so easily—they estimated that the largest ones they saw had an arm span of more than 20 feet and might have weighed as much as 250 pounds. Bavendam was diving to the north of the Cousteau team, in the Straits of Georgia that separate Vancouver Island from British Columbia, and among other things, photographed a female guarding her eggs. After laying as many as eighty thousand eggs, the female guards them until they hatch and then dies of starvation.

Despite valiant efforts on the part of scientists and the Cousteau team, many people still find the octopus a repulsive creature. Contributing to its bad reputation are its flowing shapelessness, its suckers, and, of course, its inclination to occupy closed or covered spaces (few "nice" creatures live in caves), which would seem to accord it a reputation for lurking evil. There is also the question of its beak, located where no beak is supposed to be, as well as what people perceive as a slimy texture. (Octopuses out of the water glisten before they dry out, and while they have nothing resembling a mucous covering, they look as if they ought to.) Its reputation as a malevolent monster seems to have outlived all the noble attempts to ameliorate it.

In 1935, William Outerson wrote a short story called "Fire in the Galley Stove," about the freighter *Unicorn,* disturbed by "an unusual movement of the hull, a strange shaking," which turns out to be an underwater earthquake. The quake produces a wave that almost swamps the ship (" 'Tidal wave on the port bow,' the lookout reported belatedly") and releases some strange creatures from the deep. At first the crew only *feels* the presence of these creatures ("It felt as if a floating body, soft and enormously heavy, had come to rest against the bottom of the ship"), but soon all hell breaks loose, because the creatures turn out to be giant octopuses, "a foul sight, an obscene growth from the dark places of the world, where incessant hunger is the driving force." The incessantly hungry octopuses have found that the

*The *National Geographic* has a formidable fact-checking department—I know, because I have had my facts checked by them—and although they give no sources for the "widely accepted world record," I am inclined to assume that this information was verified—and then verified again. In a short article in *Science* in 1885, W. H. Dall of the U.S. National Museum recounted his spearing an Alaskan octopus with a 32-foot radial spread. ("Having heard octopus were eatable," he wrote, "and the flesh looking white and clean, we boiled some sections of the arms in salt and water, but found them so tough and elastic that our teeth could not make the slightest impression on them.")

men of the *Unicorn* are "food . . . in the form of puny bodies that could be had for the taking," so they reach over the rails and pluck off the sailors one by one. The men put up a valiant struggle, hacking away at the tentacles with knives and hatchets, but in the end the beasts with "staring gorgon faces with great lidless eyes and a huge parrot beak" prove to be too much for the luckless crew, and every man jack of them is yanked overboard and eaten. The *Unicorn* is found with nobody aboard and her galley stove still burning, an unexpected cephalopod explanation for stories of ships that appear in perfect shape but abandoned, like the *Mary Celeste*.

The killer octopus made its first cinema appearance in 1916.

Three years earlier, Charles Williamson had designed and built a "salvage machine" that consisted of a flexible tube hung from the keel of a barge with an observation ball fitted with glass viewing ports and mechanical arms. His son, John Ernest Williamson, envisioned other possibilities, descended in the "photoscope" with a press camera, and took the first underwater photographs ever recorded in America. (The first underwater camera was built in France by Louis Boutan in 1899, and one of his first pictures was of himself.) After making some still shots, John Williamson decided to become an underwater moviemaker. In the Bahamas, he shot all sorts of fishes, then filmed a battle between a man and a shark. The fight— in which Williamson himself fought and killed a shark—was the centerpiece of *The Williamson Submarine Expedition*, which kept people coming to a Broadway movie house for almost a year. His next project was *Twenty Thousand Leagues Under the Sea*.

In the Bahamas (where forty years later Walt Disney would film the same story), Williamson obtained a ship to use for the USS *Abraham Lincoln* (which he blew up for the film), but because the navy's submarines were otherwise engaged, he had to build his own out of wood. He filmed Verne's "undersea gardens"—inhabited by several threatening tiger sharks—and outfitted the divers in hard-hat diving suits that adhered to Verne's description by using equipment that required no air hoses.* Although the *Nautilus* is attacked by a giant squid in the novel, Williamson substituted an octopus, which attacks a diver instead of the submarine. When Nemo sees the diver in trouble, he quickly dons his diving apparatus, descends on the submarine's retractable ladder, and confronts the monster. From his own *Twenty Years Under the Sea*, John Williamson narrates the encounter:

---

*It is quite astonishing to see 1916 divers walking around on the bottom with no air hoses. Williamson used a modification of the Davis Submarine Escape Apparatus (D.S.E.A.), which consisted of an oxygen lung in which the divers' exhalations were passed through caustic soda, which removed the carbon dioxide and returned pure oxygen to the diver.

*I*n the 1916 version of *Twenty Thousand Leagues Under the Sea*, Jules Verne's giant squid has become an octopus, but Captain Nemo still battles it under water.

Into the field of vision came the grotesque figure of the helmeted diver, the gallant Captain Nemo. How slowly, how very deliberately he seemed to move. Moments dragged in tense suspense. Now he was beside the native who was struggling in the clutches of the squirming python-like tentacle. A flash of his broad-bladed axe—the tentacle fell—and the struggling native shot to the surface, gasping for breath but saved!

According to Williamson, people believed the encounter was genuine. He quotes a review from the Philadelphia *Public Ledger* that said: "The struggle between the monstrous cephalopod and the pearl diver, ending in the latter's rescue by the captain, is one of the rarities of the camera. There can be no question of fake or deception. It is all there, and our vision tells us it is all true." It was, in fact, one of the first "special effects" in movie history, and the only part that was "true" was the diver. Williamson had designed a giant octopus made of canvas with halved rubber balls sewn onto the arms to represent suckers. The tentacles were spring-loaded contraptions inflated with rubber tubing that could be activated by bursts of compressed air to give them the appearance of life. The octopus machine (which Williamson patented) was controlled by a diver inside the head, and

*W*illiamson patented his man-powered octopus just in case someone wanted to steal his invention.

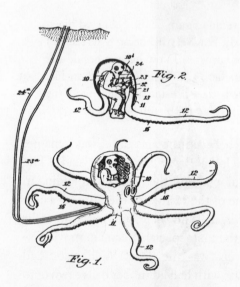

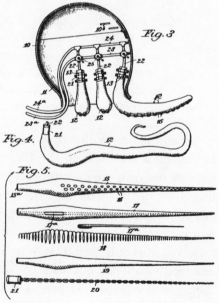

*W*illiamson's octopus was actually an elaborate contraption operated by a diver who sat in the head and manipulated the arms with springs.

the inventor felt very proud indeed of the lifelike appearance of his octopus. He wrote: "To one who did not know its inner secrets, viewing it in action was indeed a hair-raising experience. John Barrymore himself told me that in all his career on the stage and screen he had never been so thrilled, so absolutely frozen—rooted to the spot—as when he watched my octopus scenes."

In 1954, Roger Corman, the master of cheap, successful movies, had heard about an electrically powered, one-man submarine and approached the manufacturers with a proposal to use it in a film in exchange for a screen credit. They agreed, and Corman promptly wrote *It Stalked the Ocean Floor,* a story about a man-eating mutant created as a result of atomic testing. Shot in Southern California for $12,000, the film—whose title was eventually changed to *The Monster from the Ocean Floor*—included a blinking, one-eyed octopus, which Corman described as "a puppet shot from behind a cloudy fishtank," and a marine biologist who saves the pretty tourist by driving his sub into the monster's only eye. Although the film made money and launched Corman on his extraordinary career (his 1990 autobiography is entitled *How I Made a Hundred Movies in Hollywood and Never Lost a Dime*), it was less than a critical success. The reviewer Leonard Maltin described it as "a dreadful film about a squid-like creature pursued by a minisubmarine; 20,000 yawns under the sea."

From the time the atomic bomb was dropped on Hiroshima in 1945, the possibility of radioactivity creating mutant monsters became an important ingredient in monster movies. For *It Came from Beneath the Sea,* a film that was made only a year after *The Monster from the Ocean Floor,* Ray Harryhausen designed the octopus of the title. The film is an unintentionally hilarious tale of a giant radioactive octopus that emerges from the Marianas Trench because it has decided to change its diet,

A gigantic octopus wrestles a freighter in *It Came from Beneath the Sea*, made in 1955.
This was Ray Harryhausen's first monster film.

from fish to men and ships. It attacks a nuclear submarine, but the intrepid
commander Pete Matthews (Kenneth Tobey) manages to break out of the
grasp of the monster, which leaves a sample of its tissue in the bow
thrusters. It takes the scientists two weeks to determine what sort of animal
might leave a section of an arm with suckers, but they eventually decide it
is indeed a monster octopus. (In explaining the identity of the monster to
high-ranking naval officers, the scientists show them a real octopus, which
makes what follows all the more ludicrous.) It looks like an octopus, but it
moves like a rubberized robot. The monster comes ashore in Oregon,
where it grabs a couple out of a car, then heads for San Francisco, where it
inexplicably attacks the Golden Gate Bridge. Screaming crowds run
through the streets as giant tentacles pursue them, and finally the army
arrives with flamethrowers. They drive the beast back into the sea (but not
before it pulls a hunk of the bridge down). Commander Matthews fires a
special torpedo into it, and it explodes, but the lucky commander, who had
gone into the water to harpoon it with a grenade, is not harmed by the
gigantic underwater explosion. In fact, he is in such good shape that he succeeds in winning Dr. Leslie Joyce (Faith Domergue) right out of the arms

of another scientist, proving that square-jawed determination beats brains (and giant octopuses) every time.

Jules Verne's *Mysterious Island* was a sequel to *Twenty Thousand Leagues Under the Sea* and was mostly about survival under primitive conditions, à la Robinson Crusoe. As written, it contains no underwater activities, and with the exception of a dugong (see pp. 91–92), no threatening sea monsters, but the critical success of the giant squid sequences in *20,000 Leagues Under the Sea* obviously meant that some sort of threatening cephalopod had to be included in the movie sequel. Made in 1961, the film bears only a passing resemblance to the book that inspired it and probably owes more to the success of the film *20,000 Leagues Under the Sea* than it does to Jules Verne's novel. Captain Nemo (now played by Herbert Lom) appears, although his submarine remains moored in a cave throughout the movie. *Mysterious Island* is the story of some Union army prisoners who escape in a balloon, which blows out to sea and lands on an island in the middle of the Pacific (having blown all the way from Richmond, Virginia), where they encounter all sorts of bizarre monsters, including a giant crab, bees the size of Volks-

*A*lthough Jules Verne's *The Mysterious Island* contains no underwater adventures, the 1961 Hollywood version included this encounter with a giant nautiloid. The monster was designed by Ray Harryhausen.

wagens, and an enormous, crazy-looking bird that looks like a cross between a giant chicken and a kangaroo.

On a mission to raise a sunken ship, the prisoners, outfitted with Nemo's revised underwater breathing apparatus in the form of a giant shell strapped to their backs and another shell on their heads with a face mask in it, encounter a many-armed monster. As designed by Ray Harryhausen, it is a strange, cat-eyed creature that lives in a coiled, ribbed shell, like a giant hermit crab. Harryhausen invented "Dynamation," a technique of combining stop-action photography with live action that gives the "octopus" a herky-jerky movement, but after all, it would be almost impossible for any creature other than a real octopus to duplicate the sinuous motion of its arms. Although one of the prisoners is snagged by the beast, another is armed with a ray gun and zaps it so that it releases the predictable cloud of ink and then frees the prisoner. All's well that ends well in *Mysterious Island,* which could not be said for *It Came from Beneath the Sea,* in which any number of people were killed, a freighter was pulled under with all hands, and the Golden Gate Bridge was destroyed.

In 1977, only two years after *Jaws* appeared, a movie called *Tentacles* hit the screen. Obviously intending to capitalize on the shark mania of the moment, a group of Italian filmmakers managed to convince Henry Fonda, John Huston, Shelley Winters, Claude Akins, and Bo Hopkins to appear in this mess. (Unlike *It Came from Beneath the Sea,* which is so bad that it is funny, *Tentacles* is so clumsily made that it is truly offensive.) As in *Jaws,* various people are picked off by an unknown creature, but there the resemblance ends.* *Tentacles* is a witless hodgepodge of jiggling cameras, befuddled editing, missed (and occasionally dubbed) lines, and utter plotlessness. The story—what little there is of it—has something to do with the use of "illegal" high-frequency sounds that entice some sort of sea creature to go on a rampage, so we see people yanked under water or simply disappearing, that being easier and cheaper than trying to make an octopus. Every once in a while there is a murky shot of a real octopus in a tank, accompanied by ghastly tweeting noises, but otherwise, the monster never appears. After gobbling up assorted members of the cast, the octopus decides to attack a

---

*Tentacles was not the only attempt to cash in on the *Jaws* phenomenon. Also in 1977, we were treated to the appearance of *Orca,* in which the attacking animals are killer whales. They are prompted to seek revenge when a crusty old fisherman (Richard Harris) kills a female orca, inciting her mate to attack and destroy boats, docks, and, of course, the puny humans who would presume to meddle with nature. Charlotte Rampling plays a concerned marine biologist who explains the nature of the killers—never mentioning that they are really large dolphins—and the film is graced by the appearance of Bo Derek, who is seen on a slippery deck, sliding into the mouth of a vengeful killer whale.

After their sailboat sinks in the middle of the Pacific Ocean...

GIANT OCTOPUS SAVES DROWNING COUPLE!

By BEATRICE DEXTER
Correspondent

A California couple whose sailboat sank in a storm were miraculously saved from drowning — by a 100-foot-long octopus!

Betty and Richard Carter say the enormous sea beast with gentle, intelligent eyes rose out of the water, grabbed them in its tentacles and swam through giant waves toward their capsized life raft. They say he righted the raft and placed them in it, then slipped beneath the water once again.

"We thought he was going to eat us or something, but instead he came to help us," says Betty, 38, who was on the first leg of an around-the-world

raft we were stunned. It wasn't some accident — he knew what he was doing. He rescued us on purpose."

Betty and Richard had set off on their year-long trip, visited Hawaii and were on their way to Fiji when a fierce typhoon surprised them in mid ocean.

The terrified couple were buffeted miles off course and enormous 25-foot waves crashed into their 40-foot sloop.

As their boat began taking on water, the Carters frantically gathered sup-

HUGE sea beast lifted the Carters out of the water and put them in to their life raft.

storm-tossed waves, expecting to drown any moment.

"Then suddenly the water around us boiled and we saw these enormous tentacles about 20 feet thick and 80

"WE thought he was going to eat us," say Betty and Richard Carter, "but he saved our lives."

out of the water and started swimming away with us.

"His slimy suckers were plastered against us and he held us very tight. We were nearly blinded by the wind and water, but we could see the raft in the distance and after a moment we realized he was heading toward it.

"It was upside down, but when he got to it he turned it upright again and plunked us down in it. Then he swam off a ways and slipped back into the water.

"It was unbelievable."

The Carters drifted for three days before they were rescued by a passing freighter.

*N*ot everything about giant octopuses is bad.

sailboat race, so audiences see lots of boats capsizing and frightened looks on the faces of various little boys, but you never actually see what is doing the attacking. (Which is probably just as well, since the John Huston character asks if the range of a giant *squid* can be greater than thirty miles and someone else says that "the suckers on the tentacles are like the claws of a tiger.")

Bo Hopkins plays a sort of whale trainer, so he decides to take his captive killer whales to attack the monster in its lair, at which point the octopus promptly destroys the floating tank in which the whales were transported. Hopkins and his trusty sidekick leap into the water to confront the beast, only to discover that the killer whales are alive and well, after all, so while the two divers struggle with an underwater avalanche (obviously caused by the octopus), the whales attack the giant octopus. The whales squeak like mice, the octopus wheezes like Darth Vader, and one can only feel sorry for the real octopus that had to appear in the "battle" scenes, since someone was poking the poor creature with a stick that had a killer whale's face painted on the end. When the monster is vanquished, the two heroes, having lost their wives, friends, boats, and assorted acquaintances, sail off to Africa, giggling as they head into the sunset.

BIOLOGY OF THE
OCTOPUS

NOT ALL OCTOPUSES are giants; in fact, most of them are relatively small creatures that are threatening only to their prey. (The exception is the blue-ringed octopus, a brightly colored little fellow from Australia whose venomous bite can kill a human.) There are about 150 species, found in all the world's oceans, from the shallow, warm waters of tropical coral reefs to the cold depths of the abyss. Here is the diagnostic description of the family Octopodidae from Nesis's *Cephalopods of the World:*

> Body either firm, muscular or flabby, weakly muscular, but not gelatinous or semitransparent. Arms muscular, usually several times longer than the body, with 1 or 2 rows of suckers. Umbrella short or of modest size, usually not exceeding the longest arm length. . . . Third right (rarely left) arm is hectocotylized; in addition, males often have enlarged suckers in the middle of some arms, sometimes ends of all arms are modified. Eggs benthic, guarded by female, rarely she incubates them on her arms. . . . Benthic animals found from the Arctic to the Antarctic and from the littoral to the abyssal.

All eight-armed cephalopods are classified as octopuses, but they differ widely in shape and habitat. In some species (such as the banded octopus *O. horridus*), the head is small and the arms greatly elongated; while in others (the genus *Eledone*, for example), the arms are short, connected by a web, and the head is large. All octopuses have eight arms (only squid have tentacles) and a bulbous head, but after that a great variety obtains. The best-known species are shallow-water inhabitants, such as the common octopus (*Octopus vulgaris*), but in the depths of the ocean there can be found some of the most unusual octopuses—and some of the most unusual animals on earth.

Because they are soft-bodied with tissues that are made up mostly of uncompressible liquid, the deep-sea octopods are not affected by the tremendous pressure at these depths. There are authenticated records of octopuses trawled from depths of 2,425 fathoms (almost 15,000 feet), and one record of an octopus egg that was recovered from the stomach of a bottom-dwelling fish that was brought up from 7,200 meters (23,000 feet). If the shallow-water species are delicate, the deep-water octopods are almost insubstantial. Their bodies have a jellylike consistency and are so fragile that they are usually badly damaged by the act of bringing them up. The order Octopoda (all octopuses) is subdivided into two suborders, Cirrata and Incirrata. The Cirrata (commonly known as "cirrate" octopuses, from the *cirri,* or filaments, on the arms) are gelatinous, flattened animals with a deep web that often reaches the arm tips. (All other octopus species are classified as "incirrate" because they lack the fingerlike cirri on the arms.) They are also known as "finned" octopuses because there are a pair of fins located about midway on the mantle. They are usually dark-colored, ranging from purple to chocolate-brown, often with transparent elements. There is no radula and no ink sac.

The number of cirrate octopus species is small compared to the incirrate, but within that number are some very unusual animals indeed. Although they are very poorly known, it is believed that most, if not all, species are deep-water inhabitants. For example there is *Cirrothauma* (*thauma* is Greek for "wonderful"), the blind octopus, known from only a few specimens caught at depths of fifteen hundred meters or more. The eyes are much reduced, with no lens or iris and only a thread of an optic nerve. Then there is *Opisthoteuthis,* nicknamed the "flapjack devilfish" because it is a thick, flattened creature with the mantle reduced to a hump on the dorsal surface and the short arms extended from the heavy webbing.

As another example of the mysterious nature of the deep-water octopods, consider *Vampyroteuthis infernalis,* whose name can be translated as "vampire squid of the infernal depths." About 8 inches long, this deep-water denizen is among the most fascinating animals on earth.* It was first described in 1903 by Carl Chun, a German teuthologist who identified it as an octopus, because it had—he thought—eight arms. Then another pair of

---

*It obviously fascinated Grace E. Pickford, an American biologist who published extensively on the species, discussing—in different papers—its taxonomic position (it was she who erected the order Vampyromorpha), its reproductive strategies, its distribution, its eggs, and its anatomy. (The tiny squid *Pickfordiateuthis pulchella* was named for her.)

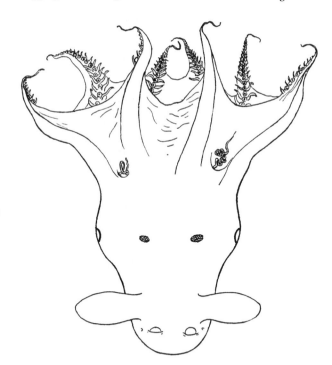

$\mathcal{D}$orsal view of an adult male *Vampyroteuthis infernalis*. The eyes are located on the bulges above the fins, and the sensory filaments (tentacles) can be seen protruding from their pockets.

thin arms was discovered, tucked into pockets outside the web that connects the eight arms. Like the cirrate octopuses, *Vampyroteuthis* has a pair of small, tongue-shaped fins situated near the posterior of the mantle, but it is not a squid and not an octopus. Taxonomically speaking, it hovers between the octopuses and the squids, in its own order, the Vampyromorpha.

The type specimen was taken on the *Valdivia* expedition in the Atlantic Ocean and was illustrated by Rübsamen, the expedition's artist. Subsequent specimens have been collected from tropical and subtropical waters all over the world, usually from depths of three thousand feet or more, in the abyss, where no light penetrates. The first specimens seemed to have two pairs of paddle-like fins, but when one with a single pair appeared, it was believed to be a separate species. Rübsamen's drawing, now in the Zoological Museum of the University of Berlin, showed only two fins, so the original description was of a two-finned animal. Further study (mostly by Pickford) revealed that in the original drawing one of the pairs of fins was erased, so it has now been concluded that only a single species exists. The very young forms have two fins, the intermediate stages have four, and when the animal reaches maturity, it reverts to its two-finned form.

For its size, *Vampyroteuthis* has proportionally the largest eyes of any animal in the world. A 6-inch specimen will have globular eyes an inch across, approximately the size of the eye of a full-grown dog. At the end of its body away from the tips of its arms, *Vampyroteuthis* has two retractable fins that have reflective surfaces, but the rest of its body is a velvety purplish black. (Between Panama and the Galápagos in 1925, William Beebe's *Arcturus* expedition hauled in "a very small but very terrible octopus, black as night, with ivory white jaws and blood-red eyes." Beebe refers to this creature as "*Cirroteuthis* spp.," but it appears to have been *Vampyroteuthis*.)

Vampyroteuthis may compensate for the blackness of the abyss in which it lives by being equipped with an astonishing series of photophores: lights all over its body—except for the inner surface of its web—that it appears to be able to turn on and off at will. In the back of the "neck" are clusters of more complex photophores, and behind the base of the paired fins there are two more light organs equipped with a sort of "eyelid" that the animal can close to shut off the light. "The lack of an ink sac," wrote Pickford, "is also in accordance with the bathypelagic habits of the species, although it strongly suggests that the animal must have other means of masking its own phosphorescence."

Based on the careful analysis of its morphology and knowing the depths at which it can be found, we can only speculate on the life-style of the vampire squid. It appears to be a weak swimmer and may not even swim at all. Instead, its gelatinous body is weak-muscled, which suggests drifting rather than darting, and its web may serve as a "parachute" to enable it to float downward in search of prey. (It also has a highly developed statocyst, the organ that controls its balance, which suggests that it descends slowly, further enhancing the idea of *Vampyroteuthis* as an almost passive predator.) The males have spermatophores, but since they possess no hectocotylus, they must transfer the sperm package to the female in some other fashion. In mature females, spermatophores are sometimes found in a special receptacle in front of each eye, where they were placed—perhaps—by the male's funnel. *Vampyroteuthis* and *Cirrothauma* have the giant nerve axons usually associated with squid, but their function in these slow-moving bathypelagic animals is unclear.

In recent years, the common octopus (*Octopus vulgaris*) has become a favorite of animal behaviorists because of the ease with which it adapts to captivity, its docile nature, and its "intelligence." (Throughout this discussion, unless the octopus species is identified otherwise, the reader is to assume that it is *O. vulgaris*.) Diving and photographing at the Isles Porquerolles, off the coast of Toulon, the Cousteau team befriended individual octopuses; they watched octopuses remove fish and crabs from fishermen's traps; and they tempted an octopus with a live lobster in a stoppered glass jar. At first the animal enveloped the jar, but when this didn't work, it poked around until it managed to insert the tip of one of its arms into a hole in the cork stopper. As soon as it had touched the lobster, the octopus proceeded to yank the cork out. "It was on the third take," said one of the Cousteau cameramen, "that [the octopus] whipped out the stopper as though it were something it had been doing all its life. When one thinks of how long it takes to teach a dog to do something as simple as sitting up or shaking hands, one must admit that an octopus learns very quickly; and that above all, it teaches itself."

Researcher Brian Boycott, author of a 1965 *Scientific American* article entitled "Learning in the Octopus," worked at the Stazione Zoologica in Naples because *Octopus vulgaris* is available along the shores of the Mediterranean. "Since it responds so consistently to the presence of prey," wrote Boycott, "the animal is readily trained." When an octopus was shown a crab and a geometric figure simultaneously, it went for the crab, but received a mild electric shock. It quickly learned to associate the crab with the shock, and after only a few tries, it refused to approach the prey when the square was visible. (In the Cousteau film, an octopus learned—after only one experience—to differentiate between a white disc and a black one if its attack on the white one was accompanied by a mild electric shock.) Curiously, while an octopus can easily differentiate between black and white, it appears that the ability is based on the relative brightness of the discs and not on the color. In a series of experiments at the Stazione in Naples designed to answer this very question, J. B. Messenger tested the octopus's color vision and concluded that "a variety of morphological, physiological and biochemical evidence make it increasingly probable that *Octopus vulgaris* is colour blind."

More recently, researchers have discovered that one octopus can learn by watching another one. At the Stazione in Naples, common octopuses were taught to discriminate between a red ball and a white one by the "reward-and-punishment" technique—the animal was given a piece of food for making the right choice and a mild electric shock for making the wrong one. An untutored octopus was placed in an adjacent tank where it could watch through the glass as the training procedures were performed. After only four observations—as opposed to sixteen tries for the "trained" animal—the "student" octopus was offered the same choices, and it chose correctly almost every time. We are not quite sure what to make of this level of learning, but in *Science*, the researchers Graziano Fiorito and Pietro Scotto wrote, "Copying of a model is reported for humans and vertebrates, and it has been considered preliminary to conceptual thought; in this sense it appears related to the cognitive abilities of the animal learning system."

The Stazione in Naples has been the scene of numerous observations of octopuses in captivity, many of which are included in the chapter on "behavior" in Frank Lane's *Kingdom of the Octopus* (first published in 1960). Like everyone else, Lane was fascinated by the boneless flexibility of the octopus, and he recounts many stories of their ability to escape from apparently closed containers. Roy W. Miner, once Curator of Invertebrates at the American Museum of Natural History, collected an octopus in Puerto Rico with about a 1-foot arm span. He put the animal in a cigar box, tied it shut, and placing it in the bottom of his dinghy, went on collecting. When he landed, he opened the box to examine his prize, but the box was empty. Miner told the story in a *National Geographic* article called "Marauders of the Sea":

> We felt as if we had been fooled by a trick of parlor magic, but upon looking into the bilge water on the bottom of the dinghy, we saw the octopus calmly peering at us from under the blade of an oar, and quickly recaptured it. Apparently the weird creature had succeeded in pushing the delicate tips of its tentacles through the tightly closed crack below the box lid, and then getting a purchase outside, had deliberately pulled its rubber-like body through the crack by flattening it to the thinness of paper.

Aboard the Cousteau vessel *Calypso,* the researchers tried to keep octopuses in tanks, but "their ability to elongate their bodies in such a way as to pass through the narrowest openings has long been the nightmare of aquarium curators. . . . We have often tried to keep specimens in jars on the rear deck, but it is almost impossible to do so because they lift the heaviest covers and slide out of the tiniest crack." Lane repeats the story told by Christopher Coates, then curator of the New York Aquarium at Coney Island, of ten octopuses that were each put into a cigar box drilled with quarter-inch holes to allow for movement of the water. The boxes were tightly tied shut and packed in a shipping tank, but upon arrival, every one of the octopuses was in the tank, not in its box.

Because of its unusual design, the octopus has perfected many different modes of locomotion. Whereas squids use their arms mostly for grasping, the tentacles of the octopus can also be employed as locomotive devices, enabling the octopus to crawl along the bottom or, in rare instances, out of the water. (An octopus too long out of the water will die of suffocation—like fishes, they breathe the dissolved oxygen in water through gills—but there have been instances where octopuses have briefly emerged from the water, usually in pursuit of a crab.) Joseph Sinel, who observed octopuses

Octopus vulgaris

for more than fifty years in the Channel Islands, wrote (of their underwater locomotion), "The octopus can proceed at a goodly rate by the simple process of walking, spiderlike, although it more frequently seems to glide along, throwing its long arms as far forward as they will reach and making fast its suckers to the ground, and repeating the operation as it brings its body up to the advanced point." Their usual direction of swimming is "backward" (i.e., away from the tips of the tentacles), with water being ejected from the funnel at the base of the arms, propelling the animal through the water, but they can also turn the funnel in the opposite direction and swim with their arm tips pointing forward.

When threatened, an octopus's first reaction is flight. (In its lair, it will retreat and anchor itself with its arms.) If this is impractical or unsuccessful, the animal then turns to "inking," a capability it shares—to a greater or lesser extent—with all cephalopods except some deep-sea octopuses and the nautilus. The ink sac of the common octopus is a pear-shaped organ attached to the funnel from which the animal can eject into the water a large quantity of a black or brownish fluid that serves either as a "smoke screen" to hide the octopus's flight or as a pseudomorph in the shape of the octopus, which causes the attacker to focus on the ink blob and not on the potential prey item. It is also believed that there is a substance contained in the ink itself that inhibits the senses of predators. When the California biologists G. E. and Nettie MacGinitie observed a captive octopus inking in the presence of a moray eel, they realized that even though the ink had dissipated, the moray could not find the octopus even when it touched it with its nose.

All cephalopods can change color, but cuttlefishes and octopuses do it better and faster than any other animals in the world.* As Packard and Sanders wrote in 1969, "No individual creature produces a wider repertoire of bodily appearances than the common octopus. For changeability it is unequalled, and if underwater snorkling had arisen earlier in our culture this animal would doubtless now occupy the place traditionally accorded the chameleon." The skin of an octopus is equipped with chromatophores, which are pigment cells that the animal can expand or contract by muscular action. These cells vary in color, and as the animal expands some or contracts others, its color changes. For the most part, the color scheme of the octopuses is in the red to orange to beige range, but by closing all the cells to pinpoint size, they can pale to a ghostly white. For an animal that is constantly changing color, it is difficult to say what its "real" color is, but when they are free swimming or relaxing, the color of the common octopus seems to be a mottled brown. A newborn octopus has about seventy-five red-brown color cells, which are replaced after four to six weeks by its adult complement of brown-black and red-orange chromatophores. By the end of its first year, the octopus has between 1 and 2 million color cells, distributed on the outer surface of the head and arms. Given the octopuses' cave- and bottom-dwelling propensities and their ability to change color, it is not surprising that they are wonderful mimics and can match their surroundings to the point where they are almost invisible. On brownish rocks, they become a variegated brown; on sand they become lighter; and there are even instances where an individual can make one half of its body one color and the other half another.

The octopus, however, is more than multiarmed, multicolored camouflage; along with its astonishing color-change abilities, it has an entire catalog of behavioral modifications that are employed for concealment, defense, courtship, and probably other functions that we can only guess at. It can change shape with remarkable facility from a flattened, formless blob to a threatening, upright shape that defies terrestrial description. Its incred-

---

*Octopuses and cuttlefishes, which are only distantly related, have independently developed many of the same color-change patterns, including the false eye spots, the dymantic display, and perhaps the most spectacular display device of all, the "passing cloud," where washes of color traverse the animal's body from mantle to tentacle tips.

𝒲ith its alternating bands of reddish-brown and white, the banded octopus is one of the most spectacular of the octopuses.

ible flexibility comes from its body musculature, which consists of fibers that run in three directions in space, permitting it to change shape like a subaqueous sylph. The arms may be loosely extended as their tips explore its surroundings (think of the complexity of processing stimuli from eight locations simultaneously), or they may be curled tightly over the head, with the suckers on the outside, in defense. The suckers, which have no chromatophores and are always whitish, can be moved independently. When the octopus strikes the pose that J. Z. Young has named "dymantic," it arises suddenly on inward-curved arms, presenting its most formidable aspect, with body made pale and its eyes enhanced by horizontal "eye-bars" of a dark color. Other behaviors designed to disrupt the coherence of the body's (already confusing) outline include changing the shape of the mantle, twisting or waving the arms, and erecting the papillae that alter the animal's texture and appearance.

There are even octopuses that glow in the dark. Among cephalopods, bioluminescence was long considered to be the particular province of the squids (and to a lesser extent, the cuttlefishes and vampyromorphs), but when a small female of the genus *Eledonella* (species undetermined) was captured in a mid-water trawl in the North Pacific, it was seen to have a ring of yellow luminescent tissue around the mouth. (As described by Robison and Young in 1981, "A peculiar circumoral organ in a pelagic bolitaenid* octopus luminesced brilliantly when treated with H_2O_2 [hydrogen peroxide].") Under treatment, the ring glowed with a strong greenish light. When additional specimens were examined, it was discovered that only the females had this "peculiar organ," and therefore the authors suggest that "it acts to attract a mate" in the darkness of the octopus's normal range, around 1,000 meters (3,280 feet) below the surface.

In addition to the chromatophores, the skin of many species of cephalopods contains iridocytes (sometimes called iridophores), which are tiny cells containing reflector platelets that impart an iridescent shimmer to the body. Although cells that light up are mostly the province of the squids (see pp. 176–78), there are some octopuses that are equipped with photophores. The blanket, or handkerchief, octopus (*Tremoctopus* sp.), whose common name derives from membranes attached to two of its dorsal arms, was reported from the Northwest Pacific with luminous organs on the dorsal webs of the females.

Tremoctopus is an interesting animal for other reasons. Originally believed to be among the smaller octopods, it has now been measured at over 5 feet in total length. It can autonomously release part of its web, which is marked with dark spots, as a decoy when it is threatened, and in 1963, E. C. Jones revealed that immature blanket octopuses equip themselves with the stinging tentacles of the Portuguese man-of-war (*Physalis*) for reasons that may have to do with either offense or defense.[†] "When a *Tremoctopus* grows big enough to kill its own prey," wrote Gilbert Voss in 1971, "it discards the man-of-war tissues." A tool-using octopus? Voss believed it was "inherited behavior . . . [and] typifies one of the extraordinary habits of Octopoda. . . ."

While most octopuses are brownish, their ability to change shape and color makes describing them more than a little complicated. Here is the

---

*In the English-language version of *Cephalopods of the World* (published in 1987), K. S. Nesis characterizes the Bolitaenidae as "body gelatinous, pigmented. Arms short, shorter than mantle, 3rd arms are longer than the others. Umbrella of modest size. Mantle aperture wide. A luminous organ—a thick ring under the integument around the mouth in adult females. . . . Ink sac present but small. 4 genera, 4–5 species. Mesopelagic and bathypelagic."

† Jones tested his theory by placing captured octopuses on his hand: "The severe pain occurred each time, but careful observation indicated that I was not being bitten by the octopus." He was also the biological detective who solved the mystery of the mysterious scooplike depressions found in the skin of various sharks, billfishes, and whales: They were being attacked by the little "cookie cutter" shark (*Isistius brasiliensis*), which has exactly the right dentition to take such bites. He made this discovery by taking a dead shark and applying its open mouth to a nectarine.

description of the "components of body patterns" of the white-striped octopus in Australian waters (from Roper and Hochberg, 1988):

> The typical cryptic body pattern in the field is a low-intensity, light, brownish-red mottle. The mantle, head, web and arms are covered with light cream to white-colored markings, the vividness of which is controlled by overlying dark chromatophores. White spots on the arms are squarish with rounded corners and arranged in two regular rows; they decrease in size towards the tips of the arms. Spots on the web and the head are oval and they become elongate interrupted stripes or streaks on the mantle.

They can have different patterns for different times of day and different patterns for different activities. Some can be prominently striped, like the zebra octopus (*O. chierchiae*), while others are identifiable by the presence of a spot (technically known as an "ocellus") on the web between the second and third arms. The Mexican species *O. bimaculatus* is commonly known as the two-spotted octopus because of the presence of these ocelli, and the white-striped octopus (*O. ornatus*) has conspicuous white markings on the mantle. Probably the most spectacular of all octopuses are the banded octopuses, sometimes known as "harlequins," which are covered from head to toes in alternating reddish-brown and white stripes. (The coloration of the striped octopuses is permanent or semipermanent, and while the animal can lighten or darken the pattern, it probably relies more on the disruptive nature of the stripes than other, more subdued species.) For the most part, octopus markings can be enlarged, reduced, or completely eliminated, depending on the "mood" of the animal. When an octopus is annoyed, it may darken in color and often turns red. (In the Cousteau book, the authors regularly refer to an octopus as "red with anger" or state, "As can be seen from its pink color, [it] is not happy.") Many species can feature a striking display of ocelli, which may intimidate predators by making them think they have encountered a large animal with scary eyes. The iridescent blue markings of the deadly *Hapalochlaena* can be enlarged or flashed at will, primarily as a warning.

Color change is stimulated by the central nervous system, and sight seems to play a major role in the animal's "decision" as to what color it will be. (It is difficult to avoid the anthropomorphic attitude that assigns volition to the octopus's color change, since there must be some sort of sequence of "conscious" reactions that controls color in a given situation.) "An octopus makes no attempt to hide its feelings," wrote Voss, "on the contrary, its emotions are closely linked to the color mechanism." While we do not really know if octopuses feel emotions, there appear to be colors that reflect certain "emotional" states. The Cousteau team tested various octopuses in the Mediterranean and concluded that livid red signifies anger or intimidation, white is fear, and so on. Alex Kerstitch described a captive octopus that became "enraged" by a mild electric shock, exhibited "a series of rapid, spasmodic, kaleidoscopic color flushes," and writhed around biting itself until it turned pale and died. Frank Lane points out that an octopus embryo still in its egg case can change color to match its surroundings, that a blind octopus can do likewise, and perhaps most startling, that the skin continues to change color even after the animal has died. Another device used by the octopus involves changing its appearance by modifying its texture. To camouflage itself on rocks or coral, for example, the animal can roughen its skin by erecting lumps, bumps, warts, and wrinkles, but when it glides through the water, the skin becomes almost slick. Alteration of texture is also believed to be indicative of the animal's "emotional" state.

The octopus is not a simple animal, even though it appears to be composed of not much more than head and arms. The head houses a remarkably complex brain, and the eyes, although not as highly developed as those of squid, are also close in structure and function to those of the "higher" vertebrates.* Although it is usually compared to that of a parrot, the lower lobe of the octopus's beak is larger than the upper, and when closed, the upper lobe fits into the lower. Sometimes it can secrete a fluid that liquefies the flesh of a victim even before it is ingested, meaning that digestion can take place outside the octopus. The octopus's tongue, known as the radula, is equipped with a series of tiny rasplike or toothlike projections that help it scrape bits of flesh from the shells of its victims.

The gravitational orientation of the octopus can be observed through the eye movements. The pupil of the octopus eye remains horizontal regardless of the animal's body position. This compensatory eye movement is known as "counter-rolling," and enables the cephalopod to maintain a stable image of the world around it, whatever its orientation. Like the similarity of cephalopod and vertebrate eyes, the development of the equilibrium system in cephalopods is another example of the principle of convergence; vertebrates and cephalopods, employing a completely differ-

---

*There is, of course, no hierarchy that ranks organisms from lower to higher except the order that we humans have devised—in order to put ourselves at the top. The invertebrates are usually considered "lower" than the backboned animals, but there is no reason for such a stratification to apply. The reasoning powers—not to mention the predatory skills, tactile sensitivity, and all-round dexterity—of certain cephalopods rivals, and in some cases clearly exceeds, the comparable capabilities of most fishes, many reptiles, and even some mammals. Fred Bavendam wrote, "Most biologists consider [the octopus] to be the smartest of all invertebrate animals, with about the same intelligence as a house cat."

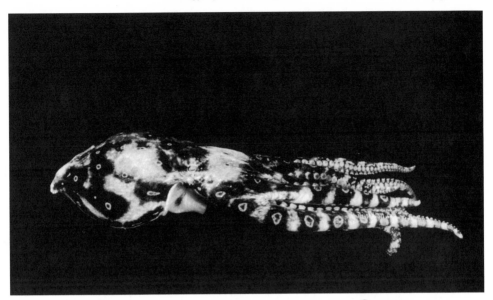

ent evolutionary strategy, have resolved a particular problem in remarkably similar ways.

A little killer with a big name, the blue-ringed octopus (*Hapalochlaena maculosa*) has a bite poisonous enough to kill a man.

Using a highly toxic venom that is stored in the posterior salivary glands, most, if not all, octopus species can also use poison to debilitate their prey, but the poison's route from salivary gland to beak to prey item is not obvious. Frank Lane says, "How it is ejected is not known for certain," but Bruce Halstead opines that the venom is discharged from the salivary glands into the pharynx and is transmitted when the animal bites. (When he was bitten by a 4-inch specimen of *O. joubini*, Craig Phillips felt "an intense burning pain like a hornet sting, which lasted for an hour or so.")

Whatever the transmission route, however, the tiny blue-ringed octopus of Australia (*Hapalochlaena* spp.) has a venom so powerful that one bite can kill a grown man.* The story is told in Australian medical literature and summarized in *Dangerous Marine Animals* by Bruce Halstead. In 1954, a diver named Kirke Dyson-Holland captured a small octopus off Darwin, and after he allowed the little animal to crawl over his arms and shoulders, it bit him on the back of the neck. He experienced a shortness of breath, a loss of muscular control, and then began to vomit. He was rushed to the Darwin hospital, where he was given a shot of adrenaline and placed on a

---

*Although commonly referred to as the "blue-ringed octopus," the genus *Hapalochlaena* actually contains at least three species, identified (by Roper and Hochberg, 1988) as the lesser blue-ringed octopus (*H. maculosa*); the greater blue-ringed octopus (*H. lunulata*); and the blue-lined octopus (*H. fasciata*), which has iridescent blue *lines* on its head and mantle, as contrasted with the rings of the other two species.

respirator, but he died two hours after being bitten. For many years, Dyson-Holland's death was attributed to an allergy to octopus bites, but when another man died after picking up a tiny octopus in Sydney Harbour and six more people became seriously ill after handling little octopuses with flashing blue spots, it became clear that *Hapalochlaena* was indeed a man killer. In 1971, Thomas Roach was bitten on the toe by an unknown animal while walking through the surf at Shoalhaven Heads, south of Sydney. He died within five minutes, and according to Gilbert Voss, "The puncture mark on his big toe was almost positive evidence of the bite of a blue-ringed octopus."

One of the truly remarkable qualities of the octopus is its ability to regenerate an injured or lost arm. Predators often grasp the cephalopod by one of its arms, and from numerous laboratory observations (mostly by Mathilde Lange), it appears that the arm can be regrown if it is pulled or bitten off. (Among the natural predators of octopuses are moray eels and other fishes, seals, sea lions, dolphins, and porpoises.) Unlike some lizards, which have a particular segment of their tails weakened to facilitate this autotomy, octopus arms have no such region, and they can apparently break the arm off anywhere along its length. It usually takes about six weeks for an arm to regenerate, and while the new limb has all the requisite suckers and chromatophores, it is usually smaller than the original. Experiments have also shown that an octopus can even regenerate part of an eye that is damaged.

Octopuses can also cast off an arm if they are in trouble, a slightly different process from having it bitten or torn off, but one that serves the same defensive function. At the Seaquarium of Miami, curator Craig Phillips tells the story (in *The Captive Sea*) of an octopus that lost an arm as he was capturing it. He kept the seven-armed octopus but threw the severed arm away. As he looked down for the lost arm, he saw that it was tightly wrapped around a killifish that had evidently approached to examine the wriggling object. "Had I not released the fish," he wrote, "it would probably have died in this condition."*

Despite their occasional bad press, most octopuses are harmless to humans. But if they are harmless to people, octopuses are deadly to shellfish. C. P. Idyll calls the octopus "the most efficient crab trap in existence," and Joseph Sinel, who wrote *An Outline of the Natural History of Our Shores*,

---

*In the case of the argonaut or paper nautilus (*Argonauta argo*), the hectocotylized arm of the male is *supposed* to go off on its own. At mating time, the specialized arm of the tiny male (he is about an inch long, as compared with the 18-inch female) breaks free and may swim around on its own until it locates a female so it can deposit its cargo of spermatophores. The hectocotylized arm of the male blanket octopus also breaks off and remains inside the female for fertilization.

included a careful and detailed study of the feeding habits of octopuses of the Channel Islands off the coast of Normandy. His book was published in 1906, so he obviously couldn't spend much time under water, but he watched the octopuses in tide pools, and he kept captured specimens in "rabbit hutches" with wire-mesh tops, firmly ballasted and kept in the rock pools. He wrote:

> If the crab is in the open, and the octopus is on the hunt, it rises above its victim, and with the tentacles so outstretched that the web that joins them part of their length forms a parachute, it descends like a cloud on its victim. . . . I have seen a moderate-sized octopus catch 17 crabs in succession, just storing them in the custody of the manifold suckers, to await their turn. The octopus does not break the shells of its victims, but simply disarticulates them, and with the slender tips of its tentacles, removes every vestige of the edible parts. The horny beak does not seem to be employed, except in taking from the tentacle suckers the portions they have removed.

Sinel also described the octopus as keeping a tentacle rolled tightly in a vertical coil until a crab happened by its lair, then unwinding the tentacle toward the crab until it has secured it with the delicate but powerful suckers on the end of its arm. The octopus hides in a crevice, or if one is not available, it builds a fortress of stones, bottles, pottery shards, or other debris. It is usually easy to identify the home of an octopus: The area immediately in front of the opening is littered with the shells and hollowed-out legs of various crustaceans.

Most invertebrates do not indulge in parental care of their offspring, that being perceived primarily as a vertebrate function. Trust the octopus to overturn that concept and display a degree of protection for its eggs that is unmatched in the world of animals without a backbone. First, however, the eggs have to get fertilized. The mating dance of these eight-armed creatures has been observed many times in captivity (even though there are very few instances where the baby octopuses survived after hatching), and it is initiated by the male. He caresses the female with the tip of his hectocotylized arm (the third arm to the left of the head), eventually inserting the tip into the mantle cavity. This arm has a spatulate end and a groove that runs its length for the transport of the sperm packets. The spermatophores are thus transferred, and the eggs are fertilized. The female then seeks a protected spot in which to lay the eggs, which are white and opalescent and about an eighth of an inch long in the common octopus. They are attached to a common strand and hung in long, vertical clusters on a permanent surface, such as the underside of an overhanging rock or the wall of a coral cave. Depending on the species and the age of the female, anywhere from 50,000 to 250,000 eggs are laid, although there are some recorded instances where the number was much higher.

Once the eggs are laid, the female guards them diligently, not leaving the nest until they hatch. She defends the nest against intruders, all the while blowing water out of her funnel to keep the water circulating around them. The eggs of the common octopus take approximately seven weeks to hatch, and when they do, a miniature version of the parent emerges. (There is no "larval" stage at which the neonates are different in any other way from the adults but size.) A newborn common octopus is about the size of a flea, and it can change color. Some species are born larger and immediately drop to the bottom, but the tiny babies of *O. vulgaris* join the vast legions of plankton, drifting at the mercy of the current and susceptible to the predation of any animal larger than they are. As observed in captive situations, the female does not eat during the time her eggs are hatching (she does nothing but guard and aerate them, so the term "incubation" does not apply), and in many cases, after the eggs hatch, she turns white and dies.

Most shallow-water octopods follow the regimen of the much-studied *O. vulgaris*, laying their eggs in an enclosed space and then protecting and aerating them until they hatch, but some deep-water species have taken the process a step further. When a specimen of *Bolitaena microcotyla* was trawled up from about 900 meters (2,952 feet) off Oahu, it was found to be a female with a "brood pouch" in which twelve recently hatched embryos were associated. (The action of the trawl evidently dislodged them, but R. E. Young believed that they had been in the pouch formed by the arms and the web.) The mouth of the 3-inch-long octopus was almost completely sealed, indicating that she had recently spawned and was therefore incapable of feeding. In 1929, Joubin described a specimen of *Vitreleldonella* that contained hundreds of hatched larvae within the mantle cavity, suggesting that there are other families of bathypelagic octopods that brood their young. In his 1972 discussion of this phenomenon, Young wrote, "All species of epipelagic octopods are known to have some means of brooding their young."

When baby octopuses hatch, they are in a group defined by their simultaneous birth, but after that brief communal moment, they are solitary creatures. With the exception of their mating rituals, they live their lives alone, concentrating on housing and feeding. Because of their soft-bodied vulnerability, octopuses protect themselves by occupying a crevice, a cave, or an artificial receptacle, such as a pottery jar or pot. (In the Mediterranean, fishermen lower a series of small pots, tied together with a length of rope, into an area known to be occupied by octopuses. In what would appear to be a manifestation of the "grass is always greener" syndrome, an octopus seems to be unable to resist a new house and will leave its rocky nest for a clay pot, only to be hauled up by a fisherman.) Unless a new domicile is offered, however, the octopus occupies a particular nest for a long time and ventures forth only to hunt for food, or in the case of the males, to look for a mate.

Because it was obviously in their interest to do so, novelists and moviemakers portrayed the giant octopus as a terrifying monster, but the very nature of the real octopus virtually dooms to failure all artificial models or "dynamation." As described by the Cousteau team, "The octopus looks like a silken scarf floating, swirling, and settling gently as a leaf on a rock," actions that lend themselves poorly to model making or stop-action photography. (Eventually, of course, we will see the image of an octopus animated by a computer, but such a creature has not yet appeared on our large or small screens.) If there is ever going to be a giant octopus in the movies, the role might best be played by an animal that has already been given the name of *Octopus giganteus*.

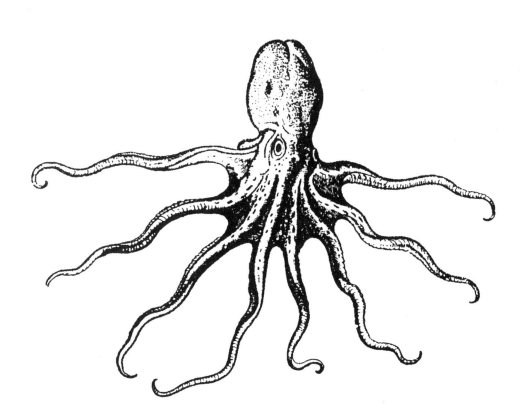

BLOBS AND GLOBSTERS

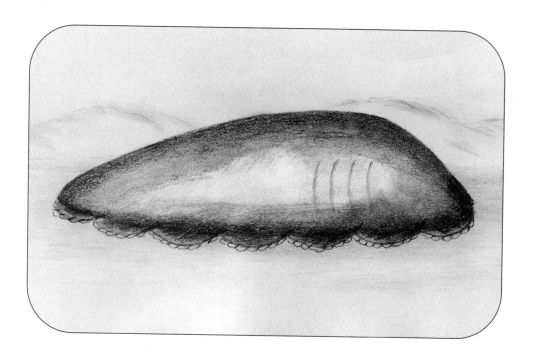

SOMETIME BEFORE NOVEMBER 30, 1896, on the shores of Anastasia Island near St. Augustine, Florida, a gigantic lump had washed up. Two boys reported it to a local physician, DeWitt Webb, who came to the beach the next day to have a look. Webb was mystified, but realized there wasn't much he could do with five tons of protoplasm, so he went home and returned the following day to have a closer look. It was composed of a white rubbery substance, and it was 21 feet long, 7 feet wide, and 4 feet high. Although it obviously could not be weighed, it was estimated to weigh between 5 and 7 tons. Dr. Webb, who was the founder of the St. Augustine Historical Society and a man with a keen interest in natural history, believed that it was the remains of a giant octopus, because when he first saw it, it appeared to have the stumps of four arms, and there was another arm buried nearby.

Because the monster was found on the beach near his hotel at South Beach, Dr. George Grant described it in a short article that appeared in the Williamsport, Pennsylvania, paper for December 13, 1896:

> The head is as large as an ordinary flour barrel, and has the shape of a sea lion head. The neck, if the creature may be said to have a neck, is of the same diameter as the body. The mouth is on the under side of the head and is protected by two tentacle tubes about eight inches in diameter and about 30 feet long. These tubes resemble an elephant's trunk and obviously were used to clutch in a sucker like fashion any object within their reach. Another tube or tentacle of the same dimensions stands out on the top of the head. Two others, one on each side, protrude from beyond the monster's neck, and extend fully 15 feet along the body and beyond the tail. The tail, which is separated and jagged with cutting points for several feet, is flanked with two more tentacles of the same dimensions as the others

and 30 feet long. The eyes are under the back of the mouth instead of over it. This specimen is so badly cut up by sharks and sawfish that only the stumps of the tentacles remain, but pieces of them were found strewn for some distance on the beach, showing that the animal had a fierce battle with its foes before it was disabled and beached by the surf.

Grant evidently wanted to drag the thing closer to his hotel, build a shed over it, and charge admission, but he was dissuaded by Webb, who staked it out, put ropes around it, and claimed it for science.

Dr. Webb engaged two men to photograph the mass for posterity, and he sent the pictures, along with his description, to J. A. Allen of the Museum of Comparative Zoology at Harvard. Allen evidently did not respond, but Webb's letter came to the attention of Prof. Addison Verrill of Yale, the nation's foremost authority on cephalopods. (From 1874 to 1896, Verrill had published twenty-seven scientific articles on the giant squid that had been washing ashore in North America, primarily in Newfoundland. For details of Verrill's descriptions of *Architeuthis,* see pp. 130–37). On the basis of Webb's description and his examination of the photos, Verrill concluded that it was indeed an octopus, and in his first publication on the subject, he even gave the animal a scientific name, *Octopus giganteus.** Verrill also wrote about the giant octopus for the New York *Herald* (January 3, 1897).

On January 16, the *Tatler,* a news sheet that reported on the visitors to St. Augustine hotels, ran this story:

The wide-spread interest in the very remarkable specimen of the giant squid, now lying on the beach a few miles below the city, is mainly due to its enormous size. It is believed to be the largest specimen ever found. Its great size and immense weight have thus far prevented its being moved for a more careful examination. A dozen men with blocks and tackle not being able even to turn it over. Another effort will be made with more extensive apparatus by which it is hoped to drag it from the pit in which it now lies and placing it higher up on the beach so that a careful and thorough examination in the interest of science can be made and the exact species determined. Professor Verrill of Yale and Profs. True and Dale [Dall] of the Smithsonian are in constant correspondence with Dr. DeWitt Webb, President of the St. Augustine Scientific, Literary and

*The rules of scientific nomenclature mandate that the first person to publish a description of a particular species shall have his name affixed to the binomial, along with the date of the publication. Thus, the full name of this creature—whatever it was—is "*Octopus giganteus* Verrill 1897."

*D*r. DeWitt Webb beside the "St. Augustine Monster," which has been hauled up on the beach. It was 21 feet long, 4 feet high, and its weight was estimated at 5 tons.

*A*fter the "monster" had been hauled up on the beach, DeWitt Webb (second from left) posed beside it with other dignitaries of St. Augustine.

Historical Society, in regard to it. Several photographs have been taken of it, but owing to its position, these have not been satisfactory. Mrs. John L. Wilson believes it to belong to an extinct species. Its hide is three and a half inches thick and its head is covered by a hood that prevents examination. Apparently it is a mass of cartilage and may have been dead in the water many days before it washed ashore on Anastasia Island.

During a storm tide between January 9 and January 15, the carcass was taken out to sea, but it reappeared on the next tide, two miles south of its original location. In order to preclude this happening again, Dr. Webb employed several able-bodied assistants, four horses, heavy tackle, and a windlass and managed to drag the thing forty feet up the beach, where it was photographed again. After Webb had succeeded in moving it farther up the beach, the *Tatler* responded with this item:

> Doctor DeWitt Webb, President of the Scientific Society, has succeeded in drawing the huge invertebrate out of the sand and securing it farther up the beach, that it can be examined by scientists. So far as can be determined at present, it belongs to no family not extinct, and is principally interesting on account of its great size, being about twenty-one feet long, without a head. Professor W. H. Dall of the Smithsonian Institute, and Professor A. E. Verrill of Yale, are naturally much interested, and may be prevailed upon to visit.

Webb also corresponded with William Healy Dall, curator of molluscs at the Smithsonian, and requested that he "come down at once," but Dall was told by his superiors that the Smithsonian could not afford to send him, nor could it afford to have the "cuttlefish" shipped from Florida to Washington. Webb then hacked off large chunks of the monster and sent them to both Verrill and Dall. In a letter to Dall dated February 5, 1897, he wrote:

> I made another excursion to the invertebrate and brought away specimens for you and for Dr. Verrill of Yale. I cut two pieces of the mantle and two pieces from the body and have put them in a solution of formalin for a few days before I send them to you. Although strange as it may seem to you, I could have packed them in salt and sent them to you at once although the creature had been lying on the beach for more than two months. And I think that both yourself and Dr. Verrill, while not doubting my measurements, have thought my account of the thickness of the muscular, or rather tendonous husk pretty large, so I am glad to send you the specimens and I will express them packed in salt in a day or two.

With the specimens on the way, Verrill published another piece in the Sunday supplement of the New York *Herald* (February 14, 1897) in which he speculated on the size, shape, and habits of *Octopus giganteus:*

> The living weight of the creature was about eighteen or twenty tons. When living, it must have had enormous arms, each one a hundred feet or more in length, each as thick as the mast of a large vessel, and armed with hundreds of saucer-shaped suckers, the largest of which would have been at least a foot in diameter. . . . Its eyes would have been more than a foot in diameter. It would have carried ten or twelve gallons of ink in the ink bag. It could swim rapidly, without doubt, but its usual habit would be to crawl slowly over the bottom in deep water in pursuit of prey. . . . We must reflect that wherever this creature had its home, there must be living hundreds or even thousands of others of its kind, probably of equal size, otherwise its race could not be kept up. . . .

In the photographs, the creature looked more like an octopus than a squid, but Verrill was evidently troubled by its size, so much larger than any known octopus. In January he submitted a note to the *American Journal of Science* in which he wrote:

> The proportions [given by Webb] indicate that this might have been a squid-like form, and not an *Octopus*. The "breadth" is evidently that of the softened and collapsed body, and would represent an actual maximum diameter in life of at least 7 feet and a probable weight of 4 or 5 tons for the body and head. These dimensions are decidedly larger than those of any of the well-authenticated Newfoundland specimens. It is perhaps a species of *Architeuthis*.

Verrill also mentions a Mr. Wilson, "who claimed to have found a portion of an attached arm, 36 feet long buried in the sand," but then decides that the statement was "erroneous and entirely misleading."*

Once he examined the samples sent to him by Webb, however, Verrill decided it was not an octopus (or any kind of cephalopod), and he suggested that it was part of a whale, but "what part of any cetacean it might have been is still an unsolved puzzle." Verrill finally withdrew his invertebrate identification (again in the *American Journal of Science*), and

---

*Wilson's actual memorandum is included in Verrill's paper and reads as follows: "One arm lying west of the body, 23 feet long; one stump of arm about four feet long; three arms lying south of body and from appearance attached to same (although I did not dig quite to body, as it laid well down in the sand and I was very tired), longest one measured over 23 feet, the other arms were three to five feet shorter."

$\mathcal{W}$orking from a photograph, A. E. Verrill drew this picture to accompany his discussion of the "Florida Sea-Monster." It is difficult to imagine anyone mistaking this for a whale.

on March 5, he wrote, "The supposition that it was an *Octopus* was partly based upon its baglike form and partly upon the statements made to me that the stumps of large arms were attached to it at first. This last statement was certainly untrue." On March 17, Webb wrote to Dall and said:

> As you already know, Prof. Verrill now says our strange creature cannot be a cephalopod and that he cannot say to what animal it belongs. I do not see how it can be any part of a cetacean as Prof. V. says you suggest. It is simply a great big bag and I do not see how it could be any part of a whale. Now that I have had it brought 6 miles up the beach it is out of the way of the tide and the drifting sand and will have a chance to cure or dry up somewhat. If it were not for the soft mass of the viscera which was so difficult to remove that we left it there would be but little odor. As it is there is no great amount.

The last time the *Tatler* made mention of the beast on the beach was on March 13. By now, the story had become embellished with the imaginative theories of some of the St. Augustine observers:

> Professor Verrill of Yale University, who recently decided that the curious something, supposed to be an octopus, was one, basing his decision on the

descriptions sent, has now concluded, after examining a piece of it, that it could not possibly be an octopus, and he cannot decide what it is. One theory advanced is that it may be a portion of some inhabitant of the sea, long since extinct, that has been fast in an iceberg for centuries, and recently washed ashore here. Another theory is that it is a portion of a deep-sea monster that on coming too near the surface was attacked by a shark, who found it too tough for a breakfast. One thing is now determined, and that is, if we do not know what it is, we know what it is not.*

Would that DeWitt Webb had published his observations and not restricted them to letters to Verrill and Dall. It seems obvious that Webb thought he saw an octopus, since his letters refer to the "mantle," the "hood," and most tantalizingly, "the viscera." Dr. George Grant, whose description of the monster ("the mouth is . . . protected by two tentacle tubes about eight inches in diameter and about 30 feet long . . .") was published on December 16, may have embellished his account for publicity purposes, but Webb reported as accurately as he could to Verrill and Dall, and provided them with photographs as well. Verrill saw only the tissue samples and photographs and from this evidence concluded that the monster was a whale. Indeed, by March 19, Verrill was beginning to argue that it had to have been a sperm whale. Even though it didn't look anything like a whale carcass, Verrill was obviously more comfortable saying it did, and tried to make the facts fit his hypothesis. In his reversal, he made some bizarre statements, explaining why he believed the material was from a whale: "The structure of the integument is more like that of the upper part of the head of a sperm whale than any other known to me, and as the obvious use is the same, it is most probable that the whole mass represents the upper part of the head of such a whale, detached from the skull and jaw." Next sentence: *"It is evident, however, from the figures, that the shape is decidely unlike the head of an ordinary sperm whale, for the latter is oblong, truncated and rather narrow in front, like the prow of a vessel with an angle at the upper front end, near which a single blow hole is situated* [italics mine]." Since the mass does not resemble the head of a sperm whale at all, Verrill tries to "imagine a sperm whale with an abnormally large nose, due to disease or old age" and finally

*Articles in scientific journals are relatively easy to locate; all you need is the date, volume, and page numbers and a library that either has or can get copies of the journals. But copies of the St. Augustine *Tatler* for 1897 are much harder to find—or know about, for that matter—and for their inclusion in this study, I am indebted to Gary Mangiacopra of Milford, Connecticut, who has spent the better part of twenty years looking for (and usually finding) photographs, newspaper articles, and even personal correspondence pertaining to the St. Augustine monster. That he has willingly shared his hard-won gains with me is an indication of his unselfish eagerness to get this story before the public.

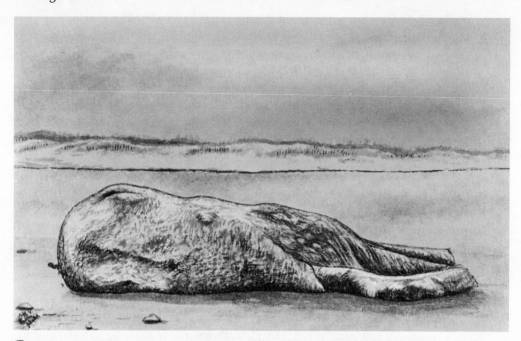

It might be possible to see this as the nose of a sperm whale, but the crease where the blowhole would be was identified as a cut, and there are still those "tentacles" to explain.

searches for some explanation, but "it seems hardly probable that another allied whale, with a big nose, remains to be discovered." To paraphrase Verrill's apologia, the mass looks a little like the head of a sperm whale except that it has somehow become detached from the skull and lower jaw; it isn't really shaped like a sperm whale's head; and if only we could find a big-nosed whale out there (preferably with no blowhole), it would explain everything. Verrill may have reversed himself because he was embarrassed to be promoting a cryptozoological creature.

And in May 1897, in the *Journal of Science,* Verrill published his final word on the subject in an article he entitled "The Supposed Great Octopus of Florida; Certainly Not a Cephalopod." (In the interests of science, this entire article is reproduced as Appendix C in this volume.) Verrill's reversal prompted this wry observation in the British journal *Natural Science* (May 1897): "The moral of this is that one should not attempt to describe specimens stranded on the coast of Florida, while sitting in one's study in Connecticut."

The tissue samples that Webb sent to New Haven have disappeared (when Gary Mangiacopra tried to track them down, he was told that "many specimens were lost during the period between the time the old museum was torn down in 1911, and the new one built in 1926"), but Webb had also sent "several large masses of the thick and firm integument" to Professor Dall at the U.S. National Museum (now the Smithsonian). The story, like the integument, languished for another sixty years, until Forrest Wood, a curator at Marineland of Florida, found a yellowed newspaper clipping in the files. It contained a drawing of the "octopus" and a caption saying that Professor Verrill had examined the remains, "which alone weighed over six tons . . . [and] that the living creature had a girth of 25 feet and tentacles 72 feet in length."*

Wood pursued every lead, including obtaining copies of the Webb-Dall correspondence, and when he learned that a sample of the integument was preserved in the Smithsonian, he persuaded the curators to send a sample to his colleague, Joseph Gennaro, a cell biologist at the University of Florida. Gennaro examined the tissue under a polarizing microscope and compared it to his controls, tissue from known octopus and squid species. He wrote (in "The Creature Revealed"):

> After seventy-five years, the moment of truth was at hand. Viewing section after section of the St. Augustine sample, we decided at once, and beyond any doubt, that the sample was not whale blubber. Further, the connective tissue pattern was that of broad bands in the plane of the section with equally broad bands arranged perpendicularly, a structure similar to, if not identical with, that in my octopus sample.

"The evidence appears unmistakable," concluded Gennaro, "that the St. Augustine sea monster was in fact an octopus, but the implications are fantastic. Even though the sea presents us from time to time with strange and astonishing phenomena, the idea of a giant octopus, with arms 75 to 100 feet in length and about 18 inches in diameter at the base—a total spread of some 200 feet—is difficult to comprehend."

At the conclusion of a lengthy discussion of "Octopus giganteus Verrill" in *Searching for Hidden Animals* (1980), Roy Mackal wrote: ". . . It seems probable to me that the evidence presented, consisting not only of native rumors, but also including so-called hard evidence—that is, tissue samples on which recent analyses with modern techniques have been car-

---

*The credit for breaking this story goes entirely to Wood. After the initial detective work, he published a three-part article in the March 1971 issue of *Natural History* magazine entitled "An Octopus Trilogy." Part I ("Stupefying Colossus of the Deep") is the story of the original discovery; Part II ("The Creature Revealed") was written by Joseph Gennaro and explains his laboratory work; and in Part III ("In Which Bahamian Fishermen Recount Their Adventures with the Beast"), Wood discusses some fishermen's recollections of what may have been a giant octopus.

A previously unpublished photograph of the St. Augustine monster, showing
something that appears to be an arm extending from the body of the creature at the right

ried out—establishes beyond reasonable doubt that very large octopuses
exist somewhere in the Atlantic off the Florida coast."*

Mackal is a biochemist at the University of Chicago (and, it must be
pointed out, a founding member of the International Society of Cryptozoology, as was Wood), and he managed to get a piece of the tissue to test it
for himself. In an article in *Cryptozoology* in 1986, he wrote, "Gennaro carried out comparative histological examination of the tissue, and concluded
that it most resembled contemporary octopus tissue. While these results
were highly suggestive, further biochemical work was required for an
unambiguous identification of the tissue." Mackal tested the tissue for various amino acids and compared the results with the known amino acid
composition from the tissues of a giant squid, a spotted dolphin, a beluga,
and two species of octopus. He concluded:

> On the basis of Gennaro's histological studies and the present amino acid
> and Cu [copper] and Fe [iron] analyses, I conclude that, to the extent the

*In a 1990 novel called *The Ghost from the Grand Banks,* science-fiction (and science) writer
Arthur C. Clarke repeats the story of the St. Augustine "monster" as background for the appearance
of a living 200-foot octopus that is hanging around a Newfoundland oil rig. Clarke's novel is about
attempts to raise the *Titanic* in 2012, a century after the sinking, and the giant octopus—which turns
out to be harmless—plays only a peripheral part in the story.

preserved *O. giganteus* tissue is representative of the carcass washed ashore at St. Augustine, Florida, in November of 1896, it was essentially a huge mass of collagenous protein. Certainly, the tissue was not blubber. I interpret these results as consistent with, and supportive of, Webb and Verrill's identification of the carcass as that of a gigantic cephalopod, probably an octopus, not referable to any known species.

In *Octopus and Squid,* Cousteau and Diolé briefly discuss the St. Augustine monster and the reports of giant octopuses in the waters between Florida and the Bahamas. With no verifying references, they then add,

> Incidents of this kind were so numerous and well-attested that an expedition was organized. Its purpose was to photograph the animal in question, and, for this, a flash camera was attached to a line in such a way as to be activated by traction. The animal was, in fact, hooked on the line, but broke it. When the camera was recovered, it was found that shots had been taken at 300 and 600 feet, but they showed only an unidentifiable stretch of brown flesh.

Another mention of a powerful octopus can be found in Bruce Heezen's discussion of whales trapped in submarine telegraph cables (see p. 248). Off Málaga, Spain, in 1951, a tangled and broken cable was brought up for repair. The captain of the cable-repair ship *Mirror* described a "one pound lump of tough, amorphous fish tissue, highly odoriferous [that] was tightly wrapped around the cable and subsequently cut clear with difficulty." It came from twelve hundred fathoms (seventy-two hundred feet) and, for reasons unknown, the captain suggested that the break was caused by an octopus and "concluded that the animal was large and powerful, judging from the extent of the damage inflicted to the fairly new cable."

The giant octopus is probably the most cryptic of all cryptozoological creatures, for it may actually exist, although the evidence is far from conclusive. The first indication that there may be such a monster was the story of the St. Augustine mound of flesh, which, to this day, has not been satisfactorily explained. The giant squid, whose existence was originally postulated on the basis of sailors' yarns, did not permit its flesh to be examined by a scientist until 1871, but we have a piece of the Florida animal that can be analyzed.* If the St. Augustine blob were the only such hunk of myste-

---

*The story of the tissue has a strange—but fitting—ending. After Gennaro cut off the two "finger-sized pieces" for his histological examinations, he left the remaining hunks in their original jar at the Smithsonian. According to Gennaro, the original Smithsonian material has now been lost, and all that remains is the piece he took; it looks, he said, "like that piece of pork when you open a can of baked beans." Gennaro has donated the remaining material to the St. Augustine Historical Society—whose early president was DeWitt Webb.

rious protoplasm in the record, it would be possible to dismiss it as a misinterpretation of known data or the anomalous ramblings of some cryptozoologists who want desperately to prove the existence of another unknown animal. Perhaps the experts are reading the evidence incorrectly, and it is the "case" of a sperm whale or the mantle of a large squid. But there are other blobs.

In a remote part of western Tasmania, in August 1960, two Tasmanian drovers, Jack Boote and Ray Anthony, discovered a huge mass of tissue while rounding up cattle with their employer, Ben Fenton. On the beach near the Interview River, they came upon a lump of flesh that they described as measuring 20 by 18 feet and weighing between 5 and 10 tons. It had no smell and did not appear to be decomposing. Fenton told a number of people about his find—and even drew a picture of it—but he could not engender any scientific interest until a year and a half later, when he convinced G. C. Cramp, a trustee of the Tasmanian Museum, to assemble a team of zoologists and naturalists to have a look for themselves. The expedition consisted of Bruce Mollison and Max Bennett of the CSIRO (Com-

The Mercury
Established 1854

Vol. CLXXXIX. No. 28,444   HOBART: 63 Macquarie St. Phone 2 5001 (9 lines).   HOBART: FRIDAY, MARCH 9, 1962   Registered at General Post Office, Hobart,   20 PAGES
LAUNCESTON: 70 St. John St. Phone 2 2201 (3 lines).   for transmission by post as a newspaper.

NEARLY AS BIG AS A HOUSE!

IT WAS COVERED WITH FINE HAIR

ABOUT 20ft. long, 18ft. wide and about 4½ft. thick, with an estimated weight of between five and 10 tons.

These are the dimensions of the "sea monster" found on the far West Coast, according to the investigating party.

The part exposed was hard and rubbery and in an extremely good state of preservation. Gulls, Tasmanian devils, native cats, and crows had been tearing at it for months to no avail.

The party described it in general outline as like a huge outline, without appendages.

It was initially covered with fine hair, described by stockmen as being like sheep's wool, with a greasy feel. They likened it to a three months' coat of a Border Leicester.

The animal had a hump of about four feet in front and tapered gradually to about six inches to what they presumed to be the back.

There were five or six gill-like hairless slits on each side of the fore part. There were four

large hanging lobes in the front, and between the centre pair was a smooth, gullet-like orifice.

The margin of the hind part had crashes like protuberances about 5ft. wide by 18in. deep, and each of these carried a single row of spines, sharp, and hard, about as thick as a pencil and quill-like. There was no appearance of eyes or other organs.

The party said a strong acidic reek came off the flesh, very similar to battery acid, and dogs and horses were unwilling to approach it.

They made a deep incision in the high part and encountered a resilient flesh which appeared to be composed of numerous tendon-like threads welded together with a fatty substance.

At no stage in the investigation did they encounter any bone material in the decayed flesh. Samples of the flesh were taken for chemical analysis. It was obviously extremely durable and had withstood weather particularly well.

"SEA MONSTER" FIND MAY BECOME WORLD TOPIC

AN expedition returned to Hobart from the West Coast yesterday with a story of a "sea monster" which could arouse worldwide interest.

They described the remains as conforming to no known animal, and examination may bring to light the fact that it is, indeed, unique.

Describing the trials and tribulations of the party, the leader of the expedition Mr. B. C. Mollison, of the CSIRO, summed up the discovery: "One imagines always to reject the fact that an animal is unknown. One is always seeking some explanation, and you try to add up"

everything, but this one does not add up yet."

"The tragedy of the whole discovery is that there was no bone material available, and it is a matter of reconstruction to determine in what order it can be placed."

The discovery which could herald a new order in zoology was the result of three prime factors:—
● The initial appreciation of the find by a stockman.
● The enthusiasm of Mr. G. C. Cramp, a trustee of the Tasmanian Museum.

who arranged an aerial search; and
● The supplementary enthusiasm of the private expedition which brought back the news.

The presence of the animal first came to light in June, 1960, when two drovers going South with a herd of cattle came across the strange object on the sands about two miles north of Interview River.

They realised they had found something unique and carried the story back to civilisation. Nothing further was done until about three weeks ago, when CSIRO members in Hobart began to piece together various reports coming to hand.

Mr. Cramp organised an aerial search to locate the object, and being successful it was still there, a private expedition was undertaken to make an exploratory survey.

Tough going for party

The exploratory party consisted of Messrs. Bruce Mollison (leader) and Max Bennett, of the CSIRO, Hobart, and Mr. L. E Wall (vice-president) and J. A. Lewis (treasurer) of the Tasmanian Field Naturalists' Club.

They left last Friday and returned to Hobart yesterday morning with a story of high adventure—a story of a trek through extremely rough country, of the wading of swollen rivers, and, above all, of a task successfully accomplished.

The original discoverers were Messrs. Jack Boote and Ray Anthony, of Smithton, and when they first saw the

● Continued on Page 2.

● This impression of the "sea monster" was drawn by a museum expert.

monwealth Scientific and Industrial Research Organization) and L. E. Wall and J. A. Lewis, officers of the Tasmanian Field Naturalist's Club. Cramp had located the object from the air, and he directed the expedition toward its destination, through the tangled and difficult terrain of Western Tasmania.

The investigating party arrived on March 7, 1962, and found that the "carcass" was almost exactly where it had been a year and half before. They reported back to Hobart, and the front page of the Tasmanian *Mercury* (March 9, 1962) bore the headline, "Sea Monster May Become World Topic. Nearly as Big as a House!" The newspaper story gave many of the details of the discovery, describing the thing as follows:

> Hard and rubbery and in an extremely good state of preservation. Gulls, Tasmanian devils, native cats, and crows had been tearing at it for months to no avail. . . . It was initially covered with fine hair, described by the' stockmen as being like sheep's wool, with a greasy feel. . . . The animal had a hump of about four feet in front and tapered gradually to about six inches to what they presumed to be the back. There were five or six gill-like hairless slits on each side of the fore part. There were four large hanging lobes in the front, and between the center pair was a smooth, gullet-like orifice.

The investigators found that "it had no visible eyes, no defined head, and no apparent bone structure" (Greenwell, 1988). Mollison, the leader of the ground forces, was quoted as saying, "One tends always to reject the fact that an animal is unknown. One is always seeking some explanation, and you try to add up everything, but this one does not add up . . . the more I looked, the more I was convinced that it conformed to no known animal."

On March 16, somewhat surprised by the worldwide publicity, the Australian government mounted a second expedition to investigate, and this time various scientists—some from CSIRO but excluding Mollison—came to examine it. By this time, the lump had acquired the name of "globster." The investigators cut out a hunk of the tissue and brought it back to Hobart, where, once again, various scientists could not agree on what it was. Prof. A. M. Clark of the University of Tasmania said it was a giant ray and "that it was clearly not a whale."* Interviewed later, Mollison said that

---

*A whale has an outer covering of blubber, which is the layer of fat that serves as insulation in the heat-absorbing water in which it lives. As the old whalers knew, you could peel the blubber layer off, leaving the meat and muscle beneath. The thickest known blubber layer is found on the bowhead whale, a resident of the Arctic, where the fat layer can be as much as two feet thick. A five- or ten-ton solid mass of tissue, with no meat or bones in it, has nothing whatever to do with cetacean blubber.

the Tasmanian globster "wasn't fish, fowl, or fruit. It wasn't a whale, seal, sea elephant, or squid."

Perhaps because so much time was lost between the discovery and the first expedition, or perhaps because the authorities were embarrassed by their inability to identify the mass in the face of considerable contradictory evidence, the Australian government decided that it was a whale. Sen. John Gorton, who was later to become prime minister, issued a terse statement in which he said, "In layman's language, and allowing for scientifc caution, this report means that your monster is a large lump of decomposing blubber, probably torn off a whale." In later interviews, Bruce Mollison was quoted as saying, "I hacked into the ivory-colored flesh with a hunting knife, but it was far too tough to get out a decent chunk. It was like thick leather." With its boneless structure, its stringy, durable composition, and the presence of gill slits, it was obvious that this was no whale. (Ivan Sanderson, writing about the Globster in *Saga's UFO Special* in 1972, asked, "Have we destroyed a creature from outer space?" The idea of giant globs landing on earth without benefit of spaceship is indeed an intriguing one.)

Then, in 1968, another Pacific Globster appeared, on the beach at Muriwai, on North Island, New Zealand. It was described as being 30 feet

The New Zealand Globster: a gigantic mound of unidentified stringy tissue that washed ashore at Muriwai, on the east coast of North Island, in 1968.

long and 8 feet high, and J. E. Morton, chairman of the Zoology Department at the University of Auckland, was quoted as saying, "I can't think of anything it resembles."

It is rare that lightning strikes twice in the same place and rarer still that a man finds two globsters. Ben Fenton, the Tasmanian stockman who discovered the first one, came across another in 1970. This one was a mere 8 feet long, but that was the part showing above the sand. "I've got no idea what the rest of it buried in the sand is like," said Fenton, "and I don't intend to try and find out." Fenton made a drawing of the first "monster," and there were several artists' interpretations published in the Tasmanian *Mercury,* but apparently there are no available photographs of the Tasmanian globsters. Greenwell (1988) reproduced a couple of photographs of the New Zealand globster, but they are without specific identification or credit, and in one of the captions, he wrote, "Details of the investigation and conclusions are unknown at this time." We are no closer to identifying the origin of the tissue of these animals than Addison Verrill was when he kept changing his mind about the St. Augustine monster.

In May 1988, Teddy Tucker, a fisherman and treasure hunter, found what became known as the "Bermuda blob" in Mangrove Bay. Tucker (in an interview with me) described the blob as "2½ to 3 feet thick . . . very white and fibrous . . . with five 'arms or legs,' rather like a disfigured star." He estimated that it weighed a couple of thousand pounds and said that three people could not turn it over. The blob had no bones or cartilage, and it was "very dense and solid"—not unlike the St. Augustine monster. In trying to cut it with a knife, Tucker remarked that "it was like trying to cut a car tire." Photographs were taken of the blob and sent to various experts: Clyde Roper, the Smithsonian's expert on giant squid; Forrest Wood, the marine mammalogist who published the story on the St. Augustine monster in 1971; and Roy Mackal, the biochemist and cryptozoologist who devoted an entire chapter of *Searching for Hidden Animals* to the Florida monster. None of these experts was able to give an opinion about the blob. (If the St. Augustine monster was really *Octopus giganteus,* then perhaps the Bermuda blob was another individual of the same species. Certainly the description of the Florida monster's "hard elastic complex of connective tissue fibers of large size" compares well with the Bermuda blob's "stringy" fibers.)

Perhaps the various "blobs" are the remains of whales, decomposed beyond recognition. Certainly that is what some of the scientists tell us. But how do we explain the analysis of the St. Augustine monster, where biochemists identified the 22-foot-long lump as resembling octopus tissue? In Part III of the "Octopus Trilogy," Forrest Wood quotes respected fishermen

*T*eddy Tucker tries to cut a hunk
from the "Bermuda blob," in
Mangrove Bay. He described it
as "like trying to cut a car tire."

of the Bahamas who claim to have seen giant octopuses, one of which was
said to be 75 feet long, that came into shallow water only when sick or
dying. Wood then writes:

> Perhaps even a skeptical biologist could be forgiven for being impressed
> with this information. Anecdotal evidence is properly mistrusted, but the
> source must always be considered, and my informant had demonstrated
> his reliability in other matters. He had given me fairly precise data as to
> where, when and by whom the giant scuttles had been encountered. And
> certainly, if they indeed existed, the account of their behavior was reason-
> able enough.

Wood was a respected scientist, with a healthy interest in mysterious
animals. Following up his investigations on Verrill's "Florida Sea-Monster,"
he wrote to Frederick A. Aldrich, director of the Marine Sciences Labora-

tory at the Memorial University of Newfoundland and an authority on giant squid. Aldrich answered Wood by saying, "Frankly, I would tend to favor a cephalopod identification for the material you mentioned and per the articles you sent. Cephalopod tissue, particularly squid tissue in my experience, is firm and does not easily decompose beyond a certain stage, and actually hardens and toughens upon exposure."

All the blobs appear to share one characteristic, which might be useful in narrowing down the possibilities. In every instance where someone tried to cut a piece off, they found the material almost impossible to cut. Dr. Webb wrote a letter to Verrill (unearthed by Wood and quoted in his article) in which he said, "The hood [of the monster] is so tough that when it is exposed to the air, an axe makes very little impression on it." When Webb sent him the first samples of the "Florida Sea-Monster," Verrill described them as "white, and so tough that it is hard to cut them, even with a razor, and yet they are somewhat flexible and elastic." (In 1962, when Joseph Gennaro tried to cut the same material, he used a pathologist's knife and had to replace the blade four times just to get two finger-sized pieces.) Bruce Mollison cut a hunk out of the Tasmanian globster of 1960 and said, "It was far too tough to get out a decent chunk. It was like thick leather," and Teddy Tucker likened his experience, as mentioned above, to "trying to cut a car tire with a knife."

In a letter of support for Verrill (published in *Science* on March 19, 1897) Dr. F. A. Lucas, curator of comparative anatomy at the U.S. National Museum, wrote, "The substance looks like blubber, and smells like blubber, and it *is* blubber, nothing more nor less." But it seems to have been something more than blubber, since blubber is fat and there are very few descriptions of fat being impervious to ax blows or impossible to cut with a razor. (As far as I know, no one has ever compared flensing a whale to cutting rubber with an ax.) And even if it was possible for the monsters to have been parts of sperm whales, which parts would they be? The head is usually equipped with a skull and lower jaw and filled with oil. (The mass of the blobs is always described as solid, not hollow.) The body of a whale is like the body of any other mammal, only larger: It has viscera, bones, meat, and muscle. None of the blobs had anything at all resembling the organs of a known creature, vertebrate or invertebrate.

Despite all the evidence, past and present, most investigators still insist that the St. Augustine monster was a whale. One has only to read the descriptive material and look at the pictures to realize that this is a misidentification. Indeed, if one examined the pictures with no information about the size of the object, there would be no question regarding the animal: It

*T*his photograph ran on the front page of the Hobart (Tasmania) *Mercury* for March 9, 1962, with the following caption: "The Director of the Tasmanian Museum and Art Gallery (Dr. W. Bryden) (left), and Mr. G. C. Cramp, a museum trustee, discuss a drawing of the mysterious monster found on the west coast with Mr. B. C. Mollison of the C.S.I.R.O. (right). Mr. Cramp organized an aerial search for the stranded monster which now presents a problem for scientists."

was an octopus. Furthermore, Verrill, who saw only photographs, evidently chose to ignore Webb's very careful identification of "two pieces of the mantle and two pieces of the body," which would certainly indicate some differentiation of form and texture in parts of the actual carcass.

All the blobs and globsters have been found dead on the beach—or rather, parts of something have been found on the beach. (We assume that they are parts of living animals even though we don't know what parts of what kind of animals.) No one has ever seen a giant octopus, except, of course, if the blobs are parts of giant octopuses.* But there is a story circu-

---

* In December 1989, according to a summary in the ISC *Newsletter* (Winter 1990), which was quoting a report carried on the AP wires, a motorized craft was attacked and overturned by a giant octopus in Iligan Bay, southeast of Manila: "Suddenly the waters began to bubble," stated Agapito Caballero, one of the witnesses. " 'Then, with the use of a flashlight, we saw something that looked like a giant octopus. It was as huge as an imported cow.' His brother Alfredo stated that the cephalopod attached itself to the pontoons of the craft, overturning it. The 12 occupants were not attacked and the octopus then reportedly submerged."

lating around Bermuda that may have something to do with a live giant octopus. A fisherman named John P. "Sean" Ingham has been having a lot of trouble with his traps. Ingham is a deep-water crab and shrimp fisherman whose traps are regularly lowered to between one thousand and two thousand fathoms. Recently, these specially reinforced traps have been coming up bent and damaged, or, in some cases, not coming up at all.

On September 3, 1984, Ingham was winching up a trap that had been on the bottom at five hundred fathoms. About halfway up, the line broke. It would take a weight of over six hundred pounds to break the line, which was polyethylene rope. Dr. Bennie Rohr, a biologist with the National Marine Fisheries Service Southeast Laboratory at Pascagoula, Mississippi, suggested that it might be the work of a giant octopus, since a full cage of tasty shrimp or crabs would be the perfect bait for it. (Giant squid presumably feed on faster-moving prey, such as fishes and other, smaller squid.) On another occasion, when a smaller trap was being hauled up from 480 fathoms, the trap seemed rooted to the bottom as if something very heavy were holding it, and the line, with a forty-five-hundred-pound breaking strain, was beginning to give. As if to prove that the trap was not snagged on the bottom, whatever was holding it began to pull the fifty-foot boat. When Ingham put his hand on the line, he felt "thumps like something was walking."

Peter Benchley based some of the novel *Beast* on his conversations with his friend Teddy Tucker. The "beasts" in the novel turn out to be 100-foot anthropophagous giant squid, but their attacks on the fish traps of "Whip" Darling are straight out of Sean Ingham's logbook. In the novel, Darling is pulling his traps in deep water when the mate, Mike, tells him, "Something's not right." At Mike's suggestion, Darling puts a hand on the rope, which is "trembling erratically. There is a thud to it, like an engine misfiring." As the line is hauled up, the stainless-steel cable that holds the cage appears at the surface, but the trap is gone. "Bit," says Darling. "Bit clean through." Four more traps are pulled, and four more cables are bit clean through. The last of the cables comes up whole, but the trap had been wrapped around its weights so hard "it was as if everything had been melted together in a furnace."

Mike stares at it for a long moment, then says, "Jesus, Whip. What kind of sumbitch do that?"

"No man for sure," says Darling. "No animal, neither. At least no animal I've ever seen."

* * *

AS THIS BOOK was going to press, I received a copy of a paper written by Sidney K. Pierce, Gerald N. Smith, Timothy K. Maugel, and Eugenie Clark entitled "On the Giant Octopus [*Octopus giganteus*] and the Bermuda Blob: Homage to A. E. Verrill." (An earlier theory of Dr. Pierce's is discussed on p. 363 of this book.) The paper was still in manuscript when I read it, and was to be submitted to the *Biological Bulletin*. That means that it has not been refereed, and, in fact, might not even be published at all. Until the paper is accepted for publication, its contents cannot be verified (or even read) by anyone else, but since one of the authors (Eugenie Clark) sent it to me because she knew this book was about to be published, I am prepared to add the following information:

Pierce *et al.* analyzed the amino acids in tissue from the St. Augustine "monster" and also from the "Bermuda Blob," and have concluded that the two samples, both of which appear to be pure collagen, did not come from the same kind of animal. "Neither carcass," they write, "is from a giant octopus nor from any invertebrate." The huge St. Augustine mass, they say, came from a homeothermic (warm-blooded) animal, while the Bermuda tissue appears to have come from a poikilothermic (cold-blooded) vertebrate like a fish or a shark. The authors conclude that the St. Augustine tissue came from an "enormous warm-blooded vertebrate" and suggest that it was "the remains of a whale, likely the entire skin." All the amino acid references sound convincing—at least in debunking the giant octopus theory—but there is no suggestion as to how the entire skin of a whale might have become detached from its original owner. (When whalers flensed a whale, they peeled the blubber off in strips.) The sample from the Bermuda specimen tested out as "the skin of a poikilothermic vertebrate . . . either a large teleost or elasmobranch," but how can we compare the dense white mass of the Bermuda Blob to the "skin" of a large fish or shark? Shark or fish skin is composed of scales or denticles, and, furthermore, there is no shark or fish with a skin so thick that it could solidify into a three-foot-thick solid mass. Despite "the profound sadness" the authors express "at ruining a favorite legend," we must conclude that the mysteries remain unsolved and the legend endures.

THE SHARK

*T*HERE IS NO WAY of identifying those who first mythologized the shark, but it appears regularly throughout the folklore of littoral or otherwise sea-related civilizations, from the Aegean to the Polynesian. Even the origins of the English word "shark" are shrouded in etymological mystery. The *Oxford English Dictionary* (*O.E.D.*) initiates its full-page discussion by saying, "The word seems to have been introduced by the sailors of Captain (later Sir John) Hawkins's expedition, who brought home a specimen which was exhibited in London in 1569. The source from which they obtained the word has not been ascertained." For the origin of the word, the *O.E.D.* seems to favor the German *schurk*, or *schurke*, meaning a scoundrel or a villain. In the past, almost all connotations and uses of the word appear to have been pejorative; among the other contemporary uses for the word "shark" are as a noun: a lawyer; and as a verb: to prey upon, steal, or swindle.

A creature whose very name conjures up such negative images is more than likely to acquire a commensurate reputation. Indeed, the shark has come down through history with a reputation as an ancient, mindless, man-eating, ship-following, eating machine that should by rights be eradicated from the face of the earth. As with all myths, this one has some grains of truth embedded in a substantial matrix of fantasy.

An enduring myth about sharks is the one that assigns them an unchanged evolutionary history that stretches back some 300 million years. For this fantasy, the rough framework applies but hardly any of the details. There have been sharklike fishes since the Devonian period, which was about 300 million years ago, but not one of these species has survived to the present day. The early sharks, in fact, didn't look much like the sleek, streamlined creatures we think of when the word "shark" is mentioned.*

Even though the earliest sharks, like their descendants, had skeletons composed mostly of cartilage that does not fossilize, there are some species in which the entire animal was preserved in stone, so we can get an idea of what some of the earliest sharks looked like. In the Paleozoic era, some 450 million years ago, in what is now America's Midwest, there swam a 4-foot-long creature that we have named *Cladoselache*. It is classified as one of the earliest chondrichthians ("cartilaginous fishes") because of its nonbony skeleton. There have been *Cladoselache* fossils found with remnants of bony fishes inside them, silent witness to the predatory nature of these early elasmobranchs. Some species of Paleozoic sharks had long, curved spines projecting from the dorsal fin, and others had vertical spirals of serrated teeth, like the blades of a circular saw. About 200 million years ago, the sharks took on some of the forms we now recognize, but many of these varieties did not make it into the present. It was "only" about 100 million years ago—long after most of the bony fishes had appeared—that sharks as we know them today began to appear in the fossil record. We must therefore recognize that there is nothing "primitive" about the sharks; they arrived after the bony fishes. They are not "living fossils"; they are the products of 350 million years of evolution, and like most life forms, they are still evolving.

There are more than 350 species of sharks today, ranging in size from the 6-inch-long dwarf shark (*Squaliolus laticaudus*) to the whale shark (*Rhincodon typus*), the largest fish in the world, reaching a length of 50 feet. (In addition to the cartilaginous skeleton that all sharks possess, the smallest and the largest shark share one additional characteristic: They are harmless to people.) Of the other sharks, only a few are large enough to inflict serious damage on a human swimmer or diver, and of the species that are large enough, only a few are really considered dangerous. It is not the biology of sharks that concerns us here, but the way people have thought about them and responded to them over the years. In the *Halieutica*, the second-century Greek poet Oppian wrote,

And they raved for food with increasing frenzy, being always hungered and never abating the gluttony of their terrible maw; for what food shall

---

* Even today, there are tiny sharks that do not get much longer than 12 inches; bottom-dwelling angel sharks that look as if they were flattened by a steamroller; hornsharks that have the face of an aquatic bulldog and pavementlike teeth that are used for crushing shellfish; bramble sharks that are covered with spiny lumps; goblin sharks with protruding jaws underneath a flattened sword; and even a frilled shark that looks more like an eel than a shark. Nevertheless, it is the white, the mako, or the tiger shark that we think of when we talk of the quintessential shark, the shark responsible for the fantasy and the fear.

*T*he largest fish in the world, the harmless whale shark (*Rhincodon typus*), photographed off Bermuda

be sufficient to fill the void of their belly or enough to satisfy and give respite to their insatiable jaws?

The first seafarers were aware of the sinuous shapes trailing their ships, ready to eat anything that fell or was thrown overboard—including sailors, dead or alive.* By the time John Hawkins brought his shark to England in 1569, its reputation was fully formed. Thomas Pennant, an early British ichthyologist writing in 1776, told this story in his *British Zoology:*

> A master of a Guinea ship informed me that a rage of suicide prevailed among his new bought slaves, from a notion the unhappy creatures had, that after death, they should be restored again to their families, friends, and country. To convince them at least that they should not reanimate their bodies, he ordered one of the corpses to be tied by the heels to a rope, and lowered into the sea, and, though it was drawn up again as fast as the

---

*The name of some sharks (requiem) is believed to be derived from the French and has something to do with the Christian mass for the dead, and indeed, it sounds as if it ought to. But as Paul Budker points out in *La Vie des réquins* ("The Life of Sharks"), "this explanation is a little too good to be true," and French etymologists are now more inclined to assume the word came from the coincidental modification of an existing word, perhaps even *chien.*

A strange furry shark menaces a Javanese boatman.

united force of the crew could be exerted, yet in that short space the sharks had devoured every part but the feet, which were secured at the end of the cord.

When Pennant collected information on sharks for his four-volume *British Zoology,* he had to rely on previously published works—of which there were precious few—and anecdotal information. Of the white shark, he wrote, "They are the dread of all sailors in all hot climates, where they constantly attend the ships in expectation of what might drop overboard; a man that has this misfortune inevitably perishes; they have been seen to dart at him, like a gudgeon to a worm." And later in the description, "Unfortunately for mankind, this species is almost universal in both the southern and northern hemispheres. It frequents the seas of *Greenland,* feeds on holibuts and the greater fish, on seals and young porpesses, and will even attack the little skin boats of the *Greenlanders,* and bite the person whose lower parts are lodged in it, in two."

The American painter John Singleton Copley (1738–1815) immortalized an event that took place in 1749, when a young man named Brook Watson, swimming in Havana harbor, was attacked by a huge shark. Watson's leg was bitten off below the knee, but quite miraculously—given the state of surgery and anesthesia at the time—he survived. In fact, he became the lord mayor of London and commissioned Copley to paint the picture in 1778. The shark itself, with its strange "lips" (suggesting that Copley painted it from a set of jaws), is like no shark ever known, but that is not the point. The painting, which was the sensation of the Royal Academy exhibition in London, exposed a previously ignorant segment of the population to the terrors of sharks.

Forty years after Pennant, in 1852, Samuel Maunder published *The Treasury of Natural History,* an encyclopedia of "animated nature." His description of the behavior of sharks was as dire as his predecessor's:

They devour with indiscriminating voracity almost every animal substance, whether living or dead. They often follow vessels for the sake of
picking up any offal that may be thrown overboard, and, in hot climates
especially, man himself becomes a victim to their rapacity. No fish can
swim with such velocity as the shark, nor is any so constantly engaged in
that exercise; he outstrips the swiftest ships, and plays round them, without exhibiting a symptom of strong exertion or uneasy apprehension; and
the depredations he commits on the other inhabitants of the deep are truly
formidable.

Until *Jaws* was published in 1974, sharks did not figure prominently in
literature. As might be expected, however, they appear in force (and in error)
in *Twenty Thousand Leagues Under the Sea*. When Captain Nemo takes his
prisoners for a stroll along the bottom of the ocean, he exposes them to all
sorts of dangers, not the least of which are the sharks. Aronnax, Conseil,
Ned Land, and the captain encounter their first sharks while returning from
an underwater walk. They see "huge shapes leaving streams of phospho-
rescense behind them," and Professor Aronnax describes his reactions:

The blood froze in my veins. I saw we were being threatened by two formidable dogfish, those terrible sharks with enormous tails and dull glassy
eyes, who secrete a phosphorescent substance through holes around their
snouts. They are like monstrous fireflies who can crush an entire man in
their jaws of iron! I don't know if Conseil was busy classifying them, but
as for me, I was observing their silver bellies and huge mouths bristling
with teeth from a not altogether scientific point of view—rather as a
prospective victim than as a naturalist.

The sharks pass harmlessly overhead ("very fortunately these voracious
animals have bad eyesight"), and the hunters return to the *Nautilus* safe and
sound. The "dogfish," however, previously described as "monstrous fireflies," put in another appearance in the South Atlantic, and from the references provided by Professor Aronnax, we are able to take an educated guess
at the species.

We also saw some large dogfish, a voracious species of fish if ever there
was one. Even though fishermen's stories are not to be believed it is said
that in one of these fish was found a buffalo head and an entire calf; in
another, two tuna and a sailor still in uniform; in another, a sailor with his
saber; and in yet another, a horse with its rider. It must be said, though,
that these stories seem a bit doubtful. In any case, none of these animals
ever allowed itself to be captured in the *Nautilus'* nets, and I therefore had
no way of finding out how voracious they were.

*T*he *grand chien du mer* ("great sea dog") from the original edition of *Twenty Thousand Leagues Under the Sea*. From the impressions given in the text, it appears that Jules Verne was describing the great white shark—at least as it was known in 1870.

Only one species of shark comes close to fulfilling these—and the earlier—criteria; only the great white shark has the reputation for voraciousness and omnivorousness that Aronnax describes. It is doubtful that Verne ever observed a live one, but it is possible that he might have seen a dead one on the beach or in a taxidermist's shop. If indeed Verne's "dogfish" is a great white, it would explain the "enormous tail"—a full-grown white shark is an enormous fish—the glassy eyes (if it was a dead one), and finally, the "phosphorescent substance" they secrete "through holes around their snouts." Of course, white sharks do not secrete a phosphorescent substance, but they do have the ampullae of Lorenzini, a pronounced series of pores around their snouts, which could, in Verne's fertile imagination, exude phosphorescence. The great white shark was originally known as *Canis carcharias,* which can be translated as "dog shark," and throughout the early history of popular ichthyology, sharks of all kinds were known as dogfishes or sea dogs. (In the original, Verne called this shark *grand chien du mer,* which can be translated as "great sea dog"—not much help in determining the species.)

In a book called *The Broad, Broad Ocean and Some of Its Inhabitants*, published in 1886, William Jones devotes a chapter to sharks, incorporating as many rumors, seamen's tales, and horror stories as he could find. Most of these stories involve man-eating sharks, some of which "bound several feet out of the sea, and seize the unwary sailor occupied in the rigging of the vessel when in full sail, [or] leap into fishing boats and grapple with the men at their oars." Our elasmophobic author also discusses various techniques for dispatching these "pirates of the ocean," including hooking them, lassoing them, and baiting them with hot bricks. No mercy should be shown to this voracious beast, which he describes thusly:

> His appearance exhibited every character of ferocity. The head is large; the mouth wide and grasping; but the teeth, the most appalling features of the animal, are remarkable for their power of mischief: there are six rows in the upper jaw and four in the lower; the teeth are triangular, and sometimes two inches in breadth, sharp-edged and notched like a saw, and as they are so planted in the jaw that each tooth is capable of independent action, being furnished with its own muscles, and as the strength of the jaws is enormous, they form a most terrific and formidable apparatus of destruction.

Although it would be difficult to identify the most lurid reaction to sharks in the catalog of antishark literature, a prime candidate might be found in Capt. William Young's *Shark! Shark!* Young was a man who hated all sharks and devoted almost his entire adult life to killing them. Born in 1875 in Southern California, Young migrated to the Hawaiian Islands around 1900, where he saw his first sharks:

> There they were, the savage, armored sea tigers which had become my fetish, my totem. I thrilled to the sight. As I leaned there, staring in utter fascination, my throat contracted. Tingling shivers ran up and down my spine, to my finger tips and toes. I wished for a harpoon, a rifle, anything that would give me a chance to make my first shark kill.

Young and his brothers went into the garbage-hauling business in Honolulu harbor, which gave them many opportunities to see and kill sharks. Young traveled around the world, occasionally employed by the Ocean Leather Company of New Jersey, a major producer and marketer of shark leather. In his book, "Sharky Bill" Young defines his attitude toward sharks:

When one sees or hears the word "shark" a powerful mental image is gen-
erated of a cold-blooded rover of the deep, its huge mouth filled with
razor-sharp teeth, swimming ceaselessly night and day in search of anything that might fall into the cavernous maw and stay the gnawing hunger
which drives the rapacious fish relentlesly on his way; a terrible creature,
in short, afraid of nothing and particularly fond of tasty human flesh.
There is something peculiarly sinister in a shark's appearance. The sight of
his ugly triangular fin cutting zigzags in the surface of the sea, and then
submerging to become a hidden menace, suggests a malevolent spirit. His
ogling, chinless face, his scimitar-like mouth with its rows of gleaming
teeth, the relentless and savage fury with which he atacks, the rage of his
thrashing when caught, his brutal insensibility to injury and pain, will
merit the name of *Afriet,* symbol of all that is terrible and monstrous in
Arabian supersition.

If these words had been written by anyone else and under any other circumstances, one would be inclined to regard them as hyperbolic nonsense
(which they are), but Young actually believed that all sharks were "rapacious
monsters" and "savage killers" and communicated his antipathy throughout
the book. *Shark! Shark!* was first published in 1933 and went through many
editions (one of which was bound in sharkskin), no doubt adding to the
fish's reputation as a mindless man-eater that should be eradicated from the
oceans by any and all means.

Because of its size, not to mention its reputation, the white shark has
long been considered a prime target for sport fishermen. The heaviest fish
ever caught on rod and reel (as recognized by the International Game Fish
Association [IGFA]) is a 2,664-pound white shark, taken by Alf Dean off
Ceduna, South Australia. While this monster, which weighs as much as a
small car, holds the official record, much heavier ones have been brought
in—they just weren't caught in accordance with IGFA rules. In 1976, off
Albany, Western Australia, Clive Green took a 16-foot female that weighed
3,388 pounds, almost a half ton heavier than the previous record, and in
August 1988, while fishing with Frank Mundus out of Montauk, Donnie
Braddick reeled in a 3,427-pounder.

If one had to devise a situation that would be the most conducive to
attracting large sharks, one could not do better than to use for bait a large,
dead mammal, preferably bleeding. Therefore, when they wanted to attract
white sharks off Durban in 1968, the producers of the documentary film
Blue Water, White Death lowered the shark cages from a whale catcher with
a dead sperm whale alongside. Unfortunately, no white sharks appeared
(they would have to go to South Australia to find them), but they did get

*A*lf Dean with the largest fish ever
caught on rod and reel as recognized by
the International Game Fish Association: a 2,664-pound white shark caught
at Ceduna, South Australia,
April 21, 1959

some of the most spectacular underwater shark footage ever filmed, for they
left the protection of the cages and swam among feeding whitetips, blues,
and tiger sharks. In the days of the Yankee sperm-whale fishery, the flensers
did their cutting from "stages" hung over the starboard side of the whale
ship, which put them directly over the whale—and the sharks. Herman
Melville wrote *Moby-Dick* in 1850, and it was published at approximately
the same time as Maunder's *Treasury of Natural History*. Although the
behavior of the sharks is more or less the same, Melville naturally does a
better job of describing it:

> . . . these two mariners, darting their long whaling spades, kept up an
> incessant murdering of the sharks, by striking the keen steel deep into
> their skulls, seemingly their only vital part. But in the foamy confusion of

their mixed and struggling hosts, the marksmen could not always hit their mark; and this brought about new revelations of the incredible ferocity of the foe. They viciously snapped, not only at each other's disembowelments, but like flexible bows, bent round and bit their own; till those entrails seemed swallowed over and over again by the same mouth, to be oppositely voided by the gaping wound.

It is in this chapter ("The Shark Massacre") that the cannibal harpooner says, "Queequeg no care what god made him shark . . . wedder Fejee god or Nantucket god; but de god wat made shark must be one dam Injin."

Another whaleman turned writer was Frank Bullen. In *Denizens of the Deep,* a collection of supposedly accurate descriptions of various sea creatures, he states that he once "purposely wrote in a ridiculously inflated style. . . . It never occurred to me that anyone would believe this story, it was so obviously absurd." But this is exactly what he does in *Cruise of the "Cachalot."* He inserts a frightful tale of a moonlight battle between a sperm whale and a giant squid or describes humpback whaling in a cave in Tonga with giant sharks swimming around, producing eerie phosphorescent trails. When it comes to describing sharks, Bullen tells some pretty tall tales:

> Many of these fish were of a size undreamed of by the ordinary seafarer, some a full thirty feet in length, more like whales than sharks. Most of them were striped diagonally with bands of yellow, contrasting curiously with the dingy grey of their normal colour. . . . He eats man, as he eats anything else eatable, because in the water man is easily caught, and not from natural depravity or an acquired taste begetting a decided preference for human flesh. All natives of shores infested by sharks despise him and his alleged man-eating propensities, knowing that a very feeble splashing will suffice to frighten him away even if ever so hungry.

EVEN BEFORE Peter Benchley chose to glorify it, the great white shark was already firmly ensconced in the pantheon of sea monsters. It is the largest predatory fish in the world; the longest accurately measured specimen is 21 feet long. This monster was captured in Cuba in 1948 and weighed 7,300 pounds. A 22-footer was captured off Kangaroo Island, South Australia, in 1987, and in the Mediterranean off Malta in 1988, a fisherman named Alberto Cutajar hauled in a 23-footer. A shark this size weighs as much as a full-grown rhinoceros.

Carcharodon carcharias is the quintessential shark, equipped with all of the components that characterize the most-feared fish in the sea: razor-sharp teeth, exquisitely honed senses, a blood lust that is unequaled by any vertebrate in the sea (and perhaps on land as well), a healthy appetite for warm-blooded prey, a black eye that stands for the unplumbed depths of evil, and the cliché of all shark clichés, a triangular dorsal fin knifing through the water. E. O. Wilson, known more for his sociobiological and entomological work than for his involvement with sharks, loves the great white. He wrote:

> The ultimate product of all this evolution, in my admittedly humble opinion, is the great white shark, *Carcharodon carcharias*. It has rightfully been called a total carnivore, a killing machine, the last free predator of man—the most frightening animal on earth. We're not just afraid of predators, we're transfixed by them, prone to weave stories and fables and chatter endlessly about them, because fascination creates prepared-ness, and preparedness, survival. In a deeply tribal sense, we love our monsters.

Apart from all other predators, moreover, *Carcharodon* has established a reputation as a man-eater, in California, in Australia, in South Africa, and in the North Atlantic. Unlike the giant squid, the white shark has been

"*B*ruce," the artificial shark, rising out of the water in *Jaws*. From this angle, the shark appears to have jowls.

sighted sporadically, cruising off the world's beaches. It can also be seen in some predictable locations, such as South Australia, South Africa, and central California, where divers, scientists, photographers, and fishermen seek it out for their particular purposes.

Benchley says he conceived the idea of a novel about a marauding shark that terrorizes the beaches after he had been fishing with Capt. Frank Mundus out of Montauk. The novel *Jaws* dominated the hardcover and paperback best-seller lists for months, but the movie made box-office history. Filming took place in 1974, in Martha's Vineyard, off the coast of Massachusetts, and featured Robert Shaw as Quint, Roy Scheider as Chief Brody, Richard Dreyfuss as the oceanographer Hooper, and Benchley himself in a cameo role as a television reporter. Steven Spielberg directed these

actors, but the real star of the film was "Bruce," a full-sized model of a great white shark.

According to Carl Gottlieb, who wrote *The Jaws Log,* an account of the making of the movie, the producers "had innocently assumed that they could get a shark trainer somewhere, who, with enough money, could get a white shark to perform a few simple stunts on cue in long shots with a dummy in the water, after which they would cut to miniatures or something for the close-up stuff." Of course, white sharks are notoriously uncatchable, not to mention untrainable, so producers Richard Zanuck and David Brown had to go back to the drawing board of Bob Mattey. Mattey had cut his teeth, as it were, on the giant squid for *20,000 Leagues Under the Sea,* and his designs for "Bruce" produced an engineering marvel as well as a thoroughly convincing menace.

For the underwater shots of

*C*over of the paperback edition of *Jaws,* the novel that made everyone think twice before going for a swim.

free-swimming sharks, the filmmakers used footage shot in South Australia by Ron and Valerie Taylor, but for all the scenes where the shark attacks boats and cages and glides through the water with its dorsal fin slicing the surface, they used the models, which were positioned on trolleys below the surface. (There were actually three models; one that was to be filmed from the right side, one from the left, and one in the round.) Throughout the film, the shark picks off swimmers, fishermen, and divers, evidently incited by no motive other than malice. Even more than the novel, the movie *Jaws* created a full-blown shark frenzy throughout the country; many were afraid to go swimming. (Until *Star Wars* came along in 1977 and *E.T.* in 1982, *Jaws* was the highest-grossing movie in Hollywood history.) It is not surprising, therefore, that *Jaws* was followed by *Jaws 2* (1978), *Jaws 3-D* (1983), and *Jaws IV* (1987). Although the shock value was somewhat diminished in the

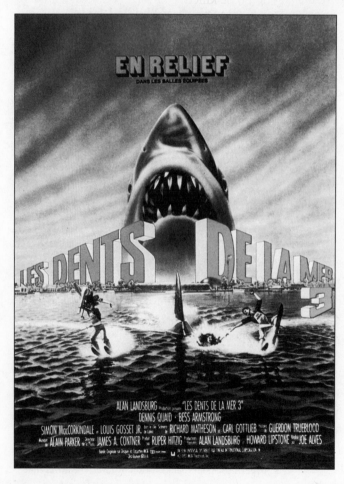

Les Dents de la mer means "the teeth of the sea" and is the French title for *Jaws*. This is the poster for the 3-D (*en relief*) version.

sequels, the reputation of the white shark as a malicious killer was certainly enhanced.

In addition to its appearance in bookstores and movie theaters, the white shark began to show up in even less likely places: on people's torsos, for instance. A shark T-shirt obviously signified that its wearer shared some of the ferocity of the shark. White shark teeth also appeared as totems around the necks of brave men (and some women), who might never have been closer to a shark than a gift shop or the loge of a movie theater. And to cash in on the shark mania, a flood of cheap books and magazines materialized almost instantly, with titles like "Jaws of Death!," "Killer Sharks!," and "Maneater!" Unlike the "Save the Whales" material, which indicated that the wearer or user was ecologically sensitive, the "Jaws" and "Killer Shark" items broadcast almost the opposite viewpoint: Sharks attack people; they are therefore evil, and they should be killed by brave people like us. Sharks are not benign creatures; they are predators and must kill living prey to eat. Although *Jaws* was fiction, it was based on fact.

In the novel, Benchley made reference to a series of grisly shark attacks that occurred off New Jersey during the summer of 1916. On July 1, Charles Vansant was playing in the surf some fifteen yards from shore in Beach Haven, when he was bitten on the left thigh. His companions dragged him to shore and applied a tourniquet to his wound, but he had lost so much blood that he died two hours after being bitten. Five days later, at a resort some forty-five miles north of Beach Haven, Charles Bruder was killed by a shark that bit off both of his feet. Then eleven-year-old Lester Stillwell was the victim of another fatal strike at Matawan Creek on July 12, and when Stanley Fisher dove in to rescue Stillwell, he, too, was attacked, and he died on the operating table. The last event in this gruesome series also occurred on July 12 in Matawan Creek when young Joseph Dunn was bitten on the left leg. Although he was severely lacerated, he made a full recovery.

Because the attacks ceased after a fisherman named Michael Schleisser caught a 7.5-foot white shark in Raritan Bay on July 14, people seemed ready to regard this shark as the perpetrator. It was believed that all the assaults had been committed by a single "rogue" white shark; in fact, *Jaws* is predicated on the same reasoning. But there are certain inconsistencies in this theory. First of all, the attacks took place over great distances—the first was ninety miles from the last—and there is no basis for the assumption that a single shark would travel so far just to bite people. (In none of the attacks was any significant amount of tissue removed, indicating that the shark was probably not feeding.) Second, the three attacks in Matawan Creek occurred in fresh water, and white sharks are not known to enter fresh water. And finally, the "rogue shark" theory, originally introduced by an Australian surgeon named Victor Coppleson, has been completely repudiated. Sharks simply do not alter their diet after tasting human flesh, and even more important, sharks are probably not interested in eating people.

We still do not have an explanation for shark attacks, but recent studies suggest that the sharks may be protecting their territory or even mistaking swimmers or surfers for seals. From the shark's vantage point, a surfer on a short surfboard, arms and legs extended, probably looks a lot like a sea lion. Sharks are not great intellects, and since they have been feeding on things that look like seals for millions of years, they are probably programmed to attack anything that resembles one. People have been swimming recreationally for only about 150 years, so the sharks cannot be blamed for not adjusting their habits quickly enough. Prior to the invention of swimming, diving, and surfing, anything in the shark's domain was fair game.

A much more likely culprit in the 1916 attacks is the bull shark (*Carcharinus leucas*), which is common off the New Jersey coasts. It regularly enters fresh water (one was found one thousand miles up the Mississippi); and instead of a single "rogue shark," we can substitute several bull sharks. Of this species, shark expert Leonard Compagno has written (in his comprehensive *Sharks of the World*), "It would not surprise the writer if this species turned out to be the most dangerous living shark because of its large size, massive jaws and proportionately very large teeth, abundance in the tropics . . . indiscriminate appetite and propensity to take largish prey, and *close proximity to human activities in both fresh and salt water.*" During July 1916, there were many more "human activities" taking place in the Jersey surf, for the East Coast was in the grip of a massive heat wave. It follows, then, that with so many more potential victims in the water, there just might be an increase in the number of shark attacks. The bull shark may be even more dangerous to humans than the white, but with its mouse-gray coloring and smaller size, it looks comparatively nondescript next to the fabled man-eater. The maximum length for a bull shark is 10 feet; for a white shark, over 20, and the white shark can reach a weight of 3.5 tons, compared with a 400-pound bull.

Probably the strangest of all white-shark incidents occurred—or rather, didn't occur—in the Azores, islands in the middle of the Atlantic. In 1982, rumors began to circulate about a 29.5-foot white shark that had been harpooned by the sperm whalers of Fayal. A photograph of the shark was circulated, leading to all sorts of investigations, including one by me. Although

I tried, I could find no evidence of a 29-footer having appeared anywhere in the Azores. That great whites exist in Azorean waters is demonstrated by the presence of a mounted 15-footer in the museum of Ponta Delgado and even references in the local newspaper to swimmers being attacked by *tiburãos brancos*. But since even the most meticulous investigation cannot produce negative evidence, some people adhere to their original beliefs, unwilling to give up just because an investigator couldn't find the creature in question.

IF THE WHITE shark, at 20 feet in length, with a mouth big enough to swallow a small child whole, isn't terrifying enough, try to imagine a creature that is more than twice as long, probably four times as heavy, and with a mouth large enough to swallow a cow. This is the stuff of nightmares. Monster lovers will be delighted to learn that this creature actually existed, but those who swim in the world's oceans will be grateful to know that it is extinct. The giant shark, which most paleontologists believe became extinct about 100,000 years ago, was called *Carcharodon megalodon; Carcharodon* because it is believed to be a close relative of the white shark

*M*egalodon (background), a great white shark, and a diver, to show relative sizes. Megalodon, at more than 50 feet long, was probably the most terrifying predator that ever lived. It has been extinct for over a million years. (We hope.)

(*Carcharodon carcharias*), and *megalodon*, meaning "big teeth." How big was it? The largest white shark tooth is about three inches high, measured along its diagonal serrated edge. The longest Megalodon tooth—a stonelike fossil—is almost eight inches long, approximately the size of a grown man's hand.

In a 1968 paper entitled "Serpents, Sea Creatures, and Giant Sharks," James F. Clark contended that a "giant shark of the magnitude of *C. megalodon* presently inhabits the deep sea. This beast, ranging between 60 and 120 feet, is intimately related to the living *C. carcharias*, if indeed it is not simply a gigantic representative of that species." It is not the intention of this discussion to dissect a misguided undergraduate paper, but Clark's essay came to the attention of Peter Matthiessen, who referred to it in *Blue Meridian: The Search for the Great White Shark*, his popular (and otherwise excellent) 1971 book about Peter Gimbel's search for the great white shark. Matthiessen acknowledges Clark's contribution and thanks him for "permission to paraphrase his arguments in support of the hypothesis that the white shark's giant relative *Carcharias* [sic] *megalodon* still exists." Because Matthiessen's book predates Perry Gilbert's 1973 revelation that the 36.5-foot "Port Fairy" white shark in the British Museum was a typographical error (the specimen was actually no longer than 16.5 feet in length), Matthiessen can be forgiven for assuming that the maximum known length of the white shark is 36.5 feet. But when he follows Clark in his arguments that "it seems much more correct to recognize but a single species of *Carcharodon* on the basis of tooth morphology," he makes a significant error. The teeth of the two species are different enough to classify them as distinct; so distinct that some paleontologists suggest that they do not even share the same ancestor.

Several scientists have also postulated the existence of giant man-eaters. One was the late Gilbert Whitley, an Australian ichthyologist whose 1940 publication *The Fishes of Australia, Part I: The Sharks*, contains this statement:

> Large flat triangular teeth with serrated edges have long been known to geologists from the various divisions of the Tertiary formation throughout the world. They are the remnants of sharks which must have attained enormous dimensions, and which were evidently similar in general form to "The Great White Shark" (*Carcharodon carcharias*) of present times. This recent species attains a length of forty feet, at which size it has teeth about three inches in length; since the fossil teeth are sometimes six inches long, it has been assumed that the extinct species reached a length of

eighty feet. Fresh-looking teeth measuring 4 by 3¼ inches have been dredged from the sea-floor, which indicates that if not actually still living, this gigantic species must have become extinct within a recent period.

Although he refers to "fresh-looking teeth," Whitley does not come right out and say that this gigantic fish exists, only that it "must have become extinct within a recent period."

Probably the most spectacular citation in all the literature can be found in David G. Stead's *Sharks and Rays of Australian Seas,* published in 1963. This book contains a description of "the most terrible monster that the seas of Mother Earth have produced"—and he is referring only to the great white. Like everyone else who wrote before 1972, including Whitley, Stead assumes that the 36.5-foot Port Fairy shark was accurately measured and includes it as "the largest recorded in Australian waters." He lists other known specimens that ranged from 16 to 20 feet, but then he launches into what he calls "the most outstanding of all stories relating to the gigantic forms of this fish ever to come to light—I mean, of course, accounts which really appeared to be founded on fact." Here is the story, as told by Stead:

In the year 1918 I recorded the sensation that had been caused among the "outside" crayfish men at Port Stephens, when, for several days, they refused to go to sea to their regular fishing grounds in the vicinity of Broughton Island. The men had been at work on the fishing grounds— which lie in deep water—when an immense shark of almost unbelievable proportions put in an appearance, lifting pot after pot containing many crayfishes, and taking, as the men said, "pots, mooring lines and all." These crayfish pots, it should be mentioned, were about 3 feet 6 inches in diameter and frequently contained from two to three dozen good-sized crayfish each weighing several pounds. The men were all unanimous that this shark was something the like of which they had never dreamed of. In company with the local Fisheries Inspector I questioned many of the men very closely and they all agreed as to the gigantic stature of the beast. But the lengths they gave were, on the whole, absurd. I mention them, how-ever, as an indication of the state of mind which this unusual giant had thrown them into. And bear in mind that these were men who were used to the sea and all sorts of weather, and all sorts of sharks as well. One of the crew said the shark was "three hundred feet long at least!" Others said it was as long as the wharf on which we stood—about 115 feet! They affirmed that the water "boiled" over a large space when the fish swam past. They were all familiar with whales, which they had often seen pass-ing at sea, but this was a vast shark. They had seen its terrible head which was "at least as long as the roof of the wharf shed at Nelson's Bay." Impossible, of course! But these were prosaic and rather stolid men, not given to "fish stories" nor even to talking at all about their catches. Further, they knew that the person they were talking to (myself) had heard all the fish stories years before! One of the things that impressed me was that they all agreed as to the ghostly whitish color of the vast fish.

Summarizing, Stead writes that he has "little doubt that in this occurrence we had one of those rare occasions when humans have been vouchsafed a glimpse of one of those enormous sharks of the White Death type, which we know to exist or to have existed in the recent past, in the vast depths of the sea. While they are probably not abundant they may yet be so." Even the smaller of Stead's figures (115 feet) offers a sense of the captivating fascination of the giant shark.

When the first fossilized shark's teeth were found, people did not know what to make of them. Pliny wrote that they fell from the sky during eclipses of the moon. Later analysts decided that they were the tongues of serpents that St. Paul had turned to stone while visiting the island of Malta, and they acquired the name *glossopetrae,* or "tongue stones." Because they were thought to be the petrified tongues of snakes, they were believed to contain power against the bite of any reptile, and they were worn or carried as talismans in the Middle Ages.

But in 1666, young Niels Stensen, scientist and physician to Ferdinand II, grand duke of Tuscany, examined the head of a large white shark that had been brought to Florence and published a report in which he noted the

GLOSSOPETRÆ

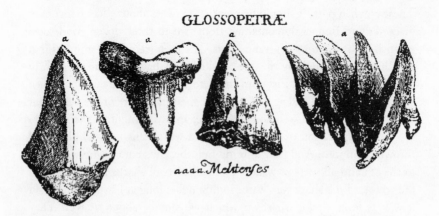

W hen people first encountered the fossilized teeth of large sharks, they believed they were the tongues of serpents that St. Paul had turned to stone—hence, *glossopetrae* ("tongue stones").

*T*he head of a great white shark, dissected by Niels Stensen (Steno) in 1667

similarity of the *glossopetrae* to the teeth of the shark he had examined. He concluded that the "tongue stones" were actually the teeth of sharks, and while he was unable to identify the process by which the tooth was turned to stone, he suspected something organic. (Up to that time, fossil remains were thought to be accidental aggregations of minerals that just happened to assume familiar shapes.) Stensen has been called the father of modern geology and paleontology, and as an ordained Catholic priest and later as a bishop, he was among the first to make science acceptable to the Church.

The only evidence we have for the existence of Megalodon is its fossilized teeth. Because their teeth are replaced many times over, these cartilaginous fishes may have thousands of teeth during their lifetime. They fall out or are otherwise displaced, which makes for a whole lot of fossil shark teeth on the ocean floor. Normally, the presence of fossil teeth leads only to paleontological discussions of the previous owners, but in the case of giant sharks, which may be the perfect monsters, people are not so willing to give up on their existence. Throughout the popular literature (as opposed to the scientific), there are repeated references to giant sharks, but very few popular writers want to come right out and say that these monsters are extinct.

J. L. B. Smith, the man who identified the coelacanth in 1938 (and therefore had a vested interest in the discovery of sensational new fishes), has written, "Teeth 5 ins. long have been dredged from the depths, indicating sharks of 100 ft. with jaws at least 6 ft. across. These monsters may still live in deep water but it is better to believe them extinct. Such a shark could swallow an ox whole."

In *Blue Meridian*, we read:

> The many sightings of enormous white sharks have led a few ichthyologists to wonder if *C. megalodon* might still exist. It has even been argued that fossil teeth of small *C. megalodon* are so similar to those of living *C. carcharias* that the two may represent a single species. . . . The oceans are still supporting whales, which have a higher metabolic rate than sharks, and possibly *C. megalodon*, like the sperm whale, feeds in the ocean depths on squid, which have been found in the stomach of the white. A giant shark would not need to surface as whales must do, nor scavenge on the continental shelf, where the smaller whites are mostly seen.

In fact, the teeth of the two *Carcharodon* species are quite different.* The teeth of the white shark are white, since they are composed of dentine and enamel, while the teeth of Megalodon are always fossilized and range in color from beige to black. Megalodon teeth are made of stone. In addition, the teeth of the giant Megalodon have a "chevron" above the root, which is lacking in the teeth of the living white shark, and much smaller serrations. Only the discovery of a fresh white Megalodon tooth would confirm the creature's current existence.

PERHAPS OF ALL the monsters, the giant shark is the most enduring. It incorporates virtually every element that we require of our mythological sea beasts: great size, mysterious habits, verified anthropophagous inclinations, and a history that goes back to the beginnings of recorded time. More than leviathan, more than the sea serpent, more than the kraken, Megalodon may be the ultimate monster.

In this technological age, the new mythology is a function of communications. In the past, epic poems, rumors, scuttlebutt, and newspaper accounts sufficed to spread the word of krakens sinking ships or mermaids

---

*Recently, some paleoichthyologists decided that the two species do not even belong in the same genus. Because the teeth of the white shark more closely resemble those of an ancestral mako known as *Isurus hastalis*, it has been suggested that the white is descended from *I. hastalis* and that the 50-foot monster should henceforth be known as *Carcharocles megalodon*.

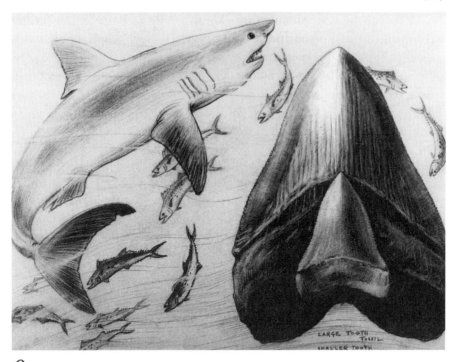

C archarodon megalodon, shown alongside a drawing of one of its teeth, and for comparison, a recent *Carcharodon* tooth (erroneously identified as having come from a 36-foot specimen). Drawing by Charles R. Knight, the renowned illustrator of prehistoric creatures.

enticing sailors to their death, but what better symbols for this age of hype than the blockbuster best-seller, or even better, the blockbuster movie? "Leviathan" has been replaced by a benign, almost symbolic whale; we now revere the gentle giants that our ancestors slaughtered into near oblivion. Sea serpents no longer threaten oceangoing vessels (if indeed they ever did), and the sirenians, far from their mythological, seductive forerunners, are now considered endangered, harmless, placid creatures, vulnerable to the ravages of powerboats. But the mythology of the shark and the squid endure, primarily through the efforts of Peter Benchley, and, to a lesser extent, novelists like Victor Hugo and Jules Verne.*

*Even though Benchley was the first, he was not the only author to produce novels about giant man-eating sharks. In 1981, Robin Brown wrote *Megalodon,* in which the protagonist is a 200-foot-long shark that roams the oceans' abyssal depths, gobbling up nuclear submarines, until it is dispatched by a trained sperm whale that scientists have airlifted in. Then George Edward Noe published a novel that he titled *Carcharodon.* It is even more preposterous than Brown's, for in this story, an 80-foot shark that had been entombed in an iceberg for "millions of years" thaws out, wakes up, and goes on a rampage destroying and eating every fish, boat, and human in sight. Neither *Megalodon* nor *Carcharodon* (published in 1987) received (or deserved) anything like the publicity avalanche that accompanied the publication of *Jaws.*

Although he was undoubtedly planning only to write action thrillers accompanied by some pertinent natural history, Benchley has become the preeminent mythologist of our time, working within a formula that is as old as time and as modern as the computer. At first, the very existence of these man-eating animals is doubted, but over the course of the books, they burst forth to threaten the puny efforts of those who would restrain or eliminate them. Benchley's white shark and giant squid have taken their places at the pinnacle of contemporary sea-monster mythology, their histories and habits available to millions through print and cinema. Unlike their predecessors, Benchley's creatures can be shown to *exist*, which, after all, is our ultimate hope—and our ultimate nightmare.

Since man first ventured out on the ocean, he has feared and despised the shark. Equipped with a vile disposition, insatiable hunger, and endless rows of teeth, these machines of destruction would attack anyone and anything that happened to share the same spot in the ocean. "The only good shark is a dead shark," we said, so we tried as hard as we could to kill as many of them as possible. We hooked them, shot them, dynamited them, caught them for leather, for fins, for food, all the while congratulating ourselves for cleansing the ocean of vermin. For most of recorded history, sharks have been perceived as ravenous demons, driven into a frenzy by a molecule of blood; waiting hungrily offshore for us to bleed or bumble into them. Then they would rip us to shreds with their razor-sharp teeth and dart crazily through the bloodstained water snapping at whatever morsels remained. And if one of their number were injured, they would tear it to pieces also; they were merciless killers that lived only to eat.

The *Jaws* phenomenon did nothing to alleviate these preconceptions; in fact, the novel and the four subsequent movies lent further credence to all the stories about man-eating sharks; only now they had added another element to their arsenal of terrors: They were able to seek out individuals and hunt them for *revenge*. Sharks come in all shapes and sizes, from sleek, streamlined ocean rangers to flattened pancakes that lie on the bottom. Some of them are capable of taking a full-sized sea lion, while others are harmless to anything but clams. Some live so far offshore or at such depths that humans have nothing to fear from them. All of these variations meant nothing to those who saw all sharks as potential threats, and they took to the boats to eradicate the lot. That they did not succeed was not for want of effort. After *Jaws* (the novel) appeared in 1974, the great white, the quintessential shark, became the object of a concentrated sport fishery, and every macho fisherman wanted a set of jaws to hang over his mantel or at least a tooth to wear on his chest. Aquariums tried to capitalize on this craze; they

Montauk Monster?

First Photo Of Great White Shark

Remember the great white shark hunt off Montauk Point? Well, according to professional photog Alvin Maley, this is the one that got away after being harpooned June 23. Maley made this picture on July 2 from small plane flying at 500 feet 30 miles south of Block Island. Maley says white spot behind dorsal fin is where harpoon pulled loose after fish towed boat for hours. John Casey, marine biologist for National Marine Fishery Service and author of a book on shark identification, says he's convinced fish in picture is indeed a great white shark and a big one at that.

*T*he "Montauk Monster" turned out to be a basking shark.

sent collecting crews and fishermen all over the ocean looking for a live one to put on exhibit.*

Curiously, once the *Jaws* mania had subsided, there was a sort of backlash that favored the sharks. There was no "Save the Sharks" movement, and no one was able to generate a lot of sympathy for a fish that could bite a swimmer in half—and sometimes did—but people began to think differently about sharks.† Perhaps it was the popularity of the sharks that changed people's attitude; every nature program on television seemed to show brave men in steel cages in South Australia heroically taking pictures of the great whites as they bit savagely at the chunks of horsemeat and tuna that were used to attract them. They were powerful, graceful animals, and if they

---

*To date, no one has succeeded, but in 1980, the Steinhart Aquarium of San Francisco put a 7.5-footer on exhibit for three days. When it became disoriented and looked as if it were going to die, the director sensibly released it to the open ocean.

† In a 1985 article called "In Praise of Sharks," E. O. Wilson wrote, "The conservation of shark species hasn't begun, although a case can already be made for the protection of such conspicuous and harmless giants as the whale and basking sharks. . . . It stirs the blood to realize that large wild animals still roam free in an unexplored part of the world."

occasionally bit people, perhaps it was the people that didn't belong in the shark's element rather than vice versa.

Through the various media—including movies, books, and television—sharks appeared as dangerous as ever, but there was a new sensitivity to the plight of all animals, and it was no longer necessary to view sharks as unreconstructed killers. Many of the myths had been (or were being) dispelled. For instance, the "feeding frenzy," so long the favorite of cheap novelists, was shown to be a behavior that existed mostly as an artifact of experimenters or filmmakers. You could whip the sharks into a frenzy, but you had to keep throwing food at them, a situation that rarely occurs in nature. Were sharks really driven mad by a minute amount of blood in the water? Think about it. Sharks usually eat living prey (there are no vegetarian sharks), so whatever they eat is likely to bleed, and it is ridiculous to assume that an animal is going to be driven crazy by its normal feeding behavior. (Sharks are attracted by blood, and they have an extremely effective sensory system that allows them to locate the source, but that is a far cry from being made crazy.) Do sharks attack people in order to eat them? And once they have tasted human flesh, do they forsake their normal diet?

Although we are still not sure why some sharks occasionally attack some people, it is becoming increasingly clear that it is not out of hunger. (Simple logic leads to the conclusion that sharks—which are quite numerous in some locations—do not regard swimmers as potential meals. If they did, no beach in the world would be safe for swimming.) *Jaws* notwithstanding, even when a shark attack has occurred, the offending animal does not usually remain in the vicinity. More often than not, after an attack, the perpetrator is not caught.*

If sharks are not mindless eating machines, what are they? They are extremely efficient, beautifully designed apex predators, serving a useful function in nature and deserving of our respect, not our hostility. Conflicts between man and shark almost always end in favor of the man, especially if the man is in his own element and not in the shark's. If the man is in his own element and the shark is in the water, the conflict is called "fishing."

Probably the most surprising event in the history of shark conservation

---

*Unfortunately for those who would defend them, sharks continue to pursue their occasional antisocial behavior. In July 1991, off the coast of Monterey, California, surfer Eric Larsen was attacked by a white shark and required 200 stitches and 135 stainless-steel staples to sew him together. A fatal attack occurred off Aldinga Beach, South Australia, in September 1991. In July 1992, a diver was killed off Matsuyama, Japan, and in October of that year, Michael Docherty was surfing off Moreton Island, Queensland, when he was killed by a shark. Then, on June 7, 1993, Therese Cartwright, a mother of four, was diving off northern Tasmania when she was attacked, and only two days later, at Julian Rocks, north of Sydney, diver John Ford was killed. In all these cases, the attacker was believed to have been a white shark.

occurred in South Africa in 1991. After a spirited campaign spearheaded by Leonard Compagno, an American ichthyologist transplanted to Grahamstown, the South African government declared the white shark a protected species. The announcement was made at a news conference in Cape Town by Louis Pienaar, the minister for environmental affairs. Mr. Pienaar said:

> Evidence is mounting that many international shark trophy hunters are now starting to focus their attention on the South African coasts. . . . The notoriety surrounding the great white shark as a ruthless "maneater" forcefully enhanced in the public eye, by amongst others, the motion picture *Jaws,* is not borne out by the low, and probably incidental human mortalities inflicted by great whites. An indiscriminate and vindictive hunt for great whites cannot be tolerated.

Although several detailed and comprehensive studies of the *Carcharodon carcharias* have been published in recent years and two symposia have been convened devoted solely to this species, it still remains one of the least-known large animals on earth. Naturally, there were South Africans who felt that protecting the "maneater" was the height of folly, but the proposal had enough scientific and political support to push it through.

South Africa, particularly the Natal coast, is probably the most shark-conscious nation on earth. In 1966, the Natal Anti-Shark Measures Board was established to protect the popular tourist beaches along the Indian Ocean. A system of mesh nets was deployed that trapped many sharks, thereby alleviating the fears of the tourists. But the nets also trapped and drowned small, harmless sharks—not to mention dolphins, turtles, and seabirds—and there were many objections to what was deemed, literally and figuratively, overkill. In other locations where shark attacks are considered a hazard—Australia and California, for example—swimmers know the dangers and swim at their own risk. Only South Africa has taken such extreme steps to protect the tourists—often at the expense of the wildlife.*

Up and down the eastern seaboard of the United States, commercial fishermen have been hauling sharks from the water in unprecedented numbers, primarily for the lucrative Asian shark-fin market. Only a few species are sought for their fins; most of the others are discarded. The cartilaginous filaments in the fins of some species are used in the preparation of shark-fin

---

*E. D. Smith, a South African electrical engineer, has invented an "electric shark barrier" that he maintains will keep the sharks away and at the same time totally eliminate the danger to other marine wildlife. The device has been tested in South African and Australian waters and shown to be completely effective, but to date, despite the potential saving of money and wildlife, it has not been installed in the waters of the Natal beaches.

soup, and the dried fins—particularly the larger ones, which have the longer filaments—may sell for fifty-three dollars a pound. In a Hong Kong restaurant, shark-fin soup may cost fifty dollars a bowl. Because of the economics of the fishery, the practice of "finning" (removing the fins and throwing the rest of the carcass overboard) has resulted in a catastrophic reduction in shark populations. According to an article in the *New York Times* in December 1992, "The peak year was 1989, when an estimated 488,000 large coastal sharks were killed. The catch has dropped off somewhat since then to 370,000 in 1991 . . . but killings nevertheless continue to outstrip reproduction, suggesting that the population is shrinking."

For years, shark tournaments (also known as "shark derbies") attracted fishermen who came to kill as many as they could in a limited time. In the early history of these tournaments, after the sharks were weighed and measured, they were discarded either at sea or in garbage dumps. It was painfully obvious that this was a waste of edible meat, not to mention good predators. Scientists who monitored these tournaments (at places like Bay Shore and Montauk, Long Island), including Jack Casey, Wes Pratt, and Chuck Stillwell of the National Marine Fisheries Service (NMFS) laboratory at Narragansett, Rhode Island, began a program of encouraging fishermen to tag the sharks they caught instead of killing them. In this way, Casey, Pratt, and Stillwell were able to assemble a formidable data base on the habits and migration patterns of the sharks of the northwestern Atlantic and in the process educate fishermen to the pointlessness of their vendetta.

Because of their concern for the sharks of the North Atlantic, Casey and his colleagues have developed an NMFS management plan with the following objectives: to prevent overfishing of shark resources; to encourage the management of shark stocks throughout their range; to establish data collection, research, and monitoring programs; and to optimize the benefits derived from shark resources in the United States while minimizing waste. The plan also sets a limit for the commercial quota, of fifty-eight hundred metric tons for the first year. After extensive public hearings, the proposal was revised to include the segregation of sharks into three managerial groupings—large coastal, small coastal, and pelagic—quotas tailored to these groupings; a minimum size for makos; no sale of recreational catch; a prohibition on landing fish at a ratio of not greater than 5 percent per carcass; a 50 percent reduction on commercial landings from the 1990 levels; and bag limits for all recreational shark fishermen. After many bureaucratic delays, the plan went into effect in the spring of 1993.

If sharks in New England waters are being killed for the Asian market,

Shark carcasses at the Bay Shore Mako Tournament. The man in the white coat is cutting off the fins for shark-fin soup.

we can imagine what is happening to the sharks of Asia. Even in remote areas like the Indonesian archipelago, observers report that the shark populations have declined noticeably.* Whereas before carcharhinid sharks (gray reef, silvertip, blacktip) were plentiful—and, of course, an important element of the local fauna—now there are almost none. Local fishermen who previously would have ignored the sharks are now seen with tails and fins dangling from their proas, and on shore, even in the smallest villages, shark fins are drying on bamboo racks. (Because they lack refrigeration, Indonesian fishermen capture the things they can dry—and that they can sell.) It is difficult to imagine a region more removed from the pressures of commercial fishing than these tiny atolls and volcanic islands, but greed knows no geographic limits, and the sharks of Indonesia are being killed for soup thickeners.

Longline fishermen around the world, seeking billfishes and tuna,

*The report on the Indonesian shark fishery was personally communicated to me by John McCosker, director of the Steinhart Aquarium in San Francisco. McCosker has been leading dive trips to Indonesia for several years, and when he told me of the decline of the shark populations, I asked him to write up his observations for me.

often find various species of sharks on their lines. Previously, shark appeared on the menu as "steakfish," or "flake," and it was often the "fish" in fish and chips, but now that shark meat has become a popular item in upscale American restaurants, one often finds grilled mako, blackfin, or thresher shark listed on the menu alongside salmon and swordfish. In 1980, the U.S. commercial catch of sharks was less than 500 tons; by 1989, it was 7,144 tons. (By 1990, however, the catch had dropped by 20 percent because of a dramatic reduction in the shark populations.)

In the past, even those who studied sharks believed they were so numerous that it would be impossible to affect their numbers. In 1970, Jacques and Philippe Cousteau, writing about the possible extinction of whales in *The Shark: Splendid Savage of the Sea,* stated, "The sharks need have no fear of such a fate. The majority of the races of squali, to which sharks belong, are perfectly adapted to their mode of life and their enormous number makes their extermination extremely difficult, if not impossible." They were very, very wrong. Because of their fecundity rate, sharks can be dramatically affected by predation. Unlike the bony fishes, some of which lay millions of eggs every year, sharks give birth to a small number of live young. With such a low reproduction rate, shark populations take a very long time to recover after a massive assault on their numbers.

Among the leaders of the nascent save-the-sharks movement is Samuel ("Sonny") Gruber of the University of Miami. He admires the sharks for their efficiency, but he is worried that they are losing the battle for survival. They are slow-growing, late-maturing animals that produce small numbers of well-formed young, a combination that ecologists call "K-selected." As opposed to fast-growing, precocious animals that produce large numbers of offspring, K-selected animals cannot withstand a concentrated onslaught on their numbers. The shark fishermen who are longlining sharks for the shark-fin market are not only decimating the populations; they are fishing themselves right out of business. Under such intense pressure, populations will soon be reduced to the point where they will be economically, if not biologically, extinct.

Gruber believes that there are good reasons to save the sharks, including the possible answers to some intriguing medical questions: Why are sharks so resistant to cancer? Why does a shark's serious wound heal within twenty-four hours without treatment? Why does a lacerated cornea, which in any other creature would permanently cloud over and cause blindness, remain clear and functional and heal rapidly? What is it about shark-liver oil (called "squalene") that causes the Japanese to pay five hundred dollars a pound for it and use it for a wide variety of medicinal applications?*

In a 1973 article (that was co-authored with his wife, Claire), Perry Gilbert, a shark expert and then director of the Mote Marine Laboratory in Sarasota, Florida, sang the virtues of sharks:

> The shark, with a modicum of fine traits, might be considered one of the most successful animals that has ever lived. To other animals it is far from delicious. Its tough hide makes it almost inedible, and while it has the grace that sheer power bestows, it is not really beautiful. . . . It has, however, one enviable attribute and this has contributed greatly to its success. . . . Cancer is virtually absent from its primal myomeres.

Some researchers believe that shark cartilage contains a protein that inhibits the angiogenesis needed to provide nourishment for tumor and cancer metastasis. Tumors need a large supply of blood to survive, and cartilage contains substances that prevent the formation of new blood vessels. Since 1979, at the Mote Marine Laboratory in Sarasota, Carl Luer has been exposing nurse sharks and clearnose rays to powerful carcinogens, including aflatoxin B_I and methylazoxymethanol, and has been absolutely unable to get tumors to grow. Working with A. B. Bodine, Luer has seen that the carcinogens reach the DNA of the elasmobranch cells, but then the cells seem to be able to repair themselves before any sort of a mutation can result. Interviewed in the Washington *Post* in December 1991, Luer said, "In other animals, we can study how cancer forms. In sharks, we can study how cancer does not form." In an article in the *Journal of the National Cancer Institute* in 1992, James Mathews wrote, "Most researchers agree that continued study of the shark's intriguing anatomy may yield answers to treating cancer in humans." Certainly an animal that is so successful in resisting cancer is worth more to medical researchers than to those who would hack off its fins and make soup out of them.

Despite the total absence of evidence, someone is prepared to cash in on the possibility that shark cartilage might prevent cancer in humans, and a New Jersey company called "Cartilage Consultants, Inc." obtained a patent for pills made of powdered shark cartilage. But, says the *Journal of the National Cancer Institute*, "there is no proof that it is effective when taken

---

*In 1981, Eugenie Clark introduced the questions about squalene in a *National Geographic* article, writing, "Recently squalene has been promoted as an effective treatment for both major and minor diseases. Thousands of Japanese pay the equivalent of nearly a dollar for a single capsule of products known by such names as Marine Gold. The manufacturer, and even some Japanese doctors, recommend two to nine capsules of squalene a day for treatment of virtually everything from constipation to cancer."

this way," and Luer, in an article written for the Mote Marine Laboratory, said, "The statements made by cartilage pill promoters that it is cartilage that gives sharks their immunity to cancer, then, are inaccurate and irresponsible." We are still a long way from finding—or even suggesting—a shark-related cure for cancer. Indeed, while irresponsible medical research might serve no useful purpose for humans, it might further endanger the sharks. In February 1993, the CBS program *60 Minutes* aired a story on shark cartilage as a treatment for cancer in humans, bringing forth an outraged response from the people who were actually doing the research. Carl Luer wrote (in the March issue of the *American Elasmobranch Society Newsletter*), "We regret that some of the companies involved in promoting such therapies are implying a link between the results of the Mote research and their product. We cannot support the marketing of shark cartilage for this application, especially since the promoters of the product intend to rely on the natural resource as an endless supply of material." If it were true that shark cartilage could somehow prevent cancer in humans, perhaps the take of sharks might be justified, but since no such evidence exists, they should not be caught and ground up for their components. In a letter to the same newsletter, Kumar Mahadevan, the director of the Mote Marine Lab, wrote, "No evidence—not even a logical connection—exists at this stage to assume that shark cartilage tested on blood vessel growth in the laboratory should produce significant tumor regression when given to cancer patients."

The idea of preserving endangered species for medical reasons is obviously not unique to the shark researchers. It is an integral element in the manifold arguments against the human extinction of any species, articulated here by Paul and Anne Ehrlich in *Extinction: The Causes and Consequences of the Disappearance of Species:*

> Extracts from some marine animals related to those that built the giant coral reefs show some promise as anticancer agents, and broad-spectrum antibiotics have been extracted from marine sponges. There appear also to be potential anticancer drugs in a wide variety of other marine mammals, including sea anenomes, segmented worms, clams, sea cucumbers, moss animals, proboscis worms, sharks, and stingrays. Marine animals have yielded substances with a broad range of potential uses in medicine, from antiviral and antibacterial action to anticoagulants, contraceptives, and the control of ulcers and hypertension.

As always, the shark presents a paradox. The disastrous reduction in various populations has brought concerned scientists to the fore, but there are far more people affected by the *Jaws* experience than by the population dynamics of sharks. In a 1990 article in *Life*, Robert Hueter of the Mote Marine Laboratory in Sarasota is quoted as saying, "Everybody talks about saving the whales and the rain forest. It's not that easy to ask people to save sharks because of their age-old image. But the same principle applies. If you change the balance of the ecosystem, you'd better be prepared for some consequences. Right now we haven't done enough research to know how extensive these consequences will be." And in September 1990, in the *Wall Street Journal*, Daniel Machalaba wrote an article called "Forget What You Thought of Sharks, They're Really Neat." He wrote, "Shark propaganda?

WOMAN MARRIES A SHARK!

By JOE BERGER / *Staff writer*

Bashful bachelor gal Andrea Lyons longed to say "I do" and settle down, but every guy she took a liking to left her high and dry — so dingbat Andrea married a man-eating shark!

As 40 flabbergasted guests looked on, the elated lady tied the knot with her pet shark Archie in a seaside ceremony at her home in Sydney, Australia.

"Everybody says Archie is dangerous and that someday he's going to eat me alive — but compared to the men I've met lately, he's an absolute angel," the blushing bride gushed to reporters.

"He's gentle and he kisses nice and he doesn't leave his dirty underwear lying all over the house. As far as I'm concerned, he's one helluva catch."

Adoring Andrea, 32, tied the knot with her beady-eyed beau in late September, but she actually landed her dream fish five months earlier when she hauled him aboard her brother's 50-foot boat off the Australian coast.

"I was shocked as hell when I realized I had a shark on my line, and I'll tell you, he fought like crazy," the flaky saleslady recalled. "It took more than an hour before I finally brought him in, and by that time we were both exhausted.

"The guys started to club him to death, but he was lying there looking at me with those kind eyes and I just couldn't let 'em do it. We put some water in the fish box and put Archie in there and strapped the lid down tight and took him home with us.

"I guess it was love at first sight for both of us."

Infatuated Andrea transferred Archie to a king-size tank behind her home and the kooky twosome have been soul mates ever since.

"There was a surfer killed by a shark out in that area two days before I caught Archie and people are saying Archie's the one that ate him," said the starry-eyed bride. "But I swim and cuddle with him every day, and to me he's a real sweetheart."

Still, daffy Andrea didn't decide to get hitched to the fish till a bank turned down her credit card application because she didn't have a hubby to help her pay the bills.

"I make $23,000 a year and have a good life, but everybody treated me like I had leprosy because I wasn't married," she said. "And the harder I tried to find Mr. Right, the more I realized most guys are jerks. Finally I decided I'd just marry Archie and put the singles scene behind me."

So, decked out in a swimsuit and scuba gear, the loonytunes lady said "I do" to her toothy groom and an embarrassed pastor pronounced them shark and wife.

Moments later, ecstatic Andrea gave her new hubby a big, wet kiss and headed into the house for champagne and cake with her guests.

"I asked 100 people to my wedding, but only 40 showed up," the nutty newlywed said. "I guess when you send out invitations announcing your marriage to Archie the Shark, some folks think you've gotta be joking."

> **'He's a lot better than any man!'**

HAPPY bride Andrea Lyons gives her new hubby a big, wet kiss!

A graphic demonstration of the way the attitude toward sharks has changed in recent years

Its time has come. The pro-shark folks are on the rise." To support this contention, he quotes Quentin Dokken of the Texas State Aquarium: "Sharks are really very timid animals; they aren't the bloodthirsty killers they are made out to be," and then mentions Sid Cook of the pro-shark newsletter *Chondros,* who has written critical letters to the makers of games, movies, toys, books, and foods that perpetuate a negative view of sharks.

Formed in 1988, the American Elasmobranch Society is composed primarily of scientists who study sharks. *Chondros* is a newsletter "Dedicated to Rational Use and Conservation of Sharks, Skates and Rays" that began publication the following year. Some people want to save the sharks, while others, still convinced that they are a menace to civilization, want their wholesale eradication to continue. Whatever our attitude, however, it is clear that the sharks have gained a new level of notoriety and respect. They are no longer considered simple killers, but they are now recognized as important elements in the complex web of life in the ocean. In the *New York Times* of December 8, 1992, William K. Stevens wrote,

> The shark, that mythic terror of the deep, has been top predator of the seas for nearly 400 million years. But sharks themselves are now being wiped out en masse by the human appetite for shark flesh, and their disappearance could disrupt the ecology of the world's oceans. The threat comes just as scientists are reaching beyond the "Jaws" image of the shark as a primitive, mindlessly malevolent eating machine that has long shrouded the beast's true nature. Behind the legend, researchers are finding a wondrously sophisticated animal whose biology, once understood, could also yield important medical benefits.

And this is the "reason" that we must preserve the sharks and all the other "monsters." Not only because they might provide us with an anticoagulant; not only because they are important pieces of a totality that we do not understand and by removing random elements, we might unbalance a critical and complex system; and not because they are powerful, graceful, and efficient predators. The reason not to eliminate an entire class of animals is that there should be no reason. In the past, our motivations have been warped; our perceptions wrong; our prejudices misguided. The headline of the *New York Times* article read "Terror of the Deep Faces Harsher Predator." If indeed there are any real monsters left, we have only to look in the mirror to find them.

THE NEW MYTHOLOGY

OF MONSTERS

There are more things in heaven and earth, Horatio, than are dreamt of in your philosophy.

—Hamlet

I BEGAN THIS BOOK with healthy skepticism; I didn't really believe in monsters, but I was willing to read through the literature and wait to be convinced. For the most part, I remain skeptical. There are rational explanations for many monster sightings, from sea serpents that were probably giant squid to beached carcasses that turned out to be basking sharks. Many monsters were shown to be something other than sea serpents, often because a legitimate animal appeared. The monster seen by Captain M'Quhae of the *Daedalus* looks like a giant squid (and was explained as such by Henry Lee), even when we look at the drawings that were intended to show that it wasn't. When the first coelacanth appeared in South Africa in 1938, the door was opened for all sorts of hypothetical monsters to wander in. The expected argument was forwarded that if this "living fossil" actually exists, then how can we deny the possibility of plesiosaurs, giant snakes, superotters and 100-foot eels just because we haven't seen one yet? The unexpected discovery of the first megamouth in 1976 fortified the "anything is possible" school.

It was easy enough to dismiss the stories when one or two witnesses saw a strange, large animal, usually off some exotic locale, like the Cape of Good Hope or northern Norway, and decided to report it as a sea serpent. In many later cryptozoological sightings, the viewers forgot their camera, had no film, or left the lens cap on. The stories of the Loch Ness monster are typical; despite a half century of concentrated inquiry, no one has been able to authenticate a sighting, and whatever "evidence" there is has been so controversial that books have to be written to defend or explain it. In the case of "real" monsters, such as the coelacanth or megamouth, the existence of a carcass—preferably one that doesn't resemble any other known animal—goes a long way toward silencing the doubters.

What are we to make of the sightings around Gloucester in 1817 and again in 1819? Shall we assume that hundreds of reputable citizens were deluded or victims of mass hysteria? Were they all participants in some enormous practical joke? If so, on whom? Or shall we accept the more parsimonious explanation, that they saw *something* and their descriptions of a 100-foot-long snakelike creature are based on some sort of reality? Lacking anything but eyewitness accounts that are almost two centuries old, we obviously cannot "prove" that the Gloucester animal actually existed (or that it didn't), but it will remain one of the great unsolved mysteries of sea-serpent lore. (The identification of a deformed three-foot blacksnake as its "spawn" added nothing to the verisimilitude of the Massachusetts monster.)

There are a few instances, however, where even the carcass—or a piece of it—is not enough. When Dr. DeWitt Webb found a gigantic, octopus-shaped hunk of stuff on a St. Augustine beach in 1896, it was verified by Prof. Addison Verrill, who later withdrew his identification and then decided it was really a piece of a whale. In this case, a fragment of the original tissue still exists (the rest having been lost over the years, through what must be one of the most flagrant examples of scientific irresponsibility in history), and there are photographs and detailed descriptions of a lump of protoplasm that obviously resembles the remains of a giant octopus. No reading of the original description would lead anyone to conclude that this object had anything whatever to do with a whale, and yet the skeptical view still obtains. Biochemical analyses of the tissue strongly indicate that it came from some sort of octopus, yet there is no mention of this monster in the "respectable" literature. Other "blobs," washing ashore in Tasmania, New Zealand, and Bermuda, would seem to lend support to the "giant octopus" theory, but to date, these pieces of protoplasm have appeared only in local newspaper stories and the *Cryptozoology Newsletter.* In all these cases, there is physical evidence, not just seamen's stories, and although it fits quite nicely into an "octopus" framework, we are forced by convention—as was Professor Verrill—to invent a whole new kind of whale rather then accept the obvious explanation. (There is no reason why a 200-foot-span octopus should not exist. There are known [but smaller] octopuses that live at depths of twelve thousand feet or more; their soft bodies could easily withstand the pressures of the depths, and besides, we already accept the existence of a giant squid 60 feet long and living at great depths.)

With the advances in technology that now allow scientists to analyze the molecular and genetic structure of animal tissue, it ought to be a simple matter to examine the tissue of the St. Augustine monster or the Bermuda blob—assuming such tissue is available—and identify its previous owner.

(No samples are known to exist from the Tasmanian or New Zealand specimens.) As mentioned earlier, however, most of the St. Augustine tissue was lost, and the Bermuda blob floated out to sea on a high tide after Teddy Tucker had managed to saw off a couple of chunks. But Eugenie Clark, a zoologist (and cryptozoologist) at the University of Maryland, managed to get a sample of the St. Augustine tissue from Gennaro and also a piece of the Bermuda blob and had them analyzed by Skip Pierce, a molecular biologist also on the faculty. Pierce tentatively concluded that they were not octopus or squid tissue but pure collagen. Such a conclusion raises more questions than it answers, since collagen is the fibrous constituent of bone, cartilage, and connective tissue and normally does not exist in two- or three-ton lumps. It might be a "collagen tumor," but it is difficult to imagine the sort of animal that could drag around a tumor so large. Besides, if sharks don't get tumors, it would have to have come from a whale, and nowhere in the literature have I encountered a reference to whales with gigantic tumors. Even if the various blobs were tumors, the most likely candidates would appear to be giant cephalopods, which brings us right back to where we started, but with the additional problem of an unknown and heretofore undemonstrated pathology.

Verrill may have recanted because he was worried about ridicule from his colleagues. It is difficult enough to mount a proper defense of a sea monster, but when one is likely to be characterized as a charlatan, a lunatic, or a grossly inept scientist, the problem is compounded exponentially. Of course, the impossibility of proving a negative proposition encourages all true believers to persevere; as long as it cannot be demonstrated that the monsters do not exist—and it cannot—they will continue to hope. The case of the giant squid fuels the cryptozoological fires, possibly more than any other creature, real or imaginary. Tales of ship-grabbing monsters are as old as seafaring, but it was not until some still unexplained oceanographic anomaly in the late nineteenth century that specimens of *Architeuthis* began appearing on the rocky beaches of Newfoundland. Because the giant squid is such an incredible animal, it is actually easier to assume that it is a mythological creature rather than a real one. (During the preparation of this book, I spoke to several people who believed the giant squid was an imaginary creature and were quite surprised to discover that it actually existed.) Its appearance in melodramatic novels such as *Twenty Thousand Leagues Under the Sea* and *Beast* has supported its assignment to the world of fiction; like the white whale, *Architeuthis* seems too big and dangerous to be true.

The Australian David Stead wrote about fish and fishing, whales and whaling, and occasionally monsters. (In *Sharks and Rays of Australian Seas*, he described the gigantic shark discussed on pp. 343–44 of this volume.) He obviously believed that Australians had been shortchanged in the sea-serpent department, so in *Giants and Pygmies of the Deep* he recounts several Australian sightings. The first occurred off Bellambi Reef, New South Wales, in 1930, and observers described a "vast monster of the serpent type," with a mouth like a pelican's beak. It is obvious to Stead that the open-mouthed beast could only have been a rorqual whale, probably a minke. Only two days later, however, another monster appeared off Scarborough ("a few miles north of the first occurrence"), but this time it could not be so easily explained away. It looked like a huge black snake, some 80 or 90 feet long, and it threw its huge head in the air, then ducked below the surface, giving the impression that it was feeding. Stead concludes that this really was a monster, "a great Calamary or Cuttlefish or giant Sea Squid, of the type frequently called *Polypus*." He then discusses several additional Australian sightings and concludes by saying, "In all of these and in many others there seems to me to be enough evidence to identify the beasts seen, not as any kind of real serpent, but the terrible gigantic Calamary."

In a curious book (*Sea Serpents*) published in 1991, Charles Bright skims the surface of sea-serpent lore, occasionally discussing interesting aspects of the more spectacular sightings but too frequently getting the details wrong. (The book is "curious" because it was published by Bowling Green University Press, but it has no bibliography and no index, and long passages are often incorporated without even a suggestion about where they might have come from.) In his conclusion, Bright quotes an 1880 *New York Times* article as follows: "We have borne the yoke of science long enough. Let us have a great protestant revival and proclaim our emancipation from scientific tyranny by maintaining the existence of the sea serpent." The last sentence in his book—just before the place where the references should have been—is "What do you think?"

Like all the other authors who have attempted to survey the vast and often contradictory history of sea serpents, I have formed some opinions of the stories. Of course, I do not believe that we should "proclaim our emancipation from scientific tyranny" by accepting all the sightings as gospel, but some seem to be more legitimate than others. Even if we assume that the aquatic dinosaurs are gone and that there are no giant eels, giant snakes, giant seals, or giant otters, we are still left with some sightings that are difficult to explain. It is perfectly natural for untrained persons to attribute "monster" characteristics to strange creatures seen at sea. Most people have never seen a giant squid—except perhaps in the movies—so how could they possibly reconcile some strange, many-armed commotion with what David Stead called the "terrible gigantic Calamary"?

Heuvelmans, Bright, and others quote the tale of the Grace Line steamer *Santa Clara* sailing from New York to Cartagena in 1947. Some 118 miles off North Carolina, the ship struck a marine creature. Third Officer John Axelson saw

> a snakelike head rear out of the sea about 30 feet off the starboard bow of the vessel. His exclamation of amazement directed the attention of the other two mates to the Sea Monster, and the three watched it unbelievingly as in a moment's time it came abeam of the bridge where they stood and was left astern. The creature's head appeared to be about 2½' across, 2' thick, and 5' long. The cylindrically shaped body was about 3' thick, and the neck 1½' in diameter. . . . The visible part of the body was about 35' long.

Since none of the descriptions include a mouth or eyes—features that would probably attract immediate attention—it seems possible to assign all the elements of the *Santa Clara* sighting to the giant squid. The "snakelike head" could be the club end of one of the long tentacles, with the suckers turned away from the viewer, and the "neck" would be the tentacle itself. The given dimensions coincide with those of the club of a large squid's tentacle, and even the "cylindrically shaped body" is the right size. In other words, there is nothing in this description that might not refer to *Architeuthis*.

I do not propose to assign all sea-serpent sightings to *Architeuthis*, but there is a strong possibility that many of those seamen and passengers who reported a "monster" of some sort were actually seeing the giant squid. Let us examine the serpents of the Scandinavian ecclesiatics Bishops Egede and Pontoppidan. As Henry Lee points out in *Sea Monsters Unmasked*, Egede's illustration of a sea serpent can be easily made to look like a giant squid if we eliminate the eye and the mouth and have the "blow" come from the funnel instead of from the mouth. Pontoppidan's accounts are based largely on hearsay and the reports of Von Ferry and Benstrup, but he also mentions the carcasses that washed ashore with regularity on the coasts of Norway. Is it not possible that mid-eighteenth-century Norway saw an invasion of giant squid like the one that occurred in Newfoundland in the late nineteenth century?

In the *Pictorial Magazine* for 1849, in an anonymous article about sea serpents, we read an account that, the author tells us, "will suffice to show that the sea-serpent in no stranger in the waters of the northern and east-

THE GREAT SEA SERPENT
(according to Hans Egede.)

*H*ans Egede's 1734 illustration of a sinuous, snakelike sea serpent

ern hemispheres." The description is attributed to the Reverend Mr. Deinboll, the archdeacon of Molde:

> On the 28th of July, 1845, four men were out on the Ramsdale-fiord, fishing. About seven o'clock in the evening, a long marine animal was seen slowly moving forward. The visible part of the body appeared to be forty to fifty feet in length, and moved in undulations like a snake. Body round, dark color, and several feet thick. Its fore part ended in a sharp snout, and its immense head was raised above the water in a semi-circular form. The color of the head was dark brown, the skin smooth. No eyes were noticed, nor mane nor bristles on the throat.

When British naturalist Philip Henry Gosse wrote *The Romance of Natural History* in 1861, he concluded with a chapter entitled "The Great Unknown" in which he summarized much of what was known about sea monsters up to that time. He retells the Romsdalfjord incident of 1845:

> They saw a large marine animal, which slowly moved itself forward, as it appeared to them, with the help of two fins, on the fore part of its body near the head, which they judged from the boiling of the water on both

 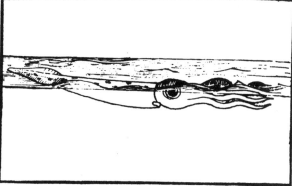

sides of it. The visible part of the body appeared to be between forty and fifty feet in length, and moved in undulations like a snake. The body was round and of a dark colour, and seemed to be several ells (an ell = two feet) in thickness. As they discerned a waving motion in the water behind the animal, they concluded that

According to Henry Lee's Sea Monsters Unmasked, this is "the animal which Egede probably saw," and on the right, Lee's explanation for the Daedalus's serpent.

part of the body was concealed under water. That it was one connected animal they saw plainly from its movement. When the animal was about one hundred yards from the boat, they noticed tolerably correctly its fore-part, which ended in a sharp snout; its colossal head raised itself above the water in the form of a semicircle; the lower part was not visible.

Gosse wrote, "Few seacoasts have been more sedulously searched, or by more acute naturalists . . . than those of Norway. Krakens and sea-serpents ought to have been living and dying thereabouts from long before Pontoppidan's time to our day, if all tales were true; yet they have never vouchsafed a single fragment of the skeleton to any Scandinavian collector." Eleven years later, a kraken "fragment"—consisting of an entire giant squid— would appear off Newfoundland, and now that an explanation appeared, it became possible to interpret Gosse's story as a description of what the Norwegians now call *kjaempeblaekspruten*. Particularly significant are the "waving motion" behind the animal (the arms); the "head" (a tentacular club); and the absence of eyes.

A hundred and one years later, in Vike Bay in the very same Romsdalfjord, a giant squid measuring thirty feet in total length was found by fishermen. One cannot fault those who believed that the 1845 animal was a sea serpent; how could they know that a real animal fitting that description would eventually appear? In fact, in describing the 1946 incident, Bjorn Myklebust wrote that before the squid stranded, it had been seen swim-

*O*ne of the illustrations that accompanied the original report of a "sea serpent" sighted from the ship *Daedalus* in 1848 off the Cape of Good Hope. It is probably easier to see this creature as a giant squid—with its tail above the surface—than as a sea serpent.

ming around the fjord. "It is therefore possible," he wrote, "that the observed sea serpents may simply have been . . . giant squids that were lying and splashing at the surface. . . . It thus seems likely that many stories about sea serpents can be reduced to stories about giant squids."

With a dark "body," pointed head, no mouth, and only the faintest suggestion of an eye, the illustration that accompanied the description of the *Plumper*'s sighting looks like no living creature—except possibly a giant squid.* If we look at the drawing of the *Daedalus* monster with *Architeuthis* in mind, the identification of the "monster" leaps off the page. We see not an "enormous serpent" but rather the tail section of an enormous cephalopod. Captain M'Quhae obligingly drew an eye where he thought it ought to go, but in his description he never mentions it. He does write, however, that "no portion [of its anatomy] was used in propelling it through the

*Heuvelmans labors to assign this creature to some inflexible type of sea serpent, writing that the illustration shows "an animal stiff as a log of wood, but there is no reason for gibes at his expense, for he would certainly not have taken a lifeless log for a living animal, and did not Aristotle talk of 'animals like beams of wood'?"

water, either by horizontal or vertical undulation." No vertebrate can move through the water without some visible means of propulsion, but a squid, which uses water ejected from the funnel or the mantle to move, could easily conform to M'Quhae's description. Then there is the case of the *Pauline*, where a sperm whale was observed in a struggle with what was described as "a monstrous sea-serpent coiled twice round a large sperm whale" (see p. 240). Since we already know that sperm whales regularly engage in battles with giant squid, it does not require a leap of imagination to see the *Pauline*'s monster as none other than *Architeuthis*.

Let us look again at the *Valhalla* sighting of 1905, as reported by the naturalists Meade-Waldo and Nicoll:

> . . . a great head and neck rose out of the water in front of the frill; the neck did not touch the frill in the water, but came out of the water in *front* of it, at a distance of certainly not less than 18 inches, probably more. The neck appeared to be about the thickness of a slight man's body, and from 7 to 8 feet was out of the water; head and neck were all about the same thickness. The head had a very turtle-like appearance as had also the eye. I could see the line of the mouth, but we were sailing pretty fast, and quickly drew away from the object, which was going very slowly. It moved its neck from side to side in a peculiar manner.

It is certainly possible to read this description as a monster with a "frill," but it is almost as easy to see it as a description of a giant squid swimming at the surface: The frill could be one of the tail fins; the neck (not attached to the "frill"), one of the long tentacles; and the head, its flattened end. The "turtle-like" appearance of the head is admittedly a problem, but if something looks like the "head" of an animal, we expect to see an eye *somewhere*, and Meade-Waldo and Nicoll may have only imagined it. (There have been many "sea-monster" sightings that can be explained as *Architeuthis* if we assume that the observers misidentified the eye.) As for the "peculiar" movement of the neck (which Nicoll described as "a curious wriggling movement"), it is more likely that they were describing an object that was *not* a neck but something else—a tentacle, perhaps. We know virtually nothing about the locomotion of giant squid at the surface (if indeed they ever locomote there), but there may be a possibility that these creatures swim with a tentacle out of the water, which would go a long way toward explaining the sightings of a large-bodied animal with a long neck. (If a giant squid ever swam with both of its tentacles out of the water, we would probably have reports of two-headed monsters.)

The Gloucester sea serpent is considerably more difficult to explain

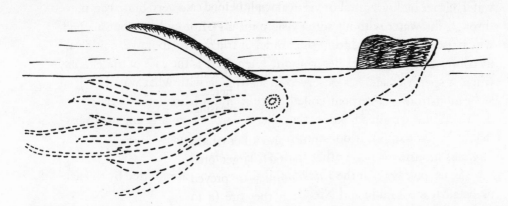

*T*he Nicoll drawing adapted to conform to the giant squid hypothesis. (See p. 65 for the original.)

away. None of the contemporaneous descriptions would appear to have any connection with giant squid—or any other known animals, for that matter— and the fact that it was seen regularly by so many people militates against hoax or hallucination. I have tried to analyze the sighting data with the idea that many of them can be explained by existing phenomena, but I can make no suggestions about the true identity of the Gloucester monster.

In the conclusion to his book, Heuvelmans has written:

The legend of the Great Sea-Serpent, then, has arisen by degrees from chance sightings of a series of large sea-animals that are serpentiform in some respect. Some, like the oarfish, the whale-shark and Steller's sea-cow, have been unmasked in the last few centuries. But most remain unknown to science, yet can be defined with some degree of exactitude, depending on the number and precision of the descriptions that refer to them.

He does not mention the giant squid in this passage, but 30-foot tentacles are surely more "serpentiform" than any parts of the whale shark or Steller's sea cow. (He devotes a chapter to "The *Kraken* and the Giant Squid," but it serves more to introduce the creature and its colorful history than to explain its sea-serpent possibilities.) The giant squid does not explain everything; there are many sightings by reputable persons that cannot be conveniently dumped into a basket woven of squid tentacles. Some monsters have been oarfish; others, basking sharks, whales, or their deformed carcasses. There are some, like the Gloucester monster, that simply cannot be encompassed by any rational explanation.

In *Why Big Fierce Animals Are Rare,* ecologist Paul Colinvaux discusses the numerical imbalance between the large predators and their prey:

For flesh eaters, the largest possible supply of food calories they can obtain is a fraction of the bodies of their plant-eating prey, and they must use this fraction both to make bodies and as a fuel supply. Moreover their bodies must be the big active bodies that let them hunt for a living. If one is higher still on the food chain, an eater of flesh-eater's flesh, one has yet a smaller fraction to support even bigger and fiercer bodies. Which is why large fierce animals are so astonishingly (or pleasingly) rare.

Colinvaux lists the white sharks and killer whales as the sea's biggest and fiercest predators, but there are, in fact, larger predators in the sea. If one accepts the hypothesis that most animals are preyed upon by other animals approximately ten times larger than they are (a formulation advanced by Charles Elton, the father of modern ecological theory), then the feeding habits of the sperm whale—which is certainly much larger than any shark or killer whale—can only be explained if the cachalot feeds on the smaller squid species. Of all known squid species, only *Mesonychoteuthis* approaches *Architeuthis* in size; all the others are considerably smaller. How can it make sense for a large-prey predator like the sperm whale to attack (presumably to eat) a creature like the giant squid, which may be much lighter in weight but might be as long as or longer than its attacker? And even more problematic, if the giant squid is such a formidable antagonist, can any animal afford to prey on it if it might turn the tables and become the predator instead of the prey?*

The exceptions to the Eltonian rule are the baleen whales, which are considerably larger than any other predators, but they circumvent the model by skipping the middleman; that is, they feed directly on the high-mass, high-protein prey items (krill) that would normally require a couple of additional stages to get to them. In this way, they resemble the very large land herbivores, like the elephant, getting their energy from plants that they do not have to be particularly fierce to capture.

The one creature that does not fit the model is the carnivorous dinosaur *Tyrannosaurus rex,* which was much larger than any terrestrial predators before or since. "If natural selection could fashion a tyrannosaur at that time," asks Colinvaux, "why not in all subsequent time? Why in particular was there nothing like a tyrannosaur in the great age of mammals . . . when all the plainslands of the earth held herds of game that make the herds of modern Africa seem trivial by comparison?" Perhaps "natural selection" has

---

*Descriptions of the fantastic battles between the giant squid and the sperm whale often have the squid throwing a tentacle over the single nostril of the whale, to prevent it from inhaling at the surface. Although this conceit is quite far-fetched, it would probably be the only way a squid could incapacitate a whale, since it does not use its arms for constriction, and its beak, although formidable, could take bites only from the whale's blubber.

fashioned a tyrannosaur for our time, and perhaps it is the one with 50-foot-long arms and eyes the size of dinner plates.

IT WOULD appear that today's monsters have much more to fear from us than we do from them. The last mermaids to torment a man were probably the sirens of the *Odyssey*. The ship-attacking kraken turns out to be a myth, although the giant squid is very real indeed. Victor Hugo's *poulpe* has been replaced by *Octopus dofleini*, a very large octopus, but no threat to swimmers. (But there may very well be 200-foot-long octopuses; we have just never seen a whole one.) The sperm whale, the largest predator ever to have lived on earth, poses a hazard mostly to squid, and with the exception of some "attacks" on whaleboats, most of which were defensive reactions to the pain of a lance plunged into their vitals, there are few records of belligerent, aggressive cachalots.* For their benevolence, for their unwitting generosity in giving themselves to us so that we might make corsets, margarine, lipstick, and shoe polish, we slaughtered the whales by the millions and drove many species toward the abyss of extinction.

The whale and the shark vie for the honor of having swallowed the biblical Jonah. From its occasional habit of eating giant squid, we know that a sperm whale is certainly capable of swallowing a man, but with one exception that we know of, it has not happened.† Although tradition holds that it was a whale that swallowed Jonah, there are those who believe the "great fish" was a shark. In his *Life of Sharks*, Paul Budker not only discounts the likelihood that a whale was the swallower but actually identifies the shark by species. Basing his arguments on the writings of the French naturalist Guillaume Rondelet, Budker suggests "that the impossibility of passing a man down the narrow throat of a whale led Rondelet to search for a marine animal capable of swallowing such a large prey and bringing it up whole later on. *Carcharodon*, the white shark, was not a bad choice." Further on, he quotes from Linnaeus's Latin description of the white shark (*Sq. dentibus*

---

*Between 1810 and 1820, a bull sperm whale nicknamed "Mocha Dick" (obviously an inspiration for Melville's novel) terrorized the shipping lanes by sinking ships without provocation, but most other instances of whales attacking *ships* (rather than whaleboats) seem to have resulted from the whale having been harpooned. In 1807, a sperm whale attacked and holed the *Union*, a whaler out of Nantucket; in 1820, an enraged whale stove and sunk the Nantucket whaler *Essex;* in 1851— the year *Moby-Dick* was published—the *Ann Alexander* out of New Bedford was sunk by a whale; and in 1902, as square-rigged whaling was coming to an end, the bark *Kathleen* was rammed and sunk by a sperm whale in the Atlantic.

† In a letter to the editors of *Natural History* magazine in 1946, E. Y. Davis told of his experience as a surgeon aboard a sealer out of Newfoundland, where a man fell overboard in proximity to a sperm whale. After swallowing the unfortunate sailor, the whale was shot. When it was opened, the badly mangled corpse of the man was removed.

triangularibus serratis) and concludes that "one should, therefore, substitute 'shark' for 'whale' in the story of Jonah, and even, for the sake of complete accuracy, *Carcharodon carcharias*."

*J*onah on the way out of the water, having been ejected from the belly of a "large fish," which is shown with two sets of very mammalian canine teeth

From the beginning, giant man-eating sharks have been among the most terrifying animals on earth. Elasmophobia was primarily restricted to seafarers, however, since the sharks were originally perceived as a threat to sailors who fell overboard. No sooner did people take up bathing at the beach as a recreation than the dire predictions about sharks turned out to be true. Given the opportunity, they ate—or at least they attacked—people in the water. As long as we were going to serve as food for the sharks, they were going to accept our invitation to the table. (Never mind that sharks really don't attack in order to eat people; what mattered is that we *thought* they did.) Soon snorkeling, scuba diving, and surfing were added to the list of human aquatic entertainments, and accordingly, the more people there were in the water, the more the sharks attacked. By 1960, the problem was so bad in South Africa that the government initiated antishark measures, designed specifically to reduce the number of dangerous sharks in the waters of the Natal Coast. Also in the early 1960s, white sharks began to attack divers off the coast of South Australia, killing two and maiming another within a three-year period. Australia, too, enacted protective measures against the sharks. In 1974, Peter Benchley wrote *Jaws*, and the reputation of the anthropophagous shark took off like a roman candle. Never mind that there are 100,000 sharks killed every year, while there may be fifty to seventy-five shark attacks annually, with five to ten fatalities. The balance is overwhelmingly in favor of *Homo sapiens*, the most efficient predator on earth; next to us, the shark looks like an amateur.

Sharks are durable creatures; they seem to have survived the vicissitudes of time and tide with their bloodthirsty reputations intact. (Along with squid and octopuses, sharks have had their malevolent stature enhanced by an appearance in the sensational literature and movies.) Sharks were revered in some cultures, such as that of the early Hawaiians, where there were numerous shark gods, but for the most part, we still think of them as potential man-eaters. Now that we understand that it is not our job to decide which species shall live and which shall die, we are beginning to learn that even the predators are an important part of life. Of course, it is not as simple as the deer huggers make out; the absence of wolves in Pennsylvania and Michigan is not solely responsible for the explosion in the whitetail deer population, and the hunters are not replacing the predators by taking out the bucks. (In fact, removing the large bucks is genetically devastating to the population; if the hunters would perform the same function as the natural predators, they would be shooting the aged does and the youngest fawns, thereby allowing the more successful deer to breed and pass along their genes.) Great white sharks are an important part of the oceans' cycle, and we probably do not need a reason not to eliminate them. It should suffice that they were plying their trade long before men decided to go for a swim and the oceans are their territory, not ours.

Why do we need monsters? As mythological creatures, they are obsolete, and as commercial objects, they seem to have outlived their usefulness. As endangered species, however, they serve to remind us of our own frailty—and also of our responsibility to preserve the planet—which may actually be their most important function. Monsters have always been with us, sometimes in ways that defy explanation: If size were the sole criterion, the blue whale would be our paradigmatic monster. But the blue whale is a harmless plankton eater, and despite its gargantuan dimensions, it has never been regarded as a threat. The same can be said of the whale shark and the basking shark, which never attack anything larger than a plankter. To qualify as a proper monster, the creature has to be large and mysterious, but it also has to pose some sort of a threat. They have always been a part of our collective psyche, just out of the range of the calculations of scientists and the classifications of taxonomists. As E. O. Wilson wrote in *Biophilia,* they provide "a sweet sense of horror, the shivery fascination with monsters and creeping forms that so delights us today even in the sterile hearts of the cities, that could see you through to the next morning."

In a 1990 article in *Cryptozoology,* Bernard Heuvelmans cites the whale shark and the manta ray as creatures whose existence was suspected and then embellished by folklore. In the early nineteenth century, actual specimens were collected, dispelling the myths but advancing the animal into what he calls "zoological status." Other animals—not necessarily aquatic—that have moved from fable to fact are gorillas (originally perceived as hairy, bloodthirsty carnivores) and the Komodo monitor lizard, the largest of all the lizards, believed in Indonesia to be a true dragon. Concluding his article, Heuvelmans wrote:

> Supported thus jointly by folklorists and cryptozoologists, monsters are not about to die. Not that they are eternal: surely they were born with human thought and will vanish with it. Yet I wish a long survival to all the animals of flesh and blood that were successively embodied in them, that somehow fed them and kept them alive, all for the comfort of our souls. We owe them that at least.

The new mythology is that of the media. The shark, consistently reviled throughout the history of seafaring man, has not become a lovable creature, but rather has become elevated by novels, newspapers, movies, and television to a level of infamy that would have been impossible in the past. Now most everyone knows about the great shark, waiting just offshore (or just after dark) to savage innocent swimmers. How many of us who read or saw *Jaws* can truly say that they have not experienced a twinge of fear upon entering the ocean for a swim? Jules Verne (with the not inconsiderable help of Walt Disney Studios) made a contemporary mythological monster out of the giant squid, and then Peter Benchley, the novelist who engineered the apotheosis of the shark in *Jaws,* propelled the kraken even more firmly into the pantheon of twentieth-century sea monsters with his novel *Beast.* Victor Hugo did the same with the giant octopus in *Toilers of the Sea,* although to a much lesser extent, since he did not have the benefit of the contemporary publicity apparatus. And finally, Herman Melville chronicled the passage of the whale from myth to monster to myth—the last, a myth of his own devising.

Alongside the media, another sort of mythology exists; the apotheosis of endangered species. As the custodians of the planet, particularly its wildlife, we have not done a very good job of fulfilling our responsibilities. Instead, we are eliminating species and habitats at an alarming rate. So for guilt-laden mankind, the ultimate expiation is to acknowledge the precious status of the "endangered species." These are the icons of *Homo ecologicus*—the names we invoke when we want to demonstrate our new concern for the welfare of the planet. And of the "monsters," several of them have already achieved this lofty distinction: Instead of fearing them, we fear *for* them. Only the giant squid, a mysterious inhabitant of the abyssal depths, is safe from the predations of man, primarily because we could not affect it if we wanted to; it is not much better known today than it was when its existence was first verified in 1857. Of all the sighted monsters, only *Architeuthis* retains its full mythological and cryptozoological status.

The whale, once the terror of unknown seas, became familiar as a product of commerce, and then, when it was almost too late, engendered a massive, worldwide campaign to save the remnants of its populations from extinction. The mermaid, originally believed to be a siren that called seamen to their doom, became instead the harmless, hapless manatee whose welfare is now the concern of conservationists all over the world. The shark, originally perceived as a threatening, pelagic menace, later became an inhabitant of aquariums, then the anthropophagous star of a best-selling novel and four Hollywood movies. Some sharks—including that quintessential man-eater the great white—are now considered endangered, and instead of protecting us from them, we are now protecting them from us.

One of the defining characteristics of monsters is their evasiveness. If we could view them in an aquarium or even a protected bay or fjord, they would lose much of their mystery. To date, however, most monsters have escaped the puny efforts of their would-be captors. Current technology precludes the incarceration of the gigantic whales and squid; there is no tank large enough to hold them, and even if there was, we could not possibly feed them. Of course, there have been octopuses and sharks in captivity, but these have been the smaller varieties. No white shark—not even a small one—has been successfully maintained in an aquarium tank, and we can hardly exhibit a giant octopus that might not even exist. Of the known sea monsters, only the humble manatee can be seen regularly in inshore waters or in aquarium tanks. The animal that evolved from an enticingly deadly siren into a mermaid and then into a species threatened by powerboats and extinction has become our only manageable monster.

APPENDIX A

The Linnaean Society's Questionnaire

Boston, August 19, 1817

The Committee appointed by the Linnaean Society have concluded on the following method of proceeding in the execution of their commission.

I. The examination to be confined to those persons professing to actually have *seen* the animal.

II. Such persons to be examined as may be met with by either of the Committee or by the Honourable Lonson Nash, who is requested by a letter addressed to him from the Committee to undertake this service.

III. All testimony on the subject to be taken in writing, and after being deliberately read to the person testifying, to be signed by him and sworn before a magistrate, the examinations to be separate, and the matter testified by any witness not to be communicated until the whole evidence be taken.

IV. The persons testifying to be requested first to relate their recollections on the subject, which being taken down, the following questions to be proposed:

THE TWENTY-FIVE POINTS

1. When did you first see the animal?
2. How often and how long at a time?
3. At what times of day?
4. At what distance?
5. How near the shore?
6. What was its general appearance?

7. Was it in motion or at rest?

8. How fast did it move and in what direction?

9. What parts of it were above the water and how high?

10. Did it appear jointed or only serpentine?

11. If serpentine, were its sinuosities vertical or horizontal?

12. Were any distinct portions out of the water at one time?

13. What were its colour, length, and thickness?

14. Did it appear smooth or rough?

15. What were the size and shape of its head, and had the head ears, horns, or other appendages?

16. Describe the eyes and mouth.

17. Had it gills, or breathing holes, and where?

18. Had it fins or legs, and where?

19. Had it a mane or any hair, and where?

20. How did the tail terminate?

21. Did it utter any sound?

22. Did it appear to pursue, avoid, or notice anything?

23. Did you see more than one?

24. How many other persons saw it?

25. State any other reasonable fact.

APPENDIX B

Giant Squid Sightings and Strandings

Authenticated records of *Architeuthis* sightings and strandings. Because some of the specimens had tentacles that were lost or damaged, some of the overall lengths include tentacles, and some do not. (In one instance, it was *only* a tentacle that was found.) In some cases, the original description was not seen by me, and I have had to use a secondary source as a reference.

DATE	LOCATION	SIZE	AUTHOR
1639	Thingøresrand, Iceland	?	Steenstrup (1849)
1673	Dingle Bay, Ireland	19′	More (1875)
1785	Grand Bank, Newfoundland	?	Thomas (1795)
1790	Arnarnesvik, Iceland	39′	Steenstrup (1849)
1798	Denmark	?	Packard (1873)
1802	off Tasmania	6–7′	Peron (1807)
1817	Atlantic Ocean	400 lbs.	Quoy and Gaimard (1824)
1853	Raabjerg, Denmark	(beak only)	Steenstrup (1857)
1855	Bahamas	——	Steenstrup (1857)
1860	Hillswick, Scotland	23′	Jeffreys (1869)
1861	*Alecton* (Canaries)	20–24′	Bouyer (1861)
1862	North Atlantic	——	Crosse and Fischer (1862)

DATE	LOCATION	SIZE	AUTHOR
1870	Waimarama, New Zealand	15' +	Kirk (1880)
1870	Lamaline, Newfoundland	40'	Verrill (1879)
1871	Lamaline, Newfoundland	45'	Verrill (1879)
1871	Grand Bank, Newfoundland	15' +	Packard (1873)
1871	Wellington, New Zealand	16'	Dell (1952)
1872	Bonavista Bay, Newfoundland	46'	Verrill (1879)
1872	Coombs Cove, Newfoundland	52'	Verrill (1879)
1873	Conception Bay, Newfoundland	44'	Harvey (1874)
1873	Logy Bay, Newfoundland	31'	Murray (1874)
?	Labrador	52'	Verrill (1879)
1874	Fortune Bay, Newfoundland	36'	Verrill (1879)
1874	Buøy, Norway	——	Grieg (1933)
1874	*Strathowen + Pearl* (Indian Ocean)	——	Lane (1974)
1875	Connemara, Ireland	30' tentacles	More (1875)
1875	St. Paul Island	——	Velain (1877)
?	Cape Sable, Newfoundland	43"	Verrill (1879)
1876	Hammer Cove, Newfoundland	——	Verrill (1879)
1876	Cape Campbell, New Zealand	20'	Kirk (1880)
1877	Lance Cove, Newfoundland	44'	Verrill (1879)
1877	Trinity Bay, Newfoundland	——	Verrill (1879)
1877	St. Paul Island	——	Velain (1877)
1877	Catalina, Newfoundland	39.5'	Verrill (1879)
1878	Thimble Tickle, Newfoundland	55'	Verrill (1879)
1878	Three Arms, Newfoundland	31'	Verrill (1879)
1879	James's Cove, Newfoundland	40' (?)	Verrill (1879)
1879	Brigus, Newfoundland	8' arms	Verrill (1879)
1879	Lyall Bay, New Zealand	(beak only)	Kirk (1880)
1880	Tokyo Fish Market	——	Hilgendorf (1880)
1880	Island Bay, New Zealand	55'	Kirk (1880)
1880	Tønsvik, Norway	——	Grieg (1933)

DATE	LOCATION	SIZE	AUTHOR
1880	Kvaenangen, Norway	———	Grieg (1933)
1880	Grand Bank, Newfoundland	66″ tentacles (juvenile)	Verrill (1880)
1881	Portugal Cove, Newfoundland	21′	Verrill (1879)
1886	Cape Campbell, New Zealand	———	Robson (1887)
1887	Lyall Bay, New Zealand	55′	Kirk (1880)
1895	Tokyo Bay	12.5′	Mitsukuri and Ikeda (1895)
1896	Hevnefjord, Norway	32′ 2″	Brinkmann (1916)
1896	Hevnefjord, Norway	32′	Nordgard (1928)
1898	North of Bahamas	———	Steenstrup (1898)
1902	*Michael Sars* (off Faroes)	9.35′	Murray and Hjort (1912)
1903	Mjóifjördhur, Iceland	tentacle	Murray and Hjort (1912)
1911	Senjen, Norway	20.3′	Grieg (1933)
1911	Monterey Bay, California	30′	Berry (1912)
1912	Monterey Bay, California	ca. 500 lbs.	Berry (1914)
1912	Japan (fishing net)	———	Pfeffer (1912)
1912	Smølen, Norway	28′ 4″	Brinkmann (1916)
1914	Belmullet, Ireland	27′ (in sperm whale)	Hamilton (1914)
1915	Bergen, Norway	23′ 8″	Brinkmann (1916)
1916	Helgeland, Norway	———	Grieg (1933)
1916	Hevnefjord, Norway	20′ tentacles	Nordgard (1928)
1917	Skateraw, Scotland	———	Ritchie (1920)
1918	Kilkel, Ireland	———	Hardy (1956)
1918	Tokyo Fish Market	———	Heuvelmans (1965)
1919	Øyvagen, Norway	———	Nordgard (1923)
1920	Hebrides, Scotland	———	Ritchie (1920)

DATE	LOCATION	SIZE	AUTHOR
1922	Caithness, Scotland	————	Ritchie (1922)
1924	Bluff, New Zealand	16'	Dell (1952)
1924	Margate, Natal	————	Heuvelmans (1965)
1927	Kalveidøy, Norway	24.6'	Grieg (1933)
1928	Ranheim, Norway	46'	Nordgard (1928)
1930	Kaikoura, New Zealand	41'	Dell (1952)
1930–1933	Pacific between Hawaii and Samoa	————	Grønningsaeter (1946)
1933	Scarborough, Yorks.	19'	Clarke (1933)
1933	Dildo, Newfoundland	————	Frost (1934)
1935	*Palombe* (Gulf of Gascogne)	26'	Cadenat (1936)
1935	Harbour Main, Newfoundland	20'	Frost (1936)
1937	Arbroath, Scotland	24.5'	Stephen (1937)
1937	Petone, New Zealand	22' tentacles	Dell (1952)
1945	Pahau River Mouth, New Zealand	————	Dell (1952)
1946	Vike Bay, Norway	30'	Myklebust (1946)
1948	Wingan Inlet, Australia	28'	Allan (1948)
1949	Bay of Nigg, Scotland	19' 3"	Rae (1950)
1949	Shetland, Scotland	(beak only)	Stephen (1950)
1952	Madeira	34'	Rees and Maul (1956)
1952	Carnoustie, Scotland	————	Hardy (1956)
?	off Mississippi Delta	————	Voss (1956)
1954	Ranheim, Norway	30'	Clarke (1966)
1955	Porto Pim, Azores	34' 5" (in sperm whale)	R. Clarke (1955)
1956	Makara, New Zealand	5.9' mantle	Dell (1970)
1958	Bahamas	47'	Voss (1967)
1961	Madeira	57 mm mantle (juvenile)	Roper and Young (1972)
1961	King's Cove, Newfoundland	"small"	Aldrich (1968)

DATE	LOCATION	SIZE	AUTHOR
1963	off Chile	45 mm mantle (juvenile)	Roper and Young (1972)
1964	Conche, Newfoundland	28.76'	Aldrich (1991)
1964	Chapel Arm, Newfoundland	4' mantle	Aldrich (1991)
1965	Lance Cove, Newfoundland	16' tentacle	Aldrich (1991)
1965	Springdale, Newfoundland	19.82'	Aldrich (1991)
1966	Sweet Bay, Newfoundland	56" mantle	Aldrich (1991)
1966	Wild Cove, Newfoundland	41" mantle	Aldrich (1991)
1966	Eddies Cove, Newfoundland	poor condition	Aldrich (1991)
1970	off St. Pierre, Grand Bank	———	Aldrich (1991)
1971	Sunnyside, Newfoundland	69" mantle	Aldrich (1991)
1972	off Durban	——— (in sperm whale)	Roeleveld and Lipinski (1991)
1972	off South Africa	——— (blue shark)	Nigmatullin (1976)
1974	off South Africa (trawl)	———	Péréz-Gándaras and Guerra (1989)
1974	Green Point, South Africa	14.82'	Roeleveld and Lipinski (1991)
1975	Bonavista, Newfoundland	51" mantle	Aldrich (1991)
1976	off South Africa	34.5'	Péréz-Gándaras and Guerra (1978)
1977	Lance Cove, Newfoundland	———	Aldrich (1991)
1978	Ft. Lauderdale, Florida	6.5" mantle	Toll and Hess (1981)
1978	Cheynes Beach, Western Australia	———	*Sea Frontiers*
1979	St. Brendan's, Newfoundland	60" mantle	Aldrich (1991)
1980	Southern California	tentacle only	Robison (1989)
1980	South Africa	2.65' mantle	Péréz-Gándaras and Guerra (1989)
1980	off Oregon (trawl)	5.3' mantle	Nesis et al. (1985)

Appendix B

DATE	LOCATION	SIZE	AUTHOR
1980	off California (trawl)	2.5′ mantle	Nesis et al. (1985)
1980	Plum Island, Massachusetts	30′	Roper (1982)
1980–1981	East North Pacific (trawls)	14 specimens	Nesis et al. (1985)
1981	Hare Bay, Newfoundland	29.96′	Aldrich (1991)
1981	Orange River mouth (South Africa)	2.63′	Nesis et al. (1985)
1981	Vavilov Ridge (off Zaire) (trawl)	3.25′ mantle	Nesis et al. (1985)
1982	Bergen, Norway	33′	Brix (1983)
1982	Sandy Cove, Newfoundland	65″ mantle	Aldrich (1991)
1982	Sydney, Australia	16.5″ mantle	Jackson et al. (1991)
1984	off Namibia	4′ mantle	Péréz-Gándaras and Guerra (1989)
1984	Aberdeen, Scotland	——	Boyle (1984)
1986	Aberdeen, Scotland	14′	Boyle (1986)
1986	Orange River mouth (South Africa)	15′ 6″	Roeleveld and Lipinski (1991)
1987	off South Africa	2.6′ mantle	Péréz-Gándaras and Guerra (1989)
1991	Soetwater, South Africa (off Cape Town)	13′ 2″	Natal *Mercury*
1991	Cape Point (off Cape Town)	1.4 m mantle	Roeleveld (pers. comm.)
1992	Kommetjie (South Africa)	(head only)	Roeleveld (pers. comm.)
1992	Cape Columbine (South Africa)	1.77 m mantle	Roeleveld (pers. comm.)
1993	Mauritius	4.5 m mantle	Staub (1993)

APPENDIX C

A. E. Verrill's Account of the Florida Sea-Monster

(American Naturalist, *April 1897. 31: 304–7*)

On the 5th of December, 1896, a portion of a very large marine animal was cast ashore on the beach twelve miles south of St. Augustine, Florida. When it first came ashore it was much mutilated at one end, and had evidently been dead for some time, and was, apparently, in an advanced state of decomposition. Contrary to expectation, it has resisted further decay, and still remains, after nearly three months, nearly in the same state as at first. It was first brought to my notice by Dr. DeWitt Webb, who has devoted a great amount of time and labor to its investigation and preservation. Through him I have received a dozen different photographic views of it, taken at different times, and showing it both in its original state and when it had been moved and partly turned over. Quite recently he has sent me several large masses of the thick and firm integument, of which the mass is mainly composed. By his efforts it has recently (with much labor) been moved several miles nearer to St. Augustine, to the terminus of a railroad, and protected from the drifting sand. It is likely to keep some months longer without much change, and to be visited by large numbers of people. The figures now given are copied from photographs made two days after it came ashore. At that time the sand had collected around it to a depth of about eighteen inches.

Its length is 21 feet; breadth about 7 feet; height about 4½ feet, when the sand was removed. Its weight was estimated at about 7 tons.

As shown by the figures, it has an elongated, pear-shaped form, broadly rounded at the larger, closed end, and considerably flattened toward the smaller and much mutilated end. At this end, as shown in both views, there are large divergent ridges covered by the frayed-out fibrous tissues. These ridges are folds of integument, but were at first mistaken for the stumps of arms, like those of an *Octopus*, and were so described in letters received by me. Moreover, Mr. Wilson, who visited it when first found, claimed to have found a portion of an attached arm, 36 feet long, buried in the sand. This last statement, in the light of later investigations, must have been erroneous and is totally misleading.[1] At that time, however, it seemed quite consistent with the form and appearance of the mass which was described by Dr. Webb as closely similar to the body of the common small octopus. The photographs show this resemblance very clearly; and the ridges at the mutilated end, then supposed to be the stumps of mutilated arms, seemed to confirm the view that the mass was the mutilated body of a huge octopus,[2] and as such it was described by me in the *American Journal of Science* and elsewhere.

As soon as specimens of the tissue were sent to me, even a hasty examination was sufficient that this view was not correct, for instead of being composed of hardened muscular fibers[3] as had been supposed, the thick masses of tissue were found to consist almost wholly of a hard, elastic complex of connective issue fibers of large size. The masses sent vary from four to ten inches in thickness. They are white, and so tough that it is hard to cut them, even with a razor, and yet they are somewhat flexible and elastic. The fibers are much interlaced in all directions, and are of all sizes, up to the size of coarse twine and small cords. The larger fibers unite to form bundles extending from the inner s urface radially. According to Dr. Webb, who opened the mass, these cords were attached in large numbers to a central saccular organ, which occupied a large part of the interior of the thicker part of the specimen. This might, perhaps, represent the spermaceti case. Naturally, most of the interior parts had decomposed long before it was opened,[4] so that we lack details of the interior structure. Externally there is but little trace of cuticle. The surface is close-grained and somewhat rough, with occasional gray patches of what may be remnants of the outer skin, much altered by decay. The thick masses contain a slight amount of oil, and smell like rancid whale oil, but they sink

---

1. The memorandum written by Mr. Wilson and forwarded to me by Dr. Webb is as follows: "One arm lying west of the body, 23 feet long; one stump of arm about 4 feet long; three arms lying south of body and from appearance attached to same (although I did not dig quite to body, as it laid well down in the sand and I was very tired), longest one measured over 23 feet, the other arms were three to five feet shorter."

2. This was also the opinion of a large number of naturalists who saw the photographs sent to me.

3. A highly contractile muscular integument is an essential feature of all cephalopods.

4. It should be stated after visiting the specimen, two days after it came ashore, Dr. Webb did not again see it for several weeks, owing to very stormy weather and its distance from St. Augustine. Nor did anyone suppose, at that time, that its tissues could be preserved or utilized for study, owing to its apparently advanced decomposition. The outer skin rapidly decayed, but the fibrous mass seems very durable.

quickly in water owing to their great density. No muscular tissue was present in any of the masses sent, nor were there any spaces from which such tissues might have disappeared by decay.

Statements that the creature cannot be an Octopus, but is of cetacean nature, were published by me in several local daily papers within a day or two after the specimens were first examined by me, and shortly afterward in the *New York Herald* and *Science*.

It is evident that such a dense and thick covering of fibrous connective tissue could not have come from any mobile part of any animal, but must have served for passive resistance to great pressure or concussion.

The structure of the integument is more like that of the upper part of the head of a sperm whale than any other known to me, and as the obvious use is the same, it is most probable that the whole mass represents the upper part of the head of such a whale, detached from the skull and jaw. It is evident, however, from the figures, that the shape is decidedly unlike that of the head of an ordinary sperm whale,[5] for the latter is oblong, truncated and rather narrow in front, "like the prow of a vessel," with an angle at the upper front end, near which the single blow-hole is situated. No blow-hole has been discovered in the mass cast ashore. There is a depression, shown in the side-view, near the large end, that I at one time thought might be a blow-hole, but Dr. Webb states that it is a "sulcus" or pit two feet long and six inches deep, apparently not connected with the interior cavity and probably due to mutilation. The specimen was doubtless floated ashore by the gases of decomposition accumulated in the interior cavity, indicating the absence of any free external opening to it, from which the gas could escape.

Photographs made of the under side of the thicker part, when it was turned up by powerful tackle, show an irregular roughness on that side, extending well forward, but not to the end. The roughness may be due to abrasion, or it may show where the skull was attached. If the mass really came from the head of a sperm whale, it would seem that it must have projected farther forward beyond the upper jaw than does the nose of an ordinary sperm whale, and it would, apparently, have been much broader and blunter, or "bottle-nosed." It is possible, of course, that its form has changed considerably since death; but in view of its wonderful toughness and firmness, no great change of the larger end, supposed to be the anterior, or nose-end, is probable. All the pulling and hauling and turning of it partly over, by the aid of six horses and strong tackle, have not served to change its shape materially, or rather its elasticity serves to restore it to its for-

5. The dimensions of the head of a large sperm whale, 84 feet long, are given as follows: Length, about 25 feet; depth, 8 to 9 feet; breadth, 5 to 6 feet. The blow-hole is like a slit, about a foot long, and has a sigmoid curve. It is on the left side, close to the tip of the nose. The spermaceti case occupies a large space within the right side of the head. It is supported by strong fibrous tendons.

mer shape. Its toughness and elasticity remind one of the properties of thick vulcanized rubber.

It is possible to imagine a sperm whale with an abnormally enlarged nose, due to disease or extreme old age, which, if detached, might resemble this mass externally at least. It seems hardly probable that another allied whale, with a big nose, remains to be discovered. Notwithstanding these difficulties, my present opinion, that it came from the head of a creature like a sperm whale in structure, is the only one that seems plausible from the facts now ascertained.

BIBLIOGRAPHY

ABRAHAMSON, D. 1992. Elusive Behemoth [Giant Squid]. *Rodale's Scuba Diving* October 1992:106; 118.

ACKERMAN, J. C. 1957. Now, About Those Stories of Sea Serpents . . . *New Bedford Standard Times* Sept. 15, 1957:12.

ADAMS, A. 1860. On the Probable Origin of Some Sea Serpents. *Zoologist* 18:7237.

AKIMUSHKIN, I. I. 1963. Cephalopods of the Seas of the U.S.S.R. *Izdatel'stvo Akademii Nauk SSSR*. Moscow. (Israel Program for Scientific Translation. Jerusalem. 1965.)

ALDIS, W. S. 1883. The Sea Serpent. *Nature* 27:338.

ALDRED, R. G., M. NIXON, AND J. Z. YOUNG. 1978. The Blind Octopus, *Cirrothauma*. *Nature* 275(5680):547–9.

ALDRICH, F. A. 1968. The Distribution of Giant Squids in N. Atlantic and Particularly about the Shores of Newfoundland. *Sarsia* 34:393–8.

———. 1991. Some Aspects of the Systematics and Biology of Squid of the Genus *Architeuthis* Based on a Study of Specimens from Newfoundland Waters. *Bull. Mar. Sci.* 49(1 & 2):457–81.

ALDRICH, F. A., AND M. M. ALDRICH. 1968. On Regeneraa, Architeuthidae). *Canadian Jour. Zool.* 46:845–7.

ALDROVANDI, U. 1613. *De Piscibus libri V et de Cetis liber unus*. J. C. Unterverius. Bologna.

ALLAN, J. 1948. A Rare Giant Squid. *Aust. Mus. Mag.* 9:306–8.

———. 1955. The Kraken—Legendary Terror of the Seas. *Aust. Mus. Mag.* 11:275–8.

ALLEN, G. M. 1940. The New England Sea Serpent. *New England Naturalist* 8:28–9.

ANDERSEN, H. C. 1840. *The Little Mermaid and Other Fairy Tales*. 1958 edition, Flensted Publications, Odense, Denmark.

ANDERSON, C. 1934. The Sea Serpent and Its Kind. *Aust. Mus. Mag.* 5:204–8.

ANON. 1849. The Sea-Serpent. *Pictorial National Library* 3(19):263–8.

ANON. 1849. Mermen and Mermaids. *Pictorial National Library* 3(19):67–70.

ANON. 1892. Another Sea Serpent. *Scientific American* 34(Supplement):14115.

ANON. 1895. Another Sea Serpent. *Scientific American* 73:211.

ANON. 1984. Skeptical Eye—The (Retouched) Loch Ness Monster. *Discover* 6(3):6.

ANON. 1991. Megamouth Reveals a Phantom Shark's Realm. *National Geographic* 179(3):136.

ANON. 1992. A Puzzle Unloched. *The Economist* 324(7774):76.

APPLEGATE, S. P. 1967. A Survey of Shark Hard Parts. In P. W. Gilbert, R. F. Mathewson, and D. P. Rall, Eds., *Sharks, Skates, and Rays*, pp. 37–64. Johns Hopkins Press.

ARNOLD, J. M. 1962. Mating Behavior and Social Structure of *Loligo pealii*. *Biol. Bull.* 123(1):53–7.

———. 1965. Observations on the Mating Behavior of the Squid *Sepioteuthis sepioidea*. *Bull. Mar. Sci. Carib.* 15:216–22.

———. 1984. Reproduction in Cephalopods. In A. S. Tompa, N. H. Verdonk, and J. A. M. van den Biggelar, Eds., *The Mollusca, Vol. 7*, pp. 419–54. Academic Press.

———. 1990a. Evolution and Intelligence in Cephalopods. In D. L. Gilbert, W. J. Adelman, and J. M. Arnold, Eds., *Squid as Experimental Animals*, pp. 3–9. Plenum.

———. 1990b. Squid Mating Behavior. In D. L. Gilbert, W. J. Adelman, and J. M. Arnold, Eds., *Squid as Experimental Animals*, pp. 65–75. Plenum.

———. 1990c. Embryonic Development of Squid. In D. L. Gilbert, W. J. Adelman, and J. M. Arnold, Eds., *Squid as Experimental Animals*, pp. 77–92. Plenum.

ARNOLD, J. M., AND R. O'DOR. 1990. *In Vitro* Fertilization and Embryonic Development of Oceanic Squid. *Jour. Ceph. Biol.* 1(2):21–36.

ARVIN, N. 1950. *Herman Melville*. William Sloane Associates. Reprinted 1972 by Greenwood Press.

ASHTON, J. 1890. *Curious Creatures in Zoology*. John C. Nimmo. London.

ATZ, J. W. 1940. The Timid Octopus. *Bull. N.Y. Zool. Soc.* 43(2):48–54.

ATZ, J.W. 1976. *Latimeria* Babies Are Born, Not Hatched. *Underwater Naturalist* 9(4):4–7.

AYLING, T. 1984. *Collins Guide to the Sea Fishes of New Zealand*. Collins. Auckland.

BAIRD, S. F. 1856. The Sea-Snake Story a Fiction. *Zoologist* 14:4998.

BAKER, M. 1979. *Folklore of the Sea*. David & Charles.

BAKKER, R. 1993. Jurassic Sea Monsters. *Discover* 14(9):78–85.

BALDRIDGE, H. D. 1974a. Shark Attack: A Program of Data Reduction and Analysis. *Cont. Mote Mar. Lab.* 1(2):1–98.

———. 1974b. *Shark Attack*. Berkeley.

BANSE, K. 1990. Mermaids—Their Biology, Culture, and Demise. *Limnology and Oceanography* 35(1):148–53.

BARBER, V. C. 1968. The Structure of Mollusc Statocysts, with Particular Reference to Cephalopods. *Symp. Zool. Soc. London* 23:37–62.

BARCLAY, J. 1811. Remarks on Some Parts of the Animal That Was Cast Ashore on the Island of Stronsa, September, 1808. *Mem. Werner Nat. Hist. Soc.* (Edinburgh) 1808–1811 1:431–41.

BARNUM, P. T. 1866. *The Humbugs of the World*. Carleton.

———. 1871. *Struggles and Triumphs, or, Forty Years' Recollection*. American News Company.

BARTHELMESS, K., AND J. MÜNZING. 1991. *Monstrum Horrendum: Wale und Waldarstellungen in der Druckgraphik des 16. Jahrhunderts und ihr motivkundlicher Einfluss*. Kabel. Hamburg.

BARTSCH, P. 1917. Pirates of the Deep—Stories of the Squid and Octopus. *Rep. Smithson. Inst.* 1916:347–75.

———. 1931. The Octopuses, Squids and Their Kin. *Smithsonian Science Series* 10:321–56.

BASSETT, F. 1892. *Legends and Superstitions of the Sea and of Sailors*. Morrill, Higgins.

BASSLER, R. S., C. E. RESSER, W. L. SCHMIDT, AND P. BARTSCH. 1931. *Shelled Invertebrates of the Past and Present, Vol. X.* Smithsonian Scientific Series.

BAUER, H. H. 1982. The Loch Ness Monster: Public Perception and the Evidence. *Cryptozoology* 1:40–5.

———. 1986. *The Enigma of Loch Ness.* University of Illinois Press.

BAVENDAM, F. 1991. Eye to Eye with the Giant Octopus. *National Geographic* 179(3):86–97.

BEACH, D. W., AND M. T. WEINRICH. 1989. Watching the Whales. *Oceanus* 32(1):84–8.

BEALE, T. 1835. *A Few Observations on the Natural History of the Sperm Whale.* London.

BECK, H. 1973. *Folklore of the Sea.* Wesleyan University Press.

BEEBE, W. 1926. *The Arcturus Adventure.* Putnam's.

———. 1934a. The Depths of the Sea. *National Geographic* 61:65–8.

———. 1934b. *Half Mile Down.* Harcourt, Brace.

BEL'KOVICH, V. M., AND A. V. YABLOKOV. 1963. The Whale—an Ultrasonic Projector. *Yuchnyi Tekhnik* 3:76–7.

BELON, P. 1551. *L'Histoire naturelle des étranges poissons marins avec la vraie peinture et description du Dauphin, & de plusiers autres de son espece.* R. Chaudière.

———. 1555. *La nature et la diversité des poissons avec leurs portraits, représenté au plus prés du nature.* C. Estienne.

BENCHLEY, P. 1974. *Jaws.* Doubleday.

———. 1976. *The Deep.* Doubleday.

———. 1982. *The Girl of the Sea of Cortez.* Doubleday.

———. 1991. *Beast.* Random House.

BENHAM, W. B. 1943. The Octopodus Mollusca of New Zealand. 3. The Giant Octopus *Macrotopus maorum* (Hutton)—in Youth, Adolescence and Maturity. *Trans. Royal Soc. N.Z.* 73:139–53.

BENNETT, F. D. 1840. *Narrative of a Whaling Voyage Round the Globe, from the Year 1833 to 1836 . . . with an Account of Southern Whales, the Sperm Whale Fishery, and the Natural History of the Climates Visited.* Richard Bentley.

BENWELL, G., AND A. WAUGH. 1961. *Sea Enchantress: The Tale of the Mermaid and Her Kin.* Hutchinson.

BERCAW, M. K. 1989. Melville's Borrowings. *The Log of Mystic Seaport* 41(2):35–44.

BERGMAN, B. 1982. Tentacled Encounters. *Equinox* 3(3):130.

BERRA, T. M., AND B. HUTCHINS. 1990. A Specimen of Megamouth Shark, *Megachasma pelagios* (Megachasmidae) from Western Australia. *Rec. West. Aust. Mus.* 14(4):651–6.

———. 1991. Natural History Notes on the Megamouth Shark, *Megachasma pelagios*, from Western Australia. *West. Aust. Nat.* 18(8):224–34.

BERRY, S. S. 1952. The Flapjack Devilfish, *Opisthoteuthis*, in California. *Calif. Fish and Game* 38:183–8.

———. 1955. The Male Flapjack Devilfish. *Calif. Fish and Game* 41(3):219–24.

BERZIN, A. A. 1972. *The Sperm Whale.* Izdatel'stvo "Pischevaya Promyshlennost" Moskva 1971 (Israel Program for Scientific Translation 1972).

BESTON, H. 1928. *The Outermost House.* Holt, Rinehart & Winston.

BEZANSON, W. E. 1986. *Moby-Dick:* Document, Drama, Dream. In J. Bryant, Ed., *A Companion to Melville Studies*, pp. 169–210. Greenwood Press.

BIGELOW, J. 1820. Documents and Remarks Respecting the Sea-Serpent. *Amer. Jour. Sci.* 12:147–64.

BIRD, C. 1878. The Sea Serpent Explained. *Nature* 18:519.

BLAKE, J. H. 1909. A Giant Squid. *Nautilus* 23:33, 43–4.

BLECKMANN, H., B.-U. BUDELMANN, AND T. H. BULLOCK. 1991. Peripheral and Central Nervous Responses Evoked by Small Water Movements in a Cephalopod. *Jour. Comp. Physiol.* 168:247–57.

BODINE, A. B., C. A. LUER, AND S. GANGEE. 1985. A Comparative Study of Monooxyegenase Activity in Elasmobranchs and Mammals: Activation of the Model Pro-Carcinogen Aflatoxin B$_I$ by Liver Preparations of Calf, Nurse Shark and Clearnose Skate. *Comp. Biochem. Physiol.* 82C(2):255–7.

BODINE, A. B., C. A. LUER, S. GANGEE, AND C. J. WALSH. 1989. *In Vitro* Metabolism of the Pro-Carcinogen Aflotoxin B$_I$ by Liver Preparations of the Calf, Nurse Shark and Clearnose Skate. *Comp. Biochem. Physiol.* 94C(2):447–53.

BOORSTIN, D. J. 1983. *The Discoverers.* Random House.

BOREAL INSTITUTE FOR NORTHERN STUDIES. 1988. *Small-Type Coastal Whaling in Japan.* University of Alberta.

BOSCHMA, H. 1938. On the Teeth and Some Other Particulars of the Sperm Whale (*Physeter macrocephalus* L.). *Temminckia* III:261–2.

BOUYER, M. 1861. Poulpe géant observé entre Madere et Ténériffe. *Comptes Rendus des Séances de l'Académie des Sciences* (Paris).

BOWEN, S. L. 1974. The Probable Extinction of the Korean Stock of the Gray Whale. *Jour. Mammal.* 55(1):208–9.

BOYCOTT, B. B. 1953. The Chromatophore System of Cephalopods. *Proc. Linn. Soc. London* 164:235–40.

———. 1954. Learning in *Octopus vulgaris* and Other Cephalopods. *Pubbl. Staz. Zool. Napoli* 25:67–93.

———. 1965. Learning in the Octopus. *Scientific American* 212(3):42–50.

BOYD, E. 1975. Monster Teeth of Chesapeake Bay. *Skin Diver* 24(1):5–9.

BOYLE, P. R. 1984. Giant Squid Strands in Scotland. *Porcupine Newsletter* 3:12.

———. 1986. Report on a Specimen of *Architeuthis* Stranded near Aberdeen, Scotland. *Jour. Mollusc. Studies* 52:81–2.

BRADBURY, R. 1992. *Green Shadows, White Whale.* Knopf.

BRADLEY, K. 1991. Monster from the Deep. *St. Augustine Record* Sept. 14, 1991:1.

BRANSTETTER, S. 1990. Shark Early Life History—One Reason Sharks Are Vulnerable to Overfishing. In S. M. Gruber, Ed., *Discovering Sharks,* pp. 29–34. American Littoral Society.

BRELAND, O. 1953. Which Are the Biggest? *Natural History* 62:67–71.

BREWINGTON, M. V., AND D. BREWINGTON. 1965. *Kendall Museum Paintings.* Kendall Whaling Museum.

———. 1969. *Kendall Museum Prints.* Kendall Whaling Museum.

BRIGHT, C. 1991. *Sea Serpents.* Bowling Green State University Press.

BRIGHT, M. 1985. The Big Blob. *BBC Wildlife* September 1985:430–3.

BRIGHT, M. 1992. *There Are Giants in the Sea.* Robson.

BRINKMANN, A. 1916. Kjaempeblekspruten (*Architeuthis dux* Stp.) i Bergens Museum. *Naturen* 40(6):175–82.

BRIX, O. 1983. Giant Squid May Die When Exposed to Warm Water. *Nature* 303:422–3.

BROWN, C. M. 1990. A Natural History of the Gloucester Sea Serpent: Knowledge, Power, and the Culture of Science in Antebellum America. *American Quarterly* 42(3):402–36.

BROWN, J. R. 1846. *Etchings of a Whaling Cruise, with Notes of a Sojourn on the Island of Zanzibar. To Which Is Appended a Brief History of the Whale Fishery, Its Past and Present Condition.* Harper & Brothers. Reprinted 1968 by Harvard University Press.

BROWN, R. 1981. *Megalodon.* Coward, McCann & Geoghegan.

BROWNLEE, S. 1985. On the Track of the Real Shark. *Discover* 6(7):26–38.

BRUSSARD, P. F. 1986. The Likelihood of Persistence of Small Populations of Large Animals and Its Implications for Cryptozoolgy. *Cryptozoolgy* 5:38–46.

BRUUN, A. 1945. Cephalopoda. *Zoology Iceland* 4(64):1–15.

———. 1956. *The Galathea Deep Sea Expedition, 1950–1952.* Macmillan.

———. 1959. Why I Believe in Sea Monsters. *Popular Science Monthly* 175:99–103, 270.

BRUTON, M. N., and S. E. COUTIVIIDIS. 1991. An Inventory of All Known Specimens of the Coelacanth, *Latimeria chalumnae*, with Comments on Trends in the Catches. *Env. Biol. Fishes* 30:371-90.

BRUTON, M. N., and R. E. STOBBS. 1991. The Ecology and Conservation of the Coelacanth, *Latimeria chalumnae. Env. Biol. Fishes* 30:313-40.

BRYANT, J. 1982. Trends in Melville Scholarship: Dissertations in the 1970s. *Melville Society Extracts* 50:12–13.

BRYANT, P. 1979. The Baja Sperm Whale Mass-Stranding. *Whalewatcher* 13(2):10.

BUCHANAN, J. Y. 1896. The Sperm Whale and Its Food. *Nature* 1367(53):223–5.

BUCKLAND, F. T. 1867. *Curiosities of Natural History, Second Series.* Richard Bentley.

BUDELMANN, B.-U. 1980. Equilibrium and Orientation in Cephalopods. *Oceanus* 23(3):34-43.

———. 1990. The Statocysts of Squid. In D. L. Gilbert, W. J. Adelman, and J. M. Arnold, Eds., *Squid as Experimental Animals,* pp. 421–2. Plenum.

———. 1992. Hearing in Nonarthropod Invertebrates. In D. B. Webster, R. R. Fay, and A. N. Popper, Eds., *The Evolutionary Biology of Hearing,* pp. 141–55. Springer-Verlag.

BUDELMANN, B.-U., AND H. BLECKMANN. 1988. A Lateral Line Analogue in Cephalopods: Water Waves Generate Microphonic Potentials in the Epidermal Head Lines of *Sepia* and *Lollinguncula. Jour. Comp. Physiol.* 164:1–5.

BUDELMANN, B.-U., U. RIESE, AND H. BLECKMANN. 1991. Structure, Function, Biological Significance of the Cuttlefish "Lateral Lines." In E. Boucaud-Comou, Ed., *The Cuttlefish,* pp. 201–9. Centre de Publications de l'Université de Caen.

BUDKER, P. 1959. *Whales and Whaling.* Macmillan.

———. 1968. Stranding of Pilot Whales (*Globicephala melaena* [Traill]) on the Coast of Normandy, France. *Norsk Hvalfangst-Tidende* 57(1):17–19.

———. 1971. *The Life of Sharks.* Columbia University Press.

BULLEN, F. T. 1898. *The Cruise of the "Cachalot": Round the World After Sperm Whales.* Appleton.

———. 1902. *Deep-Sea Plunderings.* Appleton.

———. 1904. *Denizens of the Deep.* Revell.

BURTON, M. 1954. *Living Fossils.* Thames & Hudson.

———. 1957. *Animal Legends.* Coward-McCann.

———. 1959. *More Animal Legends.* Muller.

BUSCHBAUM, R., AND L. J. MILNE. 1960. *The Lower Animals: Living Invertebrates of the World.* Doubleday.

BUSSE, P. 1993. Underwater Slaughter [Sharks]. *SF Weekly* 12(7):10–11.

BYRNE, M. ST. C. 1926. *The Elizabethan Zoo: A Book of Beasts Both Fabulous and Authentic.* Based on Topsell's *Historie* [1608], Pliny's *Natural History,* and Gesner's *Historia Animalium.* Haslewood Books.

CADENAT, J. 1935. Note sur la Première Capture dans le Golfe de Goscogne du Céphalopode Géant (*Architeuthis nawaji.*). *C. r. Ass. fr. Avanc. Sci.* 59:513.

———. 1936. Note sur un Cephalopod Géant (*Architeuthis harveyi* Verrill) Capturé dans le Golfe de Gascogne. *Bull. Mus. Nat. Hist. Nat. Paris* 8:277–85.

CALDWELL, D. K., AND M. C. CALDWELL. 1970. Consider the Loch Ness Monster: Fact, Fiction, or Pilot Whale? *Underwater Naturalist* 6(3):16–17.

———. 1985. Manatees—*Trichecus manatus, Trichecus senegalensis,* and *Trichecus inunguis.* In S. H. Ridgway and R. J. Harrison, Eds., *Handbook of Marine Mammals, Vol. 3,* pp. 33–6. *The Sirenians and Baleen Whales.* Academic Press.

CALDWELL, D. K., M. C. CALDWELL, AND D. W. RICE. 1966. Behavior of the Sperm Whale, *Physeter catadon* L. In K. S. Norris, Ed., *Whales, Dolphins and Porpoises,* pp. 678–717. University of California Press.

CAMPBELL, E. M., AND D. SOLOMON. 1973. *The Search for Morag.* Walker.

CAMPBELL, R. R. 1988. Status of the Sea Mink *Mustela macrodon* in Canada. *Canadian Field Naturalist* 102(2):304–6.

CAMPBELL, S. 1991. *The Loch Ness Monster: The Evidence.* Aberdeen University Press.

CAPPETTA, H. 1987. Chondrichthyes II: Mesozoic and Cenozoic Elasmobranchii. Vol. 3B in *Handbook of Paleoichthyology.* Gustav Fischer Verlag.

CARRINGTON, R. 1957a. *Mermaids and Mastodons: A Book of Natural and Unnatural History.* Rinehart.

———. 1957b. Sea Serpent: Riddle of the Deep. *Natural History* 66:183–7, 222.

CASEY, J., H. PRATT, N. KOHLER, AND C. STILLWELL. 1990. Draft Secretarial Shark Fishery Management Plan for the Atlantic Ocean. *Chondros* 2(4):1–2.

CHASE, R. 1949. *Herman Melville: A Critical Study.* Macmillan.

CHUN, C. 1903. Ueber Leuchtorgane und Augen von Tiefsee-Cephalopoden. *Verh. dtsch. zool. Ges.* 13:67–91.

———. 1914. Cephalopoda from the "Michael Sars" North Atlantic Deep-Sea Expedition. *Rep. Sars N. Atl. Deep Sea Exped.* 3:1–28.

CHURCH, V. 1992. Danger: No Sharks. *Newsweek.* Dec. 14, 1992:64–5.

CLAIR, C. 1967. *Unnatural History: An Illustrated Bestiary.* Abelard Schuman.

CLARK, E. 1981. Sharks: Magnificent and Misunderstood. *National Geographic* 160(2):138–87.

———. 1992. Whale Sharks: Gentle Monsters of the Deep. *National Geographic* 182(6):123–38.

CLARK, F. N., AND J. B. PHILLIPS. 1936. Commercial Use of the Jumbo Squid, *Dosidicus gigas. Cal. Fish and Game* 22(2):143–4.

CLARK, J. C. 1991. The Legendary Giant Octopus Resurfaces. *Orlando Sentinel* Sept. 6, 1991:1, 7.

CLARK, J. F. 1968. Serpents, Sea Creatures, and Giant Sharks. Unpublished ms.

CLARKE, A. C. 1953. *Childhood's End.* Ballantine.

———. 1957a. "Big Game Hunt." In *Tales from the "White Hart."* Ballantine.

————. 1957b. *The Deep Range*. Harcourt, Brace.

————. 1962. "The Shining Ones." In *More Than One Universe*. Bantam.

————. 1990. *The Ghost from the Grand Banks*. Bantam.

————. 1992. Squid! A Noble Creature Defended. *Omni* 14(4):70–2.

CLARKE, M. R. 1962a. Stomach Contents of a Sperm Whale Caught off Madeira in 1959. *Norsk Hvalfangst-Tidende* 51(5):173–91.

————. 1962b. The Identification of Cephalopod "Beaks" and the Relationship Between Beak Size and Total Body Weight. *Bull. Brit. Mus. Nat. Hist. Zool.* 8(10):419–80.

————. 1966. A Review of the Systematics and Ecology of Oceanic Squids. *Adv. Mar. Biol.* 4:91–300.

————. 1970. The Function of the Spermaceti Organ of the Sperm Whale. *Nature* 228:873–4.

————. 1976a. Observation on Sperm Whale Diving. *Jour. Mar. Biol. Assoc. U.K.* 56:809–10.

————. 1976b. Cephalopod Remains from Sperm Whales Caught off Iceland. *Jour. Mar. Biol. Assoc. U.K.* 56:733–49.

————. 1977. Beaks, Nets and Numbers. In M. Nixon and J. B. Messenger, Eds., *The Biology of Cephalopods,* pp. 89–126. Symposia of the Zoological Society of London. Academic Press.

————. 1978. Structure and Proportions of the Spermaceti Organ in the Sperm Whale. *Jour. Mar. Biol. Assoc. U.K.* 58:1–17.

————. 1979. The Head of the Sperm Whale. *Scientific American* 240(1):128–41.

————. 1980. Cephalopoda in the Diet of Sperm Whales of the Southern Hemisphere and Their Bearing on Sperm Whale Biology. *Discovery Reports.* 37:1–324.

————. 1983. Cephalopod Biomass—Estimation from Predation. *Mem. Nat. Mus. Victoria* 44:95–107.

————. 1985. Cephalopods in the Diet of Cetaceans and Seals. *Rapp. Comm. int. Mer Medit.* 29(8):211–19.

————. 1986. *A Handbook for the Identification of Cephalopod Beaks*. Clarendon Press.

————. 1988. Squids. *Biologist* 35(2):69–75.

CLARKE, M. R., AND G. E. MAUL. 1962. A Description of the "Scaled" Squid *Lepidoteuthis grimaldi* Joubin 1895. *Proc. Zool. Soc. London* 139(1):97–118.

CLARKE, M. R., AND N. MERRETT. 1972. The Significance of Squid, Whale and Other Remains from the Stomachs of Bottom-living Deep-sea Fish. *Jour. Mar. Biol. Assoc. U.K.* 52:599–603.

CLARKE, M. R., E. J. DENTON, AND J. B. GILPIN-BROWN. 1979. On the Use of Ammonium for Buoyancy in Squids. *Jour. Mar. Biol. Assoc. U.K.* 59:259–76.

CLARKE, M. R., N. MACLEOD, AND O. PALIZA. 1976. Cephalopod Remains from the Stomachs of Sperm Whales Caught off Peru and Chile. *Jour. Mar. Biol. Assoc. U.K.* 180:477–93.

CLARKE, R. 1955. A Giant Squid Swallowed by a Sperm Whale. *Norsk Hvalfangst-Tidende* 44(10):589–93.

CLARKE, W. J. 1933. Giant Squid (New to Science) at Scarborough. *Naturalist* 918:157–8.

COERR, E., AND W. E. EVANS. 1980. *Gigi: A Baby Whale Borrowed for Science and Returned to the Sea.* Putnam's.

COHEN, D. 1970. *A Modern Look at Monsters.* Dodd, Mead.

COLBERT, E. H. 1955. *Evolution of the Vertebrates.* Wiley.

COLE, K. S., AND D. L. GILBERT. 1970. Jet Propulsion of the Squid. *Biol. Bull.* 138:245–6.

COLES, R. J. 1916. Natural History Notes on the Devilfish, *Manta birostris* (Walbaum) and *Mobula olfersi* (Muller). *Bull. Amer. Mus. Nat. Hist.* 35:649–57.

————. 1919. The Large Sharks of Cape Lookout, North Carolina: The White Shark or Maneater, Tiger Shark and Hammerhead. *Copeia* 69:34–43.

COLINVAUX, P. 1978. *Why Big Fierce Animals Are Rare.* Princeton University Press.

COLLODI, C. 1882. *The Adventures of Pinocchio.* 1946 edition, translated by M. A. Murray, Grosset & Dunlap.

COLUM, P. 1960. *Legends of Hawaii.* Yale University Press.

COMPAGNO, L. J. V. 1981. Legend vs. Reality: The Jaws Image and Shark Diversity. *Oceanus* 24(4):5–16.

————. 1984. *FAO Species Catalog. Sharks of the World. An Annotated and Illustrated Catalog of Shark Species Known to Date. Vol. 4, Part 1: Carcharhiniformes.* UN Development Programme.

————. 1991. White Shark Gains Government Protection in South Africa. *Chondros* 2(7):2–3.

CONNIFF, R. 1993. From *Jaws* to Laws—Now the Big, Bad Shark Needs Protection from Us. *Smithsonian* 24(2):32–42.

COOK, S. F. 1990. Trends in Shark Fin Markets: 1980, 1990, and Beyond. *Chondros* 2(1):3–6.

CORMAN, R., AND J. JEROME. 1990. *How I Made a Hundred Movies in Hollywood and Never Lost a Dime.* Delta.

COSTELLO, P. 1974. *In Search of Lake Monsters.* Coward, McCann & Geoghegan.

COUCH, J. 1867. *A History of the Fishes of the British Islands, Vol. I.* Groombridge.

COURTENAY-LATIMER, M. 1989. Reminiscences of the Discovery of the Coelacanth, *Latimeria chalumnae* Smith. *Cryptozoology* 8:1–11.

COUSTEAU, J.-Y. 1953. *The Silent World.* Doubleday.

COUSTEAU, J.-Y., AND P. COUSTEAU. 1970. *The Shark: Splendid Savage of the Sea.* Doubleday.

COUSTEAU, J.-Y., AND P. DIOLÉ. 1973a. Last Dance on the Mating Ground. *Natural History* 82(4):45–8.

————. 1973b. *Octopus and Squid: The Soft Intelligence.* Doubleday.

CROKER, R. S. 1934. Giant Squid Taken at Laguna Beach. *Cal. Fish and Game* 20(3):297.

————. 1937. Further Notes on the Jumbo Squid, *Dosidicus gigas. Cal. Fish and Game* 23(3):246–7.

CROPP, B. 1972. The Mini-Killers: Australia's Deadly Little Cephalopod Beauty. *Oceans* 5(1):40.

————. 1982. Timeless Hunters. *Oceans* 15(6):16–20.

CROSSE, H., AND P. FISCHER. 1862. Nouveaux Documents sur les Céphalopodes Gigantesque. *J. Conch. Paris* 10:124–40.

CZERKAS, S. M., AND D. R. GLUT. 1982. *Dinosaurs, Mammoths and Cavemen: The Art of Charles R. Knight.* Dutton.

DAETZ, G. 1955. Meet and Eat the Octopus. *Natural History* 64:210–13.

DALL, W. H. 1873. Aleutian Cephalopods. *American Naturalist* 7:484–5.

————. 1885. The Arms of the Octopus, or Devil Fish. *Science* 6:432.

DAMPIER, W. 1697. *A New Voyage Round the World.* Knapton. 1927 edition, Argonaut Press.

DANCE, P. 1976. *Animal Fakes & Frauds.* Sampson Low.

DARLING, J. 1994. Seeing Ghosts: Gray Whales in the Orient. *Ocean Realm* January 1994:18–19.

DAVIDSON, M. E. M. 1929. Baird's Beaked Whale at Santa Cruz, Calif. *Jour. Mammal.* 10:356–8.

DAVIS, E. Y. 1946. "Man in Whale." Letter to the Editor. *Natural History* 6:241.

DAVIS, F. H. 1912. *Myths and Legends of Japan.* Harrap.

DAY, D. 1987. *The Whale War.* Routledge & Kegan Paul.

DEAR, J. 1991. Answers to Cancer May Lie with Sharks Under the Sea. *Washington Post* December 10:28.

DEARDEN, J. C. 1958. A Stranding of Killer Whales in Newfoundland. *Canadian Field Naturalist* 72:166–7.

DE LATIL, P., AND J. RIVOIRE. 1956. *Man and the Underwater World.* Putnam's.

DELL, R. K. 1952. The Recent Cephalopoda of New Zealand. *Dominion Mus. Bull.* 16:1–157.

———. 1970. A Specimen of the Giant Squid *Architeuthis* from New Zealand. *Rec. Dominion Mus.* 7(4):25–36.

DE MONTFORT, P. D. 1802. *Histoire naturelle genérale et particulière des mollusques.* From Sonnini's expanded edition of Buffon's *Natural History.*

DENTON, E. J. 1974. On Buoyancy and the Livers of Modern and Fossil Cephalopods. *Proc. Royal Soc. London* B 185(1080):273–99.

DEWHURST, H. W. 1834. *The Natural History of the Order Cetacea, and the Oceanic Inhabitants of the Arctic Regions.* London.

DEXTER, R. W. 1986. Cape Ann Visits of the Great Sea Serpent (1639–1886). *American Neptune* 46:213–20.

DIETZ, T. 1992. *The Call of the Siren: Manatees and Dugongs.* Fulcrum.

DILLY, P. N. 1972. *Taonius megalops,* a Squid that Rolls Up into a Ball. *Nature* 237(5355):403–4.

———. 1973. The Enigma of Colouration and Light Emission in Deep-Sea Animals. *Endeavour* 31(115):25–9.

DILLY, P. N., AND P. J. HERRING. 1978. The Light Organ and Ink Sac of *Heteroteuthis dispar* (Mollusca: Cephalopoda). *Jour. Zool., London* 186(1):47–59.

———. 1981. Ultrastructural Features of the Light Organs of *Histioteuthis macrohista* (Mollusca: Cephalopoda). *Jour. Zool., London* 195(2):255–66.

DILLY, P. N., M. NIXON, AND J. Z. YOUNG. 1977. *Magistoteuthis,* the Whiplash Squid. *Jour. Zool., London* 18(4):527–59.

DOMNING, D. P. 1981. Manatees of the Amazon. *Sea Frontiers* 27(1):18–23.

DONOVAN, D. T. 1977. Evolution of the Dibranchiate Cephalopoda. In M. Nixon and J. B. Messenger, Eds., *The Biology of Cephalopods,* pp. 15–48. Academic Press.

DOTTRENS, E. 1965. Un Curieux Diable de Mer. *Musées de Genève* 6(51):6–8.

DOUGLAS, C. 1770. An Account of the Results of Some Attempts Made to Ascertain the Temperature of the Sea in Great Depths, Near the Coasts of Lapland and Norway, and Also Some Anecdotes. *Phil. Trans.* 60:39–43.

DOUGLAS, N. 1929. *Birds and Beasts of the Greek Anthology.* Cape.

DOUGLAS, S. 1982. To Save a Vanishing Floridian. *Oceans* 15(6):8–15.

DOZIER, T. A. 1976. *Dangerous Sea Creatures.* Time-Life Books.

DUDOK VAN HEEL, W. H. 1962. Sound and Cetacea. *Netherlands Jour. Sea Res.* 1:405–7.

DUGAN, J. 1956. *Man Under the Sea.* Harper.

DUNCAN, D. 1941. Fighting Giants of the Humboldt. *National Geographic* 79(3):373–400.

DUNCAN, N. 1940. "The Adventure of the Giant Squid of Chain Tickle." In E. Johnson and C. E. Scott, Eds., *Anthology of Children's Literature,* pp. 621–3. Houghton Mifflin.

DYBAS, C. L. 1993. The Oarfish "Sea Serpent" Remains Mystery of Science. *Oceanus* 36(1):98–100.

EARLE, S. A. 1991. Sharks, Squids, and Horseshoe Crabs—The Significance of Marine Biodiversity. *BioScience* 41(7):506–9.

EARLE, S. A., AND A. GIDDINGS. 1980. *Exploring the Deep Frontier.* National Geographic Society.

EDGERTON, H. E., C. W. WYCKOFF, R. H. RINES, R. NEEDLEMAN, AND J. C. RINES. 1989. AAS Underwater Elapsed Time Camera Silhouette Photography Experiments at Loch Ness, 1989. *Cryptozoology* 8:58–63.

EGEDE, H. 1745. *A Description of Greenland.* London.

EHRLICH, P., AND A. EHRLICH. 1981. *Extinction: The Causes and Consequences of the Disappearance of Species.* Random House.

EISELEY, L. 1978. "The Long Loneliness." In *The Star Thrower,* pp. 37–44. Times Books.

ELLIS, R. 1975. *The Book of Sharks.* Grosset & Dunlap.

———. 1980. *The Book of Whales.* Knopf.

———. 1981. A Visitor from Inner Space. *Animal Kingdom* 84(4):5–11.

———. 1982. *Dolphins and Porpoises.* Knopf.

———. 1986. The Hagiography of the Whale. *Whalewatcher* 20(1):11–15.

———. 1987a. The Legendary Shark. In J. D. Stevens, Ed., *Sharks,* pp. 170–85. Golden Press. Drummoyne, Australia.

———. 1987b. Why Do Whales Strand? *Oceans* 20(3):24–9, 63.

———. 1987c. Australia's Southern Seas. *National Geographic* 173(3):286–319.

———. 1989. The Exhibition of Whales. *Whalewatcher* 23(4):11–14.

———. 1991. *Men and Whales.* Knopf.

———. 1993. *Physty: The True Story of a Young Whale's Rescue.* Running Press.

ELLIS, R., AND J. E. MCCOSKER. 1991. *Great White Shark.* HarperCollins and Stanford University Press.

ELLIS, W. S. 1977. Loch Ness: The Lake and the Legend. *National Geographic* 151(6):758–79.

EVANS, W. E., AND E. S. HERALD. 1970. Underwater Calls of a Captive Amazon Manatee, *Trichechus inunguis. Jour. Mammal* 51(4):820–3.

EYLES, V. A. 1954. Nicolaus Steno, Seventeenth-century Anatomist, Geologist, and Ecclesiastic. *Nature* 174:8–10.

FERNICOLA, R. G. 1987. *In Search of the "Jersey Man-Eater."* George Marine Library.

FICHTER, G. S. 1980. Tentacles of Terror. *International Wildlife* 10(1):12–16.

FIORITO, G., AND P. SCOTTO. 1992. Observational Learning in *Octopus vulgaris. Science* 256:545–7.

FISCUS, C. H., AND D. W. RICE. 1974. Giant Squids, *Architeuthis* sp., from Stomachs of Sperm Whales Captured off California. *Cal. Fish and Game* 60(2):91–3.

FISCUS, C. H., D. W. RICE, AND A. A. WOLMAN. 1989. Cephalopods from the Stomachs of Sperm Whales Taken off California. *NOAA Technical Report NMFS* 83:1–12.

FITCH, J. E., AND R. J. LAVENBERG. 1968. *Deep-water Fishes of California.* University of California Press.

FLECKER, H., AND B. C. COTTON. 1955. Fatal Bite from Octopus. *Med. Jour. Aust.* 1:464.

FLEISCHER, R. 1993. *Just Tell Me When to Cry: A Memoir.* Carroll & Graf.

FLETCHER, H. O. 1959. A Giant Marine Reptile from the Cretaceous Rocks of Queensland. *Aust. Mus. Mag.* 13(2):47–9.

FORD, C. 1966. *Where the Sea Breaks Its Back.* Little, Brown.

FORSTEN, A., AND P. M. YOUNGMAN. 1982. *Hydrodamalis gigas.* 165:1–3. American Society of Mammalogists.

FORTI, A. 1929. Su un Basilico. *Rivista di Venezia* 1929:1–8.

FRANK, S. M. 1989. "Unequal Cross Lights": Melville's Pictures and the Aesthetics of a Sometime Whaleman. *The Log of Mystic Seaport* 41(2):45–55.

FRASER, F. C. 1934. Report on Cetacea Stranded on the British Coasts from 1927 to 1932. *Bull. Brit. Mus. (Nat. Hist.)* 11:1–41.

———. 1946. Report on Cetacea Stranded on the British Coasts from 1933 to 1937. *Bull. Brit. Mus. (Nat. Hist.)* 12:1–55.

———. 1953. Report on Cetacea Stranded on the British Coasts from 1938 to 1947. *Bull. Brit. Mus. (Nat. Hist.)* 13:1–48.

———. 1974. Report on Cetacea Stranded on the British Coasts from 1948 to 1966. *Bull. Brit. Mus. (Nat. Hist.)* 14:1–65.

FRASER, F. C., AND P. E. PURVES. 1960. Hearing in Cetaceans. *Bull. Brit. Mus. (Nat. Hist.) Zool.* 7:1–140.

FRAZIER, J., AND H. HATHORNE. 1984. 20,000 Leagues Under the Sea: The Filming of Jules Verne's Classic Science Fiction Novel. *Cinefantastique* 14(3):32–53.

FRICKE, H., J. SCHAUER, K. HISSMAN, L. KASANG, AND R. PLANTE. 1991. Coelacanth, *Latimeria chalumnae*, Aggregates in Caves: First Observations on their Resting Habitat and Social Behavior. *Env. Biol. Fishes* 30: 281–85.

FRICKE, H., J. SCHAUER, O. REINICKE, L. KASANG, AND R. PLANTE. 1991. Habitat and Population Size of the Coelacanth, *Latimeria chalumnae*, at Grand Comoro. *Env. Biol. Fishes* 30: 287–300.

FROST, N. 1934. Notes on a Giant Squid (*Architeuthis* sp.) Captured at Dildo, Newfoundland, in December 1933. *Rep. Newf. Fish. Comm.* 2(2):100–14.

———. 1936. A Further Species of Giant Squid (*Architeuthis* sp.) from Newfoundland Waters. *Rep. Newf. Fish. Comm.* 2(5):89–95.

FRY, R., AND P. FOURZON. 1977. *The Saga of Special Effects.* Prentice-Hall.

FUSON, R. H. (ED.) 1987. *The Log of Christopher Columbus.* International Marine Publishing Company.

FUSSMAN, C. 1991. Hunting the Hunter. *Life* 14(10):22–30.

GARMAN, S. 1884. In Regard to the "Sea-Serpent" of Literature. *Bull. U.S. Fish. Commission* 4:128.

GASKIN, D. E., AND M. W. CAWTHORN. 1967. Diet and Feeding Habits of the Sperm Whale (*Physeter catodon* L.) in the Cook Strait Region of New Zealand. *N.Z. Jour. Mar. Freshwater Res.* 1(2):156–79.

GENNARO, J. F. 1971. The Creature Revealed. *Natural History* 80(3):24, 84.

GEORGE, W. 1969. *Animals and Maps.* Secker and Warburg.

GERACI, J. R. 1978. The Enigma of Marine Mammal Strandings. *Oceanus* 21:38–47.

GERMAN, A. 1992. This Must Be That Animal Called the Sea-Serpent: Captain M'Quhae's Sea Monster. *Log of Mystic Seaport* 44(3):74–5.

GESNER, C. 1551–87. *Historia Animalium.* Zurich.

GILBERT, P. W., AND C. GILBERT. 1973. Sharks and Shark Deterrents. *Underwater Journal* 5(2): 69–79.

GILMORE, R. M. 1957. Whales Aground in the Cortés Sea: Tragic Strandings in the Gulf of California. *Pacific Discovery* 10:22–7.

———. 1959. On the Mass Strandings of Sperm Whales. *Pacific Naturalist* 1:9–16.

GILPIN-BROWN, J. B. 1977. The Squid and Its Giant Nerve Fibre. In M. Nixon and J. B. Messenger, Eds., *The Biology of Cephalopods*, pp. 233–60. Symposia of the Zoological Society of London. Academic Press.

GLASS, K., AND K. ENGLUND. 1989. Why the Japanese Are So Stubborn About Whaling. *Oceanus* 32(1):45–55.

GOLDER, F. A. 1925. *Bering's Voyages*. American Geographical Society.

GOLDSMITH, O. 1774. *An History of the Earth and Animated Nature*. 8 Vols. J. Nourse.

GOODRICH, S. G. 1859. *Illustrated Natural History of the Animal Kingdom, Being a Systematic and Popular Description of the Habits, Structure, and Classification of Animals*. New York.

GOODWIN, G. G. 1946. The End of the Great Northern Sea Cow. *Natural History* 55(2):55–61.

GORDON, D. G. 1987. What Is That? (Cryptozoology). *Oceans* 20(4):44–9.

GORDON, D. G., AND A. BALDRIDGE. 1991. *Gray Whales*. Monterey Bay Aquarium Foundation.

GORE, R. 1992. Dinosaurs. *National Geographic* 183(1):2–53.

GOSLINE, J. M., AND M. E. DEMONT. 1984. Jet-propelled Swimming in Squids. *Scientific American* 252(1):96–103.

GOSSE, P. H. 1861. *The Romance of Natural History*. James Nisbet.

GOTTLIEB, C. 1975. *The Jaws Log*. Dell.

GOULD, R. T. 1930. *The Case for Sea-Serpents*. Philip Allen.

———. 1934. *The Loch Ness Monster and Others*. Geoffrey Bles.

GOULD, S. J. 1989. *Wonderful Life: The Burgess Shale and the Nature of History*. W. W. Norton.

GRAVES, W. 1976. The Imperiled Giants. *National Geographic* 150(6):722–51.

GREENWELL, J. R. 1983. "Sea Serpents" Seen off California Coast. *ISC Newsletter* 2(4):9–10.

———. 1985a. Second Megamouth Shark Found. *ISC Newsletter* 4(1):5.

———. 1985b. Giant Octopus Blamed for Deep Sea Fishing Disruptions. *ISC Newsletter* 4(3):1–6.

———. 1988a. Bermuda Blob Remains Unidentified. *ISC Newsletter* 7(3):1–6.

———. 1988b. Third Megamouth Found. *ISC Newsletter* 7(4):4.

———. 1991. Megamouth Caught Alive and Studied. *ISC Newsletter* 10(2):1–3.

GREGORY, W. K. 1934. The Loch Ness Monster. *Natural History* 34(7):674–6.

———. 1935. Nature's Sea Serpent. *Natural History* 35(5):431–7.

GRIEG, J. A. 1933. Cephalopods from the West Coast of Norway. *Bergens Mus. Aarb.* 1(4):1–25.

GRIMBLE, A. 1952. *A Pattern of Islands*. John Murray.

GRØNNINGSAETER, A. 1946. Sjørmen-blekksprutten. *Naturen* 70:379–80.

GRUBER, S. H. (ED.) 1990. *Discovering Sharks*. American Littoral Society.

GRUBER, S. H., AND C. A. MANIRE. 1989. Challenge of the Chondrichthyans. *Chondros* 1(1):1–3.

———. 1990. The Only Good Shark Is a Dead Shark? In S. H. Gruber, Ed., *Discovering Sharks*, pp. 115–21. American Littoral Society.

GRUBER, S. H., AND J. F. MORRISSEY. 1990. Shark vs. Man: Are Sharks Losing the Battle? *Underwater Naturalist* 19(1):3–7.

GUDGER, E. W. 1934. Jenny Hanivers, Dragons, and Basilisks in the Old Natural History Books and in Modern Times. *Scientific Monthly* 38:511–23.

———. 1940. Whale Sharks Rammed by Ocean Vessels. *N. Eng. Nat.* 7:1–10.

GUITART-MANDAY, D., AND J. MILERAS. 1974. El Monstruo Marino de Cojimar. *Mary Pesca* 104:10–11.

HAGELUND, W. A. 1987. *Whalers No More*. Harbour Publishing.

HALEY, D. 1978. Saga of Steller's Sea Cow. *Natural History* 87(9):9–17.

HALL, A. 1976. *Monsters and Mythic Beasts*. Doubleday.

HALL, A. J. 1984. Man and Manatee: Can We Live Together? *National Geographic* 166(3):400–13.

HALL, H. 1991. Mugged by a Squid! *Ocean Realm* Spring 1991:6–7.

HALSTEAD, B. W. 1959. *Dangerous Marine Animals*. Cornell Maritime Press.

HALSTEAD, B. W., AND D. D. DANIELSON. 1970. Death from the Depths. *Oceans* 3(6):14–25.

HAMILTON, J. E. 1914. Belmullet Whaling Station. Report of the Committee. *Rep. Br. Ass. Adv. Sci.* 125–61, 137–8.

HAMILTON, R. 1845. *Amphibious Carnivora*. In William Jardine, Ed., *The Naturalists's Library: Mammalia*, W. H. Lizars.

HANLON, R. T. 1982. The Functional Organization of Chromatophores and Iridescent Cells in the Body Patterning of *Loligo plei* (Cephalopoda: Myopsida). *Malacologia* 23:89–119.

———. 1990. Maintenance, Rearing, and Culture of Teuthoid and Sepioid Squids. In D. L. Gilbert, W. J. Adelman, and J. M. Arnold, Eds., *Squid as Experimental Animals*, pp. 35–64. Plenum.

HANLON, R. T., AND B.-U. BUDELMANN. 1987. Why Cephalopods Are Probably Not "Deaf." *American Naturalist* 129(2):312–7.

HANLON, R. T., AND R. F. HIXON. 1980. Body Patterning and Field Observations of *Octopus burryi* Voss, 1950. *Bull. Mar. Sci.* 30:749–55.

HARDY, A. C. 1956. *The Open Sea: Its Natural History. Part I: The World of Plankton*. Houghton Mifflin.

———. 1959. *The Open Sea: Its Natural History. Part II: Fish and Fisheries*. Houghton Mifflin.

———. 1967. *Great Waters*. Harper.

HARMER, S. F. 1927. Report on Cetacea Stranded on the British Coasts from 1948 to 1966. *Bull. Brit. Mus. (Nat. Hist.)* 14:1–65.

———. 1928. The History of Whaling. *Proc. Linn. Soc. London* 140:51–95.

HARRIS, D. 1972. Vagabundos del Mar: Shark Fishermen of the Sea of Cortez. *Oceans* 5(1):60–72.

HARRIS, N. 1973. *Humbug: The Art of P. T. Barnum*. Little, Brown.

HARTMAN, D. S. 1969. Florida's Manatees: Mermaids in Peril. *National Geographic* 136(3):342–53.

———. 1979. *Ecology and Behavior of the Manatee (Trichechus manatus) in Florida*. Spec. Publ. No. 5. American Society of Mammalogists.

HARVEY, E. N. 1952. *Bioluminscence*. Academic Press.

HARVEY, M. 1874. Gigantic Cuttlefishes in Newfoundland. *Ann. Mag. Nat. Hist.* 13:67–70.

———. 1879. Article in the *Boston Traveller* January 30, 1879.

———. 1899. How I Discovered the Great Devil-fish. *Wide World Magazine* 2:732–40.

HASEGAWA, Y., AND T. UYENO. 1978. On the Nature of a Large Vertebrate Found off of New Zealand. In *Collected Papers on the Carcass of an Unidentified Animal Trawled off New Zealand by the Zuiyo-Maru*, pp. 63–5. Société Franco-Japonaise d'Oceanographie. Tokyo.

HASS, H. 1952. *Manta: Under the Red Sea with Gun and Camera.* Rand McNally.

HAWLEY, T. M. 1989. The Whale, a Large Figure in the Collective Unconscious. *Oceanus* 32(1):112–20.

HEATH, H. 1917. Devilfish and Squid. *Calif. Fish and Game* 3(3):1–6.

HEEZEN, B. C. 1957. Whales Entangled in Deep Sea Cables. *Deep-Sea Res.* 4:105–15.

HEILNER, V. C. 1953. *Salt Water Fishing.* Knopf.

HELM, T. 1962. *Monsters of the Deep.* Dodd, Mead.

HERRING, P. J. 1977. Luminescence in Cephalopods and Fish. In M. Nixon and J. B. Messenger, Eds., *The Biology of Cephalopods,* pp. 127–59. Symposia of the Zoological Society of London. Academic Press.

HERRING, P. J., AND M. R. CLARKE (EDS.). 1971. *Deep Oceans.* Praeger.

HEUVELMANS, B. 1965. *In the Wake of the Sea-Serpents.* Hill & Wang.

———. 1984. The Birth and Early History of Cryptozoology. *Cryptozoology* 3:1–30.

———. 1990. The Metamorphosis of Unknown Animals into Fabulous Beasts and of Fabulous Beasts into Known Animals. *Cryptozoology* 9:1–12.

HIGH, W. L. 1976. The Giant Pacific Octopus. *Mar. Fish. Rev.* 38:17–22.

HILGENDORF, F. 1880. Über Einen Riesegen Tintenfisch aus Japan, *Megateuthis martensii,* g.n., sp.n. *S.B. Ges. Naturf. Fr. Berl.* 65–7.

HILL, D. O. 1975. Vanishing Giants. *Audubon* 77(1):56–107.

HOCHBERG, F. G. 1974. Southern California Records of the Giant Squid, *Moroteuthis robusta. Tabulata* 7:83–5.

———. 1986. Of Beaks and Whales. *Bull. Santa Barbara Mus. Nat. Hist.* 95:1–2.

———. 1988. The Skin of Cephalopods—A Living Tapestry of Color and Texture. *Bull. Santa Barbara Mus. Nat. Hist.* 122:1.

HOCHBERG, F. G., AND W. G. FIELDS. 1980. Cephalopoda: The Squids and Octopuses. In R. H. Morris, D. P. Abbott, and E. C. Haderlie, Eds., *Intertidal Invertebrates of California,* pp. 429–44. Stanford University Press.

HOFBAUER, C. 1964. Sea-Cows—The Sirens of the Odyssey? *Animals* 4(8):220–3.

HOFMAN, R. J. 1989. The Marine Mammal Protection Act: A First of Its Kind Anywhere. *Oceanus* 32(1):21–8.

HOHMAN, E. P. 1928. *The American Whaleman.* Longmans, Green.

HOLDER, C. F. 1899. Some Pacific Cephalopods. *Scientific American* 80:253.

HOLIDAY, F. W. 1969. *The Great Orm of Loch Ness: A Practical Inquiry into the Nature and Habits of Water-Monsters.* Norton.

HOLMES, W. 1940. The Colour Changes and Colour Patterns of *Sepia officinalis* L. *Proc. Zool. Soc. London* 110:17–35.

HOME, E. 1809. An Anatomical Account of the *Squalus maximus,* etc. *Phil. Trans. Royal Soc. London* 98:206–20.

HOYLE, W. E. 1904. Reports on the Cephalopoda from the "Albatross" Expedition. *Bull. Mus. Comp. Zool.* 43(1):1–71.

HOYT, E. 1993. Courting Oblivion [Northern Right Whales]. *Equinox* 12(2):32–43.

HUDNALL, J. 1977. In the Company of Great Whales. *Audubon* 79(3):62–73.

HUDSON, H. 1625. Divers Voyages and Northern Discoveries of Henry Hudson. In *Purchas his Pilgrimes.* London.

HUGO, V. 1866. *Toilers of the Sea.* Paris.

HUNTER, R. 1978. *To Save a Whale: The Voyages of Greenpeace.* Chronicle Books.

———. 1979. *Warriors of the Rainbow: A Chronicle of the Greenpeace Movement.* Holt, Rinehart & Winston.

HUSAR, S. L. 1977. *Trichechus inunguis* (Amazonian manatee). *Mammalian Species* 72:1–4. American Society of Mammalogists.

———. 1978a. *Dugong dugon* (Dugong). *Mammalian Species* 88:1–7. American Society of Mammalogists.

———. 1978b. *Trichechus senegalensis* (African manatee). *Mammalian Species* 89:1–3. American Society of Mammalogists.

HUSTON, J. 1980. *An Open Book.* Knopf.

HUTCHINS, B. 1992. Megamouth; Gentle Giant of the Deep. *Aust. Nat. Hist.* 23(12):910–17.

HUTCHINS, J. 1968. *Discovering Mermaids and Sea Monsters.* Shire Publications.

IDYLL, C. P. 1971. *Abyss: The Deep Sea and the Creatures That Live in It.* Crowell.

INGALLS, E. 1987. *Whaling Prints in the Francis B. Lothrop Collection.* Peabody Museum of Salem.

INGE, M. T. 1982. Melville in the Comic Books. *Melville Society Extracts* 50:9–10.

———. 1986. Melville in Popular Culture. In J. Bryant, Ed., *A Companion to Melville Studies*, pp. 695–739. Greenwood Press.

INTERNATIONAL WHALING COMMISSION. 1950–92. *Annual Report.* Cambridge.

IRVINE, A. B., AND H. W. CAMPBELL. 1978. Aerial Census of the West Indian Manatee *Trichechus manatus* in the Southeastern United States. *Jour. Mammal* 59(3):613–17.

IVERSON, I. L. K., AND L. PINKAS. 1971. A Pictorial Guide to Beaks of Certain Eastern Pacific Cephalopods. *Calif. Dept. Fish and Game, Fish Bull.* 152:83–105.

IWAI, E. 1956a. Descriptions of Unidentified Species of Dibranchiate Cephalopods I. An Oegopsiden squid belonging to the genus *Architeuthis. Sci. Rep. Whales Res. Inst.* 11:139–51.

JACKSON, G. D., C. C. LU, AND M. DUNNING. 1991. Growth Rings Within the Statolith Microstructure of the Giant Squid *Architeuthis. The Veliger* 34(4):331–4.

JAPAN WHALING ASSOCIATION. 1980. *Living with Whales.*

———. 1987. *Whales and Traditions of Diet.*

JENKINS, M. M. 1972. *The Curious Mollusks.* Holiday House.

JOHNSON, C. S. 1978. Sea Creatures and the Problem of Equipment Damage. *U.S. Naval Institute Proceedings* August:106–7.

JONES, E. C. 1963. *Tremoctopus violaceus* uses *Physalia* Tentacles as Weapons. *Science* 139:764.

———. 1971. *Isistius brasiliensis,* a Squaloid Shark, the Probable Cause of Crater Wounds in Fishes and Cetaceans. *Fish. Bull.* 69(4):791–8.

JONES, W. 1886. *The Broad, Broad Ocean and Some of Its Inhabitants.* Warne.

JOSSELYN, J. 1674. *An Account of Two Voyages to New England.* London.

JOUBIN, L. 1929. Notes préliminaires sur les céphalopodes de croisières du "Dana" (1921–1922). *Ann. Inst. Oceanogr. Monaco* 7:1–24.

JOY, J. B. 1990. The Fishery Biology of *Todarodes sagittatus* in Shetland Waters. *Jour. Cephalopod Biol.* 1(2):1–20.

KAWAKAMI, T. 1976. Squids Found in the Stomach of Sperm Whales in the Northwestern Pacific. *Sci. Rep. Whales Res. Inst.* 28:145–51.

———. 1980. A Review of Sperm Whale Food. *Sci. Rep. Whales Res. Inst.* 32:199–218.

KEMP, M. 1989. A Squid for All Seasons. *Discover* 10(6):66–70.

KENNEY, J. 1978. Tall Tales and Sea Serpents. *Oceans* 11(4):8–12.

KENT, W. S. 1874a. Note on a Gigantic Cephalopod from Conception Bay, Newfoundland. *Proc. Zool. Soc. London* 1874:178–82.

———. 1874b. A Further Communication upon Certain Gigantic Cephalopods Recently Encountered off the Coast of Newfoundland *Proc. Zool. Soc. London* 1874:489–94.

KERSTITCH, A. 1991. Attack of the Devilfish. *Baja Explorer* Nov./Dec. 1991.

———. 1992. Primates of the Sea [Octopuses]. *Discover* 13(2):34–8.

KIPLING, R. 1893. "The White Seal." In *The Jungle Book*. The Century Company. 1950 edition, Grosset & Dunlap.

KIRK, T. W. 1880. On the Occurrence of Giant Cuttlefish on the New Zealand Coast. *Trans. N.Z. Inst.* 12:310–13.

———. 1888. Brief Description of a New Species of Large Decapod (*Architeuthis longimanus*). *Trans. N.Z. Inst.* 20:34–9.

KLINOWSKA, M. 1989. How Brainy Are Cetaceans? *Oceanus* 32(1):19–20.

KNIGHT, C. R. 1935. *Before the Dawn of History*. McGraw-Hill.

———. 1946. *Life Through the Ages*. Knopf.

KNUDSEN, J. 1957. Some Observations on a Mature Male Specimen of *Architeuthis* from Danish Waters. *Proc. Malacol. Soc. London* 32:189–98.

KOCH, A. C. 1845a. *Description of the Hydrargos sillimani (Koch), a Gigantic Fossil Reptile, or Sea-Serpent Lately Discovered by the Author, in the State of Alabama, March, 1845*. B. Owen.

———. 1845b. *Description of the Hydrargos harlani (Koch)*. B. Owen.

KOSTER, J. 1977. What Was the New Zealand Monster? *Oceans* 10(6):56–9.

KOZAK, V. A. 1974. Receptor Zone of the Video-Acoustic System of the Sperm Whale (*Physeter catadon* L, 1758). *Fiziologichnyy Zhurnal Akademy Nauk Ukrayns'koy RSR*. 20(3):317–21. Translated by Joint Publication Research Service, Arlington, Va.

KRAUS, S. D. 1989. Whales for Profit. *Whalewatcher* 23(2):18–19.

KRUTCH, J. W. 1970. Unnatural History. *Audubon* 72(6):36–40.

LACÉPÈDE, C. 1798. *Histoire naturelle des poissons*. Plassan.

LA GORCE, J. O. 1919. Devil-fishing in the Gulf Stream. *National Geographic* 35(6):476–88.

LANE, F. W. 1941. The Great Sea-Serpent. *The Field* 178:548–50.

———. 1974. *Kingdom of the Octopus*. Sheridan House.

LANGE, M. M. 1920. On the Regeneration and Finer Structure of the Arms of the Cephalopods. *Jour. Exp. Biol.* 31:1–40.

LANGTON, J. 1994. "Revealed: The Loch Ness Picture Hoax. Monster was a toy submarine." *Sunday Telegraph*, March 13, 1994:1, 3.

LARSON, L. M. (TRANS.) 1917. *The King's Mirror*. Oxford University Press.

LEBELSON, H., AND B. RUSH. 1985. Garadiavolo: The Devil Monster Hoax. *Sea Frontiers* 31(3):164–7.

LEBLOND, P. H. 1983. A Previously Unreported "Sea-Serpent" Sighting in the South Atlantic. *Cryptozoology* 2:82–4.

LEBLOND, P. H., AND E. L. BOUSFIELD. 1993. Preliminary Studies on the Biology of a Large Marine Cryptid in Coastal Waters of British Columbia. In press.

LEBLOND, P. H., AND M. J. COLLINS. 1987. The Wilson Nessie Photo: A Size Determination Based on Physical Principles. *Cryptozoology* 6:55–64.

LEBLOND, P. H., AND J. SIBERT. 1973. Observations of Large Unidentified Marine Animals in British Columbia and Adjacent Waters. *MS Rept., UBC Dept. Oceanography* 28:1–63.

LEE, H. 1875. *The Octopus.* London.

———. 1884a. *Sea Monsters Unmasked.* London.

———. 1884b. *Sea Fables Explained.* London.

LEHN, W. H., AND I. SCHROEDER. 1981. The Norse Merman as an Optical Phenomenon. *Nature* 289:362–6.

LESUEUR, C. A. 1818. Sur le serpent nommé Scoliophis: Extrait d'une lettre adressée au rédacteur. *Jour. Phys. Chim. Hist. Nat. (Paris)* 86:466–9.

LEWIS, T. A. 1990. Squid: The Great Communicator? *National Wildlife* 28(5):14–19.

LEWISOHN, R. 1954. *Animals, Men and Myths.* Harper.

LEY, W. 1941. Scylla Was a Squid. *Natural History* 48(1):11–13.

———. 1948. *The Lungfish, the Dodo, and the Unicorn.* Viking.

———. 1968. *Dawn of Zoology.* Prentice-Hall.

———. 1987. *Exotic Zoology.* Bonanza.

LEYDA, J. 1951. *The Melville Log.* Gordian Press.

LINEAWEAVER, T. H., AND R. H. BACKUS. 1973. *The Natural History of Sharks.* Doubleday Anchor.

LINNAEUS, C. 1758. *Systema naturae.* 10th ed. Vol. 1. Regnum animale. Holmiae.

LOOMIS, F. B. 1911. A New Mink from the Shell Heaps of Maine. *Amer. Jour. Sci.* 31:227–9.

LUER, C. A. 1993. Sharks and Cancer—The Real Story. *Shark Line* (Summer 1993). Mote Marine Laboratory.

LUER, C. A., AND R. E. HUETER. 1993. "60 Minutes" of Shark Cartilage: Commercially Available Product Revealed as Cancer Treatment. *American Elasmobranch Society Quarterly Newsletter* 1:1.

LUND, R. 1990. Shadows in Time—A Capsule History of Sharks. In S. M. Gruber, Ed., *Discovering Sharks,* pp. 23–8. American Littoral Society.

MACALESTER, E. G. 1981. Dark-Water Octopus. *Sea Frontiers* 27(2):79–81.

MACGINITIE, G. E. 1938. Notes on the Natural History of Some Marine Animals. *Amer. Midl. Nat.* 19:207–19.

MACGINITIE, G. E., AND N. MACGINITIE. 1949. *Natural History of Marine Animals.* McGraw-Hill.

MACKAL, R. P. 1976. *The Monsters of Loch Ness.* Swallow.

———. 1980. *Searching for Hidden Animals: An Inquiry into Zoological Mysteries.* Doubleday.

———. 1986. Biochemical Analyses of Preserved *Octopus giganteus* Tissue. *Cryptozoology* 5:55–62.

MACKINTOSH, N. A. 1956. 2,000 Feet Down: Deep-Sea Photographs Teach Us More About the Little-Known Squid. *New Scientist* 1:60.

MACLEISH, W. H. 1980. "Mysterious Creatures." In J. J. Thorndike, Ed., *Mysteries of the Deep,* pp. 242–91. American Heritage.

MADSEN, A. 1978. *John Huston: A Biography.* Doubleday.

MAGNUS, O. 1555. *Historia de gentibus septentrionalibus.* Antwerp.

MALLOY, M. 1989. Whalemen's Perceptions of "The High and Mighty Business of Whaling." *The Log of Mystic Seaport* 41(2):56–67.

MANDEL, P. 1963. Showdown for Loch Ness. *Life* 55(12):17–18.

MANDOJANA, R. 1964a. Kraken. *Pesca y Casting* 8(85):22–6.

———. 1964b. Buceando in el Pacifico Chileno. *Pesca y Casting* 8(86):36–40.

MANGIACOPRA, G. 1975. *Octopus giganteus* Verrill: A New Species of Cephalopod. *Of Sea and Shore* (Spring 1975):3–10, 51–2.

———. 1977a. The Great Unknowns of the 19th Century: Sightings of Sea Serpents Along the Northeast Coast of North America. Part I: 1869–1879. *Of Sea and Shore* (Winter 1976–77):201–5, 228.

———. 1977b. The Great Unknowns of the 19th Century. Part II: 1880–1888. *Of Sea and Shore* (Spring 1977):17–24.

———. 1977c. The Great Unknowns of the 19th Century. Part III: 1892–1899. *Of Sea and Shore* (Summer 1977):95–104.

———. 1977d. The Great Unknowns of the 19th Century. Part IV: Comments and Conclusions. *Of Sea and Shore* (Fall 1977):175–8.

———. 1980a. The Great Unknowns into the 20th Century: Observations of Large Unknown Marine Animals Along the Northeast Coast of the North American Continent. Part I: 1900–1913. *Of Sea and Shore* (Spring 1980):13–20.

———. 1980b. The Great Unknowns into the 20th Century. Part II: 1919–1939. *Of Sea and Shore* (Summer 1980):123–7.

———. 1980c. The Great Unknowns into the 20th Century. Part III: 1947–1980. *Of Sea and Shore* (Fall 1980):193–6.

———. 1980d. The Great Unknowns into the 20th Century. Part III, Continued: 1947–1980. *Of Sea and Shore* (Winter 1980–81):193–6.

MANVILLE, R. H. 1966. The Extinct Sea Mink, with Taxonomic Notes. *Proc. U.S. Nat. Mus.* 122(3584):1–12.

MASSY, A. L. 1928. The Cephalopoda of the Irish Coast. *Proc. R. Irish Acad.* 38:25–37.

MATHEWS, J. 1992. Sharks Still Intrigue Cancer Researchers. *Jour. Natl. Cancer Inst.* 84(13):1001.

MATTHEWS, L. H. 1938. The Sperm Whale, *Physeter Catadon. Discovery Rep.* 27:93–168.

MATTHIESSEN, P. 1971. *Blue Meridian: The Search for the Great White Shark.* Random House.

MATURANA, H. R., AND S. SPERLING. 1963. Unidirectional Response to Angular Acceleration Recorded from the Middle Cristal Nerve in the Statocyst of *Octopus vulgaris. Nature* (London) 197:815–16.

MAUNDER, S. 1852. *The Treasury of Natural History; or a Popular Dictionary of Animated Nature.* Longmans, Green.

MAXWELL, G. 1952. *Harpoon Venture.* Viking.

MAXWELL, J. 1993. Seeing Serpents. *Pacific Northwest* 27(3):30–4.

MAYO, M. 1984. Splash. *Cinefantastique* 14(3):15–17.

MCCORMICK, H. W., T. ALLEN, AND W. E. YOUNG. 1963. *Shadows in the Sea.* Chilton.

MCDANIEL, N. G. 1989. Arms and the Man: Twenty Years in the Grip of the Giant Pacific Octopus. *Oceans* 22(1):38–45.

MCEWAN, G. J. 1978. *Sea Serpents, Sailors, and Skeptics.* Routledge & Kegan Paul.

MCGOWAN, C. 1991. *Dinosaurs, Spitfires, & Sea Dragons.* Harvard University Press.

MCHUGH, J. L. 1974. The Role and History of the International Whaling Commission. In W. E. Schevill, Ed., *The Whale Problem: A Status Report,* pp. 305–35. Harvard University Press.

MCINTYRE, J. 1974. *Mind in the Waters.* Scribners.

———. 1982. *The Delicate Art of Whale Watching.* Sierra Club.

MCPHEE, J. 1990. *Pieces of the Frame.* Farrar, Straus and Giroux.

MCRAE, M. 1992. Misunderstood Predator [Sharks]. *Equinox* 65:40–53.

MCVAY, S. 1966. The Last of the Great Whales. *Scientific American* 215(2):13–21.

MEAD, J. G. 1980. An Analysis of Cetacean Strandings Along the Eastern Coast of the United States. In J. R. Geraci and D. J. St. Aubin, Eds., *Biology of Marine Mammals: Insights Through Strandings*, pp. 54–68. Rep. No. MMC-77/13. U.S. Marine Mammal Commission.

MEADE-WALDO, E. G. B., AND M. J. NICOLL. 1906. Description of an Unknown Animal Seen at Sea off the Coast of Brazil. *Proc. Zool. Soc. London* 2(98):719.

MELVILLE, H. 1851. *Moby-Dick*. New York. 1967 Norton critical edition, H. Hayford and H. Parker, Eds. Norton.

MERLE, R. 1969. *The Day of the Dolphin*. Fawcett.

MERRETT, N. *Lepidoteuthis grimaldi* (Cephalopoda) from the South Atlantic. *Ann. Mag. Nat. Hist.* Ser. 13, 6:635–6.

MESSENGER, J. B. 1977. Evidence that *Octopus* Is Colour Blind. *Jour. Exp. Biol.* 70:(1):49–55.

MICHELMORE, P. 1991. In the Jaws of a Shark. *Reader's Digest* 12/91:86–90.

MILLER, J. A. 1983. Super Squid Lies in State. *Science News* 123(7):110.

MILLER, W. J. 1976. *The Annotated Jules Verne: Twenty Thousand Leagues Under the Sea*. Crowell.

MILNE, L. J. 1947. Squid. *Atlantic Monthly* 180(2):104–6.

MINER, R. W. 1935. Marauders of the Sea. *National Geographic* 68(2):185–207.

MITCHILL, S. L. 1829. The History of Sea-Serpentism. *Amer. Jour. Sci.* 15:351–6.

MITSUKURI, K., AND S. IKEDA. 1895. Note on a Giant Cephalopod. *Zool. Mag. Tokyo* 7:39–50.

MORE, A. G. 1875a. Gigantic Squid on the West Coast of Ireland. *Ann. Mag. Nat. Hist.* 4(16):123–4.

———. 1875b. Notice of a Gigantic Cephalopod (*Dinoteuthis proboscideus*) which was Stranded at Dingle, in Kerry, Two Hundred Years Ago. *Zoologist* 2(10):4526–32.

———. 1875c. Some Account of the Gigantic Squid (*Architeuthis dux*) Lately Captured off Boffin Island, Connemara. *Zoologist* 2(10):4569–71.

MORELL, V. 1982. The Myth & Science of Cryptozoology. *Equinox* 1(5):22–35.

MORISON, S. E. 1971. *The European Discovery of America: The Northern Voyages A.D. 500–1600*. Oxford University Press.

———. 1974. *The European Discovery of America: The Southern Voyages A.D. 1492–1616*. Oxford University Press.

MOYNIHAN, M. 1985a. *Communication and Noncommunication by Cephalopods*. Indiana University Press.

———. 1985b. Why Are Cephalopods Deaf? *Amer. Natl.* 125(3):465–9.

MOYNIHAN, M., AND A. F. RODANICHE. 1977. Communication, Crypsis, and Mimicry Among Cephalopods. In T. Sebeok, Ed., *How Animals Communicate*, pp. 293–302. Indiana University Press.

———. 1982. *The Behavior and Natural History of the Caribbean Reef Squid Sepioteuthis sepioidea, with a Consideration of Social, Signal, and Defensive Patterns for Difficult and Dangerous Environments*. Paul Parey.

MUMFORD, L. 1929. *Herman Melville*. Harcourt, Brace.

MUNTZ, W. R. A. 1991. Anatomical and Behavioural Studies on Vision in *Nautilus* and *Octopus*. *Amer. Malacol. Bull.* 9(1):69–74.

MURRAY, J., AND J. HJORT. 1912. *The Depths of the Ocean*. Macmillan.

MYKLEBUST, B. 1946. Et nytt funn av kjempebleblekksprut i Romsdal. *Naturen* 70:377–9.

NANSEN, F. 1911. *In Northern Mists: Arctic Exploration in Early Times.* Stokes.

NEMOTO, T., AND K. NASU. 1963. Stones and Other Aliens in the Stomachs of Sperm Whales in the Bering Sea. *Sci. Rep. Whales Res. Inst.* 17:83–91.

NESIS, K. N. 1970. The Biology of the Giant Squid of Peru and Chile. *Okeanologiia* 10:108–18.

———. 1974. Giant Squids. *Gidrobiologiia* 6(706):55–60.

———. 1987. *Cephalopods of the World.* T. F. H. Publications. Translated from the Russian by B. S. Levitov.

NESIS, K. N., A. M. AMELEKHINA, A. R. BOLTACHEV, AND G. A. SHEVTSOV. 1985. The Capture of Giant Squid of the Species *Architeuthis* in the North Pacific and South Atlantic. *Zool. Zh.* 64(4):518–28.

NEWMAN, E. 1848. The Great Sea Serpent. *Zoologist* 1848:2306–24.

NIGMATULLIN, C. M. 1976. Discovery of a Giant Squid *Architeuthis* in Atlantic Equatorial Waters. *Biol. Morya Vladivostok* 4:29–31.

NISHIWAKI, M., AND H. MARSH. 1990. Dugong *Dugong dugon* (Muller 1976). In S. H. Ridgway and R. Harrison, Eds., *Handbook of Marine Mammals, Vol. 3*, pp. 1–31. The Sirenians and Baleen Whales. Academic Press.

NISHIWAKI, M., T. KASUYA, T. TOBAYAMA, N. MIYAZAKI, AND T. KATAOKA. 1981. Distribution of the Dugong in the World. *Sci. Rep. Whales Res. Inst.* 31:131–41.

NISHIWAKI, M., M. YAMAGUCHI, S. SHOKITA, S. UCHIDA, AND T. KATAOKA. 1982. Recent Survey on the Distribution of the African Manatee. *Sci. Rep. Whales Res. Inst.* 34:137–47.

NIXON, M., AND P. N. DILLY. 1977. Sucker Surfaces and Prey Capture. In M. Nixon and J. B. Messenger, Eds., *The Biology of Cephalopods*, pp. 377–434. Symposia of the Zoological Society of London. Academic Press.

NOE, G. E. 1987. *Carcharodon.* Vantage Press.

NORDGARD, O. 1923. The Cephalopoda Dibranchiata Observed Outside and in the Trondhjemsfjord. *K. norske Vidensk. Selsk. Skr.* 1922:1–14.

———. 1928. Faunistic Notes on Marine Evertebrates III. *K. norske Vidensk. Selsk. Forh.* 1(26):70–2.

NORDHOFF, C. 1856. *Whaling and Fishing.* Moore, Wilsatsch, Keys & Co.

NORMAN, J. R., AND F. C. FRASER. 1938. *Giant Fishes, Whales and Dolphins.* Norton.

NORMAN, J. R., AND P. H. GREENWOOD. 1963. *A History of Fishes.* Hill & Wang.

NORRIS, K. S., AND G. W. HARVEY. 1972. A Theory for the Function of the Spermaceti Organ of the Sperm Whale (*Physeter catadon* L.). In S. R. Galler, K. Schmidt-Koenig, G. J. Jacobs, and R. E. Belleville, Eds., *Animal Orientation and Navigation*, pp. 397–417. NASA Special Publication 262.

NORRIS, K. S., AND B. MØHL. 1983. Can Odontocetes Debilitate Prey with Sound? *Amer. Naturalist* 122(1):85–104.

ODELL, D. K., E. D. ASPER, J. BAUCOM, AND L. H. CORNELL. 1980. A Recurrent Mass Stranding of the False Killer Whale *Pseudorca crassidens*, in Florida. *Fish. Bull.* 78(1):171–6.

O'DOR, R. K. 1988a. The Forces Acting on Swimming Squid. *Jour. Exp. Biol.* 137:421–42.

———. 1988b. The Energetic Limits on Squid Distributions. *Malacologia* 29(1):113–19.

O'DOR, R. K., AND R. E. SHADWICK. 1989. Squid, the Olympian Cephalopods. *Jour. Cephalopod Biol.* 1(1):33–55.

O'DOR, R. K., AND D. M. WEBBER. 1986. The Constraints on Cephalopods: Why Squid Aren't Fish. *Canadian Jour. Zool.* 64:1591–1605.

————. 1989. Invertebrate Athletes: Trade-Offs Between Transport Efficiency and Power Density in Cephalopod Evolution. *Jour. Exp. Biol.* 160:93–112.

O'DOR, R. K., H. O. PORTNER, AND R. E. SHADWICK. 1990. Squid as Elite Athletes: Locomotory, Respiratory, and Circulatory Integration. In D. L. Gilbert, W. J. Adelman, and J. M. Arnold, Eds., *Squid as Experimental Animals*, pp. 481–503. Plenum.

OHSUMI, S. 1958. A Descendant of Moby-Dick, or a White Sperm Whale. *Sci. Rep. Whales Res. Inst.* 13:207–9.

OKUTANI, T., AND T. NEMOTO. 1964. Squids as the Food of Sperm Whales in the Bering Sea and Alaskan Gulf. *Sci. Rep. Whales Res. Inst.* 18:111–22.

OKUTANI, T., Y. SATAKE, S. OHSUMI, AND T. KAWAKAMI. 1976. Squids Eaten by Sperm Whales Caught off Joban District, Japan, During January–February. *Bull. Tokai reg. Fish. Res. Lab.* 87:67–113.

OMURA, H., K. MOCHIZUKI, AND T. KAMIYA. 1978. Identification of the Carcass Trawled by the *Zuiyo-Maru*—from a Comparative Morphological Viewpoint. In *Collected Papers on the Carcass of an Unidentified Animal Trawled off New Zealand by the Zuiyo-Maru*, pp. 55–60. Société Franco-Japonaise d'Oceanographie. Tokyo.

ORTELIUS, A. 1570. *Theatrum Orbis Terrarum.* Antwerp.

OUDEMANS, A. C. 1892. *The Great Sea-Serpent.* London.

OUTERSON, W. 1937. "Fire in the Galley Stove." In A. Hitchcock, Ed., *Alfred Hitchcock's Fireside Book of Suspense.* Simon & Schuster.

OWEN, R. 1848. The Great Sea Serpent. *Ann. Mag. Nat. Hist.* 2d ser. 2:458.

————. 1881. Descriptions of Some New and Rare Cephalopoda. *Trans. Zool. Soc. London* 11:131–70.

PACKARD, A., AND F. G. HOCHBERG. 1977. Skin Patterning in *Octopus* and Other Genera. In M. Nixon and J. B. Messenger, Eds., *The Biology of Cephalopods*, pp. 191–232. Symposia of the Zoological Society of London. Academic Press.

PACKARD, A., AND G. SANDERS. 1969. What the Octopus Shows to the World. *Endeavour* 28(104):92–9.

PACKARD, A., H. E. KARLSEN, AND O. SAND. 1990. Low Frequency Hearing in Cephalopods. *Jour. Comp. Physiol.* 166:501–5.

PACKARD, A. S. 1873. Colossal Cuttlefishes. *American Naturalist* 7:87–94.

PARISI, B. 1930. Mostri Artificiali. *Riv. Sci. Nat. "Natura"* 21:1–8.

PAYNE, R., AND S. MCVAY. 1971. Songs of the Humpback Whale. *Science* 173:585–97.

PENNANT, T. 1812. *British Zoology. A New Edition in Four Volumes. Vol. III: Class IV. Reptiles. IV. Fishes.* Wilkie & Robinson.

PÉREZ-GÁNDRAS, G., AND A. GUERRA. 1978. Nueva Cita de *Architeuthis* (Cephalopoda: Teuthoidea): Description y Alimentacion. *Inv. Pesq.* 42:401–14.

————. 1989. *Architeuthis* de Sudafrica: Nuevas Citas y Consideraciones Biologicas. *Scient. Mar.* 53:113–16.

PERON, F. 1807. *Voyage de Decouvertes aux Terres Australes, etc.* Paris.

PETERS, M. 1990. *The House of Barrymore.* Knopf.

PFEFFER, G. 1912. Die Cephalopoden der Plankton—Expedition. Zugleich eine Mongraphische Übersicht der Oegopsiden Cephalopoden. *Ergebnisse der Plankton—Expedition der Humboldt—Sifting.* 2:1–815.

PHILLIPS, C. 1964. *The Captive Sea.* Chilton.

PHILLIPS, J. B. 1933. Description of a Giant Squid Taken at Monterey, with Notes on Other Squid Taken off the California Coast. *Cal. Fish and Game* 19(2):128–36.

———. 1961. Two Unusual Cephalopods Taken Near Monterey. *Cal. Fish and Game* 47(4):416–17.

PICCARD, J., AND R. S. DIETZ. 1961. *Seven Miles Down.* Putnam's.

PICKFORD, G. E. 1940. The Vampyromorpha, Living-Fossil Cephalopods. *Trans. N.Y. Acad. Sci.* 2(2):169–81.

———. 1946. *Vampyroteuthis infernalis* Chun. I. Natural History and Distribution. *Dana. Rep.* no. 29:1–45.

———. 1949a. The Distribution of the Eggs of *Vampyroteuthis infernalis* Chun. *Sears Found. Jour. Mar. Res.* 8(1):73–83.

———. 1949b. *Vampyroteuthis infernalis* Chun. II. External Anatomy. *Dana. Rep.* 32:1–131.

———. 1950. The Vampyromorphs (Cephalopoda) of the Bermuda Oceanographic Expeditions. *Zoologica* 35:87–95.

———. 1952. The Vampyromorpha of the "Discovery" Expeditions. *Discovery Rep.* 26:197–210.

———. 1964. *Octopus dofleini* (Wülker). *Bull. Bingham Oceanographic Coll.* 19(1):1–70.

PILLERI, G., AND L. ARVY. 1981. The Precursors in Cetology from Guilleaume Rondelet to John Anderson. *Invest. on Cetacea* 12:1–258.

PINKAS, L., M. S. OLIPHANT, AND I. L. K. IVERSON. 1971. Food Habits of Albacore, Bluefin Tuna, and Bonito in California Waters. *Calif. Dept. Fish and Game Fish. Bull.* 152:1–105.

PLINY. *Naturalis Historia.* Loeb Classical Library, 1933. Harvard University Press.

POLIKOFF, B. 1953. Unnatural Wonders of the World. *Chicago Nat. Hist. Bull.* 24(12):5.

PONTOPPIDAN, E. 1755. *The Natural History of Norway.* London.

PORTER, J. W. 1977. *Pseudorca* Stranding. *Oceans* 10(4):8–15.

PORTER, W. H. 1971. Sea Serpents and Ocean Monsters. *Oceans* 4(5):60–3.

QUOY, J. R. C., AND J. P. GAIMARD. 1824. *Voyage autour du monde . . . Exécuté sur les corvettes de S.M. l'Uranie et la physicienne pendant les années 1817, 1818, 1819, et 1820.* Louis de Freycinet.

RAE, B. B. 1950. Description of a Giant Squid Stranded near Aberdeen. *Proc. Malacol. Soc. London* 28:163–7.

RAFINESQUE-SCHMALTZ, C. S. 1819. Dissertation on Water-Snakes, Sea-Snakes, and Sea-Serpents. *Phil. Mag.* 54:361–7.

RAMUS, J. 1689. *Nori Regnum, hoc est Norvegica antiqua et ethnica, sive historiae Norwegicae prima initia a primo Norwegiae Rege, Noro, usque ad Haraldum Harfagerum, etc.* Christiana.

RANDALL, J. E. 1973. Size of the Great White Shark. *Science* 181:169–70.

RATHJEN, W. F. 1973. Northwest Atlantic Squids. *Mar. Fish. Rev.* 35(12):20–6.

RECKSIEK, C. W., AND H. W. FREY. 1978. Bilological, Oceanographic, and Acoustic Aspects of the Market Squid, *Loligo opalescens* Berry. *Cal. Fish and Game Fish Bull.* 169:1–185.

REES, W. J. 1949. Giant Squid: The Quest for the Kraken. *Illustrated London News* 215:826.

———. 1950. On a Giant Squid *Ommastrephes caroli* Furtado Stranded at Looe, Cornwall. *Bull. Brit. Mus. Nat. Hist.* 1:31–41.

REES, W. J., AND G. E. MAUL. 1956. The Cephalopoda of Madeira. *Bull. Brit. Mus. Nat. Hist.* 3:257–81.

REYNOLDS, J. E. III. 1979. The Semisocial Manatee. *Natural History* 88(2):44–52.

———. 1992. Distribution and Abundance of Florida Manatee (*Trichechus manatus latirostris*) Around Selected Power Plants Following Winter Cold Fronts: 1991–1992. Florida Power and Light.

REYNOLDS, J. E. III, AND D. K. ODELL. 1991. *Manatees and Dugongs.* Facts on File.

REYNOLDS, J. N. 1839. Mocha Dick, or the White Whale of the Pacific. *Knickerbocker Magazine* May 1839:377–92. 1932 edition, Scribners.

RICHARDSON, E. S. 1966. Wormlike Fossil from the Pennsylvanian of Illinois. *Science* 151(3706):75–76.

RICKS, C. 1989. *Tennyson: A Selected Edition.* University of California Press.

RINES, R. H. 1982. Summarizing a Decade of Underwater Studies at Loch Ness. *Cryptozoology* 1:24–32.

———. 1984. Activities of the Academy of Applied Science Related to Investigations at Loch Ness, 1984. *Cryptozoology* 3:71–3.

RITCHIE, J. 1920. Occurrence of a Giant Squid (*Architeuthis*) on the Scottish Coast. *Scott. Naturalist* 133–9.

———. 1922. Giant Squids on the Scottish Coast. *Rep. Brit. Ass. Adv. Sci.* 1921:423.

ROBISON, B. H. 1989. Depth of Occurrence and Partial Chemical Composition of a Giant Squid, *Architeuthis,* off Southern California. *The Veliger* 32(1):39–42.

ROBISON, B. H., AND R. E. YOUNG. 1981. Bioluminescence in Pelagic Octopods. *Pacific Science* 35(1):39–44.

ROBSON, C. W. 1887. On a New Species of Giant Cuttlefish Stranded at Cape Campbell, June 30th, 1886. (*Architeuthis kirki*). *Trans. N.Z. Inst.* 20:34–9.

ROBSON, F. D. 1978. The Way of the Whales: Why They Strand. *Whalewatcher* 12(4):4–11.

———. 1980. *Strandings: Ways to Save Whales.* Angus & Robertson.

ROBSON, F. D., AND P. J. H. VAN BREE. 1971. Some Remarks on a Mass Stranding of Sperm Whales (*Physeter macrocephalus* L. 1758) near Gisborne, New Zealand, on March 18, 1970. *Z.f. Saugetierk* 36:55–60.

ROBSON, G. C. 1925a. On *Mesonychoteuthis,* a New Genus of Oegopsid Cephalopoda. *Ann. Mag. Nat. Hist.* 9th ser. 16:272–7.

———. 1925b. The Deep-Sea Octopoda. *Proc. Zool. Soc. London* 1925:1323–56.

———. 1933. On *Architeuthis clarkei,* a New Species of Giant Squid, with Observations on the Genus. *Proc. Zool. Soc. London* 1933(3):681–97.

ROELEVELD, M. A. C., AND M. R. LIPINSKI. 1991. The Giant Squid *Architeuthis* in Southern African Waters. *Jour. Zool. Soc. London* 224:431–77.

ROMER, A. S. 1974. *Vertebrate Paleontology.* University of Chicago Press.

RONDELET, G. 1554. *Libri de Piscibus Marinis, in Quibus verae Piscium effigies expressae sunt.* Matthiam Bonhomme.

ROPER, C. F. E. 1969. Systematics and Zoogeography of the Worldwide Bathypelagic Squid *Bathyteuthis. Bull. U.S. Nat. Mus.* 291:1–210.

ROPER, C. F. E., AND K. J. BOSS. 1982. The Giant Squid. *Scientific American* 246(4):96–105.

ROPER, C. F. E., AND F. G. HOCHBERG. 1988. Behavior and Systematics of Cephalopods from Lizard Island, Australia, Based on Color and Body Patterns. *Malacologia* 29(1):153–93.

ROPER, C. F. E., AND R. E. YOUNG. 1972. First Records of Juvenile Giant Squid *Architeuthis* (Cephalopoda: Oegopsida). *Proc. Zool. Soc. Washington* 85(16):205–22.

———. 1975. Vertical Distribution of Pelagic Cephalopods. *Smithsonian Contributions to Zoology* 209:1–51.

ROPER, C. F. E., R. E. YOUNG, AND G. L. VOSS. 1969. An Illustrated Key to the Families of the Order Teuthoidea. (Cephalopoda). *Smithsonian Contributions to Zoology* 13:1–32.

ROWLAND, B. 1973. *Animals with Human Faces: A Guide to Animal Symbolism.* University of Tennessee Press.

RUDWICK, M. S. J. 1992. *Scenes from Deep Time.* University of Chicago Press.

RUGGIERI, G. D., AND N. D. ROSENBERG. 1974. The Octopus, "Cowardly Lion" of the Sea. *Oceans* 7(4):50–5.

RYAN, P. R. 1989. Buddha and the Whale. *Oceanus* 32(1):52–3.

SAIBIL, H. R. 1990. Structure and Function of the Squid Eye. In D. L. Gilbert, W. J. Adelman, and J. M. Arnold, Eds., *Squid as Experimental Animals,* pp. 371–98. Plenum.

SANDERSON, I. T. 1948. What-Is-Its of the Sea. *True* 24(139):38–39, 86–89.

———. 1965. Australia's Strange New Sea Monster. *True* July 1965:32–3, 72–3.

SANGER, D. E. 1993. Defiant Japan to Promote Eating Whale Meat. *New York Times* January 30, 1993:6.

SASAKI, M. 1929. A Monograph of the Dibranchiate Cephalopods of the Japanese and Adjacent Waters. *Jour. Fac. Agric. Hokkaido Imp. Univ.* 10(Supplement):1–357.

SAXON, A. H. 1989. *P. T. Barnum: The Legend and the Man.* Columbia University Press.

SCHAEFER, F. S. 1992. Squids Live Fast, Die Young. *Sea Frontiers* 38(2):10–11.

SCHAEFFER, B. 1967. Comments on Elasmobranch Evolution. In P. W. Gilbert, R. F. Mathewson, and D. P. Rall, Eds., *Sharks, Skates, and Rays,* pp. 3–35. Johns Hopkins Press.

SCHEFFER, V. B. 1969. *The Year of the Whale.* Scribners.

———. 1989. How Much Is a Whale's Life Worth, Anyway? *Oceanus* 32(1):109–11.

SCHLEE, S. 1970. Prince Albert's Way of Catching Squid. *Natural History* 74(2):20–5.

SCHROEDER, W. C. 1940. The Provincetown "Sea Serpent." *N. Eng. Nat.* 7(2):1–2.

SCORESBY, W. 1820. *An Account of the Arctic Regions with a History and Description of the Northern Whale Fishery.* Constable. 1969 edition, David & Charles.

SEABURY, C. 1852. Reported Capture of the Sea-serpent. *Zoologist (London)* April 1852:3426–29.

SELMER, C. 1959 (Ed.) *Navigatio Sancti Brendani Abbatis.* University of Notre Dame Press.

SERGEANT, D. E. 1962. The Biology of the Pilot or the Pothead Whale (*Globicephala melaena* Traill) in Newfoundland Waters. *Bull. Fish. Res. Bd. Canada* 132:1–84.

———. 1979. Ecological Aspects of Cetacean Strandings. In J. R. Geraci and D. J. St. Aubin, Eds., *Biology of Marine Mammals: Insights Through Strandings,* pp. 94–113. Rep. No. MMC-77/13. U.S. Marine Mammal Commission.

———. 1982. Mass Strandings of Toothed Whales (Odontoceti) as a Population Phenomenon. *Sci. Rep. Whales Res. Inst.* 34:1–47.

SHELDRICK, M. C. 1979. Cetacean Strandings Along the Coasts of the British Isles 1913–1977. In J. R. Geraci and D. J. St. Aubin, Eds., *Biology of Marine Mammals: Insights Through Strandings,* pp. 35–53. Marine Mammal Commission.

SHEPHERD, O. 1930. *The Lore of the Unicorn.* Houghton Mifflin.

SIGURJONSSON, J. 1989. To Icelanders, Whaling Is a Godsend. *Oceanus* 32(1):29–36.

SILVERBERG, R. 1965. Hoaxes and Half-truths. *Natural History* 74(3):62–5.

SINEL, J. 1906. *An Outline of the Natural History of Our Shores.* Sonnenschein.

SIVERTSEN, E. 1955. Bleksprutt. *K. norske Vidensk. Selsk. Mus. Arb.* 1954:5–15.

SLIGGERS, B. C., AND A. A. WERTHEIM (EDS.) 1992. *Op het strand gesmeten: Vijf eeuwen potvissstrandigen aan de Nederlandse kust.* Walburg Pers. Enkhuizen.

SMITH, A. G. 1963. More Giant Squids from California. *Cal. Fish and Game* 49:209–11.

SMITH, C. L., C. S. RAND, B. SCHAEFFER, AND J. W. ATZ. 1975. *Latimeria,* the Living Coelacanth, is Ovoviparous. *Science* 190: 1105-6.

SMITH, E. D. 1974. Electro-physiology of the Electric Shark Repellent. *Trans. South African Inst. Electrical Engineers* 65(8):166–85.

———. 1989. Low Cost Installation of a Submarine Cable in a Rough Surf Zone. *Electron* 6(4):11–16.

———. 1993. Planned Introduction of Electric Barriers to Natal. *Chondros* 4(1):1–4.

SMITH, J. L. B. 1940. A Living Coelacanth Fish from South Africa. *Trans. Royal Soc. South Africa* 28:1–106.

———. 1956. *The Search Beneath the Sea: The Story of the Coelacanth.* Holt.

———. 1961. *The Sea Fishes of Southern Africa.* Central News Agency.

———. 1966. Sea Serpents. *Outlook.* December:1–5.

———. 1968. *High Tide.* Books of Africa. Cape Town.

SMITH, M. M. 1970. The Search for the World's Oldest Fish. *Oceans* 3(6):26–36.

SOUCIE, G. 1976. Consider the Shark. *Audubon* 78(5):2–35.

SOULE, G. 1981. *Mystery Monsters of the Deep.* Franklin Watts.

SPRINGER, S. 1971. It Began with a Shark. In G. Scherz, Ed., *Dissertations on Steno as Geologist,* pp. 308–19. Odense University Press.

STARBUCK, A. 1878. *A History of the American Whale Fishery from Its Earliest Inception to the Year 1876.* Part IV, Report to the U.S. Commission on Fish and Fisheries, Washington. Reprinted 1964: Argosy-Antiquarian Ltd., New York.

STEAD, D. G. 1906. *Fishes in Australia.* Sydney.

———. 1933. *Giants and Pygmies of the Deep: The Story of Australian Sea Denizens.* Sydney.

———. 1963. *Sharks and Rays of Australian Seas.* Angus & Robertson.

STEENSTRUP, J. 1849. Meddelese om tvende kiaempestore Blaeksprutter, opdrevne 1639 og 1790 ved Islands Kyst, og om nogle andre nordiske Dyr. *Førh. skand. naturf.* 5:950–7.

———. 1849–1900. *The Cephalopod Papers of Japetus Steenstrup.* 1962 English translation by A. Volsoe, J. Knudsen, and W. Rees. Danish Science Press.

———. 1855. Om den i Kong Christian IIIs tid Øresundet fange Havmand (Sømunken kaldet). *Dansk Maanedsskrift* 1:63–96.

———. 1857. Oplysninger om Atlanterhavets colossale Blaeksprutter. *Førh. skand. naturf.* 7:182–5.

———. 1898. Kolassale Blaeksprutter fra det nordlige Atlanterhav. *K. danske vidensk. Selsk. Skr.* 43(5):409–54.

STEINBACH, H. B. 1951. The Squid. *Scientific American* 184(4):64–9.

STEJNEGER, L. 1884. Contributions to the History of the Commander Islands. No. 2. Investigations Relating to the Date of the Extermination of Steller's Sea-Cow. *Proc. U.S. Natl. Mus.* 8:181–9.

———. 1887. How the Great Northern Sea-Cow (*Rytina*) Became Exterminated. *Amer. Nat.* 21:1047–54.

———. 1936. *Georg Wilhelm Steller.* Harvard University Press.

STELLER, G. W. 1781. *Journal of a Voyage with Bering, 1741–1742.* 1988 edition, translated by O. W. Frost, Stanford University Press.

STENO (NIELS STENSEN). 1667. *Elementorum Myologiae Specimen . . . Canis Carchariae Dissectum Caput.* Florence.

STEPHEN, A. C. 1937. Recent Invasion of the Squid *Todarodes sagittatus* (Lam.) on the East Coast of Scotland. *Scot. Naturalist:* 131–2.

————. 1944. The Cephalopoda of Scottish and Adjacent Waters. *Trans. Roy. Soc. Edinb.* 61:247–70.

————. 1950. Giant Squid, *Architeuthis* in Shetland. *Scot. Naturalist* 62(1):52–3.

————. 1962. The Species of *Architeuthis* Inhabiting the North Atlantic. *Proc. Royal Phys. Soc. Edinburgh* 68:147–61.

STEVENS, W. K. 1992. Terror of Deep Faces Harsher Predator: Hunted for their fins, sharks are vanishing from the oceans. *New York Times* December 8, 1992:C1, C8.

STEVENSON, J. A. 1935. The Cephalopods of the Yorkshire Coast. *Jour. Conch.* 20:102–16.

STOLZENBERG, W. 1993. The Familiar Stranger [Octopus]. *Sea Frontiers* 39(4):14–15, 58.

STRAUS, K. 1977. Jumbo Squid, *Dodisicus gigas. Oceans* 10(2):10–15.

STRONG, W. R. 1990. Instruments of Natural Selection: How Important Are Sharks? In S. M. Gruber, Ed., *Discovering Sharks,* pp. 70–3. American Littoral Society.

SUMMERS, W. C. 1990. Natural History and Collection. In D. L. Gilbert, W. J. Adelman, and J. M. Arnold, Eds., *Squid as Experimental Animals,* pp. 11–26. Plenum.

SWEENEY, J. B. 1972. *A Pictorial History of Sea Monsters and Other Dangerous Marine Life.* Crown.

TARASEVICH, M. N. 1968. The Diet of Sperm Whales in the North Pacific Ocean. *Zoologicheskiy Zhurnal* 47(4):595–601. National Technical Information Service, 1974.

TAYLOR, L. R., L. J. V. COMPAGNO, AND P. J. STRUHSAKER. 1983. Megamouth—A New Species, Genus, and Family of Lamnoid Shark (*Megachasma pelagios,* Family Megachasmidae) from the Hawaiian Islands. *Proc. Cal. Acad. Sci.* 43(8):87–110.

TAYLOR, M. A. 1986. Stunning Whales and Deaf Squids. *Nature* 323:298–9.

THIELE, J. 1921. Die Cephalopoden der Deutsch Sud-polar Expedition 1901–1903. *Dt. Sudpol. Exped.* 16(8):433–65.

THOMAS, C. 1988. The "Monster" Episode in Adomnan's *Life* of St. Columba. *Cryptozoology* 7:38–45.

THOMPSON, K. S. 1991. *Living Fossil: The Story of the Coelacanth.* Norton.

THURSTON, H. 1989. Quest for the Kraken. *Equinox* 46:50–5.

TIME-LIFE BOOKS. 1988. *Mysterious Creatures.* Time Inc.

TOLL, R. B., AND S. C. HESS. 1981. A Small, Mature Male *Architeuthis* (Cephalopoda: Oegopsida) with Remarks on Maturation in the Family. *Proc. Biol. Soc. Wash.* 94(3):753–60.

TOPSELL, E. 1607. *The Historie of Foure-Footed Beastes.* London.

————. 1608. *The Historie of Serpents.* London.

TOWNSEND, C. H. 1935. The Distribution of Certain Whales as Shown by Logbook Records of American Whaleships. *Zoologica* 19(1):1–50.

TRAILL, T. S. 1854. On the Supposed Sea-snake, Cast Ashore in the Orkneys in 1808, and the Animal Seen from the H.M.S. *Daedalus* in 1848. *Proc. Royal Phil. Soc. Edinburgh* 3(44):208.

TRYON, G. W. 1879. *Manual of Conchology; Structural and Systematic. Vol. I Cephalopoda.* Philadelphia.

TSUCHIYA, K., AND T. OKUTANI. 1991. Growth Stages of *Moroteuthis robusta* (Verrill, 1881) with the Re-evaluation of the Genus. *Bull. Mar. Sci.* 49(1 & 2):137–47.

TUCKER, D. W. 1955. An Uncollected Record of the Great Sea-serpent. *Nature* 176(4484):705.

TWEEDIE, M. 1963. Is There a Sea-Serpent? *Animals* 2(12):326–9.

VELAIN, C. 1877. Remarques Générales au Sujet de la Faune des Iles St. Paul et Amsterdam,

Suives d'une Description de la Faune Malcolgique des Deux Iles. *Archs. Zool. Exp. Gen.* 6:1–144.

VERNE, J. 1870. *Twenty Thousand Leagues Under the Sea.* 1962 edition. Bantam.

———. 1875. *The Mysterious Island.* 1986 edition. Signet.

VERRILL, A. E. 1874a. Occurrence of Gigantic Cuttlefishes on the Coast of Newfoundland. *Amer. Jour. Sci.* 7:158–61.

———. 1874b. The Giant Cuttle-fishes of Newfoundland. *Amer. Naturalist* 8:167–74.

———. 1875a. Notice of the Occurrence of Another Gigantic Cephalopod (*Architeuthis*) on the Coast of Newfoundland, in December 1874. *Amer. Jour. Sci.* 10:213–14.

———. 1875b. The Colossal Cepahalopods of the Western Atlantic. *Amer. Naturalist* 9:21–78.

———. 1877. Occurrence of Another Gigantic Cephalopod on the Coast of Newfoundland. *Amer. Jour. Sci.* 14:425–6.

———. 1879. The Cephalopods of the Northeastern Coast of America. Part I. The Gigantic Squids (Architeuthis) and their Allies; with Observations on Similar Large Species from Foreign Localities. *Trans. Conn. Acad. Sci.* 5:177–258.

———. 1880. The Cephalopods of the Northeastern Coast of America. Part II. The Smaller Cephalopods, Including the "Squids" and the Octopi, with Other Allied Forms. *Trans. Conn. Acad. Sci.* 5:259–446.

———. 1881. Giant Squid (*Architeuthis*) Abundant in 1875, at the Grand Banks. *Amer. Jour. Sci.* 21:251–2.

———. 1882. Occurrence of an Additional Specimen of *Architeuthis* at Newfoundland. *Amer. Jour. Sci.* 23:71–2.

———. 1897a. The Florida Monster. *Science* 5(114):392.

———. 1897b. The Florida Sea-Monster. *Amer. Naturalist* 31:304–7.

———. 1897c. The Supposed Great Octopus of Florida; Certainly Not a Cephalopod. *Amer. Jour. Sci.* Vol. iii, no. CLIII (no. 16):355.

VILLIERS, A. 1958. *Give Me a Ship to Sail.* Hodder & Stoughton.

VINCENT, H. P. 1949. *The Trying-Out of Moby-Dick.* Houghton Mifflin.

VIRGIL. ca. 20 B.C. *The Aeneid.* 1956 translation by W. F. Jackson Knight. Penguin Classics.

VOSS, G. L. 1956a. A Checklist of the Cephalopoda of Florida. *Q. Jour. Fla. Acad. Sci.* 19:274–82.

———. 1956b. A Review of the Cephalopods of the Gulf of Mexico. *Bull. Mar. Sci. Gulf and Caribbean* 6:85–178.

———. 1959. Hunting Sea Monsters. *Sea Frontiers* 5(3):134–46.

———. 1963. Cephalopods of the Philippine Islands. *Bull. 234, U.S. Natl. Mus.*

———. 1967. Squids: Jet Powered Torpedoes of the Deep. *National Geographic* 131(3):386–411.

VOSS, G. L., AND R. F. SISSON. 1971. Shy Monster: The Octopus. *National Geographic* 140(6):776–99.

VOSS, N. A. 1980. A Generic Review of the Family Cranchiidae. *Bull. Mar. Sci.* 30(2):365–412.

WALLACE, I. 1959. *The Fabulous Showman.* Knopf.

WATKINS, W. A. 1980. Acoustics and the Behavior of Sperm Whales. In R.-G. Busnel and J. F. Fish, Eds., *Animal Sonar Systems*, pp. 283–90. Plenum.

WATSON, P., AND W. ROGERS. 1982. *Sea Shepherd: My Fight for Whales and Seals.* Norton.

WEBB, W. 1897. A Large Decapod. *Nautilus* 10:108.

WELLS, H. G. 1905. "The Sea Raiders." In *Twenty-Eight Science Fiction Stories by H. G. Wells.* Scribners. Dover edition, 1952.

WELLS, M. J., AND R. K. O'DOR. 1991. Jet Propulsion and the Evolution of Cephalopods. *Bull. Mar. Sci.* 49(1 & 2):419–32.

WENDT, H. 1959. *Out of Noah's Ark.* Houghton Mifflin.

WHEELER, A. 1977. "New Zealand Monster," *New Scientist,* July 28, 1977:91.

WHITAKER, I. 1985. The King's Mirror (*Konungs skuggsjá*) and Northern Research. *Polar Record* 22(141):615–27.

———. 1986. North Atlantic Sea Creatures in The King's Mirror (*Konungs skuggsjá*). *Polar Record* 22(142):3–13.

WHITE, J. R. 1984. Man Can Save the Manatee. *National Geographic* 166(3):414–18.

WHITE, T. H. 1954. *The Book of Beasts: Being a Translation from a Latin Bestiary of the Twelfth Century.* Jonathan Cape.

WHITEHEAD, H. 1990. *Voyage to the Whales.* Chelsea Green.

WHITLEY, G. P. 1928. Jenny Hanivers. *Aust. Mus. Mag.* 3(7):262–4.

———. 1940. *Fishes of Australia. Part I: The Sharks.* Royal Zoological Society of New South Wales.

WHITMORE, F. C., AND L. M. GARD. 1977. Steller's Sea Cow (*Hydrodamalis gigas*) of Late Pleistocene Age from Amchitka, Aleutian Islands, Alaska. *U.S. Geologic Survey Professional Paper* 1036:19Pp. + plates. Washington, D.C.

WILEY, J. P. 1976. Cameras, Sonar, Close in on Loch Ness. *Smithsonian* 7 (3):96-100.

WILFORD, J. N. 1986. *The Riddle of the Dinosaurs.* Knopf.

WILLIAMS, J. 1974. The Bad News About Sharks. *Esquire* 81(6):121–23, 148.

WILLIAMS, L. W. 1909. *The Anatomy of the Common Squid, Loligo pealii, Leseur.* E. J. Brill.

WILLIAMS, W. 1951. Friend Octopus. *Natural History* 60:210–15.

WILLIAMSON, G. R. 1988. Seals in Loch Ness. *Sci. Rep. Whales Res. Inst.* 34:151–7.

WILLIAMSON, J. E. 1936. *Twenty Years Under the Sea.* Hale, Cushman & Flint.

WILSON, E. O. 1984. *Biophilia.* Harvard University Press.

———. 1985: In Praise of Sharks. *Discover* 6(7):40–2, 48, 50–3.

———. 1992. *The Diversity of Life.* Harvard University Press.

WOOD, F. G. 1954. Underwater Sound Production and Concurrent Behavior of Captive Porpoises, *Tursiops truncatus* and *Stenella plagiodon. Bull. Mar. Sci. Gulf and Carib.* 3:120–33.

———. 1971. An Octopus Trilogy. Part I: Stupefying Colossus of the Deep; Part II: The Creature Revealed (by J. F. Gennaro); Part III: In Which Bahamian Fishermen Recount Their Adventures with the Beast. *Natural History* 80(3):14–24, 84–7.

———. 1973. *Marine Mammals and Man.* Luce.

———. 1979. The Cetacean Stranding Phenomenon: An Hypothesis. In J. R. Geraci and D. J. St. Aubin, Eds., *Biology of Marine Mammals: Insights Through Strandings,* pp. 129–89. Rep. No. MMC-77/13. U.S. Marine Mammal Commission.

WOOD, G. L. 1982. *The Guinness Book of Animal Facts and Feats.* Guinness Superlatives Ltd.

WRAY, J. W. 1939. *South Sea Vagabonds.* Reed.

WYLER, R. 1986. *Song of the Whale.* Doubleday.

WYMANS, J. 1848. The Fossil Skeleton Recently Exhibited in New York as That of a Sea-Serpent, Under the Name of *Hydrarchos Sillimani. Proc. Boston Soc. Nat. Hist.* 2:65–8.

————. 1851. Observations on the Fossil Bones of Zeuglodon. *Proc. Boston Soc. Nat. Hist.* 3:328.

WYSS, J. 1813. *The Swiss Family Robinson.* Airmont edition. 1963.

YOUNG, J. Z. 1938a. The Giant Nerve Fibres and Epistellar Body of Cephalopods. *Q. Jour. Microsc. Sci.* 78:367–86.

————. 1938b. The Functioning of the Giant Nerve Fibres of the Squid. *J. Exp. Biol.* 15:170–85.

————. 1977. Brain, Behaviour and Evolution of Cephalopods. In M. Nixon and J. B. Messenger, Eds., *The Biology of Cephalopods,* pp. 377–434. Symposia of the Zoological Society of London. Academic Press.

YOUNG, R. E. 1972. Brooding in a Bathypelagic Octopus. *Pacific Science* 26(4):400–4.

————. 1977. Ventral Bioluminescent Countershading in Midwater Cephalopods. In M. Nixon and J. B. Messenger, Eds., *The Biology of Cephalopods,* pp. 161–90. Academic Press.

YOUNG, R. E., AND C. F. E. ROPER. 1976. Bioluminescent Countershading in Mid-Water Animals: Evidence from Living Squid. *Science* 191(4231):1046–7.

YOUNG, R. E., E. M. KAMPA, S. D. MAYNARD, F. W. MENSCHER, AND C. F. E. ROPER. 1980. Counterillumination and the Upper Depth Limits of Midwater Animals. *Deep-Sea Research* 27(9A):671–91.

YOUNG, W. E. 1934. *Shark! Shark!* (As Told to Horace E. Mazet). Gotham House.

INDEX

Illustration Credits

A NOTE ON THE TYPE

This book was set in a modern adaption of a type designed by the first
William Caslon (1692–1766), greatest of English letter founders. The Caslon
face, an artistic, easily read type, has enjoyed two centuries of ever-increasing
popularity in our own country. It is of interest to note that the first copies of
the Declaration of Independence and the first paper currency distributed to the
citizens of the newborn nation were printed in this typeface.

Printed and bound by Courier Book Companies,
Westford, Massachusetts

Designed and composed by Cassandra J. Pappas